MOTHERS

Books by Gloria Goldreich

Leah's Journey
Four Days
This Promised Land
This Burning Harvest
Leah's Children
West to Eden
A Treasury of Jewish Literature
Mothers

MOTHERS

A Novel by

GLORIA GOLDREICH

Little, Brown and Company
Boston   Toronto   London

FIRST EDITION

The characters and events in this book are fictitious. Any
similarity to real persons, living or dead, is coincidental
and not intended by the author.

Library of Congress Cataloging-in-Publication Data

Goldreich, Gloria.
    Mothers: a novel/by Gloria Goldreich.
        p.   cm.
    ISBN 0-316-31936-8
    I. Title.
    PS3557.03845M67 1989
    813'.54—dc20   89-8356
                                      CIP

10 9 8 7 6 5 4 3 2 1

FG

*Published simultaneously in Canada
by Little, Brown & Company (Canada) Limited*

PRINTED IN THE UNITED STATES OF AMERICA

For my daughter Jeanie

Acknowledgments

The author wishes to thank Dr. William S. Nelson, Chairman of the Department of Obstetrics and Gynecology of the United Hospital of Portchester, New York, for his kind advice regarding medical information.

MOTHERS

I

The two women sit beneath the oak tree, and the sunlight that filters through the young leaves filigrees their upturned faces with a lacy radiance. A small redwood table stands between them. It is set with pale green linen napkins that exactly match the soft new-grown grass, and a blue ceramic bowl filled with the still-rare first fruits of the season — clusters of tiny white cherries, ruby-colored plums, small golden peaches. Fruit knives, with glinting steel blades and delicate mother-of-pearl handles, rest against strawberry-shaped milk-glass plates. The taller woman, Nina Roth, whose silver-threaded dark hair is plaited into a loose chignon, selects a peach and turns it in her hands. She wears a white skirt that falls almost to her ankles and a loose yellow cotton sweater. The sweater is long-sleeved, and although the day is warm, she pulls the cuffs down to her wrists, and her copper bracelets jangle musically. She rolls the peach about on her lap, and it streaks the white linen with a shadow of dampness. A slat of sunlight splices her angular face, and to escape it she shifts position on the flowered cushion of the lawn chair as she slips her foot free of the soft white leather slipper and rubs it across the grass.

Stacey Cosgrove watches her intently as she eats her cluster of cherries. Daintily, one by one, she pops them into her mouth, and she swallows the pits because she does not know what to do with them. When she has finished the cherries, she studies the fruit bowl and takes up a plum. She bites into it; its golden flesh is a shade lighter than her thick, curling hair that, this morning, she has brushed loosely about her shoulders. As she eats, a crumb of pulp clings to a front tooth (the jagged incisor across which Hal likes to run his tongue), and she licks it away. She wears a short-sleeved blue dress, patterned with honey-colored flowers, and high-heeled white sandals. The dress is too small and the bodice pulls tightly across her breasts. Sweat stains form dark half-moons beneath her arms. She moves her chair back so that it is more deeply nestled in the velvet shade of the tree.

"It is hot for May," she says. Her voice is soft and breathless, betraying an almost practiced sibilance. It occurs to Nina that once perhaps, when Stacey was a young girl, someone complimented her on her charming voice, and now she is a woman who will always speak like a child.

"I like it hot," Nina replies. "I work best when it's hot." She tosses her peach pit into the rhododendron bush. It falls softly and disappears amid the wide, dark leaves.

Stacey places her own plum pit on the white strawberry-shaped plate. She wipes her hands on the green linen napkin, which she shakes loose and allows to flutter in the sudden soft breeze. It is like a flag of spring, she thinks. *A flag of spring.* The words please her and she wants to write them down. She carries a small notebook in her oversized white shoulder bag in which she copies such phrases, because recently she has begun to write poetry. But of course she cannot write in her notebook while Nina Roth watches her. She smiles at the dark-haired woman whose eyes, the color and shape of almonds, are fixed on her with a steady, intent gaze. Still, Stacey is not uncomfortable. She is used to being stared at. When she was a child, her mother has told her with foreboding melancholy, people often turned in the street to stare at her.

"What work do you do?" she asks. "I didn't think you worked."

"I'm a dancer," Nina replies and swiftly corrects herself. "That is, I used to be a dancer. Now I do choreography. I design dances — compose them in a way."

"I know what choreography is," Stacey says stiffly. "I go to the ballet a lot. Or at least, I used to."

They smile at each other then for the first time — the woman who used to be a dancer and the woman who used to go to the ballet. *A lot.* Nina slips off her other shoe and curls and uncurls her long toes.

"I don't do ballet," she says. "I'm into modern dance. It's different."

"I know." Stacey bends to remove her own high-heeled sandals as though this shared interest has given her the right to relax. "I know modern dance too. Martha Graham. Pearl Primus. Jose Limon." She offers the names eagerly, proudly. "I took an evening extension course in modern dance once. We saw films and went to a performance at Lincoln Center."

"That's wonderful." Nina's tone is warm, encouraging. Her students, particularly her less-talented students, would recognize it at once. It is reserved for the breaking point of lessons when they feel they cannot go any further and she coaxes them forward tenderly, urgently. She smiles at Stacey and feels herself break free of the tension that has locked her in its grip all morning. Her body is well-trained, and slowly her muscles relax; her pelvis curves against the chair's flowered cushion, the arch of the foot now eased, now tensed with rhythmic precision. "My brother-in-law, Dr. Roth, did tell me that you have a lot of cultural interests." Immediately she regrets her words, and a harsh flush rouges her cheeks. She did not mean to sound condescending, patronizing.

But Stacey nods proudly, pleased to have been recognized.

"I like the arts," she says. "I have always been interested in the arts." The slogan slashed across the community college brochure has become her own and she repeats it effortlessly, without self-consciousness. "I've taken a lot of courses."

She glances at her shoulder bag. In addition to her notebook, it contains the very thick paperback novel she is reading called *The Madness of a Seduced Woman.* Because it is taking her so long to finish, and because she carries it with her from place to place and from room to room, sometimes even balancing it on the kitchen counter or the baby's changing table, its cover is creased and discolored. She has patched it with tape, and she wants to show it to Nina Roth and impress her with the book's size and her own care and zeal. Each crease, each food stain, is a scar marking Stacey's tenacious

struggle to add another notch to what Hal calls her "culture score."
He uses this term not cruelly but with an indulgent indifference.
Stacey can do whatever makes her happy, he has often said, and he
means it. He baby-sits when she takes her courses, pays for her books
and tuition, and even boasts of her achievements. If Hal were here,
he might even show the book to Nina Roth (as he showed it to her
brother's wife last week), but Stacey does not want to show off. She
does not have to show off, after all. It is Nina who wants something
from her, not she who wants something from Nina. With new confidence, she swivels about in the chair and looks toward the house.

It is a beautiful house. She had recognized that at once as Dr.
Roth drove up the long circular driveway. It is a Colonial. Stacey is
familiar with architectural categories because for a long time she and
Hal spent their weekends driving to outlying suburbs. There they
toured the model homes of new tract developments that shot up out
of raw earth amid the wounded stumps of newly cleared but not quite
leveled trees. She had come to recognize the difference between Tu-
dors and Colonials, the advantages of sprawling ranches and of tidy
Cape Cods. But this white columned house makes the Colonial development houses she visited seem like flimsily constructed doll-
houses. It is girdled by a wide porch and set well back on a sloping
lawn.

When she arrived, the windows were open and sheer lemon-
colored drapes shivered in the breeze. Two workmen knelt on the
slate path, repairing the grouting between the ochre-colored triangular slabs. Their heads were bent close to their work, and it had
seemed to Stacey for a brief and wild moment that the house was a
shrine and they worshipped on their knees before it. But then one
of them rose, wiped his hands on his green pants, and lit a cigarette.
He tossed the match onto the path, and Stacey felt reassured. She
had not glanced back when Dr. Roth parked, nor had she looked
back at the house as she followed him to the garden where Nina
Roth was placing the blue bowl of fruit on the redwood table.

"My sister-in-law thought it would be more comfortable to meet
outside on a day like this," Dr. Roth had said in that soft, caring
tone that had generated her trust from their very first meeting eight
years ago.

"It's all right," she had replied in the dry, quiet voice that told him that while she did not believe him, she accepted his comfort.

She had smiled reassuringly at him when he apologized for leaving after introducing her to Nina Roth. An emergency consultation at the hospital. Surely she understood. She had understood. Of course, he would not want to be at this meeting. It was enough that he had set the process in motion.

But now she stares openly at the house, which she has not been invited to enter. She studies the glass-enclosed rear porch on which she can see a table and chairs crafted of a delicate pale wood. Silver wind chimes dangle at the entryway and sound softly as the door opens and closes. A young girl descends the steps. She is tall and dark-haired, and her features, like those of Nina Roth, are finely chiseled and seem too small for her long, angular face. But her hair is cut into a close-fitting cap, and her eyes are a bright beryl blue. She wears a white tennis dress and her pink sneakers that match the pink cardigan knotted by the sleeves about her shoulders. Stacey thinks she resembles the girl in the television advertisement who dashes gaily toward her lover, winking all the time at the camera and chatting about the potency of her anti-perspirant. "Princess No Sweat," Stacey thinks, and she knows that is how she will describe the girl to Hal that night. She and Hal make up names for the actors in the television commercials, and often they turn the volume down and replace it with their own innovations. They lie naked on the king-sized bed and giggle at their own cleverness.

"Mom, I'm taking the car," the girl calls. She does not look at Nina or wait for her reply but strides toward the redbrick garage.

"All right," Nina shouts back. She makes no move toward the girl, and Stacey is surprised that she does not ask her where she is going, but then perhaps she knows. Of course, she knows. The girl is wearing a tennis dress. Still, there are so many places to play tennis. Stacey would ask. She feels superior now because she is a better mother than Nina Roth, and that new superiority emboldens her.

"I didn't know you had a daughter," she says. "Dr. Roth didn't mention a daughter."

"She's not my husband's daughter," Nina says, not looking at her, not asking what Dr. Roth did mention. "She's the child of my first marriage. Hildy. She's just seventeen."

"But Dr. Roth said you couldn't have children." Stacey remembers his words exactly, even the melancholy tenor of his voice as he spoke of his younger brother, David. A wonderful, talented man. An inventor. Caring and concerned. Just the sort of man who would make a wonderful father, but his wife could not have children. It was so sad. The doctor had sighed and Stacey too had sighed. Dr. Arnold Roth had delivered her three children, Evan, Jared, and Andrea. Andrea's birth had been a difficult one, and he had sat beside her all through the night, now holding her hand, now placing his own dry palms soothingly across her distended abdomen, whispering to her, cajoling her, congratulating her when she triumphed over a rending contraction, and, at last, holding Andrea out to her. The newborn infant was still glowing and slippery, red-faced but oh, so sweet and small, and she had whimpered softly until Stacey settled her quietly and comfortably against her breast.

"You're a natural," Dr. Roth had said admiringly, and Stacey had felt the warmth of his approval.

It had been that night, during the long labor, when the contractions halted suddenly but not ominously, that the doctor had first mentioned his brother, David. And then five years had passed before he spoke of him again.

Stacey watches Hildy back the car out of the garage. It is a small red sports car, not unlike the toy car that Stacey bought for Andrea's Barbie doll. It too is red, and Andrea often dresses Barbie in a white tennis outfit when she places her in the car. Andrea is right on target, Stacey thinks proudly, bitterly, and she decides that she will knit the doll a pink cardigan.

"That's true," Nina says, and sadness, like a veil, falls across her face. "There was a tumor and I had to have a hysterectomy. That was before I met David, my husband. I told him about it, of course." She says all this very quickly, the words tumbling over each other, and then she sighs deeply and drops her eyes as though embarrassed to have revealed so much.

But Stacey, unperturbed, nods sympathetically.

"Oh, I've heard a lot of stories like that," she says knowingly. She has sat on enough playground benches with other mothers to have heard of every imaginable gynecological difficulty. She knows about fibroids and about infections caused by scraps of residual placenta, ovaries punctured by the careless thrust of forceps, fallopian tubes blocked by mysterious discharges. Misfortunes and miracles of conception and delivery have been recounted during long afternoons as children quarreled in the sandbox and shrieked with delight on skyward-soaring swings.

"*They told me I couldn't conceive and then I became pregnant with Melissa.*"

"*He says that I should have my tubes tied. Jimmy was a breech and they almost did a section.*"

"*A section's not so bad except for the scar.*"

"*They can do a bikini scar. That's not so bad.*"

They are fascinated by their bodies, these playground mothers. They sit with their hands on their stomachs and brush their fingers across their breasts. Milk stains spot their blouses. Lazily they scratch their arms and rub their own cheeks with the damp washcloths they carry in small plastic bags for their children. They offer each other sample hand creams and lotions, passing the tiny plastic bottles from hand to hand, lifting them with fingers reddened by ammonia, hot water, cold water. They cake their faces with pressed powder to conceal their red eyes and the tracks of tears that fall so often and so suddenly.

They weep because a repairman has not come or a sister-in-law has said something unkind or because they are pregnant or because they cannot conceive. But they are not frightened by their tears. Moisture, intimate wastes, dominate their days, rule their nights. They know that the interior walls of their bodies shine wetly and, in the darkness, they smile to think of their own secret and slippery incandescence. Even the secrets they share with other women on the playground benches are sweetly effusive.

Stacey takes a peach and slices it carefully, arranging the segments on the white strawberry-shaped plate. She eats one piece at a time like a greedy but unhurried child. The golden juice drips down her chin, and she pats it away delicately with the green linen napkin.

"Do you want to take a walk, see the garden?" Nina asks.

"Yes." She rises but does not put on her shoes, although she lifts her heavy white bag and hoists it onto her shoulder.

Together then, both of them barefoot, they walk across the soft young grass and study rosebushes on which tightly knotted buds have just begun to form, and the delicate pink-and-purple-flowering azalea, which are at the peak of their season. Together they kneel beside the flower beds and inhale the rich, sensual fragrance of the pale narcissi and golden-throated daffodils.

Before Stacey leaves in the taxi that Dr. Roth had thoughtfully ordered for her (charging the fare and the driver's tip to his account), Nina cuts a bouquet of daffodils for her and scoops up the remaining fruit and places it in a plastic bag.

"Please take it. We may go away for the weekend, and it would just rot," she says to restore balance, to make it clear that Stacey will be doing her a favor by accepting the peaches and plums and the only remaining cluster of white cherries. "Your children may like them."

"My children eat a lot of fresh fruit. They love it," Stacey assures her proudly, as though boasting of an important talent unique to seven-year-old Evan, five-year-old Andrea, and three-year-old Jared, who, in fact, thrusts away all fresh produce with a shrill and defiant scream.

Stacey does not look out the window as the cab carries her to a neighboring suburb where the streets are narrower and the houses smaller, and where, in some backyards, laundry hung on clotheslines flaps in the breeze. She reads *The Madness of a Seduced Woman* as the flowers and fruits slide about on the cracked plastic seat and fill the cab with a clinging necrotic fragrance. She finishes half a chapter on the journey, and when she walks up the path of the small frame house, she hold Nina Roth's gifts carefully, as though they are fragile and delicate burdens. But although she places the fruit in a covered bowl in her refrigerator, she tosses the flowers into the garbage pail at the side of the house. Hal has recently developed an allergy as yet untraced, and he sniffs the air nervously each evening when he arrives home.

2

"I like her," Nina Roth tells her husband, David, as they sit across from each other at dinner that evening.

She smiles at him reassuringly. He is a tall, large-handed man, and his close-cut, sand-colored hair is still damp from the shower. In his light-blue oxford shirt and well-pressed khaki slacks, he has the look of the obedient, well-scrubbed child who has dutifully bathed and changed before dinner. He is a man who has not lost the open boyish look of innocence, an irony of a kind, Nina realizes, because his boyhood, so early touched by death, was strangely devoid of innocence.

They are dining at Luigi's, a small Italian neighborhood restaurant they favor because of its old-world booths crafted of thick dark wood that guarantee privacy and the neatly mended white linen cloths that reveal care and quality. Always the small rents in the fabric are repaired with tiny butterfly stitches fashioned of silken thread. Such symbols of parsimonious grace are important to Nina and David Roth. Besides, the food is always excellent, and tonight Luigi himself, a wizened, silver-haired man whose dark suit has been worn to a shine, pours the wine and waits for David's approving nod before withdrawing to the corner booth where he studies a ledger and a tattered pile of invoices.

"What is she like?" David asks.

It is a calculated question. His brother, Arnold, has already described Stacey to David. She is the only woman he knows, certainly his only patient, who is, Arnold said in his careful, professional language, "appropriate." He had further described her as intelligent, well-balanced, extremely healthy, and attractive. Most important, Arnold had stressed, was the fact that despite her limited educational background (which he had not discussed in detail — not yet), she had the compassion and imagination to understand the implications of their plan. And she was hardheaded and ambitious enough for her own family to understand the economic benefits that would accrue to them if she agreed. Arnold's description was accurate and clinically correct, David knows, but he wants another dimension, a subtler evaluation. That was why he wanted Nina to be the first to meet Stacey Cosgrove. Nina would know whether it was wise to proceed.

David recognizes his wife's talent for capturing elusive nuances of personality. Always, she crafts her verbal sketches with deadly accuracy, brandishing intuition and insight. She choreographs her descriptions of individuals and incidents as she choreographs her dances, slowly building toward a final, telling revelation. David has no such gift. He is a scientist, not an artist. His perceptions are surface; his judgments predictable. He perceives this limitation as a deformity, not unlike a withered arm, a weakness of sight. He is a good enough scientist, he knows, and indeed he has become wealthy because of his small inventions, switches and meters that he creates and manufactures. He is always busy with other inventions that will increase his wealth, expand his markets. But he is not deceived. His accomplishments are pedestrian and of no real importance. It is only true creation, true art that counts. He knows this because of the lesson of his father's life and of his father's death.

Amos Roth had been a painter whose chosen subjects had been working people, artisans and shopkeepers. In richly layered oils, he had captured a weary shoemaker studying his last in a dark and cluttered workshop, a white-haired tailor bent over a sewing machine, a fruit vendor wearing a built-up orthopedic shoe pushing a barrow up a hill through columns of falling rain. "The artist makes the viewer feel the silken silver texture of the rain," one reviewer wrote admiringly. Amos had, mysteriously, achieved early fame, early recognition. The rich purchased his portraits of the poor, and Art News published a profile on him, alternately calling him a "neo-realist" and a "painter of the proletariat."

Few critics in America had discussed Amos's paintings on Jewish themes. Perhaps the memory of the war was still too fresh, too threatening. It was not yet time for books and films and art about the Holocaust. Yet Amos Roth had pasted photographs from *Life* magazine on oaktag and studied them carefully. He had enlarged snapshots from an album sent to him after the war by a neighbor who had discovered it amid the rubble of the family's destroyed home. Amos had shown his sons the faded sepia prints — the pictures of infants and toddlers, of grave-eyed young men and sweet-faced young girls, of bearded men and plump, soft-cheeked women. He tried to puzzle out who they might be.

"This, I think, is my grandfather David. You are named for him. Yes. He was very proud of his beard and trimmed it every day, they said. You can see that, can't you?" His sons had studied the print, had tried to search out a resemblance to themselves, to their father, had dared not ask what had happened to that distant David.

"My great-aunt Miriam, for whom my sister is named. They look alike, I think. So fair-haired and fine-featured, both of them."

He did not speak about the pictures of the small children, although he touched them with his long, paint-stained fingers, as searchingly as he sometimes touched his own sons' faces.

And then, staring at the enlarged photos, he had painted his portraits, his brush moving swiftly, his face set in lines of such sorrow that his sons were frightened and hurried out of the studio to play in the sun-bright street.

Still, David had always looked at the completed portraits with the wonderment of a small boy trying to comprehend an adult universe. He knew about the war. Evil men in gray uniforms who barked harshly in German and wore caps embossed with the symbol of the death's head (which Arnold had explained to him in condescending tones) had tried to conquer the world and destroy the Jews. His grandparents' village had been captured and all his fathers' relatives taken to a place called Treblinka. A concentration camp, they called it, and David had a hard time understanding what that could be. He knew what *concentrate* meant. "Don't bother me, I'm concentrating," his mother often said, and for a long time he thought that a concentration camp might be a place where people were imprisoned and forced to think very hard. He understood, however, that the skeleton-faced, large-eyed children and the gaunt, bewildered men and women in his father's paintings were those who had somehow (by a miracle, his mother said sadly) survived the war. He did not understand why their faces were always turned either upward or toward the ground as though searching for something.

"What are they looking for, Papa?" David remembered asking his father.

Amos Roth had shrugged.

"I don't know. Perhaps they search for their families, their homes. Maybe a husband looks for his wife. A sister for a brother. Parents for their children. Or maybe" — and here his own voice had grown puzzled — "maybe they are listening for something — laughter or a song or the sound of someone crying. I don't know. That's how I saw them. That's how I painted them."

It had been important to Amos to explain his work to his younger son. (Later, much later, it had occurred to David, the man, that his father had perhaps had a premonition of his early death and wanted to cram as much as possible into the hours allotted to him — a fanciful thought, he knew, yet it brought him an odd comfort.) Often, Amos took David with him to his studio, where the small boy played with colored chalks and stole secret glances at his father's work. Amos talked as he painted. He told David stories of the Polish village in which he had been born, the village he had left as a child but that he had never forgotten. He and his sister, Miriam, had been sent to America to stay with an aunt and uncle. Their parents were to have followed them, but history intervened, and Amos Roth's last memory of his mother and father was somehow intermingled with the hooting of a train whistle, his mother's tears, and the fierce strength of his father's hands on his shoulders.

"He was a strong man," Amos had told David. "And he came from a family of strong men. I don't remember much, but I remember at weddings the men of the family would dance in a tight circle, stamping and swaying, around and around so that the room itself trembled, sometimes for as long as an hour."

"And what did the women do?" Amos had asked.

"Ah, the women. The women sang." And then he himself had

sung the Yiddish songs of his childhood, stumbling now and again at
a forgotten phrase, a complicated melody. "Raisins and Almonds,"
he sang, translating the Yiddish words into English. "Mama, Mama,
sing me a song." He mixed paints as he sang, and David dared not
look up from the pictures he drew with his colored chalk. He could
not bear the sadness in his father's eyes.

"It's hard to believe," Amos had said, "that so many years have
passed, and now there is no village, no family, no home. Only the
songs and the stories are left. But maybe that's enough, David. Enough
that I can teach my sons my father's songs and stories and that they
will teach them to their children. Where life continues, death is
denied. There's magic in that, David."

It was his father who was the magician, David had thought. His
father who created something out of nothing, who filled dead canvases with searching faces, singing the songs of his subjects even as
he painted them. It was his father who had denied death by having
children and sharing with them and loving them. That is how David
has always remembered Amos — a tall man, sandy-bearded, sandy-
haired (similar, oh, so similar to the grandfather David in the faded
photograph), wearing worn, paint-stained green pants and singing of
raisins and almonds in an unfurnished, sun-drenched loft.

Amos died when David was eight years old of a heart attack so
sudden and swift that David and his mother, Claire, who were in
the apartment at the time, did not realize he was dead for almost
two hours. They thought he had fallen asleep in the large black
leather chair where he often rested after a long day in the studio,
and so, deferentially, they had spoken softly to each other and moved
through the living room in stocking feet, circling the dead man's
chair. It was Arnold, arriving home from the library, who dropped
his books when he perceived the waxen pallor of Amos's skin, his
heavy immobility (because the death rigor had begun), the expression of incredulity frozen onto his face. Arnold stepped over his books
and touched the cold claw that had been his father's hand. He held
his ear to Amos's mouth and heard no hiss of breath but smelled a
bilious sourness. Weeping, he went to the kitchen and told his mother
what he thought, what he knew.

Claire Roth's long scream and then her shout of denial gave voice to the bewilderment and disbelief of her husband's face masked in the finality of death.

"Exactly what did you say to her?" David had asked his brother years later.

"I just told her he was gone, I think," Arnold replied. It is the expression Arnold still uses in his professional life, David knows. *Gone. Vanished. Disappeared.* Not dead. Never dead.

"No! No! It can't be. How can you tell me that?" Still, decades later, Claire's shriek rings in her sons' dreams, assaults the silence of their solitude.

She had been baking, and her hands were covered with flour. Her white handprints covered the dead man's face, powdered his sand-colored hair. Their neighbors, the elderly couple who lived across the hall and had, in fact, been Amos's subjects (she in her faded housedress, he in a neat cotton suit), had pulled her away from his body, pried her fingers loose from his cheeks as she tried to pinch him into wakefulness, into life. The old woman washed the dead man's face with a kitchen cloth. She did not want to explain the flour marks to the police, whom her husband summoned in quavering voice while the two boys hid behind their mother in the doorway.

David and Arnold sat beside their mother at the funeral and beside her, on overturned wooden crates, through the week of mourning. The mirrors of the house were covered with sheets, but their father's paintings — the portraits of the pale Woolworth's shopgirl at the ribbon counter, the machinist carrying a green metal lunch box, the seamstress holding a length of fabric up to the milky light Amos Roth had favored — stared down at them. Their grief was soothed by the faces of the weary poor.

The paintings of the Holocaust survivors were in the studio. Amos never hung them in his home. Claire found them too disturbing, and it was probable (as Edith observed so many years later) that he wanted to shield his sons from daily confrontation with the tragic stories they told. His last painting was never finished. It portrayed a young woman holding an infant. The child's body was outlined on the canvas, but although Amos had prepared the palette, had found the exact shade for the infant's skin (he was justly celebrated for his flesh tones), only one small foot had been painted. It was as though the unfinished infant was still curled within the womb of his imagination, a baby waiting to be born. Although many collectors expressed an interest in this last, unfinished canvas, Claire donated it to a kibbutz in Israel founded by Holocaust survivors. David did not see it again until he and Nina visited Israel for the retrospective exhibit of Amos Roth's paintings.

The visitors who came to offer their condolences during the week of mourning all shook hands with Arnold, kissed David, and offered Claire the same words of comfort.

"Yes, it's a tragedy. A terrible tragedy. He was so young, so talented. But look what he left behind." Their arms flared out to embrace the room. They patted David and Arnold as though they were not boys but inanimate objects, small memorial sculptures. They looked reverently up at the paintings. "He won't be forgotten. Look what he left behind."

Everyone said the same thing. It was the threnody of the mourning period, more powerful and reverberant than the prayers murmured by the quorum that assembled each morning and evening to say kaddish for a man they barely knew. Amos Roth had achieved immortality. His posterity was guaranteed. He had left behind two sons and enough paintings for a retrospective exhibition.

More important, he had left behind his artistic testimony to history. His sons would guarantee his own continuity, and his work would endure as imagined evidence of his people's story. "He painted from his heart," the art critic who delivered the opening remarks at Amos Roth's retrospective in Tel Aviv said so many years later. "His brush strokes recreated the soul of his people. In his colors the dead are quickened and the unborn celebrated."

"Look what he left behind," the small boy David would say aloud to comfort himself throughout that first desolate year of loss when he felt himself invisible, abandoned.

He would look in the mirror, stare at Arnold (who did not look up when his younger brother talked to himself but listened silently, sorrowfully), and then wander into the living room to look at the paintings. Slowly, Amos Roth's death was assimilated, and David and Arnold once again ran through the living room, shouted to each other in defiance of the silence of mourning, the muteness of death. Two years later, Claire Roth remarried. Nathan Silberman, her second husband, was a wealthy manufacturer who owned a small collection of proletarian art. Amos Roth lived on in Nathan Silberman's large Long Island home where his paintings hung in a large, carefully lit, and wide-windowed room. His sons argued at Nathan Silberman's dining room table; and art historians sat in his study and interviewed the stylishly dressed woman who had been married to the painter. Claire was never so much Nathan Silberman's wife (although she lived happily with him for twenty-five years) as she remained Amos Roth's widow.

Neither David nor Arnold inherited their father's gift, although they dutifully enrolled in art classes and trailed after their mother to sculpture studios. They took music lessons, and David even went to a creative writing workshop at a North Shore Y. Arnold at last discovered a small gift for poetry, and even now he fills wide-lined, soft-covered notebooks with long narrative poems. David envies his brother just as he envied the talent of John Cowper, his college roommate, who wrote short stories for the college literary magazine and whose recently published novel has received respectful reviews.

A psychiatrist friend has told David that, considering his background and the impact of his father's achievements on his life, it is not surprising that he has always been drawn to artistically creative people. It was, in fact, inevitable.

David recognizes this. The first girl he slept with was a painter and long after their affair had ended he would study the sketch pad that she had left in his room. Always, he was stirred anew to see her charcoal drawings of trees and birds in flight and delicately etched seashells. She had not been an attractive girl, he acknowledged. It was her gift, her gentle art, that had aroused him to that first mysterious surge of passion that swept him out of boyhood.

Since then, he had always been involved with creative women — clever artists and writers, musicians and dancers. Such women can enter a crowded room, glance about, and see the small dramas, the intricate mosaics in the talk and laughter that to him, despite his yearnings, remain just that — talk and laughter. Nina too has that gift, that artist's secret sight, the ability to see reality as dream and dream as reality. It is Stacey Cosgrove's dream, as she perceived it, that she offers him now as they eat their veal piccata and drink their very cold white wine.

"She's very pretty. She could be beautiful, I think, if she had the time, the money, if she knew what to do with her hair, how to dress. Instead she opts for the casual, careless approach. Wears her hair long about her shoulders, girlish — too girlish. It's a good color though — a honey gold, curly, thick."

Nina touches her own dark hair, sculptured tonight into a single long plait through which she has woven a narrow lime-green ribbon that matches her loose linen shift. She wore her hair that way the first time David saw her, the night she danced a small cameo role in *The Rite of Spring* at the northern campus of the state university. David was conducting a weekend workshop in industrial design, and he had attended the performance with John Cowper, who was on the faculty. He had watched Nina's entrance and been mesmerized by her tight, lithe body, the fierce set of her finely carved features, the glossy dark braid that whipped about her shoulders as she danced across the stage in her flame-colored leotard.

"She is like liquid fire," he had thought then, and the words had startled him because he seldom thought in metaphor, not even in awkward and clichéd metaphor. He had not spoken his thoughts aloud, not to John Cowper, who had that afternoon allowed him to read the heart-turning haiku verse he had written for his wife the night their son was born. But he had waited for Nina after the performance and invited her out for coffee, his voice strong but his hands shaking. Just as tonight his voice is strong and steady, yet the knife and fork tremble as he carves the pink meat into narrow strips.

He feels the stirring of fear. He braces himself for disappointment. He has, he recognizes, invested so much in Nina's encounter with Stacey Cosgrove. How desperately he wants his wife to think well of this young woman, whom Arnold thinks might agree to help him, help them. He needs Nina's approval, but he wants more than that. He wants her to like Stacey Cosgrove so that, in the end, she can share with her the mothering of the infant who lives now only in his imagining, in his febrile and irrational desire.

"Tall? Short?" he asks.

"Short. Five feet one, perhaps two. But she gives the appearance
of height, maybe because she has a yearning to be taller and holds
herself stretched, erect. I've taught such girls — the small ones who
want to stretch themselves into a height for the corps. She yearns —
yes, that's the right word for her. She yearns to be taller, to be better
educated, to be more at ease, more cultivated — just more." Nina's
voice grows softer. She knows what it is to yearn for perfection, to
dare to dream of greatness, even while recognizing the limitations of
talent. She has come to terms with it herself, and yet, even now,
she stares at herself in the long mirror behind her barre and says
aloud, *"This I would do and this I can do."* Instinctively, she had
understood this in Stacey, although it is not artistic perfection for
which Stacey yearns: she seeks to cultivate appreciation, understanding, to reach out to a world beyond the one into which she was
born. Nina respects this, and she smiles at David and spreads butter
across a very small piece of Italian bread.

"She has a high opinion of herself," she continues. "And she is
ambitious for her children. She is greedy, yes, but not in an unpleasant way — not for money or possessions. She is greedy for experience, opportunity."

Nina remembers suddenly how Stacey ate one fruit after another,
how she studied the golden pulp of the plum, sectioned the peach.

"What did you talk about?"

"Casual chatter for a while. The weather. Arnold. What a good
doctor he is."

"Yes. He is a good doctor," David said mildly.

He would expect Stacey Cosgrove to say as much. All Arnold's
patients speak of his goodness, his competence, his tenderness. Some
of them even fall in love with him and send him wistful notes or
impassioned pleas after their deliveries. He receives gifts on his birthday, careful and caring gifts from the women who have allowed him
to probe the mysterious canyons of their bodies and witness their
shrieks of pain, their tears of shame. They send him hand-knit scarves
if their children were born in the winter because they remember that
his neck was red and chafed with the cold when he smiled comfortingly down at them as they lay on the delivery table, their feet imprisoned in cold steel stirrups, their bodies restrained by pain. They

send him velvet-wrapped bottles of after-shave lotion and cologne because they remember his scent as he bent over them and murmured gentle words of reassurance. They try to guess at the aroma he uses and they imagine him patting the moisture onto his skin, which is so pale because he works so hard and does not take care of himself. It is Arnold's wife, Edith, who writes the thoughtful thank-you notes to which she signs his name. It is she who places the gifts in a cabinet, to be distributed to Arnold's residents and students at Christmas and at graduation.

David wonders if Stacey Cosgrove ever gave his brother a gift. He doubts it. She has no money. Arnold has told them that he decreased her bill halfway through her last pregnancy, and later, because her husband had allowed their insurance to lapse, he forgave it entirely. And, of course, if Stacey did not need money, Arnold would not have proposed her for this undertaking, which tonight seems to him to be impossible, incredible. (And yet, he knows that it is possible, it is credible. It has been done before, hundreds of times. Arnold has shown him the statistics, the case histories.)

"And we talked about dance," Nina continues.

"About dance?" He is surprised. Arnold has told him that Stacey is not educated. She was pregnant with her first child when she graduated from high school.

"She took a course in the dance. Apparently, she takes a lot of courses."

"That's encouraging." David has a special sympathy for the students who attend evening and adult extension classes like the one he himself occasionally teaches in drafting and design at the local community college. He has watched them as they arrive at the campus and approach the lecture halls. They are weary and slow of step; their faces are gray with fatigue and their eyes are dull. They step diffidently out of the way and clutch their battered briefcases defensively as energetic undergraduates dash out of the building they enter at twilight. Still, they plod determinedly to the lecture halls, which are littered with the detritus of the day students — balled-up scraps of paper, chewing-gum wrappers, chipped Styrofoam cups, pencil stubs, and dried-out Bic pens. (David recalls a woman who methodically cleaned her area of the classroom each evening before his lecture, even wiping her desk with a damp cloth.) Spurred by tenacity, such students open their notebooks, will themselves to wakefulness, and struggle to comprehend the lesson, to scavenge scraps of knowledge, to glean leavings of culture. He pities these desperate scholars and he admires them. Will he pity and admire Stacey Cosgrove? he wonders.

"Yes. It says something special about her." Nina places her knife and fork diagonally across the plate. "I got the feeling that she goes to these classes because she wants to be . . . I don't know . . . better, I guess. And because she believes that she is better."

"Better than what? Better than whom?" He is impatient. He has the scientist's urge for positive conclusions based on clear and invariable evidence. Nina offers him intuition and insight, which at once fills him with wonder and admiration, uncertainty and distrust. He lacks the artist's faith.

"Better than the life she lives. Maybe better than the people she lives it with," Nina replies slowly. Mentally she translates Stacey's yearnings into the language of dance — a leap that falls short, an aborted grand jeté, arms outstretched and then lowered in defeat, despair.

They order fresh fruit for dessert, and the waiter brings them a bowl not unlike the one Nina set out in the garden that morning. Nina takes a plum, but David lifts his cup of espresso and studies it as though searching out secrets in the dark, syrupy drink, which he has laced with too much sugar, too much Amaretto.

"Shall we go ahead then?"

"It's your decision. You'll have to meet her, talk to her."

"Of course." But his voice is very soft and he does not lift his eyes from the cup.

"It is what you want, isn't it?" Nina asks gently, reasonably.

"You know what I want. I want a child. My own child." He has spoken these words so often that they sound worn thin, like a record overplayed on a defective turntable. If he utters them yet again, he thinks, the disk will crack and the words will merge into shredded, incomprehensible syllables, a madman's gibberish endlessly repeated.

"I know." She leans across the table and grips his wrists. Her nails cut into his soft flesh. This pressure is her reassurance, her recogni-

tion of his need. Her eyes glitter with sorrow because she cannot give him the child he so desperately wants. Often, standing naked in the shower, she passes her fingers across the pale, ridged scar of the incision and curses her own body for the malignancy it carried within it — the threatening tumor that robbed her of the ability to give life and deprived David of fatherhood. She understands the intensity of his desire; she comprehends its wellspring. She had wept, as he had wept, when they stared at the photographs of children at the Yad VaShem memorial museum in Jerusalem. Later, walking from Mount Herzl to the city, he had said aloud, "Where life continues, death is denied." His father's words. She had heard them before (marveling that he remembered them, wondering if he had created the memory) and she would hear them again, but she was newly aggrieved. Because of her, he did not have the power to deny death.

"David," she says now, "I understand. Truly. Truly."

She did not have to go to Israel. She has always known. She has always understood. She loves him enough to share his yearning (again the word intrudes), to become his accomplice, his partner. His desire is her own. His child will be her child.

He lifts her fingers from his wrist, and together they stare down at the pale arcs her nails have carved into his flesh.

"I know," he says. "Darling. Nina darling. I know."

"You'll call her then?"

"Yes. I'll call her. I'll invite her to dinner."

"Lunch will be better," Nina says. "But give her the choice."

"Yes. I'll give her the choice. Nina?"

"Yes?"

"Thank you." He reaches across the table, takes her hand, and brings it to his lips. Moist and soft, his kiss grazes her palm, rests against her heart line.

Hildy is in the kitchen when they arrive home. She sits at the table in her lemon-yellow baby-doll pajamas, her long legs already tanned to an even golden brown entwined around the legs of the chair. Her newly shampooed dark hair forms a satin caplet about her angular face. She polishes her nails with scarlet lacquer as she takes sips from a large glass of milk. Her hand brushes against the glass and a scrap

of wet polish clings to it and forms a blood-red crescent against the whiteness.

"Did you have a good dinner?" she asks.

"Yes," Nina replies. "Did you eat at Alison's?"

"I ate." As always, Hildy offers a curt half answer that is no answer at all. She shoots a glance at David, and her blue eyes are bright with mischievous defiance. She anticipates his anger, his annoyance. But he says nothing.

He agrees with Nina that Hildy's rudeness is provocative. And his sister-in-law, Edith, who is a clinical psychologist, has told him that such behavior is not unusual. "She's testing you. It's an adolescent syndrome." The test is probably more arduous, he supposes, because he is not Hildy's natural father, although he adopted her when he married Nina. Hildy was six then. She wore a pale blue organdy dress to the wedding and her dark hair was caught up in two clusters of curls and tied with blue ribbons. She had hugged him when he lifted her after the ceremony and kissed him wetly and called him Daddy. Perhaps now she wants to be reassured that he will never reject her, never rescind the bonds of responsibility and affection that were formed with the adoption. A natural parent has no choice. Blood and genes cannot be denied, but an adoption agreement is, after all, only a piece of paper.

Does Hildy feel this? Does he feel this? The thought frightens him. He loves Hildy and has loved her from their first meeting. He allows memories to cascade in a kaleidoscope of reassurance — memories of him and Hildy dashing into the ocean during vacations at the Connecticut shore, Hildy on his shoulders at a birthday party, Hildy flushed with fever clutching his hand and screaming, "Daddy, Daddy, Daddy!" She no longer calls him Daddy. He cannot remember when she began to call him David. Never mind. This too will pass. It is a phase, and they will weather it, and it does not matter what she calls him.

"As long as you're not hungry," he says drily.

They turn to go upstairs, his arm around Nina as though to protect her from Hildy's anger.

"Hey, Mom."

They pause warily.

"What is it, Hildy?"

"Who was that woman who was here this morning? That dumpy, brassy blonde?"

"A friend," Nina replies coolly.

"Oh, yeah?" Hildy's harsh laughter trails after them as they walk on. Minutes later she follows them. They hear the sound of her tape deck. Madonna singing "Material Girl." It is the song they dislike the most, and they have told her so because Edith has stressed that it is important that they share their feelings. The volume is turned up and the refrain blares.

"Cause we are living in a material world and I am a material girl.
You know we're living in a material world and I am a material girl."

David cringes at the harsh words sung in that defiant, childlike voice. Nina shrugs and grimaces. Exhausted, she flings herself down across the bed.

"Come here," she says and holds her arms out.

"No room," he replies.

Their oversized bed, covered with a woven spread in the deep burgundy Nina favors, is strewn with the stuffed animals they have collected since their marriage. There is the lamb he bought in Somerset, fashioned of snow-white wool with coal-dark eyes, the peacock made with real feathers that sat on Nina's lap throughout a flight from France, the thin-legged pink flamingo she found in a Florida craft shop, the turquoise elephant Hildy bought them one anniversary, and the widely grinning Tigger, which Nina tosses at him now. Expertly, he catches the soft plush orange-and-black tiger and advances toward Nina, hiding behind it.

" 'Tiger, Tiger, burning bright in the forests of the night,' " he chants, and she fights off his advance, barricading herself behind a small pyramid of animals. He sweeps them away and lies down beside her, placing the tiger on the headboard, amid the other animals and carved figurines.

Nina turns on her side, and languidly he unzips her dress, watches her writhe out of it, and then he lies still as she unbuttons his shirt, removes his shoes, his socks. Like small children, they undress each other, and he switches the lamp off when they are naked. Their

lovemaking that night is both gentle and swift, as though they seek
to reassure each other, to demonstrate at once their tenderness and
their passion. When Nina is asleep, David gets out of bed and steps
onto the small, soft pile of animals. He scoops them up and carries
them to the chaise, smiling at the picture of himself: a middle-aged
naked man, moving through the darkness, his arms full of brightly
colored stuffed animals.

He puts on a robe, opens the door, and sees that Hildy has not
shut off the downstairs light. He will have to go down again and
make certain that the house is dark and the front door is bolted. He
has never gone to sleep without checking the bolt on the front door.
He is a careful man.

That same night, Stacey and Hal Cosgrove lie naked across their
king-sized bed and watch Johnny Carson. Because the color tube on
their television set is defective, the faces of Johnny and his guest,
sex therapist Dr. Ruth Westheimer, are a bilious green.

"She looks like a moon gremlin," Hal says. "A troll." He fiddles
with the volume so that the sound is distorted and Dr. Ruth's Vi-
ennese accent becomes the garbled speech of a diminutive alien.

Stacey laughs. Hal can always make her laugh. Even when she is
angriest with him, when she sees quite clearly that he is irresponsible
and perhaps will always be irresponsible (she does not need her father and brothers to chronicle his failings — she has indexed them
herself again and again), he can make her laugh. That is one reason
why she knows she will never leave him. He fends off the dark moods
that grip and subdue her and fill her with the fear that nothing matters, that nothing will ever matter again. Hal can break that melancholy bewitchment with his love, his laughter. He twists around
on the bed and picks up the half-finished bottle of beer on the night
table.

"Don't," she says and playfully pats his stomach. Hal is a tall, lean
man, but now a small potbelly is forming, although he tries to obscure it by pulling his belt too tight. He has a new job, managing a
downtown restaurant, and he likes the way the secretaries who eat
there look at him.

"It's your hair and eyes they go for, not your stomach," Stacey has

told him knowingly. Hal has thick dark hair, which he allows to grow just a shade too long, and narrow dark eyes. When Jared was born, he cultivated a short, neatly trimmed beard. The combination of hair and beard implies an unconventional, inquiring intellect. Many of the young women with whom Hal shares an occasional drink or a cup of coffee have urged him to go back to school, to earn a degree. He listens to them carefully and nods thoughtfully. Sometimes he sighs deeply. He speaks seriously about the wonderful programs available for older students at the Columbia School of General Studies, the City University. But of course he will never go back to school. He still gets a knot in his stomach when he thinks about school and about the years he spent staring at words he could not read, numbers he could not add.

He was promoted because the teachers loved him. He acted out the stories he could not read, relying on the pictures in the primers. They thought him clever and charming and relied on him to carry their notes from room to room. They forgave his inability to take tests. It was well known that some children just froze during examinations. It was evident that Hal Cosgrove was a bright boy. It was evident to everyone except the long-chinned young teacher who took over his sixth-grade class. The second time he turned in a blank test paper claiming nausea, she asked him to stay after school and took him into the resource room, where she proffered test after test. She resisted his excuses and explanations until at last he threw the desk over and scattered the wide-margined pages that he could not read.

"I can't do it!" he had screamed. "So what the hell. So I'm stupid."

"You're not stupid," she had said so firmly that he believed her. "You have what we call a learning disability, and now that we know that we can help you. I'll speak to your parents."

"My father," Hal had muttered. His mother was long dead, and his father, a morose, silent machinist who kept their tiny apartment immaculate and cooked bland but nutritious meals, was uninterested in Hal's schoolwork. Hal had been a "change of life" baby, born when his older brother and sister were already married and his father was too exhausted to care.

The machinist came to see the teacher but expressed no concern, nor did he take note of the fact that by ninth grade Hal was reading and had even learned to divide and multiply. But Hal had never really caught up. He was too discouraged. He had drifted through high school on the waves of that discouragement, buoyed by an ir-repressible humor, a magical charm. He did not need learning. He compensated for it with cleverness, with an almost charismatic ami-ability. Sometimes, watching late-night talk shows, he thinks that he should have been a comedian. He has always been able to make people laugh.

He can usually make his bosses laugh too. For a while at least. Until they reluctantly discover inaccuracies in his work, discrepan-cies at the register. He is not dishonest, they all decide. He is care-less. Always he receives a good reference and always there is another job, another boss. And, of course, there is always Stacey.

They have been together since their junior year in high school, when Stacey offered to type his term paper and then found she would have to write it as well. She wrote it in his bedroom (the aging machinist went to bed after the seven o'clock news), sitting naked at his desk after their first swift and energetic lovemaking. The topic he had chosen was "The Bill of Rights: What It Means to Me," and Stacey wrote it straight on the typewriter while he watched tele-vision and made her giggle by turning down the volume on commer-cials and making up his own words. She wore her golden hair short then, and he had told her that she looked like a cherub as she sat at the desk, sucking the eraser of her pencil. He had fallen asleep, and she had covered him and pulled the blanket up under his chin before she left, placing the neatly typed paper beside him.

She covers him now because the spring air is mischievous, and although the evening was warm, a sudden chill has come with the night. And then she puts on her faded blue terry-cloth robe and goes to cover the children. He lies back, his hands beneath his head. He hears her bare feet padding softly down the narrow hallway and then the boys' murmurs and Andrea's sweetly trilling laughter. She laughs in her sleep, his little girl, his beautiful small princess.

"So tell me what these Roths are like," he says when Stacey comes back into the room. It is the first time he has mentioned her visit to the Roth home, and she had wondered if he had forgotten about it, but of course Hal does not forget such things. He only makes it seem as though he does, as though to minimize their importance.

"I only met her. That's how they wanted it, Dr. Roth said."

"Why her? What's she got to do with it?" Hal asks irritably.

"She's his wife. In the end she'll be the mother."

"The mother." He laughs harshly. "I'm not too good at dictionary definitions, but I always thought the mother was the lady who gave birth to the baby."

"Hal, stop." She speaks very softly, but he does stop and pulls her closer to him as though asking forgiveness.

"She seemed very nice," Stacey continues. "She's a dancer. A choreographer. Beautiful in this sort of interesting way. And she has a daughter from a different marriage. That's important, I think. I mean, it wouldn't be like having a baby was a whole new thing to her." Stacey's voice is dreamy, as though she is talking to herself, rather than to him. Still, he listens carefully, alert to tone and inflection.

"What happens now?" he asks.

"We wait and see, I guess. I have to meet him. I suppose Dr. Roth will call or else he'll call — David Roth. And then — what about you?"

"What about me?'"

"Don't you want to meet them?"

"Meet them? Why the hell do I want to meet them?" he asks angrily. He finishes the beer in one swallow and leaps out of bed, holding his stomach taut, slapping it. "Who are they to me?"

"I don't know," Stacey says quietly, seriously, and he can see that she is trying to figure it out. That's how Stacey is. She is always figuring things out. He grins, his anger defused as swiftly as it was aroused. It doesn't matter. The whole thing will probably fall through. It's a crazy idea. He goes back to bed and kisses Stacey on the forehead, the mouth.

"Listen. Don't worry," he says gently. "It's going to be all right."

"I wasn't worried," she replies. "I was only thinking."

But she closes her eyes and does not reply. She does not want to tell him that she was thinking about the sound of silver wind chimes in the soft spring breeze and the tart taste of the white cherries in her mouth. Someone once told her that cherry trees grow wild in California, and she imagines herself and the children picking huge clusters in a roadside glen. She will dangle them like earrings about her ears and Andrea's, and she will hang wind chimes at the door of the redwood house in which they will live. She sees the house clearly. It nestles in the curve of a low hill, shaded at the rear, flooded with sunlight where their deck (their enormous deck) encroaches upon a flowering meadow. Smiling, she falls asleep, Hal's arm flung carelessly across her stomach.

3

David Roth calls Stacey Cosgrove the next morning to arrange a meeting the following week. She is hesitant, almost cagey, and he is fearful that her visit with Nina had somehow discouraged her. But all her excuses are plausible. She cannot meet him on Monday because she must take her older son to the dental clinic. Tuesday is the one day a week she volunteers at the library. ("I love working with books," she adds proudly, and he can sense the yearning Nina had stressed.) On Wednesday her daughter is in a school play, and that Thursday she is the cookie mother at her younger son's play group. Her week is gone, she says regretfully, and he suggests the following Monday.

"Fine." Her agreement is swift, breathless, as though she had feared that he might give up.

"Lunch or dinner?" he asks as Nina suggested.

"Oh, lunch, of course," she says with an edge of righteousness in her voice. "I have to be home to give my children dinner."

And lunch too, as it turns out, must be at an earlier hour than is convenient for him. She must arrange their meeting before the noon hour so that she will be at home before her children arrive from school. He acquiesces. The scales are heavily weighted on her side. He has nothing to balance against the needs of her children and her own vigilant concern for them. And that concern does impress him, he acknowledges as he hangs up, although he is nagged by the odd suspicion that Stacey Cosgrove had meant for him to be impressed.

Stacey wears the same blue dress patterned with honey-colored flowers for her luncheon with David Roth. She had wanted to wear her white suit but discovered that it was too tight. She had not lost the weight she gained while nursing Jared. It was the beer. The malt enriched her breast milk, they had told her at the La Leche League, and she had formed the habit of drinking a glass at lunch and a full bottle at dinner.

She puts the white suit back in the closet, pleased that although it is four years old its fabric has not yellowed. It has a California look, and by the time they get to California she will be thinner and she will wear the suit with a new jade-green blouse. (She sees this blouse, as yet unbought, quite clearly. It has small green buttons and a bow tie.) But for today the blue dress will have to do. She wears pale blue patterned stockings and her high-heeled white sandals. She brushes her hair for a long time, matting down the curls, but in the end she does not wear it loose but ties it back with a loosely knotted blue scarf, the way she wore it in high school. Indeed, when she enters the restaurant, David Roth thinks she is a student and so he ignores her.

Both Nina and Arnold described Stacey accurately, but he had not expected her to look so young, to glow with that cherublike innocence. In the end it is Stacey who approaches him. She walks determinedly across the small reception area, where a blond waitress in peasant costume desultorily arranges matchbooks and menus on a vinyl-topped table.

"You're David Roth, aren't you? I recognize you because you look so much like your brother."

David is flustered, disarmed. He does resemble Arnold somewhat. They both have their father's sandy hair and wide-spaced hazel eyes, straight-lashed and heavy-browed, and their mother's fair complexion. But David is tall and large-boned, while Arnold is a short man and slender of build. David's expression is open, optimistic, while Arnold always looks wary, concerned. He enters every room, Nina had once observed with shrewd cruelty, as though he is braced for tragedy, uncertainty. (David did not remind her that Arnold, after all, had entered his living room and discovered his father dead in an easy chair. He has stopped trying to forge a friendship between his wife and his brother.)

"Of course. And you are Stacey Cosgrove." He smiles at her, prepares to gain her favor, to cajole her into admiring him as she admires his brother. He is not unaware that young women are drawn to him. The technical assistants vie with each other to work with him. Edna, his secretary, works overtime cheerfully and shields him valiantly against intrusive phone calls, visitors who will waste his time. All the young women who work for him give him clever gifts at Christmas, and each year on his birthday they jointly produce champagne and a cake and giggle pleasantly at his surprise. And he is always surprised because he always forgets that they had remembered his birthday the previous year. In turn, he is solicitous of them, gentle and gentlemanly. He remembers to ask about their families, to compliment them on a pretty pin, a sweater, a new dress patterned with wildflowers. Before their lunch is over, he will have told Stacey Cosgrove that he likes her dress.

They follow the waitress to a corner table in a large, brightly lit room, which at this hour is almost empty. He orders a gin and tonic for himself, and although Stacey is hesitant, she at last orders a strawberry daiquiri. Her choice amuses him and evokes memories of his college dating years when strawberry daiquiris were the preferred drink of girls who hated the taste of liquor but were intrigued by the feminine pink of the sweet cocktail. He is more at ease when the drinks are served, when she has tasted hers and a foamy mustache crests her upper lip.

"Tell me something about yourself, Stacey," he says. It is his standard opening when he interviews young women for jobs in his office or his workroom. And he is, after all, interviewing Stacey Cosgrove. That is what this luncheon is all about.

She looks at him. Her eyes are green, a pale jade color, and she opens them wide, as children do when their innocence is startlingly and briefly affronted. But then she smiles, and her smile is friendly and disarmingly imperfect, revealing a jagged tooth to which a shred of pink-dyed citrus clings. She licks it away, her tongue moving with catlike skill.

"There's not much to tell," she says. "I got married my last year in high school. But I did graduate. I always thought I would go to college. I had good marks and I loved school. I still do. I'm always

taking courses — you know, at the community college and at evening extensions. But I got pregnant right away, and of course the
baby was more important. And then Hal and I talked about it and
we figured that it was best to have our family while we were still
young. Hal is a wonderful man, a terrific father. We were high school
sweethearts. You know — proms and class outings and all that sort
of thing. We used to study together." She blushes. She is painting
him a word picture plucked from the pages of *Seventeen* or the in-
nocent television sitcoms of vanished decades. She sees herself as a
Brady Bunch daughter, blooming with adolescent innocence coupled
with an attitude of mature responsibility.

Hildy would laugh, he knows. He imagines his stepdaughter's harsh
mimicry and recalls how he arrived home a few weeks earlier to find
her with her friends Seth and Alison sprawled on the floor giggling
wildly as they watched a rerun of *Leave It to Beaver*. The scent of
marijuana had lingered in the room despite the open windows, and
he had suspected that they had doused a joint at the sound of his car
in the driveway. Still, he had said nothing but had stood in the
driveway and watched them mock the script with deadly accuracy.
In chorus they had shouted, "Gee whiz!" and "I'll get it, Mom,"
imitating the youthful actor's tone and accent. But Stacey Cosgrove
would not mock *Leave It to Beaver*. She aspires to its tenor, its values.

"What does your husband do for a living?" David asks as he accepts the menus from the waitress and passes one to Stacey. The
menus are pretentious, leatherbound and oversized, but Stacey sets
hers aside without a glance and orders spaghetti with white clam
sauce.

"Make that two, and a green salad for each of us," he tells the
waitress.

"I always have the same thing in an Italian restaurant," Stacey
confides. "My whole family does. Me, my mom and dad, my brothers."

She is a married woman with three children of her own, he notes,
but when she speaks of her "family," it is her parents and siblings to
whom she refers. No one marries out of the *Brady Bunch*, and everyone stays the same age forever.

"Anyway, you were asking about Hal," she continues. "The thing
with Hal is that he has this learning disability. He's dyslexic and

that sort of screwed him up in school and he got too disgusted to think about college. But he has this great personality and he's really very smart. A disability doesn't mean you're stupid — in fact, a lot of dyslexic people are really brilliant. Einstein, for instance. Albert Einstein."

"I've heard that," David acknowledges.

"Hal's had a lot of really good jobs managing restaurants and clubs and stuff like that. He's a natural with people. They really like him. Our kids' friends all say they wish they had a dad like Hal. He can make them laugh. That's one thing he can always do — make people laugh." She herself laughs now as though in remembered merriment, and the waitress who sets down their plates smiles also. Stacey's good humor is contagious.

"And how would Hal feel about . . . about what we are contemplating?" David asks and recognizes at once his fear of putting the purpose of their meeting into words. Even in thought it repels him as much as it attracts him.

He had broken into a cold sweat when Arnold first suggested it, although cautious Arnold had spoken in hypothetical terms, his voice cool and edged with the disinterested restraint of the clinician. The brothers had been having dinner together after going to synagogue to say kaddish on the anniversary of their father's death. They are not religious men, but always they have said kaddish for their father at the small synagogue around the corner from their boyhood home and then eaten at the dairy restaurant Amos Roth had favored.

It had occurred to David on that particular evening that he was now exactly as old as Amos Roth had been when he died. Since his return from the exhibit of Amos Roth's paintings in Israel a few months earlier, David had been obsessed by coincidences in family histories. He had sat before the computer in the Museum of the Diaspora in Tel Aviv and watched dates, names, places, flash across the screen as family chronologies were revealed. More than once he had noted how dates repeated themselves: a father and a son sharing a birthday, mothers and daughters dying at the same age, brothers dying on the very same date in different years. He was thirty-eight. At thirty-eight Amos Roth was dead, and at thirty-eight David, his younger son, was haunted by grim forebodings.

"Thirty-eight." Arnold had nodded. "So young when you think in terms of death."

"I think I'm going to repeat what every damn visitor said during the week of shivah," David had said. "Remember: 'A tragedy, but look what he left behind.' If I were to die tomorrow, Arnold, what the hell would I leave behind?"

Bitterness soured his mouth and his eyes burned. The thought had haunted him since his birthday, weeks before. Suddenly he had become aware of the gray at his temples, the shortness of breath when he raced for his train each morning. His body had begun to betray him. The ophthamologist prescribed stronger glasses; the internist spoke warningly of cholesterol. Slowly, he was slipping across life's shadowed border. Two of his classmates had died of heart attacks in recent months, and he read his alumni bulletin with trepidation. The buffer generation that had stood between his contemporaries and death was vanishing. He went to the funerals of his friends' parents and felt the cold breath of his own mortality. Often he awakened in the night, fearful because his heart beat too fast, his extremities were cold, and the singing of mysterious birds intruded on the nocturnal silence.

"You have your family," Arnold said carefully. "Nina. Hildy. The business."

"The business." David shrugged. "I'm not underestimating my little inventions, Arnold, but they're no great contribution. And in the end, legal documents notwithstanding, Hildy's not my daughter, although God knows I've tried to be a father to her. But even if things were different with Hildy, I'd still want a child of my own. Do you know what I mean?"

"Flesh of your flesh. Blood of your blood," Arnold had replied. "Is that what you mean?"

"Exactly. Is it shameful to want some sort of continuity, some sort of guarantee of survival, of family survival? Especially when you come from a family like ours that has been virtually decimated. God, Arnold, I didn't realize until I looked up the history of our family, of Papa's village, in Yad VaShem and then in the Museum of the Diaspora, how many had been lost in the war. I understood Papa's paintings then, for the very first time. They do a sort of computer image of a family tree at the museum and I thought, 'I am the last branch. There will be no outgrowth after my name to symbolize a new generation.' I wanted to cry then, Arnold — to cry because so many had been killed and because I would never have a child to replace them. Is it wrong to want a child who is a biological link to the future, who might inherit my eyes, maybe even Papa's talent, whose birth might somehow compensate for all those terrible deaths?"

David lifted his hands pleadingly. Each word he spoke was an assault upon his marriage, perhaps a denial of Hildy. No. Nina understood his feelings and he could never deny Hildy. He loved her. But his love for her did not preclude his yearning for a child in whom he would see himself, his father, a child in whose life (as Amos Roth had said) death itself was denied.

"Not shameful," Arnold said. "Normal. Natural. I hear sentiments like that a dozen times a month in my practice. Men say it and women say it. 'Give us a child.' 'We want a child.' And they mean their own child. Flesh of their flesh. Blood of their blood. I wasn't being sarcastic."

"And what do you do for them?"

"I try my fertility tricks. Sperm count. Temperature charts. Ovulation accuracy. Fallopian examinations. And then I send them to other doctors who may have some other tricks or another perspective on the problem. Relaxation therapy, perhaps. Intercourse patterning. Some even believe in diet, vitamins, psychotherapy."

"And if all that doesn't work?"

"Then we are at the hope of the last resort. Artificial insemination. In vitro fertilization. And we suggest adoption. Foster children. The gamut. But none of these would be helpful to you, David. Nina's medical history would exclude them, and I know that you don't want to raise someone else's child."

Arnold looked down and stirred his coffee. In his consulting room, he often looks down at his desk when he speaks to patients of such matters. He cannot bear the pain in their eyes, the glances of sorrow and hurt, of accusation and recrimination that husbands and wives dart at each other when he confirms at last the cessation of hope. And always he had worried about his younger brother, worried about him and protected him. Hadn't he stood in the doorway to the living

room so that David would not see the disbelieving grimace of death
that had etched its way across their father's face?

"Of course, for Nina, with Nina, it's over," David said.

Arnold knew about Nina's hysterectomy. As David himself had
known about it from the beginning. Nina, her voice quivering, had
told him about it the first time they made love. She had wept as she
spoke, and he had kissed away her tears and then passed his lips
across the rose-dusted rise of her nipples, the pale scar that carved a
smile across her abdomen.

"It doesn't matter," he had assured her.

And it had not mattered. Not then, not all those years ago when
the future was tomorrow and he could not think beyond the moment
of their next meeting, the memory of their last exchange. He had
not thought about having his own child during those early years.
They had Hildy, who streaked through the house, climbed into bed
to lie between them, darted onto the porch in her flowered nightgown to greet him each night when he returned home. She had been
a mercurial child, radiant and swift as quicksilver, until the moodi-
ness of adolescence slowed her pace, darkened her spirit, and turned
him from "Daddy" into "David."

But even before that he had felt the stirrings of an anomalous
desire. Often, passing a young man walking with a child, he would
find himself studying their faces, searching out similarities of feature,
of stance. His friend John Cowper, newly divorced from the woman
for whom he had written the beautiful haiku verses, came to visit
with his young son. Terry was a boy soprano; he sang Purcell with a
melancholy sweetness.

"Funny," John had said. "I'm a monotone myself, but my father
had a wonderful voice. Strange how the genes surface. You'll see."

David had remained silent, yet John's words had echoed his own
feelings. Yes, he too wanted the genes to surface, he too longed for
the renewal of generations. He mourned the children who would not
be born to him, the sons and daughters in whom he might have seen
a glimmer of his father's talent, whose eyes might have been deep-
set like those of his grandfather, whose laughter might have, in some
small, mysterious way, compensated for the agony of the cousins he
had never known — the children whose faces stared up at him from

the pages of the photograph album that had survived the war. He acknowledged then (even as he refilled John's glass and poured himself a double scotch, which he did not drink) the aching emptiness that he knew to be a sense of loss, of life denied.

An unfamiliar sadness had enveloped him then, a crippling despondency that slowed his steps and his speech, that blocked his laughter. He waited, day after day, for it to disappear, to vanish like a heavy and oppressive mist, pierced at last by sunlight. And Nina waited too. He felt her worried eyes upon him, heard the bewilderment in her voice. He had never been a moody man. The change was frightening to her.

"What is it?" she asked one night, lying rigidly beside him in the darkness. She held a tiny stuffed ermine, fashioned of that animal's actual fur, which he had given her for her birthday, and as she spoke, she rubbed her cheek with it, as though to take comfort from its luxurious softness. She waited for him to tell her that he had cancer, that he was having an affair, that his business was in trouble. She had considered so many sources for his misery, braced herself for a desperate revelation. Still, she was unprepared for his reply.

"I want a child — a child of my own," he had said and recognized in his own voice the whine of a small boy who knows that his dearest wish cannot, will not, be fulfilled. Shame mingled with sorrow and he held her close.

"Are you sorry then?" she had asked him, trembling. "Would you still have married me if you had known then how you would feel now, how much you would want a child of your own?"

He looked at her. In the darkness her skin was as white as the tiny stuffed animal that she clutched still, as though this new misery had drained it of color, had blanched it.

"I don't know." He had been honest with her. "Everything changed for me when we went to Israel. You remember, Nina, how we looked at those montages at Yad VaShem — the faces of the children?"

"Yes."

"I remembered what my father had said."

" 'Where life continues, death is denied.' " How quiet her voice was.

"Yes. I said it then. And since then, not a day goes by when those words don't come back to me. I'm sorry. I've tried to rationalize it away. A mood. A midlife crisis. But the mood grows — like some damn emotional cancer. Is it selfish of me, Nina?" He had waited for her to chastise him, to reason with him, to blast him free of his yearning. Instead she had lifted her face to his, had kissed his eyes (closed against her pain), his cheeks, his lips, as her long black hair fell across his shoulders.

"What does it matter, David? It's how you feel. You can't help that. And I can't help that." Her honesty had matched his own and had, in the end, given him license to speak so openly to his brother.

And Arnold too had been honest with him that night as they spoke over dinner, on the anniversary of their father's death.

"There is a way for you to have your own child though, David. A rather radical way, but it's been done."

"How?"

"You could father your own child although Nina would not be the biological mother. A woman impregnated with your sperm would carry the child for you for a fee and give it to you and Nina for adoption. There would be a contract, consent, clear terms."

It was then that David felt the cold sweat form — small beads of ice congealed beneath his arms, across his chest and back. He was shocked that Arnold, conservative, gentle Arnold, would suggest such a radical idea. Had his desire for a child been so desperate, so nakedly apparent, that his brother would offer this unorthodox recourse — what had he called it? Oh, yes, the hope of the last resort.

"It sounds dangerous, risky to me. Unprecedented."

"Not unprecedented. There are cases on record. Several hundred, I believe, and probably ten times as many that are unrecorded, private arrangements made by lawyers and doctors acting discreetly, quietly, but within the law. And not dangerous if you make the right choice, find the right woman."

"Do you know of such a woman?" David had asked, his heart beating too fast, his body racked with a sudden tremor.

It was then that Arnold had mentioned Stacey Cosgrove for the first time.

David watches Stacey now as she eats her spaghetti, carefully curling the strands about the tines of her fork, snipping off the uneven ends with her spoon. Her concentration is such that he wonders wryly if she has taken a course in etiquette. The snobbery of the thought shames him. She is a nice woman, sweet and open, admirable, in fact, from all that she has told him, from all that Arnold has told him.

Arnold delivered her three children and has known her since her first pregnancy. Always she has been a good patient, careful of herself and the child she carried, concerned about the family at home; then too, she has been courageous (Arnold is that rare obstetrician who recognizes the courage of pregnant women), forbearing in the face of discomfort and pain. But most important of all, she loves being pregnant.

She feels best, she has told Arnold (and he believed her because her sincerity, her enjoyment was so evident), when life grows within her. She glows from the moment of gestation ("And I know when it happens — I always know," she has asserted proudly) through the long and langorous nine months as the embryo slowly takes form, swims its way into humanity, moving and shifting within the opalescent envelope of her womb, awash in the nourishing fluids of her body. She feels then that she is participating in a miracle, that each day of her pregnancy throbs with a sense of purpose. She welcomes the burden of increased weight, the clumsiness, the isolated spells of nausea, even the leg cramps and the sleeplessness of the last trimester — all proof of growth and development. She is at once creator and nurturer, and it is all effortless — effortless and wonderful and still mysterious. She looks at her children, at Evan and Andrea and Jared, and thinks, "Oh, did I make them? Oh, did they truly grow within me?"

The effort, the strain comes afterward. She loves her children, she told Arnold. She is a good mother, but what she truly loves, what has given her the greatest joy, the sweetest pleasure of her life, is the condition of pregnancy — of life within life.

She told Arnold all this a year after the birth of her last child because Hal had insisted she arrange for a tubal ligation. He did not want any more children. Three was all they could manage, all they could afford.

"And what do you want?" Arnold had asked. It was a routine

question, posed to all his patients at such consultations, because he believes that all emotional avenues must be explored. There are unforeseen situations that he would have his patients consider. What if a woman has a tubal ligation and one of her children dies? What if death or divorce terminates her marriage and she remarries and is unable to give her new husband a child? Gently he probed, questioned. Stacey was open, honest. It was then that she had spoken to him of her feelings during pregnancy, her reaction to Hal's request.

"I don't want it," she replied. "I'd get pregnant again if we could afford another child. But we can't, you know that. We can't afford anything. Our kids are bright, all three of them. I want them to go to college. But that takes money. Hal gets a job and then he loses it and then he gets another, but the truth is they're not such great jobs. I've got to bring in some income, and I can't do that if I'm pregnant and raising kids. Birth control doesn't work for us. We're too lazy or too careless or too unlucky."

"How do you see your life, your future?" he had asked. The question exceeded the usual parameters, but throughout the interview he had been haunted by the ghost of an idea, the whisper of a possibility.

"I want to get to California. All of us. It would be a new start. Hal could really make something of himself there, maybe even get his own place. He's easygoing and has this great personality. They like that casual style in the West. A lot of people have told him that. And there are a whole lot of other advantages. The climate. Good-bye to snowsuits and boots and heating bills that make me puke. And there's the state university system for my kids. I had a teacher in this course I took last year who said that California had the best educational opportunities for kids in the whole country. And he wasn't talking just community colleges or vocational schools. But before we could even start out, we'd need twenty thousand dollars, I figure, to cover fares and start-up money and settle accounts here." Stacey smiled at him apologetically. She has not forgotten that she still owes Arnold a substantial sum, although he has told her that in view of her insurance problems (but mostly because he likes her), he will forgive it.

"Twenty thousand dollars," Arnold repeated. It was not an enor-

mous sum, but it was not a small sum either. It would take Stacey
and Hal Cosgrove at least five years to save such an amount, he
estimated, and even then there would be no guarantee. Stacey might
work and begin to save, and Hal, careless, charming Hal, might
empty the account for a surefire investment that would not be surefire, for a tip on a horse, for a weekend binge. Arnold had met Hal
and liked him, but he recognized his type: the sweet-talking, infan-
tile con man, as unreliable as he was likable. Stacey's scenario for
her family's future, for the westward move (which does make sense,
he admits), is plucked from the pages of a slick woman's magazine
("How You Can Change Your Family's Life"), but it will not work.
However, if she had twenty thousand dollars, tax-free, in a single
lump sum on hand, then a new chapter might be written. It was
then that he had again mentioned his brother, David, that caring,
careful man who so desperately wanted a child.

"It would be such an act of generosity — such an opportunity to
do something for someone else and to help your own family. But, of
course, only a very special woman could do that."

Stacey had blushed as though he had paid her a compliment. She
had smiled and lowered her eyes. Hesitantly, Arnold had spoken of
compensation. Her color had deepened. Like a small girl, she sucked
a tendril of golden hair.

"I'd have to think on it," she had said at last, her little-girl voice
quivering. "Talk to Hal."

"Of course." With the courtesy he extends to all his patients, he
had walked her to his office door, where they shook hands. And
then resolutely, he had put all thoughts of Stacey Cosgrove from his
mind. Two weeks later she had called him. She had thought about
it. She had spoken to Hal. She was, in fact, hesitant but receptive.
Still, she would have to meet the man and his wife. She could only
consider doing this special thing for a special man, a special woman.

All this Arnold had reported to David that night, over dinner, on
the anniversary of their father's death. Is she hesitant but receptive
still? David wonders as Stacey eats her salad.

"What do they call this?" she asks, plucking up a piece of arugula,
the tender green leaf so delicately brushed with a carmine fringe.

"Arugula. A kind of lettuce."

"How do you spell it?" To his surprise, she reaches into her oversized white plastic shoulder bag and pulls out a small notebook and a ballpoint pen chewed away at the top.

"I think it's a-r-u-g-u-l-a," he says carefully, respectfully, "but I may be wrong."

"You wanted to know how Hal would feel about this?" she asks as she replaces the notebook. She steers the conversation back to its point of origin. She is a capable emotional navigator, he recognizes. "Well naturally, it took him by surprise at first." (Hal had, in fact, been incredulous and then furious. "What the hell — you want to be some kind of incubator for someone else's kid? Are you out of your mind?" he had shouted.) "But then we talked." (They *had* talked. She had explained everything very carefully. The physical ramifications. The legal ramifications. How it had been done before. Her own feeling that they would be doing something really fantastic for someone else. It was a good deed. The best deed. And then she had spoken of the money. Twenty thousand dollars free and clear, after all her medical expenses had been covered. A lump sum. Freedom money to cut them loose from the bitter eastern winter, the narrow, crowded frame house, the desperate cycle of one lousy job after another. It was the gateway to California, with its golden sunlight and golden oranges, and their kids all suntanned and healthy chasing after each other through groves of fruit trees. Not that she would do it just for the money, but the combination was so great — the opportunity to do something really super for someone else and get something for themselves too. Why not? Why not? She had read articles and periodicals in the local library. They would be part of a pioneering vanguard. Other people were doing it. They were just ahead of their time. It was that argument that had turned the tide with Hal. He loves being ahead of his time. Finally, he had agreed to her visit to the Roth home. The first step. And now they were at the second step.) "He's still not really crazy about it, but he thinks he's beginning to feel comfortable with it, which I'd say is a positive reaction." She loves that phrase, which she picked up in a psychology class when she was pregnant with Jared. *Positive reaction.* It offers her a gauge of a kind, an emotional barometer by which she measures herself, measures the world.

"And you — do you have anything you want to ask me, Stacey?"
David asks, addressing her by name for the first time.

"Yeah. How old is your wife's daughter?"

"Hildy?" The question surprises him. "She was seventeen a few
months ago."

"Where's her father?"

"He's dead."

He does not tell Stacey Cosgrove that Michael Ernst, Nina's first
husband, was killed in an accident on a California freeway. He had
been slightly intoxicated, and the driver of the car that jumped the
barrier and smashed into his car on the driver's side had been high
on cocaine. A seventies West Coast collision, Nina had told David
bitterly when she told him about Mike and her brief marriage. She
was eighteen years old when she met him in a dance class. He was
already dancing in the chorus of a Broadway musical — a beautiful
youth, topaz-skinned, his long-lashed eyes slate-colored, clusters of
dark curls clinging to his wonderfully shaped head. Tall for a dancer
and confident. He had trained all his life. Each muscle rippled with
controlled strength; his limbs coiled and uncoiled with wondrous
elasticity. She could not keep her eyes off him. The sound of his
voice, his laughter, hypnotized her. She had followed him into the
street, trailing after him until he turned and laughed and took her
hand. He had claimed her easily, casually. They danced, they made
love, and despite the protests of her parents (a pharmacist and a
teacher who were bewildered by their beautiful, talented daughter),
they married. Michael went on the road when she was three months
pregnant with Hildy. He returned for the birth, held his newborn
daughter as though she were a fragile toy, and told Nina he was
taking off for the Coast. He was sorry, but he was in love with someone else, a blond Swede with whom he had danced in the road
company. A week after his arrival in San Francisco he was dead.
Before Nina could mourn his desertion she was mourning his death.
She rarely speaks of Michael, and Hildy has never mentioned her
father. Why should she, after all? She never knew him.

"Well, that's okay then," Stacey says.

"What's okay?"

"I was worried that your wife was divorced and there'd be problems with her ex-husband. I mean, I wouldn't want this baby we're talking about to grow up in a house that was buzzing with a lot of unfinished business."

"We haven't talked about the baby yet," he reminds her gently.

"I know." She blushes, like a small girl embarrassed by a faux pas. "Dr. Roth told me how much you want a baby of your own. I understand that. Honestly, I do. A lot of people might say, 'So why don't you adopt?' but I think I know how you feel. I've always felt sorry for people who have no kids of their own. It's like they have no future, leave no imprint."

What must it be like, she has wondered, to pass through life leaving no trace, sparking no hope? She has swallowed the disappointments of her own life, the education and fragments of grace she must scavenge from the leavings and charity of others, the worn paperbacks she reads too late at night, too early in the morning. But she feels no defeat because her children may yet succeed. They are so bright, so beautiful; they carry within their glowing bodies her talents, her hopes, her dreams mingled with Hal's easy charm, his gift for laughter, his disarming gentleness. They are her sweet "hostages to fortune." (She will take another Elizabethan literature course this semester, she vows, as the words course through her mind, intoxicating her with their rhythm, their wisdom.) She is overwhelmed with compassion for the sad-eyed man who sits opposite her, who wants so desperately to have his own sweet hostage to fortune, who so openly yearns for hope, for continuity.

"I'd like to help you have a child of your own," she says, her eyes lowered, her voice hesitant, lingering.

"But?" He has discerned the hint of objection, of uneasiness. He is not surprised. He too objects. He too is uneasy. But there is no other way. On that Arnold had been very clear.

"But I don't like the idea of a baby being conceived like in a lab. Okay, not a lab but without contact. I'd just lie there like some prize cow and they'd inject me with your sperm. I can't see a human life beginning like that." She shivers as though anticipating the cold touch of a speculum against the moist warmth of her vulva. Now she speaks in a whisper. "A baby should be born because a man and a woman were together, came together." Her cheeks are burning and her head is lowered as though she fears his scorn, his ridicule.

And he does stare at her in disbelief.

"What do you want then, Stacey?" He asks this question patiently and she is relieved, grateful.

"What I want is for you and me to make love. To go to bed together. I know it sounds crazy, but a baby should be born because there was some kind of feeling between two people, because they were one. I can't stand the idea of test tubes or thermometers or any of that stuff. I want to feel this baby begin to happen the way I felt the beginning with my other kids. And I did feel it, each time. I knew. The doctors don't think that's possible, but I did know. And I want the same thing to happen this time. I want this baby to be conceived because of a feeling between you and me. Oh, not love. Of course not. But friendship. Sharing. Caring. I don't know. But I do know that I'm not a machine. I'm a mother. And a mother has to feel everything. Everything. From the beginning." She takes a long drink of water. She has said all that she meant to say.

"But you're married. I'm married." Frenzied, he scrambles for words, objections; he experiences a dizzying, liberating sense of relief. It is over then. This mad idea is finished, done with. He cannot, he will not, go to bed with this woman who speaks with the breathlessness of a young girl, with this plump blond child-mother.

"But it would have nothing to do with being married," she explains. "It would have nothing to do with Hal and me or with you and your wife. Nothing to do with romance. We would be together only for the baby. It wouldn't interfere with your marriage or with mine, although of course they'd have to know about it — Hal and your wife. It wouldn't be fair otherwise." She speaks in the slow, careful tone of a teacher trying to get a reluctant student to understand a complex concept.

He smiles thinly.

"Stacey, it's not that simple. Suppose, for argument's sake, I agree. Suppose we do go to bed together, have intercourse, but you don't conceive. What then?"

"It could happen," she concedes. "But it won't. I know when it's the right time. I always know."

Each month she feels the contraction of muscles, the tenderness of her breasts, as her cycle peaks to fertility. Occasionally she has even dreamed of the ovum dropping, imagined it floating through her womb, nacreous, opalescent.

David sits perfectly still, absorbing her suggestion, her claim. He neither doubts nor disbelieves her. He understands her reasoning, and now that his first shock has passed, he likes her for it. Strangely, he feels more comfortable about the situation than he has since Arnold first made the suggestion. Stacey has humanized it. She has made him feel her role, her involvement. She will not be an object, a convenient incubator. She wants to be a mother to this child (his child) from conception through delivery. Her proposal no longer sounds bizarre to him. It is possessed of a logic, of an emotional validity that he recognizes and admires.

The waitress, less sullen now that the pockets of her bright-red apron are filled with crisp bills, glides up to them.

"Dessert? Coffee?"

He orders a double espresso. Stacey has a cappuccino with whipped cream and a tortoni.

They do not speak as he drinks his coffee and she spoons tiny bits of her tortoni into the cappuccino and licks the melted ice cream from her spoon. Again, he remarks the catlike quality of her tongue. When she kissed her infant children, did she lick them? he wonders. Does she lick her husband when they make love, her acrobatic tongue caressing the soft lobe of his ear, the tender flesh between neck and shoulder? Will she lick him if they go through with this suggestion of hers? His excitement grows; he experiences an involuntary towering of desire. His face is very hot, and he dips his napkin into the glass of water and pats his brow, his cheeks.

"So?" she says at last.

"I would have to talk to my wife. You would have to talk to your husband." And yet he can hear the hint of acquiescence in his own voice, the small hum of triumph in her murmured assent.

They part, as they met, in the entry of the restaurant. They shake hands soberly in the manner of business associates who have entered into preliminary negotiations. Indeed, she grasps her handbag as though it is an attaché case. They leave, going in opposite directions, and neither of them turns to look back. It is entirely possible, they both know, that they will never see each other again.

4

Because Nina is away all that week participating in a conference on "The Dance and Contemporary Society" at Skidmore College, David does not discuss his conversation with Stacey with her until the following Saturday. Although she called each night, it was tacitly understood between them that this was not a subject to be discussed on the telephone. Instead, they discussed her work, the demonstration class she taught, the urgent project David has been working on. On Wednesday night their conversation centered on Hildy's car, which had been side-swiped in the high school parking lot. The incident had depressed and upset Hildy.

"How did it happen?" Nina asked.

"It's not my fault. You blame everything on me. Maybe it's my fault that I'm alive!" Hildy screamed into the phone.

"It's all right. We'll get it repaired," David said wearily into the extension. "I'll call the body shop tomorrow."

Hildy hung up, and to break the vacuum of silence, Nina spoke of a workshop she had attended, of the excellent restaurant where she and her old friend Bruce Connors had had lunch. She loved Saratoga. Such cunning shops and restaurants. Her hotel was an elegant old hostelry, and she missed David especially when she showered in the spacious bathroom. Her voice was soft, teasing. She would have him remember their shared showers in hotels in the Caribbean, in Athens and Paris and Jerusalem — even the ice-cold outdoor shower of a cabin in the foothills of the Adirondacks.

"I miss you too," he said. "We have a lot to talk about."

"I know." Her voice is sad, almost fearful. "Till Friday night then."

On Friday afternoon, David left work early and went uptown to visit his brother, who, since the birth of his first son, has closed his office after lunch on Fridays. Arnold and Jacob, his elder son, sat at the dining room table, working out a geometry problem. Jacob is a poor math student, and Arnold is concerned about his grades. He is, however, a very fine artist, and his teachers at the High School of Music and Art are enthusiastic about his work.

"I assume he has Papa's talent, although I don't know what Papa would have thought of his work," Arnold had said when he showed David the geometric abstract in oils that Jacob had completed as a class project. Arnold had framed it and hung it beside Amos Roth's celebrated portrait of a cobbler and just beneath his father's haunting sketch of a Holocaust survivor — a large-eyed child who leans against a barren tree.

David and his sister-in-law, Edith, had coffee in the den, which Edith also occasionally uses as an office. David studied the silver-framed photographs on the desk, the cabinet, the bookcases. Amos Roth as a young man, his painter's smock misbuttoned, his eyes squinting at the sunlight. Arnold and his mother on the day of his graduation from medical school. Arnold's young sons in shorts and tee shirts, laughing into the camera, their arms linked. David himself seated in his garden. He was struck anew by the likenesses between the boys and the men. Even their postures were similar, their shoulders thrust slightly forward, their heads tilted, as they stared gravely at the camera. They had each wet-combed their thick sandy hair but were unable to restrain the cowlicks that tumbled across their very high foreheads. And, in each photo, the gravity of the gaze is offset by the humorous, impatient curl of their full lips. They are bonded, the boys and the men, by temperament and feature.

Edith asked him about Stacey and he was not surprised. Arnold and Edith keep nothing from each other.

"I liked her. But I don't know what will happen. It's so . . . so unorthodox. What do you think, Edith?"

"I think you will always regret it if you give up the only opportunity to have a child of your own. But what I think isn't important. It's what you think, what you want."

He did not answer but looked again at the photographs. He did not tell Edith that what he wants is to see himself in his child's eyes, to teach his father's songs to a child of his own, to have his mother lift the infant born to him and say (as she said of each of Arnold's infant sons), "Can't you see Grandpa's chin? Look, look, his hair is the exact color of Amos's." And yes, he wants to show his child the photographs of the small Polish village and tell him of the family who lived there: the vanished Davids and Miriams, the cousins whose names he never knew and will never know for whom he lights a single memorial candle each Yom Kippur eve. He closed his eyes, as Edith spoke of the plans for the bar mitzvah of Aaron, her younger son, and in his mind's eye he saw the glass-enclosed flame flicker so bravely through the long hours of the Day of Atonement.

Edith kissed him when he left, and he knew that she had sensed his sadness.

David and Nina have no time to talk before they must leave for Sabbath dinner at the Goldfeins'. Seth Goldfein has been Hildy's good friend since nursery school. He is a lanky, long-faced youngster who wears his dark hair too long and dresses in faded dungarees that cling to his bony legs and oversized bulky-knit sweaters in martial shades, army khaki, machine-gun gray, metallic blue. He is obsessed with computers and speaks earnestly of modems and increased memory.

His father, Ted, is a successful cardiologist with whom David holds a joint patent for a valve on a sophisticated electrocardiogram apparatus. The Goldfein marriage is not a happy one, and it is common knowledge that Ted keeps a mistress.

Betty, Seth's mother, is overweight, overdressed, and her strawberry-blond hair is overbleached. She is, Nina has said fondly, one of the dearest and most boring women in the world.

Friday evenings at the Goldfeins' are self-conscious and laced with theatricality. When they arrive, Betty, who wears a black pants suit, covers her head with a lace mantilla and lights the Sabbath candles, singing the benediction, although it is quite dark and the official hour for candle lighting has passed. The table is set with silver cups in honor of the Sabbath, and the braided loaves of challah are covered with the embroidered cloth Betty bought in Jerusalem. Ted intones the kiddush in sonorous tones and gravely passes the silver cup from hand to hand. Still, David admires their tenacity with regard to tradition, and he is sorry that he and Nina are so lax about any kind of observance. Perhaps if they have another child . . . The thought takes him by surprise and he glances guiltily at Nina.

As Betty serves the chicken soup, Seth in his casual mischievous voice asks Hildy how her parents reacted to her slamming into that Dodge jalopy.

"I thought you were the one who got slammed into," David says mildly.

"I lied," Hildy replies and smiles. She is wearing Nina's old pale blue leotard and a long paisley skirt. Although the table is elegantly set with linen napkins, she wipes her mouth with her sleeve.

"Testing," Edith would call her behavior, David knows, and he says nothing although his mouth is sour with anger, his lips compressed with forbearance.

They reserve the quarrel for their return home.

"There was no reason to lie," Nina tells Hildy in a tone coated with ice to shield her fury.

"Maybe if you were home, if you were ever home, I'd have told you the truth. But even when you're here, you're in that damn studio."

"Don't try to make me feel guilty. It won't work." Nina's voice is shrill. "I am home more than you are. This was the first time I've been away overnight in months."

"And you couldn't wait to go, could you? Madame Choreographer. Madame Role Model. Super Mom. La Grande Dame de la Danse," Hildy taunts.

White-faced, his fists clenched, David breaks in.

"That's enough. That's too damn much. You're careless and you lie, and then you blame your mother for your behavior. Get to your room. Get out of here and go to your room."

"Hey. Hey. I'm not five years old." Hildy smiles at him, a flash of teeth, a thrust of tongue. She sits down, crosses her legs. The long paisley skirt parts and she draws it closed. "And you're not my father except on a legal document. Remember that."

"Come upstairs, Nina," he says, ignoring Hildy, but Nina does not move and he goes upstairs alone, leaving his wife and her daughter sitting opposite each other on deep green velvet easy chairs in the living room.

Miraculously, he falls asleep at once and does not awaken until the milky light of the spring dawn drifts into the room. He and Nina make love then with the practiced passion and magical swiftness of the long married. It is afterward, when their intimacy is so inviolate, when they are exhausted by their love, that he at last tells her of his meeting with Stacey Cosgrove.

Nina listens, her hand resting on his head, her fingers buried in his thick sandy hair. She smiles when he tells her that Stacey asked him to spell *arugula.* She does not smile when he tells her of the condition Stacey has imposed on their oh, so tentative agreement.

"She's a child, an immature, romantic child. Can she really be that naive? Does she think it's that simple for a man and woman to go to bed together and make love and conceive a child? Ridiculous." She laughs harshly, derisively.

"That was my immediate reaction," he replied. "When she said that I thought, 'Okay — that's it. It's over.' But then I thought about it. I have to be honest. The laboratory quality of this business bothered me from the first. Artificial insemination — a child comes into being without any human contact, any passion or affection."

"And you are not repelled by the animal-husbandry aspect of her suggestion," Nina says coldly. She sits up in bed at a remove from him and slips on her green nightgown.

"That's hardly fair," he says.

"You have your terminology. I have mine." Her voice is tight. She slips out of bed and goes into the bathroom.

Minutes later, he hears the shower. It is their habit to linger in bed on weekend mornings, to speak softly and drift in and out of sleep, her body nestling against his, breath and dreams commingling in the luxury of leisure. But this morning she has swiftly reclaimed herself and rushed to wash away his touch. The stuffed animals, scattered carelessly across the carpet, stare up at him, the discarded toys of playmates who have had a brief and sudden quarrel. He picks up the woolly lamb and places it carefully on her pillow.

"I'm going out to jog," he calls to her.

"All right."

It is a clear morning, still cool, although the light breeze is threaded
with a new warmth. As he runs, his pace slow and rhythmic, his
anger is soothed and his thoughts clarified.

Nina is in pain, he realizes, because she cannot give him a child.
He has with his new longing imposed a burden of guilt on her, although she had been honest with him from the very beginning. She
had told him that she could never have another child, and in the
glory of his love for her (his graceful darling, his princess, who seared
his heart with tenderness), he had assured her that it did not matter.
He had not anticipated then his growing yearning, the melancholy
sense of deprivation compounded year after passing year so that it
metastasized, sapping his joy, blocking his spontaneity. Nor could he
have anticipated the flood of feelings that overwhelmed him in Jerusalem, that continue to haunt him now. The dead left a mandate
for the living. His father had painted survivors in search. "*What are
they looking for, Papa?*" David the child had asked. The answer comes
to him now. They were in search of hope, in search of continuity.
Their search has become his own; it is the source of his discontent,
of the anguish, the festering lacuna within the fullness of his life.

And Nina shares his grief, he knows. Shares and empathizes and
suffers. How heavily she had leaned against him as they stood before
a photograph that showed the Germans evacuating a village in Poland. He had not dared to move closer so that he might read the
name of the village. And he had known, without looking at her,
that Nina's eyes were fixed on the blurred image of a young woman
holding a child. He had thought then of Amos Roth's last painting — the unfinished infant in his mother's arms. Later, Nina had
told him that she too had been thinking of that painting, and he
had not been surprised. So often their thoughts and feelings merge.
There is much that she would do for him. Arnold's suggestion had
not shocked her. She had met with Stacey, liked her, encouraged
him to meet with her. But now, too much has been asked of her.
Much too much.

He must, he tells himself, as his lungs fill painfully and sweat beads
his face, put this yearning into perspective, assimilate his sorrow. He
cannot, he will not, allow it to poison his marriage. He loves Nina
too much. He will call Stacey Cosgrove and thank her politely, per-

haps even send her a small gift. The decision calms him and he increases his pace.

He returns home exhausted and relaxed. Nina is in the kitchen wearing a black leotard seamed with pale sweat stains from her morning workout, her face very pale.

"Nina, I've thought it through," he begins, but she puts her fingers on his lips.

"Listen. I've been thinking about it also. I've been too damn hard and selfish in this. I feel threatened, I guess, and I suppose that's normal. But I don't want to ever think that I was responsible for the road not taken. I know what having your own child means to you. I'm not going to stand in your way."

"But there are other women we might contact who would not insist on such a condition," he protests and drinks from the glass of juice she holds out to him. The salty taste of her sweat touches his tongue.

"But I think that you yourself are intrigued by such a condition," Nina replies. "I heard it in your voice. Am I wrong?"

She knows him well. She understands that he too wants this child to be conceived in passion of a kind — if only his passion for fatherhood, for continuity, and Stacey's passion for pregnancy now romanticized into saintly altruism. Stacey will have it all, Nina thinks bitterly. Stacey will bear David a child and achieve her own family's emancipation. *Ms Magazine* will beatify her unless the tide changes, in which case they will crucify her in an in-depth article analyzing her motivation.

Nina smiles bitterly, but David sees it as a smile of acquiescence. He leans forward and kisses the soft pink bow of her lips and holds her close so that he can feel the beating of her heart against his chest. He marvels at her courage, her generosity.

"Nina. Nina. You won't be sorry," he murmurs.

She sighs. She is sorry already.

Exactly a week later, Stacey lies in bed beside Hal. They have just made love and their bodies are moist and lustrous in the darkness. His arm snakes over her shoulder, his fingers play absently with her nipple. He is, as always after lovemaking, relaxed and masterful. It is at this moment that she tells him that she has met with Arnold and David Roth.

"Yeah?" He is wary.

"It's set. I'm going to really try to have his baby."

He is silent.

"You said it was all right."

"I said it was all right. I didn't say I'd like it."

"Okay." She waits a few minutes, and then she kisses him on the lips, strokes the silken hairs of his beard. "There's something else."

"What?"

"I want the conception to be natural. No test tube, no doctor. I'm going to sleep with David Roth."

He jerks away, thrusts her away from him, sits upright, his face distorted with rage.

"Are you crazy?" he shouts. Spittle streaks whitely at the corners of his mouth. "What's the matter with you? What do you want, you want to be this guy's whore? Because that's what you are when you sleep with a man you're not married to! Check it out in your dictionary." He seizes the dictionary from the pile of books stacked on the bedside table and hurls it across the room. The black book flies open and lies facedown on the floor like a small wounded animal.

"Was I a whore when I slept with you before we were married?" Stacey asks calmly. One thing she knows for certain: when Hal begins an argument with screams and shouts, she can always subdue him, eventually, with calm and reason.

"That was different. We were in love, just kids ourselves. You're taking money from this son of a bitch."

"I'm not taking money for sleeping with him. The money is for carrying his baby. If I sleep with him and I don't get pregnant, I'm not going to take a penny, not a penny. There's a big difference between getting paid to become a mother and getting paid to be a prostitute."

"Why can't it be just the way Dr. Roth explained it to you at first? He injects you with the sperm and that's it." Hal clenches and unclenches his fists. His anger is subsiding, but a familiar fatigue overtakes him. It is the tiredness he feels when he has difficulty understanding a concept — the same sort of weariness that had caused him to sleep at his desk when he was a small boy who could not understand that the series of letters in his primers formed words.

"Because I'm a woman and not a machine, and I don't think babies should come into being that way. You want me to be inseminated like some prize mare? My womb would be an incubator, if that was how it was done. Wouldn't it be better to think of this in human terms, Hal? This baby is part of the mystery — part of a man and woman coming together."

"Mystery." He spits the word out with a contempt that does not mask a vestige of awe. He too believes in the mystery of conception and birth, in the miracle of passion and compassion. He looks at his children, especially at Andrea, and he wonders at the congregation of genes and history that have formed her heart-shaped face, colored her cornflower-blue eyes, molded her slender, graceful legs and rounded arms. The best of himself, the best of Stacey, so wondrously joined in the darkness, produced this golden-haired creature of light — Andrea, his daughter, his sweet princess. The thought thrills and embarrasses him. He is not a man who is comfortable with such insights, such abstractions. He leans back against the pillows. And Stacey, as though she reads his thoughts, moves against him in the darkness.

She strokes his back, his neck. Her breath, warm and sweet in his ear, whispers comfort, understanding.

"Not every man can understand something like this. That's what makes you so special, Hal. And I know it's because you're so unselfish, because you love me and the kids so much. Oh, Hal, we're so lucky. I'm so lucky."

He is silent. He knows what she is doing, but he knows too that she believes every word she utters. His Stacey. His sweetheart. He relaxes, soothed by her touch, her words, and she continues, her voice still soft but stronger now.

"It will have nothing to do with love. No other man could ever make me feel the way you make me feel. And you know that if I do go through with it, and if it works out, I'm doing it for you, for the kids. That's how much I love you — that's how much I love all of you." Her voice is hypnotic and he surrenders to it; he is persuaded to her belief. His anger fades and is replaced by a surge of pride.

Most guys would be intimidated if their wives made such a suggestion. But he's sure enough of himself, sure enough of Stacey.

"So what do you think, honey?"

"I'll think about it," he says and closes his eyes.

Stacey leans back, content. She has won. But then she knew she
would. There are some things she can claim effortlessly and others
for which she must campaign relentlessly. She has long accepted such
a pattern, and she does not underestimate Hal's strength.

5

On a hot afternoon late in May, the Roths and the Cosgroves arrive at Charles Norris's law office in a high-rise near the county center. They exit from separate elevators and meet in the corridor where they appraise each other in the dim interior light. There is some laughter at the coincidence of their arrival (although, in fact, they all have the same appointment), and Stacey introduces her husband.

"Nina and David Roth, Harold Cosgrove." She giggles nervously, but Hal thrusts his hand out to David and smiles widely.

"Hal, just call me Hal. It rhymes with pal." They hear his laughter for the first time. It is full-bodied and generous, scornful of serious- ness and formality; they understand why Stacey is so drawn to it. Besides, he is an attractive man, dark-haired, dark-bearded, even- featured. He wears gray slacks, a light-blue sport shirt open at the neck, and a navy-blue cotton jacket, the loose sleeves pushed up to his forearms. His outfit would not be out of place among Hildy's friends, David decides, except that they would not wear a chain of heavy braided gold — a chain that Hal touches now and again as though it is a talisman.

"Hal." David takes his hand and is startled to find it soft to his touch and limp within his grasp.

They enter the office together and the receptionist ushers them into the conference room at once. Arnold and Charles sit opposite each other at the long rosewood table and they are both frowning. David is not surprised. He had not expected Charles to approve of this step he is taking. Charles, his attorney and his friend, is conservative in both practice and politics. Soft-voiced and hard-thinking, he examines every alternative, checks every precedent, shies away from any hint of legal shadow.

He represented David during Hildy's adoption proceedings and enraged Nina by his insistence on seeing Michael's death certificate. ("Does he think I made it up?" she asked bitterly, but in the end, she had to write to the state of California and obtain a copy.) Charles acted for David in the purchase of his house and held up the closing for two months while an ambiguity in the title was resolved. He is "of counsel" to David's firm and often clashes with other attorneys over his insistence on particular language in the filing of patents, the drafting of contracts.

David trusts his friend and knows that he will have a difficult time persuading him to countenance this agreement between himself and Stacey Cosgrove. He has already met with him twice and listened to the attorney's well-taken objections. Still, Charles has reluctantly agreed to proceed.

Charles shakes hands with all of them and then glances down at the notes he has made on the yellow legal pad on the table. The two couples circle, take seats, and lean expectantly forward.

"We all know why we're here," Charles says, and his voice is resigned, sad. "I've met with David Roth and with Dr. Arnold Roth. We have spoken on the phone, Mrs. Cosgrove. I want to tell you from the outset, as I have told you before, that I do not approve of this undertaking — not that you are here to ask me for approval or disapproval. Still, I feel that it is my obligation to warn you that this is a situation that is potentially dangerous, perhaps even litigious."

"Litigious?" Hal says questioningly, and it is only Stacey who understands that he is not quarreling but asking for definition.

"Might lead to a lawsuit," she explains.

"How?"

"There are many possible scenarios. Stacey Cosgrove carries and bears the child and David and Nina Roth change their minds and decline to accept it. Stacey Cosgrove carries and bears the child and then changes her mind and declines to give it to the Roths for adoption. The child is born defective. Who will claim it? The child is born dead. Is Stacey Cosgrove's obligation fulfilled, or must she undertake another pregnancy?" Charles speaks slowly, deliberately, as though he is conducting a class and his students have confessed themselves to be slow learners.

"But isn't that why we're here? To prevent such scenarios?" Nina asks. She toys with the narrow gold belt of her tan linen dress.

"You're here, as I understand it, to draw up a contract of agreement. But I remind you, Nina, that if every contract was observed to the letter and spirit in which it was drafted, there would be no lawsuits, no complaints of breach. I would be irresponsible if I did not advise you of such possibilities." He coughs and covers his mouth with his neatly folded white handkerchief.

"I've managed to obtain copies of surrogacy agreements arrived at by other parties for Charles," Arnold says. "Two of my colleagues who were involved in similar private negotiations were kind enough to oblige me."

"And I have done some research, of course," Charles adds, "although this is virgin territory for the law."

Hal laughs aloud and claps his hands.

"Virgin. That's some choice of word, Counselor," he says, and then, as the others remain silent, he sinks back in his chair and lifts his eyes to the ceiling.

Stacey stirs restlessly. She stares out of the window into the office across the way, where a very thin gray-haired woman is speaking into an old-fashioned black phone. Her parents still have such a clumsy, ugly phone, and it is still on the high shelf in the kitchen where, as a child, she had to arch and stretch to reach it.

"I have drawn up a preliminary agreement which I would like both parties to study," Charles says. He passes copies of the agreement to Stacey and David. Stacey opens the stiff blue paper jacket and riffles the long pages on which clause tumbles after clause. *Whereas. Whereas. Whereas.* She winces and closes it.

"Let me summarize briefly for you," Charles continues in the paternal tone that has swayed so many juries to his argument. "The terms are fairly simple. Stacey Cosgrove agrees to carry a child, conceived with the sperm of David Roth, and then, at the birth of the child, she will surrender said infant to David and Nina Roth, who will then formalize its adoption, naming Nina Roth as the legal mother.

David Roth will pay for all prenatal care, hospital, and obstetrical fees. He will also pay Stacey Cosgrove the amount of twenty thousand dollars, free of any taxes or other encumbrances. She will relinquish all claim to the child. If the child is born defective, David Roth will assume responsibility for its care."

"Defective?" Nina utters the word as though it has a sour taste. "Surely, there will be a sonogram, amniocentesis?" She turns to Arnold, her brows lifted questioningly.

"There are no guarantees in life, Nina," Arnold replies. "Such tests are not always a hundred percent accurate. We will exercise every caution, but there is no certainty."

"You see my point? There are many eventualities, Nina. We can't anticipate all of them," Charles Norris says. He is the father of two sons, healthy, bright boys whose photographs stand in silver frames on his desk. He is also the father of a severely retarded daughter who was placed in an institution in Pennsylvania. She has pale blue eyes and corn-colored hair, and he keeps her faded and battered snapshot in his wallet. Her name is Lynn.

"We would take care of the baby if it were born defective," Stacey says in a small worried voice. "Wouldn't we, Hal?"

His head jerks toward her, his finger stretched forth warningly.

"Don't be crazy, Stacey," he replies harshly. There is no laughter in his tone, and painful splotches of red mottle her cheeks.

It is clear to all of them that Hal Cosgrove, for all his laughter and good humor, wields ominous power over his wife.

"There is also provision in the other agreements I've studied for a psychological evaluation of the potential mother," Charles continues more cautiously.

"Forget it!" Hal's tone is curt. "What is this, a slave market? We're going to check teeth, maybe IQ's. We don't need this. All you need is for me and Stacey to say yes."

"I am, of course, seeking advice as to whether we will require a release or a consent from Mr. Cosgrove," Charles assures him.

"I advise. I consent." Hal's good humor floods back.

"I assume you will want to share this material with your own attorney. And, of course, I'll be pleased to meet with him," Charles says.

"We don't have an attorney," Stacey murmurs, but Hal flashes her a monitory look.

"Sure we do. Sure."

He does, in fact, play poker regularly with a lawyer named Andrew Kardin. Hal became friendly with him when he was the manager of a West Side bar some years previous and Andy, who was then separated from his wife, came by regularly. Hal recognizes such men and understands them. They need a familiar room, recognizable faces, a sympathetic glance, and a friendly voice. Andy and his wife were reconciled, but he trailed Hal from job to job and is part of the regular poker game that meets wherever Hal happens to be working. Hal will show Andy the proposed contract, get his suggestions. Hell, he will even pay him. The thought of the twenty thousand dollars affords him a brief swell of power. He will be a man who can write a check.

"Please. Consult your attorney." Charles Norris is relieved. He would not want the Cosgroves to turn around in a year's time (if this damn contract goes through, and he hopes to God it won't) and claim that they had been coerced into agreement without the advice of counsel.

They all shake hands when they leave. David is reminded of the cordial farewells he and Nina exchanged with the couple from whom they bought their house, standing in this same doorway, the late-afternoon light casting the same rib of radiance across Nina's face. She smiles at Stacey and Hal now as she smiled at the elderly Rosses then. It is her facile stage smile, brilliantly flashed at an audience she will, in all probability, never see again.

Two weeks later Charles Norris calls David and tells him that he has spoken with Andrew Kardin, the Cosgroves' attorney. As a result of their conference, certain small changes have been made in the contract. The provision for a psychological evaluation has been deleted. A provision to cover the costs of maternity clothing and household and child-care help, should it be required during the course of the pregnancy, has been added.

"That's reasonable," David says. He passes his hand across the smooth surface of the polished olivewood paperweight on his desk.

He bought it in a small Jerusalem shop, just before early closing on a Friday afternoon. The shopkeeper, a wizened Yemenite, had spoken softly to David as he wrapped it, and his granddaughter, a beautiful, dark-eyed teenager, seeing David's puzzled look, had translated for him.

"My grandfather wishes you to live one hundred and twenty years. He wishes you and our people joy from your children."

"Thank you," David had said and averted his eyes lest his melancholy be revealed. He had never fathered a child. Joylessness would haunt him.

"I'll draw up the final agreement then," Charles replies, his tone flat. "You're sure, David? Really sure?"

"Charles, listen closely, listen good. I'm sure. Really sure." David laughs, the laugh of a joy that is just beginning.

6

On an unseasonably cool June evening, David Roth and Stacey Cosgrove check into the Sheraton Russell Hotel on Park Avenue. The date is of Stacey's choosing, carefully calculated. The place is of David's selection, a small but elegant hotel. He does not want Stacey to be either intimidated or offended. The quiet lobby is tastefully furnished with deep leather chairs and glass-enclosed bookshelves. While David registers, Stacey studies the titles.

"Would you like a drink before dinner?" David asks, turning to her. He has already handed the elderly porter a folded bill and their two small cases.

Dinner. She has not thought about dinner, although, of course, it is obvious that they must eat.

"All right," she says shyly.

In the small, dimly lit bar, they sit at a corner table and she looks at the sporting prints on the paneled walls.

"They shot a scene of *The Verdict* in here," David tells her. "The scene where Paul Newman smacks Charlotte Rampling."

"Really?" She looks around the room with new interest. It has, after all, been the scene of violence and excitement. She wonders how an actress feels when she is hit hard in a movie. She is only acting, but still it must hurt. The pain is real. And Charlotte Rampling had bled in that scene, she remembers, bled and wept and licked at the amalgam of blood and tears. Her pain wasn't lessened because she was acting, and her blood was the same color it would have been if she had betrayed Paul Newman in real life.

Stacey is sort of like Charlotte Rampling tonight, she reflects. She too is an actress playing a role. Right now, at this twilight hour, she is David Roth's wife (that is how they are registered because it was simply easier, he explained), and later, after dinner, she will play the part of his mistress. No. Not his mistress. The word is too casual, too aimless. She fumbles for another description, a more appropriate word. Ah, yes. She will be his surrogate wife. Like Hagar was for Abraham. Like Bilhah and Zilpah were for Jacob. She will be like the women with whom the patriarchs slept, the women who bore their children. The biblical references (learned in a comparative religion class) please her and she smiles, happy suddenly to be in this beautiful room, with a soft carpet beneath her feet, her face reflected in the smoked-glassed mirror behind the long, curving bar carved of golden wood.

She has two drinks. Two gin and tonics, the same drink David orders. She is surprised that she likes the taste, and when her second glass is drained, she sucks at the slice of lime.

"My father used to cover slices of lemon with sugar and give them to us like candy," she tells David.

"What does your father do?" David asks.

"He owns a small hardware store. My brothers work with him there."

Her two older brothers, Steve and Jeff, have always worked with her father, helping out in the store even when they were boys, after school and on weekend afternoons. Stacey had remained home with her mother, pale, sad Rose Carmody, who spent most of her day sitting at the dining room window, staring down at the street below.

Her mother had not always been sad. Stacey can dredge up memories of Rose laughing at the beach, her long golden hair, the same color as Stacey's, flecked with sand and sea. And she can remember Rose singing as she cut up celery for the chicken salad sandwiches that were a staple for their family picnics at the Botanic Gardens. But then there had been another pregnancy and the apartment was awash with whispers. *Twins. Danger. Bleeding.* Twice the doctor arrived in the night, his thin voice irritable. After the second visit, he ordered her to bed for the duration of the pregnancy.

How old had Stacey been then, perhaps seven, eight? Old enough

to make the lunches for her father and brothers, old enough to stand
on tiptoe at the bedroom window and hang the laundry on the
clothesline and then to reel it in again and sort it into clumsy, unwieldy piles. Her brothers wore unironed shirts to school and tiptoed
through the house. Her father ironed Stacey's dresses himself. A tall,
heavy man, he crouched over the ironing board that he had ordered
especially built for his wife who was barely five feet tall. He looked
like a circus contortionist as he passed the iron across ruffles and
sashes, his face set in lines of concentration.

Rose went into labor in her eighth month. Stacey was home alone
with her, watching television. Rose's screams pierced the quiet of
the afternoon, sent Stacey sprinting from the television set. Rose's
water had broken, and Stacey saw her grip the soaking counterpane,
her face distorted; she moaned and shouted, anguish and anger mingling. Stacey arched and stretched to reach the squat black telephone on the high shelf in the kitchen. She called her father, the
doctor, the woman who lived next door. Then she stood helplessly
beside her mother, clutching an armload of towels so newly plucked
from the clothesline that they were wind-stiffened and scratched her
cheek.

Rose was rushed to the hospital, but the babies, a boy and a girl,
were stillborn. The long sadness had begun. Rose returned home to
stand vigil at the window, to search the street, sometimes shading
her eyes against the impact of the sun that now seldom touched her
skin.

"What's she looking for?" Stacey had wondered querulously. "Does
she think the twins are going to come dancing around the corner?"

She pitied her mother and hated her. The mothers on the television screen would not have surrendered to such sadness. Not Mrs.
Walton. Not funny, buoyant Lucy. They would have acted with
courage. They understood pregnancy, its risks and its rewards.

Stacey's father and brothers escaped to the store, but she came
home dutifully until high school, when she too broke loose. She
discovered the library, the drama club, the cheerleading squad, the
corner luncheonette. Why go home and watch Rose sit so quietly in
the cocoon of what Stacey now recognized to be half-madness? And
then she discovered Hal Cosgrove, and she hardly went home at all.

Stacey feels sorry for her father. Her brothers are married now with their own families. Still, he has the store and one Sunday a month they all go to an Italian restaurant together — even Rose. And they do all order the same thing: spaghetti and clam sauce. They are wary of altering the slightest pattern of their lives, of up-setting Rose's tenuous balance. And they are aware, the brothers and their sister, that they are the children of a woman who has somehow lost control of her life.

"My father died when I was a boy," David says. "I missed not having a large, close family."

"But you and your brother are close?"

"Yes. We're close."

Over dinner, which they eat in the hotel dining room, he tells her about his work. He is an electrical engineer by training, but he has a talent for developing small innovative switches that are essen-tial in the production of computers and electronic devices. Origi-nally, he sold his ideas to other companies, but now he manufactures them himself and arranges for distribution as well. It is a small en-terprise, but he finds it satisfying.

Stacey is impressed. She asks intelligent questions. She admires the design of a switch that he sketches for her in ballpoint pen on the white linen napkin, and she admires too his temerity in defacing the linen.

"It will wash out," he tells her, but he is pleased at this sweet acknowledgment of what she perceives to be his courage.

By the time they take the elevator to their room, they are relaxed with each other and enveloped in the warmth of a new fondness. They have, over drinks and dinner, become friends. David thinks her very pleasant, endearingly naive. Stacey thinks him very sensi-tive and sophisticated, and she wishes that he would laugh more often and more easily. Laughter is very important to Rose Carmody's daughter.

He opens the door to the room and switches on the light. She remains at the threshold, shy and hesitant, suddenly. The room is attractively funished in the hues of innocence, pale blue and white striped wallpaper, a blue leather chair. The moldings are painted the color of newly fallen snow. The bed is turned down to form an inviting envelope of fleecy pale blue blanket and crisp white sheets.

Their view overlooks Park Avenue, and through the window they can see into the apartment across the street. A red-haired woman wearing a bright green robe lifts a child in her arms and presses her cheek against his. The child, a small black boy in a golden yellow sleep suit, laughs. Stacey watches them intently, as though they are performers on a stage, until David softly closes and then locks the door. He draws the curtains, switches on the bedlight, which offers a rosy glow, and dims the overhead light. Her bag, precariously positioned on the bed, slips soundlessly onto the thick, pale carpet. They do not move to pick it up. In the half darkness, he lifts her chin, puts his mouth against hers — a brush of lips, not a claiming kiss.

"You're so sweet, so very sweet," he says.

She lifts her hands to his cheeks and it is she who kisses him, her catlike tongue moving into the moistness of his mouth. Her soft arms encircle him, press him against her body; he is roused to strength and warmth. Affection suffuses him. How good she is to be undertaking this. How generous. How brave. Daring emboldens her. She is fascinated, enchanted by her own courage, by his matching bravery. Quickly they undress, each absorbed with zippers and buttons, the removal of shoes, socks, stockings; she with the hanging of her suit, he with the draping of his trousers on the wooden valet. They move past each other in the darkened room like ghostly silhouettes, unembarrassed, as though they are the comfortable veterans of a long companionship. And then, naked, they embrace again and slide into the bed, coming together without awkwardness, with a swift and sweet sense of purpose. Their soft sounds mingle; the darkness reverberates with delight, with relief, and, at last, with contentment.

"Oh, good," he whispers. "Oh, how good."

"Yes." She lies so still beside him, her eyes closed, her golden lashes damp against her cheeks.

He pulls the blanket up about her, and moving very quietly, he puts on his pajamas. He falls asleep at once. When he awakens, he sees that she is wearing a pink cotton nightgown. It is new. A clear plastic tag clings to its hem, and gently, tenderly, he cuts it loose

with his pocketknife, saddened somehow that she bought a new
nightgown for this, their night together.

As they agreed, he leaves before dawn, and although he bends
over her as she lies asleep, he resists the impulse to kiss her on the
brow and closes the door very softly behind him.

Three weeks later Arnold calls him.

"Stacey was just in for an examination."

"Yes?"

"She's pregnant."

He clutches the phone. Tears sear his eyes and his lips move
soundlessly as he struggles to find a reply to offer his brother.

7

Nina moves through her garden very slowly, as though each step requires singular concentration. The summer heat seems possessed of a corporeal strength that resists her slightest gesture. She bends to pluck a weed and is reminded of a dance exercise in which the dancers are told to imagine that they are resisting the power of a hot desert wind. She smiles bitterly as she remembers how she writhed with exhaustion on the floor as the "Summer" movement of Vivaldi's *The Four Seasons* wafted through the room. She had, as always, worked too hard, tried too hard, but that is her way. Each undertaking demands an intensity of involvement, an attention to detail, that absorbs and, too often, exhausts her. Even this simple summer barbecue is orchestrated with the same care she lavishes on a choreographic composition. Her own persistence irritates her and arouses David's amusement, Hildy's scorn. Even now she appraises the garden scene for color and symmetry, struggles to remember cues, to anticipate entrances and exits.

But then she does want things to go especially well today. It is, after all, the first time Stacey and her family will visit with them, and it is an invitation that David extended with care and concern.

"I want them to think of us as family," he had said. "I want to show that we are linked and involved with each other."

Of course they are linked and involved. Nina needs no reassurance, no reinforcement. She will be mother to the child Stacey is carrying — David's child. Already she is rehearsing for that new motherhood, schooling herself to think of the unborn child as her own. She is Stacey's secret sharer, her partner in this so carefully programmed pregnancy. Each morning she stands before the mirror and imagines the gentle expansion of her own abdomen, the gathering fullness and tenderness of her breasts. She has read that it is possible for women to stimulate their mammary glands so that milk flows even though there has been no pregnancy, no birth. Perhaps she will be able to nurse the baby.

She had loved nursing Hildy. Even now her nipples tense and swell when she remembers her infant daughter's soft and urgent lips rhythmically sucking at her breast. Often Hildy had fallen into the magical, satiated sleep of infancy and the milk trickled warmly down Nina's body, streaking her flesh with moonbeams of moisture. Once Nina had touched her finger to the flowing milk and licked it; she was startled by its warmth, by its strange sweetness. How vulnerable Hildy had been then, stirring slightly, her tiny fist opening, the pink and white fingers splaying out to form a delicately petaled miniature hand and curling again into a furled bud of fist. How did it happen, that the tiny trusting infant has become a sulky, wary adolescent, a tight and angry beauty? The thought strikes Nina as disloyal, and she dismisses it and turns her attention again to her garden.

She is pleased now that they never dismantled the small play area near the rosebushes. The swing and slide set that David installed for Hildy is still sturdy. The bright sun casts a silver sheen across the stainless-steel posts, and the dark-green wooden swings sway in the slight breeze. Next to it, slyly hidden beneath the umbrella of leaves formed by the converging branches of the twin maples, is the log playhouse that David built for Hildy's seventh birthday.

She remembers the spring day he and Hildy walked across the tender new grass, hand in hand, and he opened the door to the playhouse. The door was painted red and so were the shutters because red was Hildy's favorite color. David had mixed the paint himself, carefully stirring white and carmine together to achieve the shade Hildy favored.

"Oh, Daddy!" Tears and laughter had choked Hildy's voice as she leapt into David's arms and hugged him, pressing her moist, sweet lips against his cheeks. And then she examined the small structure, exclaiming over the perfection of its dimensions, the polished beauty of its hardwood floor, the small table and chairs nestled against the wall.

David and Nina stood outside and watched the sunlight dance through the shadows cast by the maple leaves. They had been reluctant then to leave, reluctant to shatter the fragile net of happiness that encased the three of them for those few moments. Even then, perhaps, they had been aware of the encroaching danger of new borders, new birthdays, of the muting of joy and the mysterious advent of harsh laughter and dry silences.

When did Hildy last enter the playhouse? Nina wonders now. She touches the door. The wood is damp and the screws that hold the knob in place have rusted. She turns it carefully and stoops to enter. The scent of roses fills the room. The windows are open, the floor is swept clean, and the table and chairs are washed down. David has done all this, Nina realizes, in preparation for the visit of Stacey's children, and she is suddenly jealous of his attention, his solicitude. The feeling shames her.

It is a misplaced, transferred jealousy, she realizes, stealthily nurtured and incubated since the night David slept with Stacey. She forgives herself for it. She is no saint. Of course she is jealous of Stacey. Still, to atone for it, she opens the small chest that contains the plastic plates and battered pots and pans scavenged by the small Hildy for her games of "house." Nina wipes them clean with her handkerchief and sets them out on the table in readiness for Stacey's children. And then she turns and, leaving the door open, hurries up to the patio.

David is checking the grill, which they are using for the first time this season. Methodically, he arranges the coals and the slabs of mesquite that he traveled to a distant village to purchase. The small can of paraffin is ready, and the long wooden matches are in the ceramic dish that Hildy fashioned one summer in arts and crafts. It is a deep blue, and David's initials are etched into a corner in Hildy's childish scrawl. Are the lives of all families littered with the artifacts of vanished childhoods? Nina wonders. Like Hansel and Gretel, children leave a small trail of their discarded toys, tarnished souvenirs and tender gifts leading back to half-remembered rooms where once they laughed and played.

"I hope I bought enough mesquite," David says worriedly.

He wears a kelly-green shirt, faded blue jeans, and brown leather sandals that Nina had contemplated giving away because he so seldom wore them. She understands that he wears them today because they are so youthful, so casual; he has made a careful selection to project an image of carelessness, to assert that he is young enough to be a new father. Still, a network of veins bulges just below his ankle, and his stomach protrudes against the bright green shirt in betrayal. Nina smiles sadly. She herself wears a gray dress of crushed cotton, full-skirted and wide-sleeved.

"You have enough mesquite," she assures him. "It's just hamburgers and hot dogs."

"Will there be enough?" he worries.

"Of course. Idiot." She tosses a strawberry to him and laughs when he catches it in his open mouth.

"I'm no idiot," he insists and feeds her a strawberry in turn. "But you're sure it will be all right?"

"Absolutely."

She has, after all, prepared a large pasta salad, bright with clusters of broccoli and pepper rings of red and green. She has arranged a fruit salad in a hollowed watermelon boat and scattered shredded coconut amid heart-shaped strawberries and circlets of pale green honeydew and cantaloupe. She studded the juicy pastel pyramids with small paper flags and tissue-paper umbrellas. Hildy and her friends loved those small favors, and always during such gatherings, they had eaten the fruit to claim the decorations. Then, triumphantly, the children had carried their prizes out to the playhouse area where they planted them in the soft earth or threaded them through maple leaves.

She is, Nina realizes, resurrecting all the small secrets of motherhood, the whimsical enchantments that pacify and please small children and create the tenuous contentment that means (in the end) that adults can continue their conversations without distraction. But why not? Within months (*seven, only seven*) she will again be mother to a newborn. This afternoon is a preface to a new era in their lives. Their garden will once again swarm with children, the green swings will soar toward the crowns of the maple trees, and gay paper flags will flutter in the gentle wind. She feels a surge of excitement and

then a swift and sudden fatigue. She is at once exhilarated and oppressed, apprehensive and optimistic, a commingling of emotions not
unfamiliar to her. She is, after all, a choreographer, a dreamer of
dances, a creator of tension in movement.

"The tables look nice," David says.

There are two tables, one round and one long, each spread with a
yellow and white cloth and set with yellow plates and white cutlery.
The children will sit at the long table and the adults at the round
one — another secret of entertaining with children recalled and acted
upon. In addition to the Cosgroves, they have invited David's friend
John Cowper, whose new novel Nina has just finished reading, and
Mandy, the young woman he will marry when they can find the
time. (Their schedules are so busy, John has explained to David.
Mandy too writes and teaches, and they both give readings on weekends. Still, they will definitely marry before the baby is born; Mandy
is four months pregnant.) They will bring Mandy's five-year-old twins,
Eric and Samantha, and John's son, Terry. It was David's idea to
invite another family. A neat balance, a semblance of normalcy, will
be achieved. John, his contemporary, is also about to become a father, and the children will be playmates for the Cosgrove youngsters.

"Hey, I didn't know you were having a party." Hildy wanders onto
the patio wearing a white man's tee shirt, her face still sleep-wreathed.
She perches on the railing and studies her toes, then adjusts the knot
on the purple and white braided cord she wears about her ankle.

"We told you we were having a barbecue today," David says in
the steady calm tone he uses when he speaks to Hildy. "John Cowper
and Mandy and their kids. The Cosgroves." He turns away from
Hildy when he mentions their name, fearful that she will ask him
questions. That is something he and Nina must decide. How are
they to explain their arrangement with Stacey to Hildy? Should they
explain it at all? But then how will they explain the infant (*his* child,
his own child!) who will share her home, be her sibling?

They have talked about it, trying not to deceive themselves. It
will be tricky, they acknowledge. They have talked of explaining the
baby as an adopted child, but they are uncomfortable with this deceit — they have tried so hard, through all these years, never to
deceive her. They anticipate her anger, her embarrassment. As for

betrayal, she has, they know, felt herself betrayed for a long time, but they are mystified as to its source. They fear to question her and even fear their own temerity. It is easier to accept Edith's explanation of "adolescent anxiety," "transitional stage," the comforting professional language with which she appeases the anguish of parents, the sadness of children.

"But you were planning to be home today?" Nina asks her daughter.

Hildy stretches and yawns. Her tee shirt hikes up and David sees the curling dark hair of her womanhood exposed. He is reminded of a small furry animal startled out of sleep. He turns away, embarrassed and ashamed and then angered. Hildy's emergence from childhood into young womanhood has surprised and unnerved him. One day she was a child cuddled beside them in their large bed, talking to their stuffed animals, pelting them with the soft, bright creatures that they in turn tossed back at her, all of them laughing and giggling, climbing across each other, their hands uplifted to catch the turquoise elephant, the golden giraffe. And then, without warning, she was a sullen adolescent, teasing them (as perhaps she herself is teased) with the mystery of her new maturity.

"I don't know if I can stay," Hildy says. "Seth and Alison talked about going to the beach today. I want to work on my tan." She stretches out her arm and studies it. Her skin is the color of raw honey.

"We'd like it if you stayed." Nina's tone is calm yet firm. She does not look at Hildy but busies herself with the flowers that she cut earlier — full pink roses and pale purple gladioli.

She notices, as she places a full-blown rose into the vase, that a furled bud, thrusting through thorns, is concealed just beneath the lush blossom; it is as though the flesh-colored, golden-hearted rose is mother to the pale bud, so tight and hard. She wonders suddenly if Stacey's pregnancy is noticeable and realizes that of course it is too early, too soon in the gestation. The baby is still a bud of a zygote, furled and tight and hard.

"I'll see how I feel," Hildy says and wanders into the kitchen.

David and Nina are silent. There is really nothing to say, nor do they have time to talk, because just then John Cowper's battered station wagon streaks noisily into the driveway and the three children spill out, loudly chanting, "Are we there? Are we almost there?" Their laughter is strident and rebellious, the defiant laughter of children who have been told too often to be quiet, to stop laughing, to stop asking the same question over and over, until the reprimand has become invitation.

The twins, Samantha and Eric, each wear one red sneaker and one blue sneaker. Their striped shirts are faded and Samantha's plaid shorts are fastened with a safety pin. Samantha's hair is cut short while Eric's hair falls in golden ringlets to his shoulders. Terry, however, wears a brown Izod shirt, trimly fitting khaki shorts, and snow-white high-topped sneakers. Lesley, John's ex-wife, has remarried. Her new husband is an orthopedic surgeon. She buys all Terry's clothes in the Lord and Taylor Boys' Shop where she flashes her green charge card with the proud authority of a survivor, a victor.

David and John embrace with the vigorous, spontaneous rush of friendship of men who enjoy a long history of affection and shared experience and hold few secrets from each other. John kisses Nina on the cheek. They are bonded by mutual respect and their shared love for David, but they do not like each other. Artists both, they judge each other severely and harbor perverse secret reservations. Nina finds John's writing brilliant but undisciplined. He will not take the trouble to rethink a complex idea, to rewrite a dense sentence. He leaps from one image to another, juggles symbols and similes with careless abandon. He, on the other hand, thinks her work too rigid, too structured. She is controlled by her own intensity, in thrall to her own aspiration.

Nina also (quite unreasonably, she knows) dislikes John's appearance. He is tall and thin; his features are hawklike and too deeply carved. His pale hair is always too long and falls unevenly across his high brow. He wears a faded black cotton tee shirt, white duck trousers that are not quite clean, and battered sandals. His breath, when he kisses Nina on the cheek, is faintly sour.

Mandy, pale-skinned, high-browed, her fine wheat-colored hair plaited into a single braid, moves toward them slowly, cautiously, as though fearful of losing her balance. Her frail form seems inadequate to the burden of her pregnancy, and she keeps her hands in the pockets of the sleeveless denim maternity jumper because she is ashamed of her nails, which are bitten down to bloodied circlets.

"Hello, Nina, David."

Mandy's voice is very soft. That softness, fading occasionally to a breathy whisper, is the secret of the popularity of her poetry readings. Audiences strain to hear her; students lean forward in their seats. Faculty members lift monitory fingers to their lips and listen closely. She rewards them with lyric secrets. She drapes their respectful silence with necklaces of words, hypnotic alliterations, startling similes, and she smiles shyly at them as she reads. They are grateful for her confidences, pleased that their attention has been rewarded by her vision.

Mandy writes long allegories about mythical women, virgins born without hymens, wives who fantasize their husbands' murders, mothers who are seduced by lithe-limbed sons. She is a popular reader on the college circuit. She reads of lust and violence in her soft, shivering voice. John Cowper had a conference the night she read at the college where he is writer in residence and because of it he arrived late. He sat in the last row, beside Eric, who fell asleep against his arm. The pressure of the boy's small golden head was numbing, but John feared to move lest he waken the sleeping child. (Lesley had left him only weeks before; bereft of his own son, he was especially tender toward strange children.) He waited then until Mandy had answered the last question and autographed the last book (her work is published by a small feminist press, and in the jacket photo her eyes are closed and her mouth is open). Then he carried Eric to the car and she carried Samantha. They spoke over the heads of the sleeping children, and although a crowd of drunken students jostled them, Samantha and Eric did not awaken.

The children slept through the ride home, and they did not awaken when they were lowered into their sleeping bags on the floor of Mandy's loft, nor did they awaken when John took Mandy in his arms and carried her, in turn, to the box spring and mattress thrust against the wall. Triumphantly, he turned her whisper into a shout, and still the exhausted children slept. Nina knows all this because John won a prize for a long narrative poem called "Love and the Sleeping Children" and she dreamed, one night, of translating that poem into a dance.

Nina gives the three children orange juice and directs them to the swings. She asks Mandy, with real concern, how she is feeling. She realizes, with a sense of loss, that she cannot recall the visceral feelings of pregnancy — the way in which she balanced herself against the increased girth and weight, how she responded to the small life growing within her. Only last night she awakened with a leg cramp, something she has not experienced since she was pregnant with Hildy. It was dream-related, she knew, although she cannot remember the dream itself. It occurs to her that she might have dreamed that she herself was carrying David's child — a thought that caused sadness to settle upon her like a gossamer film. She is newly grieved that she is incapable of giving him the child for whom he yearns, that she herself is denied the joy of bearing a baby born of their love. Still, she will love and mother his child, and always, always, she will think of that child as her own. This she promises herself, as she listens to Mandy.

"I'm feeling great. I dream a lot and then I wake up with whole poems growing in my mind. They float onto the paper."

She smiles and closes her eyes. She no longer resembles the portrait on her book jacket. Pregnancy has altered her features, and her nose and lips seem oversized on her pale, long face.

Nina, who works so hard at her choreography, envies Mandy who awakens from a deep sleep to harvest her work, envies her her pregnancy. Hard upon the envy comes the certainty of disbelief. Mandy is a liar; she is one of those people who prefers the mundane lie to the exotic truth.

"Would you like something to drink?" Nina asks her.

"Juice, please. No alcohol," Mandy says softly, righteously. She undoes her braid and allows her long, pale hair to cape her shoulders, lifting a strand to her mouth as the Cosgroves drive up.

Unlike the twins and Terry, the Cosgrove children emerge quietly from the car. They have the self-conscious yet slyly proud look of children who have been dressed in their best clothes and know that they are on display. Evan and Jared, sharp-featured dark-haired boys, wear white shirts and navy-blue shorts. Their high-topped sneakers and tube socks are snow-white, and they step carefully across the gravel path. Andrea wears a bright pink sundress, white patent-leather shoes, and white nylon anklets trimmed with ruffles of lace. Her thick golden hair is neatly parted and crowned with a pink plastic headband. Her features are delicate, and because her front tooth has fallen out, she keeps a finger lifted to her mouth to conceal the gap, an endearing act of vanity, Nina thinks.

Stacey and Hal follow their children, Hal grinning and Stacey grave-faced, clutching a gift wrapped in blue and white paper. They have dressed with determined casualness for this Sunday barbecue, Hal in loose white trousers and a red and white striped gondolier's shirt, his gold necklace pulled taut against his neck, and Stacey in a yellow sundress too tight about the waist. One seam is slightly ripped, and her salmon-colored flesh smiles through the lips of the slit fabric. The large white plastic purse swings from her shoulder, and Nina thinks that it must smell of dusting powder and aging bits of chocolate. The thought is unkind and she is angry at herself for harboring it, but still, what *does* Stacey carry in that impossible purse?

Introductions are made. The men shake hands amiably, indifferently. Stacey and Mandy acknowledge each other with graceful waves and long, searching looks. The children stare at each other and make their swift, frank judgments.

"How old are you?" Eric asks, directing his question to all the Cosgroves. "We're six." He takes Samantha's hand. He does not expect his twin to speak. She is under his protection. Actually, Nina notes, they are mutually protective of each other. They shield each other from loneliness, from their mother's vagaries, from John Cowper's careless affection (Eric pulls Samantha away as John reaches out to pat her head), from Terry, who would stand too close to them. Perhaps, Nina thinks, everyone should have a twin, a companion from birth, a lifetime guarantor against loneliness and aloneness.

It is Andrea who answers for all of them. She is the child-mother, accustomed to responsibility.

"I'm five. Evan is two years older than me. Jared is three."

"I'll show you guys a good place to play," David says, and the children follow him across the garden to the play area.

"Play nicely," Stacey calls after them.

"We will." Again it is Andrea who replies.

"She's a lovely child," Nina says.

"Well, they're all good children when they want to be." Stacey smiles complacently.

"Mine aren't. Mine are little bastards," Mandy says, and now her voice is not a whisper. She sighs and sinks clumsily into a lawn chair.

"Do you want a stool?" John asks solicitously.

"John, please. I'm only in my fourth month, you know. How far along are you?" She turns to Stacey, who smiles shyly.

"Only two months. I didn't think I showed yet."

"I can always tell," Mandy replies smugly, bitterly. Nina cannot understand either her smugness or her bitterness.

She passes tall glasses of lemonade to Stacey and Mandy as David returns carrying a small bouquet of the wild daisies that grow near the playhouse.

"Andrea's contribution. The kids are all set," David says.

He mixes gin and tonics for himself, Hal, John, and Nina. The lemonades that Mandy and Stacey hold have a medicinal froth, and Mandy puckers her lips although the drink is sweet.

"To what shall we drink?" David asks, lifting his glass.

"To the birth of healthy children," John Cowper replies, resting his hand playfully on Mandy's abdomen.

"John, please." Mandy's voice is petulant, and she brushes his hand roughly away. Nina hopes that they will not quarrel. She does not want Stacey and Hal to witness her friends at odds with each other. It will, she fears, diminish her and David in their eyes.

"John likes to pretend that we're delighted with this pregnancy," Mandy says. "He likes to pretend that it wasn't an accident and that I am the original earth mother who would rather be pregnant than at the Villa Bellaggio, where I might have had a fellowship this year."

"I think it's wonderful that you're having another baby," Stacey interjects. "Three is a good number. I think three children make the perfect family."

"If three is ideal, then why are you having another?" Mandy asks, malice beading her eyes, seething in her voice, which nonetheless maintains its softness.

"We wanted another," Hal replies easily, cheerfully. "Four kids. An even number. Maybe another girl as cute as Andrea. Two girls, two boys. Balance. Symmetry."

He stares defiantly at Nina and David, but they are silent. Nina, the careful hostess, does not want that silence to extend into awkwardness, but she knows that she does not have to worry about John and Mandy noticing the tension. Their sensitivity is self-directed, internalized. They are too involved in their own problems to recognize the difficulties and emotional strains of their friends. Nina imagines the small, bitter novel John will write about Mandy's pregnancy, unless, of course, he writes a euphoric vignette about fatherhood the second time around. Mandy will craft elegant haiku verses about her anger, about inequity and the myth of androgyny. John and Mandy do not notice that the twins wear unmatched sneakers, that the scrape on Samantha's knee is striated with pus; of course, they will not notice this uneasy silence that Hal's casual statement, his too-easy lie, has created.

And Hal is right, Nina acknowledges, instinctively right about something they have not discussed. It is not necessary for them to announce that Stacey is carrying David's child. It is, as his challenging gaze tells them, no one's damn business except their own. Still, the question nags. What will they tell their friends and relatives when suddenly there is an infant in their home? Will they say they have adopted the baby (which will, of course, be a half-truth because, as Charles Norris has carefully explained, Nina will have to legally become the adoptive mother), or will they, with self-conscious honesty, speak of Stacey and their agreement, layering their explanations with intellectual and emotional justifications? ("*David really wanted a child of his own. It only made sense. The biological mother is a wonderful woman.*")

It would have been so much simpler, Nina thinks, to have gone away for a year and then to have returned with a child they would claim to be their own. Who would know any different, and who would care? Only Hildy, of course. *Hildy.* Nina closes her eyes and

surrenders briefly to the seductive combination of the sun's heat and
the effect of the drink (into which David has wisely poured a large
measure of gin), and when she opens them Hildy is standing beside
her. Her dark morning mood is gone. The smile that she trains on
the Cosgroves as David introduces them is inviting and brilliant. She
is dressed for the beach in a bright yellow terry-cloth chemise, which
hikes up when she stands on her toes to dutifully kiss John Cowper
on the cheek.

"I just finished your novel," she tells him. "I liked it. I really did.
Are you a writer too?" she asks Mandy, whom she has not met before.

"Mandy's a poet," John says, and Stacey leans forward excitedly,
thrusting her large white bag in front of her.

"A poet." There is awe in her voice. "I love poetry. I write some
myself. I took this course and the teacher thought that some of my
work was really good — for a beginner, I mean."

Her voice trails off as Mandy looks impatiently away.

Hildy sits on the grass opposite the three couples, who turn in
their chairs to look at her, squinting against the impact of the sunlight.

"God, it's hot," she says, and she rips open her beach dress. Beneath it she wears a sleek black one-piece bathing suit that so closely
hugs her body that briefly, magically, it seems at one with her golden
skin. Mandy and Stacey move their chairs into the shade and glance
at each other in silent complicity. They share a secret that will one
day be revealed to this lithe, dark-haired girl who preens herself so
proudly in the harsh sunlight. One day she too will be stretched and
distorted by love and lust. Her abdomen will also swell with life, and
small veins will steal across the long legs she lifts so carefully, as
though examining their color, their shape.

"Do you want anything to drink, Hildy?" Nina asks.

"Uh-uh. Seth is picking me up. We're going to the beach. I didn't
realize you were coming today," she informs the guests politely, "or
I wouldn't have made a date."

"That's all right," Stacey assures her. Her lemonade glass is empty
and she watches the last sliver of ice melt. "I'm going to have some
more, Nina. Don't get up. I'll pour it myself."

She goes to the table and refills her glass, but although she balances it painstakingly, she trips over her large white handbag and

the frothy liquid spurts forward onto Hildy, staining her swimsuit, streaking her shoulders.

"Oh, I'm sorry. I'm so sorry," Stacey says, and her voice cracks.

"It's nothing," Hildy assures her. "It's only a bathing suit. It's just sticky. I'll wash it off."

She springs to her feet and plucks up the garden hose, which she turns on. Holding it aloft, she sprays the cold stream on her shoulders and the stained area of her suit.

"Ah, that feels good," she says, and, impulsively, she drenches her legs, her thighs.

"Here, let me help you." Hal seizes the hose and trains it on her. She dances before the spray with her head bent forward, butting the arc of water like a playful bull. She circles mischievously, darting from right to left as he pursues her until at last she submits. The watery whip lashes against her back, across her shoulders. She clasps her hands in a mock plea for mercy, and as she turns he spanks her buttocks with the cold spray.

"It's marvelous," she shouts. "Marvelous." She laughs with delight, and David and Nina and their friends laugh too. Stacey's giggle is nervous, high-pitched; it attracts the children, who run across the lawn from the play area.

"Me too, me too!" Samantha shouts, tossing off her unlaced sneakers and dashing into the arc of water that Hal manipulates, now unleashing it on Hildy and then on one child after another as they discard their shoes and rush toward him. He is the ringmaster and they are his playful animals, but Hildy, pirouetting before him, is his favored mascot. He is in command and she obeys the message of his whip, sprinting and kneeling as the children gleefully trail after her.

Nina dashes into the house for towels. The hose is turned off and the wet children laugh and roll about on the grass while the adults smile at them. But Hildy is shivering, and Nina tosses the towels to Stacey and Mandy and enfolds Hildy in a large white bath sheet. Even as the other women busy themselves with the small children (Stacey clucking and Mandy hissing), so Nina too rubs her child dry. Her wide gray gauzy sleeves flutter as she rubs Hildy's shoulders, the dark glistening cap of her hair, her arms and thighs. Her daughter's body is bright and hard, the black bathing suit a sleek carapace. John

Cowper (who cannot help thinking in simile) sees Nina as a vigilant gray moth, her wings encircling a bright beetle.

And then a car horn sounds and Hildy plucks up her bright yellow chemise, waves to them gaily, and rushes off, pausing only to kiss Terry on the cheek.

Hal stares after her and then goes to the car to bring in the large plastic bag in which Stacey keeps emergency changes for the children.

"That Hildy," he thinks. "That Hildy." He smiles, remembering how the water rained down her back and how a tiny prism sprouted on her shoulder.

David starts the grill and soon the aroma of roasting meat fills the garden. Stacey and Mandy busy themselves with the plates and the condiments; they compliment Nina on the beauty of the pasta salad, which, in the end, the children refuse to eat.

The children lie on the floor of the playhouse and watch the long shadows of late afternoon splash dark velvet patches across each other's bodies. They have just managed to fit into the small enclosure, giggling as they pressed their bodies against each other, squeezing to make room. They are triumphant because at lunch David had said that he did not think there would be room for all of them together.

"Hildy never played there with more than one or two friends," he said, and Nina had nodded and then closed her eyes as though trying to picture Hildy as a small girl, playing with miniature dishes.

"We'll have to tell him we made it, that we fit," Evan says proudly. "All six of us."

"That's because I'm lying on my side and Samantha and Eric are such midgets," Terry says. "And you have Jared lying on you." He is never a gleeful, triumphant victor. He is, in fact, wary of victory, as only the child of fiercely competitive parents can be, knowing (as he does) the price that must often be paid for it.

"Still, we did it," Andrea retorts. She turns to the twins. "Are you that small because both of you were born at once? Maybe there wasn't enough food while you were growing in your mother's stomach to feed both of you. Like the food gets to the baby through a cord, and maybe not enough food was going through the cord."

Andrea knows about such things because Stacey has read to her from a picture book called *The Wonderful Story of How You Were Born*.

"How does the food get into the cord?" Samantha asks.

They are silent. Jared, who has fallen asleep, rolls into the small crevice between Andrea and Terry.

"I think whatever the mother eats goes into the cord," Andrea says hesitantly, trying to remember what the book said.

"No. I think that when the father does it — you know, when he plants the baby — maybe he plants enough food for it," Eric offers.

"He doesn't plant the baby." Evan is scornful. "He shoots his sperm into the mother with his, you know, his thing."

They giggle then, shyly, knowingly.

"Sperm," Samantha repeats. It is a new word and she tests it again. "Sperm." She is, after all, a poet's child. "How does the father shoot the sperm? How does he get it into the mother's stomach?"

"He lays on top of her." This Terry knows for certain. He had watched his father lie on top of his mother, panting and groaning, and he has watched him lie on top of Mandy, listened to their wild, frightening laughter.

"Does it make them feel nice?" Samantha asks, and they giggle again.

"It gives them more room in the bed anyway," Evan says. "They're like one person. They can roll around." Once, wakened by a dream or a stomachache, he had gone to his parents' room and stood in the doorway, watching as they rolled around; draped in the counterpane they seemed to him to be a single large white animal, and the sounds they made scared him and caused him to cry.

"We need more room on this floor," Andrea says, and her laughter is not a shy giggle but a ripple of merriment. And then they all laugh aloud and shift positions, their bodies shaking, rocking with hilarity.

Evan climbs on Samantha. Terry lies across Andrea.

"You pinched me," Samantha shrieks.

"You're tickling me," Terry cries and grabs Andrea's arm. Eric tries to topple him and tumbles onto Jared, waking him. The small boy wails in bewilderment and the laughter of the other children intensifies.

"Pant! Groan!" Terry shouts, and between bursts of laughter they pant and groan while Jared screams and screams again.

Stacey and David, who have walked down to the play area so that Stacey can pick roses to take home, hear the laughter and the screams. They hurry to the playhouse and stand in the open doorway, staring down at the children, who are, quite suddenly, silent, except for the smallest boy, whose sobs rise and fall in rhythmic terror.

In an unarticulated complicity of silence, Stacey and David say nothing to the others about what they have decided to think of as "the children's game." They sit beside each other and drink their coffee and eat their fruit salad as the children assemble at their table to eat the cake and ice cream that Nina has placed on yellow paper plates. The Cosgroves are the first to leave and they shake hands with Mandy and John, who are sprawled lazily on chaises.

Hal walks ahead with the children, and Nina and David accompany Stacey to the car. She carries a plastic container filled with the leftover pasta salad, and a cluster of pink and white roses.

"We hardly had time to talk," David says. "You're feeling good?"

"Terrific. It's early yet, but I'm beginning to show." Ruefully, she touches the rip in the seam of her sundress.

"Let's go shopping together for maternity clothes," Nina suggests impulsively. "I'll call you."

"Great," Stacey agrees. She kisses each of them on the cheek and then she yawns. "I get so sleepy in the late afternoon," she says. "I did with the others too."

"I remember feeling that way." Nina also yawns and they all laugh, sharing the secret mirth of co-conspirators.

Still, a strange and heavy lassitude overtakes Nina, and when John and Mandy leave at last, she does go up for a nap. She smiles through fragmented dreams in which a baby cries and the playhouse is mysteriously filled with soft and fragrant pink and white rose petals.

David lies beside her on his back, listening for the sound of Hildy's key in the door. He is pleased with the afternoon, pleased that Stacey's children felt at home during the visit. Determinedly, he does not think about that odd incident at the playhouse. He watches Nina as she sleeps. Gently, he tickles her cheek with the tail of the stuffed peacock. The touch of the soft feather causes her to smile and she brushes his hand away.

"Idiot," she says sleepily.

"Idiot," he agrees happily and covers her with a light blanket.

But now she is awake and she pulls him to her, placing his hands on her breasts, smiling as they move expertly, lovingly across her body.

"Love me?" she asks mischievously, but there is no need for him to answer. He is already enveloping her in that love, and her moans, so sweet and deep, rising from the core of her being, mark her delight, her joyful acceptance.

8

It is late August when Nina and Stacey arrange to shop for maternity clothes. Hildy decided to drive into the city with them. She wants to browse in Tower Records, she says. She might do some shopping, maybe in the Village. And, she adds slyly, teasingly, she might go to a museum. She has been at loose ends this summer, with Seth working at a Burger King and Alison on a "teen tour" of Europe. She slides sulkily down in the rear seat so that Nina will not be able to see her in the mirror.

"Which museum?" Stacey asks eagerly. She is familiar with all the museums of New York. She has walked through them with Evan clutching one hand, Andrea the other, and Jared asleep in the Snugli at her chest. But the children were impatient and tugged at her when she paused too long before a painting, so that the museum outings have been abandoned. Now she has decided to reward herself with a museum visit after her monthly check-ups with Arnold, whose office is not far from the Metropolitan Museum of Art. She no longer tries to persuade Hal to accompany her. He is depressed by the long quiet corridors, uneasy with the soft talk or, worse, the concentrated silence. In the garden of the Museum of Modern Art, he made fun of the Rodins, speculating about the sexual prowess of the huge sculpted figures. He plodded across the flagstone walk in imitation of an elderly man who had glanced disapprovingly at him. Stacey had giggled — she had to, he was so funny — but she has not pressed him to go again.

"I might go to the Modern," Hildy says laconically.

Nina frowns. Hildy is not dressed for a museum. She wears dirty white sneakers without laces, very tight faded blue jeans, and a white sweatshirt from which the sleeves have been raggedly severed. Still, Edith has pointed out that kids wear anything these days, and it is counterproductive (*counterproductive* is a favored phrase in Edith's professional vocabulary) to argue with them, so Nina says nothing.

"Hal's restaurant is right near the Modern," Stacey says. She always refers to the places where Hal works as though they belong to him because he has taught her to do that. He thinks of them as his own, and many patrons take him to be the owner. He is so well-dressed, so self-assured, so very much in charge. He exudes an air of proprietorship as he moves through the dimly lit bar, joshing with customers, urging waiters to move more quickly, or, as he stands at the reservation book, dispensing tables with smiling largesse. It will be natural for him to have his own place in California. And she will help him with the books — perhaps even take a course in accounting or management.

"What's the name of the restaurant?" Hildy asks. She remembers Hal and she wiggles her toes, recalling the silken touch of the wet grass as she danced through the spray.

"Ramon's, it's called. It's a nice place."

"Well, I'm not sure I'll get up there. Where are you going to shop?"

"Altman's," Nina says. "They have a good maternity department."

"Aren't you getting anything for yourself, Mom?"

"No. Today is just to get Stacey some basics," Nina replies.

"I see . . . I guess."

Hildy stares out the window, her face frozen, sullen with unasked questions. She does not understand why Nina (who measures out her time as carefully as a miser measures coins, hours for practice and composition rigidly allocated) is spending an entire day shopping for maternity clothes for Stacey Cosgrove. Who the hell is Stacey Cosgrove, anyway, and why does David call her several times a week, his voice so kindly, so solicitous? "*How are you, Stacey? How are you feeling? Is everything going well?*"

Hildy listens to these calls on the upstairs extension phone, and she wonders if Nina knows about them. It has occurred to her that Stacey is David's mistress. Seth's father has a mistress — the appointments secretary in his office. Hildy feels the onset of a headache not unlike those she develops during a math class when the teacher posits a problem she cannot comprehend. She is sorry now that she has come to the city. She really has nothing to do. She clenches her hands and her long nails carve their way into her palm. She is sorry that she was ever born.

"Listen, I'm getting out here," she says. "There's a Tower store right around here. In the Fifties, Seth said." They are stopped at a red light and she tumbles swiftly out of the car, her face averted so that the women in the front seat will not see that her eyes are dangerously bright.

"What time will you be home? Do you have enough money?" Nina calls after her, but Hildy has disappeared into the crowd of milling shoppers and office workers hurrying toward their lunch appointments. Although Nina searches the street until the light changes, she does not see Hildy, who has slipped into a boutique where she stands at a counter, fingering an Indian scarf while tears she did not expect and cannot explain streak her cheeks.

Nina and Stacey have lunch in the Charleston Gardens at Altman's. Stacey has not been there before, and she is charmed by the delicate white wrought-iron tables and chairs, the subtle pastel decor. She watches the women at the other tables as they show each other their purchases, speak so softly and earnestly, their heads bent close, and study the menu with great concentration. The small restaurant is not unlike a club, a meeting place where women are guaranteed softness, frivolity, intimacy. A basket of African violets stands on the middle of the table, and Stacey gently touches a tiny blossom. It is, as she had known it would be, real.

"That's what we'll do when we have our own restaurant," she says. "We'll use only fresh flowers. It adds something, doesn't it?"

"I think so," Nina agrees. "I hope you do get your own place."

"Oh, we will. Hal is sure of it. We'll wait for maybe a year after we settle in California and then we'll look around. We have a pretty

clear idea of what we want. We even have a name for it. 'The Unicorn.' Do you like it?"

" 'The Unicorn.' Yes. I like it. It's wonderful to have something
to look forward to."

"What do you look forward to, Nina?" The intimate ambience of
the restaurant has made Stacey bold. Women tell the truth to each
other in this room designed for their pleasurable withdrawal from the
bustle of shopping, the demands of their homes, their jobs. At an
adjacent table a young blond woman inclines her head as she talks
to an older woman who is surely her mother. She is crying shame-
lessly, fearlessly even, as the waitress refills her coffee cup. Stacey
feels sorry for men who cannot go to pretty little restaurants nestled
in the corner of department stores and sit at tables set with fresh
flowers where they can cry without shame, without fear.

"I look forward to the baby. To our baby. David's and yours and
mine." Nina says this naturally because she has rehearsed it so often
in her own mind, conditioning herself to belief and acceptance.

The baby will have three parents (Nina does not consider Hal a
part of this triumvirate of nurturers), three people concerned with its
well-being, its development, its happiness. She sees their life as a
fluid dance sequence. Unhurriedly, with flowing, easy movement,
Stacey and Nina will glide into each other's positions. With effortless, generous motion, the child will pass from the arms of one to
the arms of another, with David circling about them in an arabesque
of protection. The dance will continue, segueing into a life-cycle
work. There will be leave-takings and welcomes. Stacey will be the
affectionate "aunt," sending birthday cards and gifts from California,
visiting the family on trips east, visited by them on their journeys
west. It is all so simple — simple as the movements in a choreographic pattern that falls magically into place.

"Some people will think that what we're doing is wrong," Stacey
says.

She is thinking of her brothers and their wives, of her father, and
of her mother who has, for all these years, tottered at the edge of
madness, who still sits at the window and searches the street for a
sign of her stillborn twins. How can she explain this agreement with

the Roths to them? Already her sisters-in-law, shrewd-eyed and (Stacey thinks) jealous because Hal is affectionate to the children and to Stacey, so much more alive and attractive than their own husbands (they titter flirtatiously at his jokes, preen themselves as he compliments them on a new hairdo, a new blouse), have noticed her pregnancy. *"You never tell us anything, Stacey. We have to guess everything. How far along are you?"*

She has countered their questions with shyness and blushes, the perquisites of all pregnant women. And lying awake at night, she has conceived of alternative scenarios and discussed them with Hal, who always dilutes her anxiety with laughter.

"We can tell them that the baby was born dead," she suggested; the words evoked her fears, her superstitions. Such words are a temptation to fate, an invitation to disaster.

"No. We'll just tell them that it was born with horns and we sent it back to Rosemary," Hal offered. "Rosemary's baby. Stacey's baby. Get it? Or maybe we can tell them we offered it as a prize on a quiz show like *The Price Is Right*. 'How much is this beautiful pink and white infant worth?' " And they had laughed at that too, although Stacey found the answer forming in her mind. Twenty thousand dollars. Exactly twenty thousand, not counting prenatal care, delivery, and related expenses.

Still, they will think of something. It is more important to decide what they will tell the children. Even Jared has already noticed her pregnancy and asked questions about it, poking at her with his small fingers. (*"Big Mommy. Soft Mommy. Is my mommy growing a new baby, a new Jared?"*)

But perhaps the children will have an easier time in the end than the adults. Children have a facility for accepting the extraordinary, for melding reality and fantasy. She thinks of the games Andrea and Evan invent, of the fantasy worlds they build. Kids can accept anything. She thinks suddenly of how Andrea wept to find a dead sparrow in their yard and how Evan buried it carefully.

"I'm not really burying it," he told Andrea solemnly. "I'm planting it."

Nina smiles when Stacey tells her about that.

"It must be wonderful," she says wistfully, "to have a large family so that children can grow up together and be friends."

Her own childhood was wreathed in silence, just as Hildy's was cushioned in calm. It will be different with this new baby who will have an older sister, who will toddle about in a house where doors slam, phones ring, and the stereo projects the loud egocentric music of youth. She feels a tingle of excitement, of anticipation. A new life is beginning for them, for all of them.

"Yes. It's fun, it's good, especially at holidays. Thanksgiving. Christmas." And then Stacey is silent because this baby she is carrying will not celebrate Christmas. She blushes and averts her eyes. It is the first time that she has really thought about the fact that the Roths are Jewish and that the child she delivers for them (to them) will be raised as a Jewish child. Is it important? She does not think so, but she files the doubt away in a corner of her mind to be pondered and processed.

"Yes. It's wonderful for a family to be together at holiday times," Nina says. She thinks suddenly of the Sabbath dinner to which they had been invited in Israel.

Their host was an official of a small museum in Haifa that had acquired six of Amos Roth's paintings. His home was on the Carmel, and Nina and David had reached it at sunset, hurrying uphill, David clutching a large spray of white carnations. Everyone they passed was carrying flowers, and Nina was pleased at the thought that floral fragrance would waft across almost every table in the city. The family was gathered in the dining room. The museum director, a plump, smiling man, was eager to show David his treasures. He had come over from Germany in 1936 and so his parents had been able to bring with them many of their paintings, the elegant wrought-iron lamp that burned throughout the Sabbath, the intricately carved mezuzot. His mother, so old that she could barely stand on her matchstick legs but was supported, as she blessed the candles, by her strong young granddaughter, had smiled proudly.

"That which was ours is still ours," she told David.

There were four generations at the table. The director's married son was there with his small son, and two granddaughters who lived on a kibbutz in the south were visiting. They were all very quiet as the old woman blessed the candles. Their faces were luminous in the soft light. The large dining room windows overlooked Haifa bay, and the slowly sinking sun turned the waters of the Mediterranean the color of molten gold. As darkness fell, the museum director made kiddush, and his family sang a hymn of welcome to the Sabbath. The voices of the generations mingled, and Nina and David, who did not know the songs, held hands.

David stared hard at the children. Nina felt his longing then, as though it burned in her own breast. He wanted a child to stand beside him at the sunset hour as once he had stood beside Amos Roth. He wanted the laughter and song that one generation offers to another. It was not, she had thought sadly then (and thinks sadly now), so very much to ask for. The sharing and continuity of that which is his. The touch of a child's hand in a candle-lit room. A family gathered to celebrate a holiday, to sing a hymn of welcome to the Sabbath.

Nina smiles at Stacey.

"Look," she says gently, "I don't think we have to worry about what other people will think. We know what we're doing and why we're doing it. The important thing is that we know that it's the right thing for us." Her words ring with a new certainty, and Stacey nods.

In celebration, they order strawberry shortcake with coffee for Nina and a glass of milk for Stacey, who, of course, will not drink anything with caffeine.

The maternity shop is deeply carpeted, and they walk soundlessly from rack to rack, their faces set purposefully. Stacey concentrates on skirts and tops. They are practical, interchangeable, and can often be altered and used after the pregnancy. But then even the shifts that are so fashionable this year can be used afterward if she finds the right belt or takes in the seams. She shops with the worried intensity of those women who have always had to fit their purchases to a prescribed budget, pursing their lips even as they make a selection, always asking the saleslady about returns and refunds.

Nina, however, expertly examines the diaphanous dresses in the colors of wildflowers. She flips swiftly through the racks, rejecting the rather large selection of blacks and navy blue (*Why would a woman burgeoning with life choose to dress in the colors of death?* she wonders absently), and sends the gossamer dresses spinning until, at last, she makes a selection.

"Do you like this?" She holds out a jade-green georgette dress, its sleeves delicately capped, its bodice luxuriously pleated.

Stacey shrugs uncertainly, but Nina has found another design that pleases her.

"What about this?" A daffodil-yellow dress of watered silk, it moves gently in the breeze from the air conditioner; she holds it out proudly, like a banner of triumph.

"I don't know. Let me try them on," Stacey says guardedly, shifting her own selections onto her arm. She has chosen only sale-priced garments: a navy-blue skirt and a khaki one, a plaid blouse and a white cotton one.

A blue-haired, chinless saleswoman leads them to a dressing room. There is a pale blue velvet chaise longue in one corner and Nina sinks down on it, the yellow and green dresses draped over her arm in readiness. Seriously, methodically, Stacey tries on the skirts and tops. She piles her hair high and then combs it back. Studying herself in the mirror, she stands still and then walks slowly forward, alternately frowning and smiling. She is trying to envision herself in these outfits through all the moods that will surely overtake her as her pregnancy progresses.

In the end, she decides to take both skirts and blouses, and Nina nods her approval.

"They'll be very useful," she says. "And now for the dresses which will hardly be useful at all."

They both laugh and Stacey tries on the green dress. It flares gracefully about her legs and billows softly at her waist. The cap sleeves float above her arms and emphasize their firm roundness.

"It looks terrific," Nina says. "How does it feel?"

"Marvelous." She stands on her toes, holds the skirt delicately; she has never owned anything so soft, so light.

"Now the other one." Nina helps to lift the dress over her head and notices that Stacey's breasts are full and luminous, striated with pale blue veins. Already the nipples have darkened to the color of wine. Stacey blushes.

"I know. I get big kind of early. That's good for the milk later though."

"Yes," Nina says. "It must be." She does not remind Stacey that she will not nurse this baby.

Now Stacey wears the yellow dress. It is high-waisted and gives her an elegant Elizabethan look. The color almost matches her thick hair. Nina has a tiger-eye brooch that would look just right with it. Perhaps she will give it to Stacey, who studies herself critically in the three-way mirror.

"It's more your kind of dress," Stacey says, "although I really love it."

"Actually, I think the green is more my kind of dress," Nina says.

"Try it on," Stacey says, and they giggle.

Nina slips out of her blue shirtwaist and does try on the green dress. Enveloped in its gossamer folds, she thrusts her body forward and rocks backward on her heels. She and Stacey stand before the mirror, their arms about each other, and smile. Nina does a plié and Stacey gravely copies the movement. They are at once teacher and pupil, sisterly conspirators and sharers of a mysterious and tantalizing secret.

There is a knock at the dressing room door, and the blue-haired saleswoman enters and smiles benignly at them.

"Oh, are you both pregnant?" she asks.

"Yes," Nina says. "With the same child."

She and Stacey titter, and as the saleswoman's gaze drifts solemnly from one to the other, their laughter escalates into uncontrolled hilarity. The saleswoman nods with professional insouciance. She has worked for many years in this department and is familiar with the mood swings of pregnant women.

"Did you decide on anything?" she asks.

"Everything. We're taking everything," Nina says, and the woman gathers up their purchases, including the green and yellow dresses that they have hastily removed.

"Can you imagine? She didn't believe us," Stacey says, gasping for breath, and they collapse into laughter again and sit down on the chaise longue until they recover.

9

Hildy, angry with herself because she has cried, because she seems to cry so easily, walks slowly uptown. The temperature has soared, but the heat has not diminished the energy and activity of those who rush through the streets and dash across intersections, their heads jerking nervously from right to left. Women in summer dresses and snow-white sneakers and anklets walk swiftly, imperceptibly breaking their pace as they glance at department store windows where mannequins in plaid skirts and cashmere sweaters have, on this unbearably hot day, already begun the race toward autumn.

Men sling their jackets over their shoulders, wipe the sweat from their faces with large handkerchiefs, shift their attaché cases from hand to hand. Cars careen around corners, their horns hooting maliciously at each other, at the speeding cyclists who whip teasingly from one lane to the other. A Chinese man in a wheelchair tries to propel himself up the ramp of a kneeling bus as taxi drivers scream their rage at the delay. Walking four, five, and six abreast, pedestrians grapple for pavement space, force each other to walk diagonally, listen to conversational scraps. Many speak to themselves, their lips moving soundlessly and their heads nodding as they plunge purposefully forward.

Street vendors spread their wares the length of the curb, balancing merchandise on pyramids of cartons, arraying them on strips of soiled plastic, blankets of newspapers. Narrow-faced, lean black giants from Senegal deftly leaf through pastel piles of Mickey Mouse polo shirts, looking for a size to suit a customer who is already moving impatiently on.

"Here — take two, take three. Special price." Their voices rise in chorus, at once threatening and cajoling. Mylar balloons in metallic colors float across the sluggish air. Gold chains and watches glitter in the sun, are dangled tauntingly at passersby. A blond girl pauses in her distribution of Burger King coupons and tries on a gold watch. She slips it on her thin wrist, studies it with great absorption before plunging her hand into the pocket of her brown apron and giving the vendor a folded bill. Still wearing the watch, she resumes her distribution of the coupons, but now she stares at her own outstretched arm and smiles archly as though she is possessed of a secret power.

A jazz quartet plays loudly on the steps of a church and a small crowd gathers. Coins are tossed and fall soundlessly onto the blue velvet lining of the trombonist's open case. A couple begins to dance. The girl's bright orange hair hugs her head in a close, curling cut and she wears a sleeveless white jumpsuit. Her partner, a tall black man in a blue cord business suit, balances his attaché case in one hand as he holds her close, although he does not look at her as they dance. And then, abruptly, although there has been no break in the music, they separate and walk away. Hildy glances after them and wonders if they are, after all, together. There are no rules on this broad avenue, where blocks of pavement serve as market stalls and patches of shade are snatched as arenas for street musicians.

Hildy walks on, averting her eyes from an old woman who wears a man's black winter coat (on this hot day!) and pushes a shopping cart laden with tattered shopping bags. A family has set up a canopy in front of a gourmet cheese store. The mother and father, pale and thin, wear faded jeans and long, loose cotton shirts, but their small blond daughter, her hair curled and beribboned, wears a starched pink dress and black patent-leather shoes. The woman plays the flute and the man strums a guitar as the child dances dutifully, dispiritedly, around a top hat against which a crayoned cardboard sign has been placed. PLEASE HELP US. WE HAVE NO HOME. Dollar bills and coins have been tossed in, and Hildy adds her own contribution: the ten-dollar bill that David thrust in the pocket of her jeans that morning. Sadly, she walks away, but when she looks back she sees that the little girl is purchasing an oversized coloring book from a curbside vendor, an albino who wears a large red straw hat to shield himself from the sun.

She has reached Tower Records but she does not go in. She has enough records and tapes. Besides, Seth copies tapes for her. He has an elaborate stereo system that includes a cassette deck of his own design, and when he is not working on his car he copies tapes. Hildy and Alison watch him while they all smoke the very good grass that Alison buys from her mother's cleaning woman.

Seth loves his machines and he handles them tenderly. He is careful of his tape recorders, his stereo equipment, his car. He has power over them; they perform obediently to his slightest gesture. They are reliable, unlike his mother, who bursts into tears at improbable provocations (the dry cleaner has ruined a dress; she has not been invited to a luncheon, a party), or his father, who sometimes sleeps at home and sometimes does not.

"Machines are cool," he once told Hildy. "Besides, in this world, whoever has the most machines wins."

That was the day they had counted up the machines in their homes — the food processors and video-cassette recorders, the pasta makers and humidifiers and dehumidifiers, the power lawn mowers and the electric units affixed to the trees in their yards that zapped the mosquitoes each evening.

"We could live in India for our whole lives on what we could get for just the kitchen appliances," Seth said, and they had all laughed while Alison figured out how many rupees a toaster oven, a blender, and an electric knife might be worth.

Hildy walks past the record store and turns east. She wishes she knew someone in the city to visit. On these crowded, sun-bright streets, amidst the rush and noise, she feels herself alone and lonely. She walks more slowly now, as though to forestall the familiar terror that often overtakes her at night. *Who am I? What will I become? What kind of a person do I want to be?* The questions whirl through her mind in a dizzying rush. Often in the night she awakens and sits up in bed, bewildered by dreams she cannot remember, mysterious stirrings and longings to which she can give no names. It is then that she tiptoes down the hall and stands outside her parents' bedroom door. She cannot go in. She is too old to confront them with her nocturnal sadness. Sometimes, they are awake, and standing in the hallway, she listens to the soft sound of their voices, so cushioned by relaxed intimacy. There are other nights when the gay sounds of their play resonate through the door. David roars like a lion; Nina bleats like a lamb. Hildy imagines them on the bed, amid the menagerie of their whimsical stuffed animals, playing games of jungle and field, their laughter as unrestrained as their love.

She wants to open the door then, to become part of their gaiety. She wants to move in their enchanted orbit. But most of all, she wants them to hold her very tightly, and yet she does not want them to touch her at all. *Who are they and who is she?*

Trembling suddenly, Hildy goes into a Lamston's and buys a cheap lipstick in a harsh shade of crimson and a cerise nylon scarf, which she ties jauntily around her neck. Immediately, she feels better. Loud colors, loud noise invariably make her feel better.

Calmed, she walks uptown. She will go to the gift shop of the Museum of Modern Art and buy her mother a gift. She smiles as she anticipates Nina's bewilderment, her pleasure. She walks quickly. The lunch hour is over and the streets are less congested. She is hungry and she begins to search for a burger place, a lunch counter, and almost at once sees the small restaurant. Ramon's. Of course. This is where Hal Cosgrove works. Stacey had said it was not far from the museum. Hildy does not hesitate. She pushes open the door and enters the dimly lit room.

Hal is at the cashier's desk. He looks at Hildy appraisingly but does not immediately recognize her. He notices how her white shirt emphasizes her amber-colored skin and how her black hair caps her finely shaped head. She looks familiar, but then a lot of girls look familiar. No, he knows her. She is the Roths' daughter, the girl who danced before the hose at that barbecue — the only fun he had had that day, although Stacey had enjoyed herself. Hildy. That's the girl's name. He is good with names — especially the names of women.

"Hello, Hildy," he says.

"Hi, Hal."

He is pleased that she is not surprised to see him. So she knew he worked here and sought him out. He feels flattered. He pulls his stomach in and touchs his gold chain. He is glad he wore his blue shirt today, the one Andrea says looks so terrific. She knows what she is talking about, his Andrea, his little princess.

"Stacey told me this was your place, and I got hungry just as I passed it," Hildy says.

"Good thinking. And nice timing. I'm just about ready to eat, myself. Come on. I'll tell you what's good."

He leads her to the rear of the nearly empty restaurant and they sit down at a table covered with a red cloth. A waiter approaches with menus, but Hal waves him away and grins.

"Let me order for you," he tells Hildy. "Trust me."

"Sure," Hildy says. She loosens the cerise neckerchief and reties it. "But how will you know what I like?"

"I'll read your mind. And if I'm wrong, you'll eat it anyway like a good girl. Because I ordered it."

But she does like what he orders: cold minestrone and tortellini filled with cheese and spinach. She likes the way he orders, brusquely, authoritatively. David would be solicitous, uncertain of his own choice, anxious for her to make her own selection. Hal is so daring, so assertive. She remembers suddenly how he trained the hose on her, flashing it first to one place and then to another, whipping her into obedience. The memory fills her with a strange and unfamiliar pleasure.

"You must think you know everything," she says teasingly, daringly.

"I know a lot of things," he says. "Like I know enough not to come into this circus of a city on a hot August day. My train wasn't even air-conditioned today. It was murder."

"I drove in with my mother and Stacey," Hildy says. "They're going shopping."

"Oh, yeah. For maternity clothes."

"That's right." She is somehow surprised that he knows this. The shopping excursion is the business of women. She is certain that David does not know that Nina and Stacey are at Altman's. It is not the sort of information Nina would share with him. "You know," she continues, "that's sort of funny, because my mother really doesn't even like to shop for herself." She is teasing him into a response, but he is too shrewd to be caught.

"How about you? Do you like to shop, Hildy?"

"Not especially."

"So what do you like to do?"

"You mean, what do I want to be when I grow up?" She nimbly offers questions in place of answers. "I don't know. What do you want to be when you grow up?"

"I am grown up."

"So? Is this it?" She glances around the room, plucks at the red tablecloth, which in places has faded to a pale pink.

"No. This isn't it. This is a dump." He tells her then about his plans for his own place. Not here, not in this city. New York is like a circus now. You'd have to be crazy to open anything here. The street outside, with its peddlers and homeless, its crazies and sidewalk entertainers, is like a scene from *The Rise and Fall of the Roman Empire.* (This is an observation that Stacey gleaned in a course on Contemporary Urban Civilization, and Hal has found that it impresses those to whom he repeats it.)

"So where would you open it?"

"In California when we move out there. Somewhere near San Francisco, maybe. Everything is more laid back there. More mellow. I even have a name for the place. I'm going to call it 'The Unicorn.' "

"Cute," Hildy says.

The food arrives and they eat hungrily. It is very good and they give it their rapt attention, reaching across the table for slices of oven-warmed bread and pats of butter. Their arms touch and their knives duel playfully for the remaining golden square of butter. They laugh, indifferent to the crumbs that rain down on the cloth.

"It's good. Really good," Hildy says. She has not eaten as well for days. During the summer David and Nina often eat out, but she refuses to join them. She is not in the mood, she says. She doesn't feel like eating. She has things to do. In truth, she does not go because she feels herself an outsider, an intruder on their intimacy.

She has felt that way since the morning of her graduation day from elementary school when she was awakened by clutching cramps and the rush of blood that she knew was her first menstrual period. Frightened (although Nina had prepared her for the onset of womanhood), she had gone to the room where David and Nina slept. The door was open and she stood on the rib of sunlight that slashed across the threshold. They were naked, their arms intertwined, their bodies pressed together: two become one. They moved in rhythm, their eyes closed, secret smiles on their faces. Hildy stepped away. In the hallway, she heard her mother moan softly and say, "David. David." From that time on she too called him David, and she has not called him Daddy since.

"It is good," Hal says. "I have the recipes. I figure that for a start we'll serve light suppers at the Unicorn. I've been collecting ideas. Come on. I'll show you. I've got a lot of stuff in the office."

She follows him through the empty restaurant to the small back room with its clutter of mismatched file cabinets and littered desks. The phone rings as they enter, and importantly he orders ten dozen matchbooks and a case of cocktail napkins.

"A lot of detail in this business. It's not easy," he says. "You have to think of everything."

"Yes."

He passes her a folder crammed with recipes, photographs of restaurant interiors, matchbook and napkin samples, swatches of fabric.

The waiter brings them tall glasses of iced coffee and sets them down on the table. Hildy lifts her glass, looks at the small cloud of cream.

"To the California Unicorn," she toasts.

"Hear, hear." Hal grins. They click glasses and drink. A mustache of whipped cream forms above Hildy's lip and Hal brushes it gently away with his finger.

"You're cute," he says.

"Do you think so?" She stares forlornly down at her glass, and he is startled to see that she is crying. She is thinking of the little girl in the pink dress tap-dancing on the pavement.

"You know you are," he says. "What's wrong?" His voice is tender. He speaks to her as he would speak to Andrea, his baby, his princess.

"I don't know."

"Ah, come on." He puts his arm around her and fingers the cerise neckerchief. "Everything will be all right."

He ties another knot in the scarf that so loosely encircles her throat and pulls her toward him by the silken leash. Her mouth is open and he kisses her softly, lightly. Her sadness gives him power over her, but he will not use it. Gently, he releases her, gathers up his papers, closes his folder.

"When will you be going west, Hal?" she asks.

"After the baby is born," he says. "Right after that."

"Won't it be hard to travel with a newborn?"

"Hey," he says. "That baby isn't coming with us. That baby's not mine. It's your dad's. Stacey's having it for you guys — for you and your mom and your dad. Didn't you know you were going to be a big sister?"

The mocking lilt in his tone emphasizes the absolute wild truth of his words. She stares at him and he feels a flash of fear. Stacey will be angry that he has told Hildy. That was her parents' right, she will say. But what the hell — how was he supposed to know that they hadn't told her? Still, his mouth is sour and he is awash in the sweat of fear and apprehension; he remembers suddenly that he showered three times (three times!) the night Stacey stayed in the city with David Roth.

Even now, so many weeks later, the thought of that night, of Stacey and David together, darkens his mood, triggers an anger so fierce and so wounding that it frightens him. Still, he cannot believe that it happened, that he allowed it to happen, that she wanted it to happen. *How could she? And how could I?* The questions assault him and leave him weakened and despondent.

"No, I didn't know that." Hildy's tone is flat, but there is no disbelief in her voice. Rather, it is as though Hal has confirmed a vague, unarticulated suspicion.

She drains her glass and sets it down on a corner of the desk, where spilled food has congealed into a glinting, greasy stain. She feels again the growth of the headache, the early stirrings of a nausea that will not lead to vomiting. The air-conditioning unit hums noisily but the tiny office is suffocatingly hot.

"Well, now you do," Hal says.

He kisses her again, this time with a bitter harshness, his teeth crushing her lips, his fingers gripping her arms, until the phone rings and he releases her to answer it. She hurries out then, and despite her headache, despite her nausea, she goes to the gift shop of the Museum of Modern Art, where she buys Nina a black scarf threaded with strands of silver and gold.

That night Nina shows David the jade-green maternity dress that she will take to her dressmaker to be shortened for Stacey. Stacey, of course, does not have a dressmaker, nor does she have time to alter the dress.

"Very nice," he says and turns away.

"No. Look."

Nina puts the dress on and studies herself in the long mirror that hangs on their closet door. She loosens her dark hair and brushes it so that it falls in silken waves about her shoulders. She dusts her eyelids with pale-green shadow and drapes a long string of pearls around her neck.

"How do I look? How do I look?"

"Beautiful," he says. "Beautiful."

"Pregnant. I look pregnant." She laughs enticingly. "Imagine that I am having the baby — your baby. That *I* am pregnant."

She moves before him, her abdomen thrust forward. She rocks back and forth on her heels. The dress swirls softly about her legs, billows over her body. She takes his hand and places it on her breasts, slides it down across her waist, her hips.

"Feel," she commands huskily. "Feel life. Feel our baby."

He smiles and touches her knowingly, tenderly, tracing her breasts.

"Our baby." He kneels before her and kisses her abdomen. "I love our baby."

"And I love our baby's daddy." Her voice is at once teasing and tender. There is a new excitement between them. They are conspirators engaged in a daring and dangerous undertaking, sharers of a wondrous secret. The unborn child (their child, *theirs*) fires their energy, fevers their love. Nina breaks away from him, and he watches as she dances across the room in the diaphanous green dress, her outstretched arms cradling the air.

10

Hildy no longer listens on the extension when David talks to Stacey. The mystery of such conversations is solved, and besides, she is too busy. The fall semester has begun, and she feels a new urgency about school. This is her senior year, and she must apply to colleges. Achievement tests and multicolored applications loom before her. She travels to Manhattan once or twice a week, ostensibly to do research at the New York Public Library or to visit NYU and Columbia. She wants to get a feel for the urban campuses, she tells Nina and David, who raise no objections. They are, in fact, pleased and relieved that she is showing such positive interest in her academic future, and they encourage her to visit colleges in other parts of the country as well.

"Why? Do you want to get rid of me?" she asks languidly, and then, slyly, "How far away do you want me to go?"

Their protests come in an effusive, apologetic rush. Of course they do not want her to go far away, but neither do they want to limit her. They want her to have many options, to develop independence, even as they cannot help worrying about her.

"When will you be home?" Nina invariably asks when Hildy leaves for the city.

Her answers are vague. When the library closes. She may want to go to a lecture at Columbia, a film at NYU. She'll try to call.

In actuality, on most of her trips to the city, she meets Hal and they sit over mud-colored cups of bitter reheated coffee in Ramon's. The shabby restaurant is deserted in the late afternoon; the bar area where Hal and Hildy sit is dimly lit, and long shadows glide between empty tables. The swinging doors that lead to the kitchen yawn open, and they hear the dishwasher sing sadly in Spanish until the cook orders him harshly to shut up. Hal tells Hildy jokes, makes her laugh. He reaches across the table and cups her head protectively in his large hand.

"Did they tell you yet?" he asks. They speak in the code of conspirators, seldom using names or mentioning events.

"Not yet."

"Do you think that they know that you know? About it?"

"No."

They smile smugly, as though their complicity confers superiority. Hal always walks her to the door and kisses her. Sometimes his kiss is a brotherly brush of lips against her cheek; sometimes he gravely presses his mouth against hers, arches his body dangerously close, then laughingly releases her. Mischievously, they play a game of their own design, inventing the rules as they progress from week to week.

"Hang in there," he says as she leaves, and she nods.

She will hang in there. Now that the initial shock of Hal's revelation has passed (and it was shock she experienced, she knows, recalling still the sudden iciness of her fingertips, the wave of nausea that washed over her when he told her about the baby), she relishes their secret. It balances David's deceit, Nina's betrayal. It gives her an advantage in the teasing game of tag she now plays when she is at home. She is the pursuer, the incisive detective; David and Nina are her unsuspecting suspects.

Occasionally, after dinner, she stalks David. She follows him into his study and stares at him when he reaches for the phone.

"I won't bother you," she says. "Go ahead. Make your call."

"No," he protests. "It wasn't important. I've changed my mind."

An hour later she trails him into the kitchen and surprises him with his hand on the receiver.

"Oh, I didn't know you were on the phone, David," she says, and she wonders if Stacey appreciates these calls, his anxious questions. ("*How are you feeling, Stacey? Did you have a good day? You're not doing too much, are you?*")

One night Hildy walks barefoot into their bedroom and finds Nina reading *The Mother Knot*.

"Going backward?" she asks. "I mean, you're through with all that mother stuff, aren't you?" She lifts the pile of magazines on the bedside table and finds the battered paperback copy of *The Magic Years*. "You're really on a kick, aren't you? How come?"

"I'm thinking about a dance on the theme of mothering," Nina says, and this, at least, is true.

Nina is, these days, obsessively absorbed in the relationship between mothers and their children, the bonding and the separation. She watches women and their children in the streets and stores, marks the way mothers walk slowly, mincing their steps to accommodate their toddlers. She has already notated a movement in which a woman dances with an infant in her arms, swirling exuberantly across the stage, lifting the child toward a ray of sunlight, a rainbow, swooping low to examine a fragile shell, a tender blade of grass. She thinks of adding another child to the sequence and toys with the memory of Stacey holding Andrea's hand while balancing Jared on her other arm.

Nina visits Stacey once or twice a week now. She has, in fact, helped Stacey to rearrange her living room furniture, given her tickets to a local concert, and accompanied her to hear Mandy read her poetry at a church in a distant suburb.

Hildy snorts derisively.

"So all the time you spend with Stacey Cosgrove is research?" she asks, but she leaves the room before Nina can reply.

David and Nina are not indifferent to Hildy's careless questions, her stealthy treks.

"She senses something, of course. You know how sensitive she is," Nina says.

"We have to tell her," David insists worriedly. "It's not fair to her."

"We'll tell her after we know the outcome of the CVS," Nina says firmly. She refers to a new dateline, a new decision in this perilous course they have undertaken.

Arnold has strongly recommended a procedure called chorionic villus sampling, during which fetal tissue is tested to determine the health of the fetus. He explained it carefully to them, although, as always, he avoided Nina's gaze as he spoke.

"I encourage the sampling because it is a sensible precaution," Arnold told them as they lingered over coffee after a Sunday brunch. Nina listened carefully as she watched, through the picture window, Edith and Hildy's slow stroll about the garden. Her sister-in-law and her daughter share a penchant for the sere lawns and brittle leaves of autumn.

"A precaution against what?" David asked, lighting a cigarette, although he knows that Arnold is troubled by his smoking. Their father had been a heavy smoker, and often he painted his subjects with cigarettes dangling from their lips. Indeed, one of Amos Roth's famous paintings, the one that hangs in the Whitney, is a depression scene in which a skeletal man, dressed in a shabby dark suit, sits on a debris-strewn stoop rolling a cigarette. Still, David smokes. It is the smallest of revolts against the fraternal solicitude that has cushioned his life since the afternoon Arnold discovered their father's stiffening body in the black leather armchair.

"A precaution against the possibility of Stacey giving birth to a genetically impaired infant," Arnold replied and fanned the smoke away.

Nina smiled bitterly; always she is amazed at the breadth of the medical profession's vocabulary of euphemisms. Arnold speaks of major surgery as "an insult to the system"; his patients do not die, they "pass on." Still, "genetically impaired" does sound better than "deformed," "retarded," "defective."

"I recommend CVS in special cases," he continued, "because we can do it earlier than we can do amniocentesis — sometime between the ninth and twelfth weeks of the pregnancy. For amnio we'd have to wait at least another month, and then we'd have to wait for another several weeks to get the results. With CVS we have a reading much sooner. You can see why it's preferable."

David and Nina nodded in solemn acquiescence. They understood the importance of the time element. At an early stage of pregnancy there is no movement, the mother does not experience the sensation of life stirring and growing within her. Nina knows a dancer who underwent amnio in her fifth month and was told that the child she carried would be a Down's syndrome baby. She had confided in Nina during a rehearsal coffee break, speaking in the quiet, steady tone in which women who are not close friends exchange intimacies.

"I could feel the baby growing, becoming stronger every day. I felt it moving, kicking, and I began talking to it, telling it stories. Sometimes, when I couldn't sleep I got out of bed and danced with my baby. Around and around the room I whirled, my arms around my stomach, around my baby. We were partners, sharers. My baby did not stir after I danced, and when I went back to bed I thought, 'Ah, my baby knows that rest must follow dance.' I was so proud of its wisdom. I was so happy to dance with my baby. And then my doctor told me my baby was damaged. That was the word he used. *Damaged* — a word that they use for merchandise on a shelf, things that you wouldn't want to bring home. It might have been different if he had said that before I felt life and movement, before I danced with my baby, my poor, damaged, never-born little baby." The dancer's voice had broken and she had bent double in the booth as though to shield herself from the invasion that had, in fact, taken place months earlier.

She had, of course, opted for an abortion, and during the procedure she had held her hands against her ears and squeezed her eyes shut. She feared that when the fetus was ejected from the safety of her womb it might emit a scream; she feared that her dancing baby might jerk its still-unformed legs in a wild jig of death.

Nina had listened and offered only the comfort of silence, the touch of her hand on the younger woman's outstretched fingers. She had not been surprised to learn, months later, that the dancer had left the company and was once again pregnant. The announcement of her daughter's birth was posted on the company's bulletin board. "I can certainly see the advantage of getting results as early as possible in the pregnancy," Nina said.

"It's a relatively simple process," Arnold continued, still looking only at David. "We do it intravaginally and it's absolutely painless."

"But there is some difficulty?" David asked. He blew a smoke ring and the pale blue wisp curled through the air, took the shape of a minuscule womb, unraveled to form a quivering question mark.

"There is a high risk of spontaneous abortion — miscarriage. Almost seven percent." Arnold offered the statistic softly, as though the incompetence of his profession embarrassed him.

"What would you advise?" David asked.

"I think that given the unorthodox circumstances of this pregnancy, we should opt for CVS."

"Have you spoken with Stacey about it?"

"Yes. I'm afraid she's fairly resistant. She's apprehensive, of course, about the danger of miscarriage, but more than that she doesn't see the need for any testing at all. She didn't have amnio with her other children and she says, quite accurately, that given the fact that this is her fourth pregnancy and she is in her mid-twenties, she is not in a high-risk group. More importantly, to all of us I think, she insists that even if the results of the test are negative, she is not sure she would opt for abortion." Arnold sighed and cradled his chin in his hands.

"I see," David said. Stacey's reaction did not surprise him. It was, he recognized, both sentimental and selfless, endearing and immature. "Seven percent makes the procedure high risk."

"Some say it's closer to eight percent," Arnold admitted.

David stood and went to the window. He was a scientist, a businessman, and he knew how he would decide if such an ominous statistic haunted a proposed project. But this was an entirely different sort of decision. It involved his own child, his posterity.

"This test is vital," Arnold persisted.

David did not answer. Arnold was right, of course. He did not, could not, deny that. But he himself ached with a fear that caused his limbs to grow heavy. What if the fetus were defective? He trembled to think of what the loss of this unborn child would mean to him. There had been a photograph in the Jerusalem museum of a father sitting on the curb of a street in an unnamed ghetto, the body of a child in his outstretched arms, his mouth open in what surely must have been a wail of agony and despair. Nina, who stood beside him, had leaned heavily against him.

"How terrible. Nothing worse. To lose a child." Tears stood in her eyes, and he had not realized until he touched his own cheek that he too was weeping.

And now he himself, not yet a father, was threatened with just such a devastating loss. His heart beat faster, and Nina, as though sensing his distress, reached for his hand. She held it tight, and the tension in her fingers betrayed her. Please, she thought. Please. Let our baby be healthy. Please. We don't want our baby to die.

He led her to the window. Together they watched Hildy and Edith pause before the dwarf maple whose leaves were already bloodied by the crimson hues of autumn.

"You know, we have no choice," Nina said softly. "Stacey must be persuaded."

"Of course. I'll talk to her."

Now it remains for Stacey to be persuaded, and then, after the CVS results are known, when they are certain that the pregnancy will progress, then they will tell Hildy. Only then.

David arranges a lunch date with Stacey, again choosing the Italian restaurant where they first met. This time he does not mistake Stacey for a schoolgirl. She is in her eleventh week of pregnancy, and her plaid maternity blouse flares buoyantly as she walks across the reception area to greet him. She has also had her honey-gold hair cut in such a way that the thick curls frame her face. Nina suggested the style, and it was Nina's own hairdresser who sculpted Stacey's long swathes of hair into soft, fulgent aureoles that radiate brightly against her rose-white skin. David, watching her as she glides toward him, thinks that she looks like a Botticelli madonna. He had thought her attractive from the first, but now he thinks her beautiful. She kisses him on the cheek, and as they follow the hostess to their table, he notices that other men stare after her, and he feels a flexing, self-congratulatory pride because this beautiful woman who walks beside him is pregnant with his child.

Her voice is different; the fluting girlish tone is replaced by a lyrical womanly firmness. She does not order spaghetti with clam sauce. Instead she selects veal piccata, a favorite of Nina's, although he does not comment on this. She is not unaware of the reason for this lunch.

"I know you want to talk to me about this CVS procedure," she says at once.

"Yes." Again he is impressed by Stacey's frankness, by her utter lack of dissimulation. Will his child inherit this disarming candor? Is such a quality genetically transmitted? He feels a surge of gratitude to Arnold for having placed him in contact with Stacey Cosgrove, who is so beautiful and who radiates such health and wholesomeness.

"I think it's too risky," she continues. "And it's not a worthwhile risk. I mean that even if the test shows there's something wrong with the baby, I'm not going to have an abortion."

"Stacey, under the terms of our agreement, if there is something wrong with the child it is my responsibility — mine and Nina's. Is it fair to impose that upon us?" He struggles to contain his own anxiety.

"I'm thinking about what's fair to the baby," she insists. "I mean, this is a living baby, a human being growing inside me — a baby that I wanted to have, that you wanted to have."

"We want a healthy baby. You know that. We talked about it."

Their food arrives and they stare down at the pink flesh, so artistically arranged on their plates. He is sorry now that he too ordered the veal. The delicate meat is the color of a baby's skin, and he wonders how he can bear to plunge his fork into it. Instead he picks up the strawberry that nestles on a corner of the plate, and his mouth fills with the tart juice. Stacey too eats her strawberry, and he thinks that if their lips met, the shared taste would commingle, the liquid of their mouths would interchange and again they would achieve a sweet unity. Stacey cuts her meat. She eats it with sharp, determined bites, her tongue darting skillfully, acrobatically, to lick at a vagrant drop of sauce. He is ashamed because his maleness is stirred and he blushes as he struggles to control the involuntary erection that has come upon him so suddenly.

"It's good," Stacey says. "And this meat is very good for the baby. Low in fat and high in protein."

"I'm sure it must be." He concentrates on the food, willing himself to reasonableness. That, after all, is why he is meeting Stacey, to encourage her to be reasonable.

"All my babies have been healthy." She continues their conversation effortlessly. "There's no reason to think that this baby won't be. I've been so careful — I think even more careful than I was with the others."

"I know all that, Stacey, and I appreciate it. But there's always a chance of something being wrong, and that's why they have these tests — the CVS, the amnio."

"And I think you should know," he goes on, bracing himself for what he will say next (because he and Nina have decided on a course of action, and they know that it will shake Stacey even as it shakes them), "that if you have the baby and it is not normal and cannot live a normal life, we will not care for it at our home but we will place it in a state institution."

She stares at him as though seeing him for the first time, as though she is newly aware of a dimension to his personality that repels her and reverses all previous feelings. The papers that week have been laced with exposés of atrocities at state institutions — babies found awash in their own feces, adolescents sexually abused by "therapy aides." The brightness vanishes from her face, and she nervously buttons the top button of her plaid blouse so that he can no longer see the soft triangular cleft where her very white neck rises from between the gentle curve of her fleshy shoulders.

"You never said that. Not when we talked about it in the lawyer's office."

"According to the terms of the agreement, all I'm required to do is provide custodial care for such a child."

Her eyes fill with tears, and he leans across the table and takes her hands in his own, stroking them as he sometimes stroked Hildy's hands when, as a child, she would sink beneath an inexplicable burden of sadness and weep with bewilderment at her own misery.

"Stacey, I'm sure the baby will be born healthy. But we want to be absolutely certain. You know that Hal wouldn't want to care for a sick child. He said that at once. And you wouldn't want your baby — our baby — in an institution."

"Oh, it's so hard," she says in despair.

"Only if you make it hard." He keeps his voice firm, monitory. "It's such a simple procedure, absolutely painless."

"Do you think I'm worried about the pain?" she asks in the petulant tone of a child who has only just realized that she has not been understood and perhaps will never be understood.

Her tears fall again, and he dabs at her eyes with the checkered napkin, dipping it into the glass of cold water, indifferent to the fact that two women at a neighboring table stare at them knowingly, their mouths curled into bitter smiles.

"Well?" he asks as they part.

"I'll think about it." Her voice is so faint that he must lean forward to hear her.

David returns to his office and calls Charles Norris. The lawyer listens without commenting and calls to his secretary for a copy of the agreement between Stacey Cosgrove and David Roth. David hears the rustle of papers and then Charles Norris's introductory cough.

"We may have mentioned prenatal testing in the office, David, but we didn't stipulate it in the agreement. There is no way to legally force her to agree to undergo the procedure. My mistake. I took it as a given that she herself would elect such a course of action. I suppose lawyers should never take anything as a given."

"No one should take anything as a given," David replies caustically. He wonders if Charles Norris is staring at the photographs of his sons; he wonders if he thinks often of his retarded daughter, who must now be in her twenties. David sighs. The burdens of paternity are heavy; he wonders, disloyally, uneasily, if they outweigh the joys.

Nina is not at home that evening to hear about his lunch with Stacey. She is en route to a creative arts festival in Maryland, driving south with Mandy, whose poetry reading will precede the dance portion of the program. A new alliance has sprung up between Nina and Mandy. They speak often and with great intimacy. Nina asks Mandy questions about her pregnancy, her mood swings, her dreams. She reads the poems Mandy is writing and probes their meaning. David realizes that Nina asks Mandy all the questions she cannot (or will not) ask Stacey.

Nina's absence does not distress David. He is, in fact, relieved, because he is strangely fearful that she will somehow divine everything that transpired between Stacey and himself — the words spoken and unspoken, the involuntary rush of arousal. He and Hildy are home alone, but he is, for once, indifferent to her edgy barbs, and when she goes out he does not ask where she is going or when she will be home. In consequence, perhaps, she calls later to tell him that she is at Seth's house, that Alison is also there, and she will be home within the hour.

When Stacey arrives home from her lunch with David, she finds Hal and Andrea seated at the kitchen table. They are coloring in a big coloring book that is spread open between them, and they each work on a separate picture, plucking crayons from the large box of Crayolas. Hal colors a castle, lightly filling in the crenellations with peacock blue. Andrea colors the stars in her picture a beautiful magenta, outlining their shape in silver.

"Look at this, Stacey. This kid has some imagination. Magenta stars." Everything Andrea does delights Hal. She is his small miracle, his precious princess. He is a good father to the boys — he tosses baseballs to Evan, rides Jared on his shoulders — but it is Andrea who consumes his heart, absorbs his thoughts.

Andrea beams with pleasure. She climbs onto Hal's lap and kisses him. When Stacey draws closer she presses her golden head against Stacey's abdomen.

"When will I feel the baby? When?" She remembers still how she slept pressed against her mother and felt Jared's firm kick *in utero.*

"Soon. Very soon."

Stacey runs her fingers through Andrea's tightly clustered curls. She inhales the soapy scent of her daughter's skin, lifts her small palm (Magic Marker–stained and smelling of peanut butter) to her lips and kisses it. Andrea is more than daughter to her. She is sister and friend. They giggle and whisper together; they skip down the street singing nonsense songs. Sometimes Andrea is a little mother who brings Stacey a pillow, a glass of juice. It is Andrea who senses (and forgives) Stacey's fatigue, who whispers away her anger (because Stacey is so often angry; she explodes with fury because a sneaker has been lost, a toilet has overflowed, Evan has been rejected from math enrichment, Andrea has not been invited to a birthday party). Sometimes in the late afternoon, Stacey and Andrea watch television together; they switch the sound off and snuggle close to each other in the silence, locked in sweet, shared melancholy.

In bed that night, her head resting on Hal's outstretched arm,

Stacey tells him about her meeting with David. Sleepily, her words muffled, she tells him that she cannot see herself undergoing the CVS procedure. She is unprepared for Hal's reaction. He jerks his arm away and sits up in bed. He pulls viciously at the cord of the bedside lamp, and in its dim glow she sees that his face is white with fury.

"Are you crazy? Are you nuts? Of course you're going to have that damn chorionic villus whatever the hell it is. We're not playing house here, Stacey. This is for real. That's a baby growing in you, not a doll. You're not an actress on some goddamn soap opera. Roth doesn't want to be saddled with some mongoloid and neither do I. So you get your head straight and go take that test. I went along with this because you wanted it and because I saw that it could be good for us. Don't pay me back by acting like an idiot." His voice is cold as steel, honed by invincible rage, and she begins to weep softly.

"But how could I have an abortion?"

"You'll have an abortion if the test shows anything's wrong with the kid."

"But how can we be sure the test is accurate? What if the baby is healthy and they make a mistake in the lab?" She has heard dozens of stories of such medical errors as she sat on playground benches and listened to the litany of biological woes shared by women trapped in similar circumstances. Their bodies are treacherous battlefields, each organ threaded with mines: mysterious acids poison lengths of intestines, grapefruit-sized tumors grow in inoperable spheres, blood flows from ulcerated colonic sources and will not be stanched. And the doctors make error after error. Misjudgments are compounded. Healthy organs are excised and malignancies remain undiscovered. Viable fetuses are aborted and deformed children are resuscitated in operating rooms where masked features can never be identified. Women of childbearing age are obsessed by their bodies, and their obsessions are marked and serviced. Each month Stacey notes articles in McCall's, Redbook, Ladies Home Journal. "The Operation That Almost Failed." "They Said I Couldn't Survive Surgery." "Health Quiz: One Hundred Questions About Your Body."

"No more talk." Hal turns, seizes her arms, shakes her punish-

ingly. "Tomorrow morning you get on the goddamn phone and make
an appointment with Roth for that test. Tomorrow. First thing. You
hear me?"

His fingers press down against her flesh and his face is threaten-
ingly close to her when he speaks. She is, not for the first time,
frightened of him, fearful that his anger may explode into violence.
Hal, who can make her laugh, can also make her weep. She trembles, but he releases her and shuts off the light. His back is turned.
He has said all that he will say and will tolerate no argument, no
soft assault of reason. Unlike David Roth, he will not coax or cajole.
She touches his shoulder, but he remains immobile, a statue who
punishes her with his silence. He makes no move to comfort her
when she weeps. Still, in the morning, he awakens early and makes
the children's breakfasts, sees them off to school.

When Stacey looks at herself in the mirror, she sees the marks of
his fingers against her arms. Before drinking the coffee (which Hal
has set down on her night table), she calls Arnold Roth's office and
schedules an appointment for the CVS.

David drives Stacey to the hospital on the appointed day. Hal has
asked him to do this because he himself must meet with Herb Green,
the owner of Ramon's, who wants to talk to him about expanding
the restaurant. Hal hates Herb, a smug rich man's son who treats
the restaurant as a toy and Hal as a caretaker. Hal will let him begin
renovations, let him get steeped in the crap of construction, and
then tell him that he's taking off for California. The timing will be
just right.

"I figured you'd want to be there," Hal told David Roth when he
asked him to drive Stacey. He added this with his eyes narrowed, his
gaze a shaft of cruel shrewdness of the sort that makes him a dangerous adversary in domestic arguments. ("Hal knows how to get under
your skin," Stacey's brothers have often said to their wives — an
observation that, strangely, evokes the women's respect.)

David and Stacey speak very little during their drive into the city.
They are both very tired. Stacey slept badly and David's sleep was
haunted by fragmented dreams, one tumbling over the other so that

he awakened again and again, struggling to remember the terrors that had sent him racing over the precipice into wakefulness, his body drenched in the acrid sweat of terror.

He does remember one dream with disturbing clarity, and he plays it back as he drives. In that dream, robed in white, he stood beside Arnold, in front of a black leather armchair. The chair was tilted upward and Stacey lay across it, her legs splayed open, her body draped with a pale blue paper gown. Arnold was masked; his hands, gloved in luminous white rubber, flashed in and out of Stacey's body. He reached blindly for his instruments, silver specula, steel forceps, fulgent needles, never rising from his knees, his eyes fixed on Stacey's exposed dark vaginal canyon. His sleek gloves became flecked with scraps of body tissue, spongy petals of rose-colored blood. Stacey moaned and Arnold breathed hard.

"Look," he said to David. "It's coming — your baby is coming."

David knelt beside him. A fetid odor oozed from Stacey's body, and he saw a small shiny skull, blue-veined and striated with silken strands of hair, edge forward. His heart pounded. Suddenly a second skull appeared and he saw two sets of matching ears, as delicate as seashells, two mouths contorted with fury. The two heads writhed and locked against each other, the wrinkled, tender foreheads collided, and the terrified cries mingled. A single neck supported them both. His child was a monster, two-headed, four-eared. And it would not stop shrieking.

He awakened then and, in the darkness, heard the terrible swiftness of his own heartbeat and felt not fear, not surprise, but resignation, acceptance. An unnatural child had been born of this unnatural pregnancy. Immediately, his wakened self banished the thought, condemned it. *A dream. Only a dream.* He reached out to touch Nina's dark hair (dark as the tendrils that covered the infant skulls) and fell again into the grip of dreams.

David escorts Stacey to Arnold's office in the hospital.

"An hour probably. Perhaps less. Provided there are no complications," the smiling nurse tells him.

Stacey is pale, grave-eyed.

In the waiting room he closes his eyes, and as though assembling scattered pieces of a jigsaw puzzle, he reviews the fragments of those elusive dreams. He remembers, quite clearly, that he and Nina sat together in an empty park. Beautifully lacquered playground equipment, swings painted a bright red, a jungle gym of sunshine yellow, are unused, and although there is no wind, the swings move slowly, rhythmically, back and forth. Nina begins to cry. "We are in the playground of the murdered children," she says. "Who will swing on the swings, climb the jungle gym?" Her voice is plaintive. But even as she speaks, Amos Roth, wearing his paint-spattered green pants, approaches them. He carries an infant that he places in Nina's arms, and then he vanishes. Nina holds the child. Its skin is grayish, but as she touches the baby, the limbs take on a healthy, rosy color, and David understands that his father has brought him the infant left unfinished in his very last painting. He smiles to think that Amos has such trust in him, and he watches as the baby in Nina's arms begins to grow, within minutes evolving into a toddler and then a sturdy child who runs off to climb the sunshine-yellow jungle gym. And suddenly the playground area is filled with children, laughing, shouting children who call to each other in a language he does not understand but that his child speaks rapidly, effortlessly.

Of course. Here, in the waiting room, the dream is clear to him. The playground was the one in which he and Nina had rested as they walked down from Mount Herzl after their visit to Yad Va-Shem. He had taken pictures of the children playing that day — wonderful pictures that he will enlarge and frame. And he will hang one in his child's room — the child who will be born to him, rescued from his father's imagination to continue his father's dream. Now he opens his eyes, but still he holds the memory of this dream close because it comforts him. He will tell Nina about it. He must tell Nina about it.

He is not alone in this room. A middle-aged man and woman sit side by side on the blue plastic couch reading paperback books. Their faces, like those of patients in a dentist's waiting room, are set in masks of resignation, frozen to accept the unpleasant. But the woman is crying. She turns a page, lifts a handkerchief to her eyes, and continues reading. David imagines her moving efficiently through her home, weeping as she slices vegetables, sorts laundry, answers correspondence. She is a woman who accommodates herself to the rhythm of her sorrow.

David glances at his watch. An hour has passed. An hour, the nurse had said, perhaps less. *If there were no complications.* Then there must have been complications. He thinks of the grim statistic: seven percent, almost eight percent. He has opted for safety, and so his child has been lost, washed away in blood and pain. Briefly, bitterly, he is angry with Nina, with Arnold, who so strongly advocated this course. Probably Nina never wanted the baby. Immediately, he recognizes the unfairness of the thought. Now he schools himself to accept the news his brother will bring him. He summons up his dream, dwelling on each detail: the angry faces of his two-headed child, its single neck glowing red, the lucency of its shell-shaped ears. The dream had been a warning. Better no child at all than a monster baby or one whose handicap would cloud all their lives with sadness.

"It's all right," he tells himself as a man in a blue jogging suit sits next to him and the middle-aged woman, still weeping, closes her paperback novel.

And then Arnold is standing in the doorway, wearing a wrinkled pale green hospital gown; a minute fleck of blood adheres to the steel frame of his glasses. Arnold's eyes are bright with worry and David's hands tense. But it is the middle-aged couple who rise and hurry to speak to Arnold, who, paternally, places his arm on the woman's shoulder, nods comfortingly to the man. Slowly, with measured step, the three of them walk down the hall. Angered, relieved, David leans back in his seat. It has been this couple's daughter who has occupied Arnold all this time. In all probability, he has not yet turned his attention to Stacey.

And then, even as he begins to breathe more easily (because when he saw Arnold, he found himself gasping for breath as though the mucus of disappointment had blocked his lungs and settled in a bilious film across his throat), the couple return and gather up their books, their coats.

"She's going to be all right," the woman tells David, as though picking up the thread of an interrupted conversation. "Our daughter. She's pregnant and our son-in-law is out of town, so we brought her here. She felt some pain and she's lost two other babies, so we were frightened. We were lucky that Dr. Roth was here to see someone else. He says she's fine and the baby too. You get so fearful at a time like this."

"Mildred. Please." Her words embarrass her husband as her tears did not.

"Good luck to her, to you," David says.

"Oh, yes. And to you too. I hope your wife is all right, your baby healthy." Blushing, as though she has said too much (it is one thing to reveal her own secrets and quite another to guess at those of a stranger), she hurries out, clutching her husband's hand.

And now David wills himself to calmness. He wonders if he should call Nina, who had been so nervous that morning she could barely drink her coffee. No, he will call when he has news. Instead he tries to read Mandy's book of poems, but the mythological symbolism eludes him. Who was Ceres? he wonders as Arnold comes in at last, smiling, beaming.

"Sorry for the delay, but the other case might have been an emergency. Anyway, all went well and Stacey was wonderful. There's no pain involved, but a lot of women get so tense — it is an invasion, after all. But Stacey is a trouper. We came through fine. The pregnancy is intact and we'll have the results of the sampling in a few days." Arnold is smiling, and David can sense the depth of his brother's relief. Solemnly, they shake hands.

He and Stacey leave the hospital, and he takes her to the restaurant of the Metropolitan Museum of Art, where they order Napoleons, fresh strawberries, and cappuccino.

"I come to the museum after every visit to Dr. Roth," Stacey says, and he smiles approvingly. How wonderful she is, how endearing in her aspirations, her yearnings. "I'm going to take Andrea with me next time," she continues. "She's old enough for us to do things like that together. I want to take her to concerts too."

"You should," David agrees. "Andrea's such a sensitive girl."

"It's so much easier to share things with a girl. Not that my boys aren't wonderful."

"I think I understand what you mean," David says gently, although all he wants, all he will ever want, is a healthy child, be it son or daughter. It occurs to him that in his dream, there was no indication of the sex of the infant whom Amos Roth, his father, placed in Nina's arms.

And yet, as he thinks about it, driving home alone after leaving Stacey at her home, he finds himself smiling at the thought of a daughter, an infant girl born with all the ova of her reproductive life already in place. That tiny body then contains the promise of generations, the seed of the future. The miracle, the mystery, so overwhelms him that he pulls over to the curb for a moment. *A daughter.* His mother had told him once that his father had always wanted a daughter.

"He felt so close to your aunt Miriam," she had said. "She was the one who knew all the family stories, who called to remind him about the holidays, about family obligations. Yahrzeits. 'Remember to light the candle, Amos.' " His mother had mimicked his aunt's voice. "I used to grow so angry at her, but what was there to be angry about? Don't I call you now before your father's Yahrzeit and remind you to light the candle? It's women, you know, women who nurture a family, keep it together. Mothers. Daughters." Her voice had trailed off sadly, made faint by grief for the daughter who had never been born to her.

"A daughter," David says aloud. "I want a daughter."

His own daring frightens him, and he drives speedily home.

A week later Arnold calls to tell him that an examination of the fetal tissue shows no sign of abnormality.

"Can you tell the sex?" David asks.

"In this case, yes. A girl."

"Thanks. Thanks a lot," David says, and he remains with the receiver balanced in his hand, his heart beating a tympani of joy, for a long minute after Arnold hangs up.

That night Nina and David take Hildy out to dinner. They sit opposite her at Luigi's. It occurs to David that they are at the same table where he and Nina first talked about Stacey. Again, Luigi himself sits at a corner table bent over his account books. There is something reassuring about the old man's constancy, about his insistence on the good linen so impeccably mended, and about the old-fashioned wooden corkscrew with which the waiter opens their chilled bottle of Chianti.

"A glass for the signorina?" the waiter asks.

David glances inquiringly at Hildy.

"A Coke, please," she says, and he is relieved. He does not want to do battle with her tonight.

"So what's it all about?" Hildy asks, playing with her salad.

"What's what all about?" Nina volleys question with question. A delaying tactic. Her hands are cold and the wine is sour in her mouth.

"A special dinner out in the middle of the week. It's no one's birthday. You're not getting divorced, are you? Alison said her parents took her to dinner here the night they told her they were splitsville. She had shrimp marinara, and ever since then she gets nauseous when she sees a shrimp."

Hildy relates this with strange relish, although she had held Alison's hand when her friend told her the story. Alison had wept as she spoke. That had been the year of Alison's tears, of her endless weeping. ("I mean, why did we have to go to a restaurant so they could tell me? They could have told me at home. Except they were probably afraid that at home I'd make a scene — cry or yell or something — and they knew I wouldn't do that at Luigi's, in front of a lot of people. They were covering their asses, that's what they were doing," Alison had said and wept again.)

Hildy thinks that Nina and David may also be protecting themselves from her — that they too are using this quiet, elegant restaurant, with its old-world charm (so unlike Ramon's with its tacky red cloths and plastic cruets and salt and pepper shakers), as an emotional fortress.

"Well, we do have to talk to you about something important," Nina says. She coughs uncertainly. She has spent much of the afternoon thinking of ways to explain the situation to Hildy. What if Nina herself were pregnant? She would simply say that one day soon Hildy would have a brother or a sister. But of course this is not so simple.

David covers Hildy's hand with his own. Her painted nails peek out like small jewels from between his large, freckled fingers.

"You know, Hildy," he says, "one of the great things about marrying your mother was getting you as a daughter."

She moves her hand away. She can feel the pressure of his love seeping into her flesh, and it shames and embarrasses her because, just now, at this moment, she hates him for what she knows he will say to her.

The waiter arrives with their dinner. They are all having chicken cacciatore, and Hildy wonders if, from now on, the sight of chicken will make her nauseous. When they have all been served, David speaks again.

"I love being a father to you. I just love being a father. Maybe that's what makes me want to have another child. Because it's been so wonderful having you, being with you.

"There's another reason too." He bites his lip and leans toward her. The words come slowly. His voice is hoarse, almost broken by his own intensity. "Things changed for me when your mother and I went to Israel. We told you about our visit to Yad VaShem. There are photographs of children there — children who were killed in the camps, who died in the ghettos. One of them reminded me of you — a dark-haired girl, slim like you with such beautiful, sad eyes. And some of them reminded me of your cousins, of Aaron and Jacob. I can't describe how I felt. Such a sadness. Such a terrible sadness."

"We cried," Nina says softly. "Both of us. We stood in that room and cried."

Hildy grips her knife, her fork. She herself may weep at any moment. She looks away and fiercely begins to butter her bread.

"We saw so many other terrible things that day," David continues. "A mountain of children's shoes. Little shirts, little dresses. Hair. The hair of children who had died."

"Why are you telling me all this? Why?" Hildy's voice is shrill and her eyes glitter.

"Because that day was the beginning. I thought about my father, about the children he had painted. I thought of all the children who had died before they knew what it was to live, and of how they took lives with them. A whole generation will never be born. And then we went to a park where children were laughing, playing, and I knew what I wanted: a child of my own who would somehow balance the death of just one of those children."

He is quiet, aware of Hildy's burning gaze. Has anything that he has said made sense to her? (Does it make sense to him?) He wants her to ask a question, to venture an opinion, even to laugh harshly, cruelly. But she says nothing and he continues, speaking more quickly now.

"I talked to your mother about my feelings. She understood. It took her time, but she understood. And we hope you'll understand. We know that you'll have to think about it."

"It was hard," Nina says, and Hildy turns to her as though surprised by her voice, her presence. David's words, despite her resistance, had absorbed her, but she finds her mother's comment strangely jarring.

"We talked about it, about what we could do. How I could have a child of my own. Your uncle Arnold made a suggestion, a very good one. Stacey Cosgrove had been a patient of his, and he had an idea which may sound strange to you at first," David continues.

Hildy looks at him. The spell is broken.

"I know everything," she says, and her voice is newly hard, strangely flat. "I know that Stacey is pregnant with your baby."

"How do you know?" Nina speaks in a whisper. She thinks bitterly of how she and David worried themselves over this conversation, how they planned and rehearsed their words, how they feared that Hildy would think they had deceived her, betrayed her, while it is she who has deceived them, betrayed them.

"Hal Cosgrove told me," Hildy said. "Weeks ago."

"Do you think it was fair not to tell us that you knew?" David asked.

"Do you think it was fair not to tell me what was happening?" she counters.

The weights on the scales of deception are evenly balanced. They are matched adversaries now.

"Hildy, we wanted to be certain that all would go well before we

told you. There was a certain test . . . other considerations. But the
baby will be wonderful for our family. You'll be a big sister."

"How will I be a big sister? That baby will be nothing to me."

"It's my baby," David replies. "And you're my daughter."

"I'm not your daughter. I'm a name on an adoption decree. You
married my mother. I was part of the deal." She shivers at the cruelty of her own words, still feeling the warmth of his palm on the
back of her hand, the seeping of his love. But, if he loves her, why
must he have another child (*his own child*)? Isn't she enough? Isn't
she anything?

"Hildy. Try, please, try to understand." Nina's voice breaks. She
stares down at her plate. The red sauce bloodies the pale chicken.
She sets her knife and fork down and lifts her wineglass, fearful that
she will weep before her daughter (her beautiful, angry daughter,
whose face is sharp with pain) and that her tears will in themselves
be a confession, an admission.

They finish the meal in silence and speak little on the drive back
to their home, where a single light burns palely in an upstairs
bedroom.

11

───────── ❧ ─────────

Stacey dreams. Waking and sleeping, as her pregnancy progresses, dreams converge upon her, seduce her into stillness. She grows languid, tumescent of mind and body. It is an earned laziness that she feels, and she surrenders to it without guilt or qualm. She awakens early to send Andrea and Evan to school, to bring Jared to his daycare center, but often she does not dress. She shrugs a heavy coat over her nightgown, pulls boots on over her sleep socks. She propels herself forward, comforted by the knowledge that when she returns home she can return at once to bed and resume her sleep, her dreams. This is her work for the next months, the work for which she is being paid.

Always, Andrea is the first of the children to arrive home, and often Stacey is still in bed. Andrea climbs in beside her and they lie together in the nest they form out of the sleep-sour linens, the layers of blankets. Andrea's golden head rests against the soft expanse of Stacey's abdomen and she sleeps, cushioned by her mother's flesh. Often they awaken together. They stare at each other and smile with pleasure because they are so warm and so well rested and the house is so quiet.

"Did you have a dream, Andrea?" Stacey asks, and if Andrea has not had a dream, she happily makes one up. They always take place in California, in large houses, and involve families in evening dress, waiting cars, wondrous surprises. *The little girl opened the package and inside the big box was a tiny emerald ring. The little girl ran to the window and saw a beautiful fat pony.*

Stacey is always happy to tell Andrea her own dreams, which are so complicated (threaded as they are with mountains looming above rainbowed horizons, sudden turnings on endless roads) that the small girl stops listening and instead plays with her mother's hair. She takes up the comb and brush from the bedside table and perches on the pillows behind Stacey. Stacey loves the flutter of Andrea's fingers as she lifts and drops lengths of curls; she quivers with pleasure as Andrea vigorously draws the brush down, tenderly teases the ends with the handle of the comb. Andrea uses her own barrettes and ribbons to form a colorful tiara, an intricate arrangement of rosettes. Now and again, Stacey playfully seizes the brush and comb and makes Andrea her prisoner, trapping her between her thighs and holding her still as she in turn twists the golden curls (thicker and silkier than her own) into a topknot, a ponytail. Always, they laugh happily at the results, holding the mirror up to reflect each other's pleasure. Once a week they paint their fingernails, always deciding carefully on the color.

"Isn't this fun, Andrea?" Stacey asks insistently. It is the kind of fun her own mother, poor Rose Carmody, could never offer her, so busy was she watching at the window for her stillborn twins to turn the corner.

"It is fun," Andrea always answers truthfully. Other girls in her class make play dates, but Andrea would rather be with her mother, who is free to dream and play. Andrea is glad that Stacey no longer takes classes or works at part-time jobs. She understands that all Stacey's energy is concentrated on the new baby, who grows and now begins to swim so that Andrea, her hands pressed against Stacey's abdomen, can feel its movement. She is Stacey's companion in this mysterious, adventurous pregnancy.

One afternoon Nina and Hildy Roth arrive as Stacey and Andrea sit at the kitchen table, an assortment of nail-polish bottles spread before them. Nina had found a black woolen cape that she had worn during her own pregnancy. Hildy had wanted to come along for the ride (a suggestion that Nina had taken as a positive sign — a melting of the icy carapace of feigned indifference into which Hildy has withdrawn since the night they told her about the baby). Hildy looks about the small house without masking her curiosity. She glances into the bedroom, and Stacey is ashamed that the bed is not made, that Hal's faded striped pajama top drapes the television set like a tattered banner. Hildy is thirsty, and she washes the glass she plucks up from the drainboard before using it.

"What are you guys doing?" she asks.

"We're polishing each other's nails," Andrea replies gravely. "I chose magenta. Mommy wants blush pink. What color do you like?"

"Purple," Hildy says decisively. "I want mine to be purple. What about you, Mom?"

"Rose," Nina says. It has been years since she polished her nails, but she and Hildy shed their tweed coats and sit opposite each other at the table.

Stacey switches the radio on and Roberta Flack's voice fills the small kitchen. They do not listen to the words, but they know she is singing of a woman's deep and desperate pain. The two mothers sway to the music and delicately, tenderly move the tiny brushes across their daughters' fingernails. Hildy and Andrea hum, wave their hands to dry, and spread their fingers wide.

"Let's try two different colors, Andrea," Hildy says. "Your mom will do your other hand purple and my mom will do my other hand magenta."

"Okay." Andrea is pleased that Hildy knows how to play, wants to play.

When both their hands are done, they lift them to each other. Hildy presses her palms against Andrea's and teaches her a clapping game. They sing in chorus, "I am a pretty little Dutch girl, as pretty as can be. And all the boys around my block are crazy over me."

The afternoon light fades, but they remain at the table, enveloped in the gathering shadows, laughing and talking as now the daughters paint their mothers' nails. And this is how Hal finds them when he arrives home — Nina and Hildy, Andrea and Stacey, their voices bell-like in the half darkness, their laughter sweetly contagious. The mothers' fingers, splayed across the kitchen table, are pale in the dimness. Their nails glow like iridescent stars.

The smell of the lacquer sickens Hal, and he feels himself ignored, excluded (although they all turned to welcome him). Abruptly, he turns on the light and switches the radio to another station.

Stacey keeps Andrea out of school and takes her to the city when she visits Arnold Roth for her monthly checkup. Afterward they go to the Museum of Modern Art and drift through the permanent collection. Andrea makes up stories about the paintings. Rousseau's sleeping gypsy is actually a prince in disguise, en route to reclaiming his kidnapped princess. Matisse's bathers are members of a single family who gather once a year at the water's edge to celebrate their mother's birthday. Their mother, of course, is a mermaid.

Stacey laughs with delight and hugs her daughter (because she too has always made up stories about the paintings and has never had anyone with whom to share them) and takes her to the cafeteria, where they eat the soft yogurt that comes out of the machine in frothy swirls.

Stacey notices proudly, forgivingly, that people stare at them. She is not surprised. Andrea is adorable in her plaid winter coat, her golden curls twisted into chubby bunches that frame her heart-shaped face. And she knows that Nina's black cape becomes her, gives her a dramatic look. Carefully, she adjusts the black beret she bought to wear with it, setting it at a jaunty angle on her own hair, which turns burnished gold in the winter, making it a shade darker than Andrea's. When they leave the museum they skip down Fifth Avenue until Stacey grows breathless and briefly fearful because she has forgotten her pregnancy for a moment. They walk slowly then, hand in hand, like sisters, like friends, like mother and daughter.

12

Nina invites the Cosgroves for Thanksgiving. Stacey hesitates because she has always spent the holiday with her family, but then it develops that her brothers have accepted invitations to their wives' families and her parents will accompany her older brother.

"You're welcome too, Stacey," her sister-in-law says.

"I'll think about it," Stacey replies, and she realizes that her family has embarked on an almost self-conscious pattern of separation. It has been three months since they gathered for Sunday dinner at the Italian restaurant, and she speaks only infrequently to her brothers and their wives. (It occurs to her that this distancing coincides with the onset of her pregnancy, and she is vaguely troubled by the thought that the Roths, in a way, have replaced her own family.)

She accepts Nina's invitation without consulting Hal, and she is surprised by his anger.

"What are we, their pals, their charity case? This is a business deal we have with them, Stace. We're getting too involved."

"It's not a business deal," Stacey replies, and Hal is surprised by the firmness of her tone, by the way her blue eyes go flat and hard. This pregnancy has changed Stacey. She is less malleable, more resistant; her new strength challenges and excites him. "Besides," she adds, "if you feel that way, maybe you shouldn't be seeing so much of Hildy."

She knows that Hildy has formed the habit of visiting Hal at Ramon's. It is convenient, Hildy has said, because she is doing a term paper on the history of the nineteenth-century theater and she does much of her research at the Donnell Library. It's great to have a place nearby to grab a bite. And Hal is so funny, so smart, she confides to Stacey. He makes her laugh. He makes her see things differently. She means this as a compliment, Stacey knows. If Hildy admires Stacey's husband, she must also admire Stacey.

"Hildy's a good kid," Hal says defensively, but Stacey has made her point and he no longer protests Nina's invitation.

On Thanksgiving morning Hildy, Seth, and Alison drive to the northern part of the county to pick up the gallon jugs of cider and the sack of chestnuts that Nina purchases each year from a discourteous and disgruntled farmer named Mancredi. During her days in a summer repertory dance troupe, Nina's company had boarded at Mancredi's farm and Nina had formed a mute friendship with George Mancredi. Michael Ernst, Hildy's father, had been in that troupe, and Mancredi had occasionally lent Nina and Michael his battered car. Once he had invited them to share a pizza with him in the village and had told them how he hated his farm, his rural community, his overweight, dull-eyed wife. His confidences embarrassed them, but they were strangely grateful for his friendship and defended him to the other dancers who were angered by a rudeness that bordered on abuse.

The first time Nina brought Hildy to Mancredi's farm he had stared at her and said, in his flat, angry voice, "Looks like her father, doesn't she?"

Nina had felt grateful because sometimes it seemed to her that her marriage to Michael Ernst had been a dream — perhaps he had never existed, had never made love to her, and, of course, had never died on a California freeway. Mancredi, taciturn and angry, validates her past and each Thanksgiving she rewards him by buying his cider (which is, in fact, very good) and the chestnuts, which she packs in plastic bags and distributes to her friends. This year she has no time to go to the farm herself, but she knows that Mancredi will cast a surly look at Hildy and mutter that she has Michael's eyes. Surely, it is good for Hildy to realize that her natural father had eyes as dark as her own, that he was lithe-limbed and small-boned and possessed of such beauty that he is remembered still by a man like Mancredi.

The farmer goes even farther this year. He stands before Hildy with his hands shoved deep into the pockets of his faded green pants.

"If I saw you coming down the street I'd know you were Michael's girl," he says. "The way you walk, the way you hold your head."

Hildy thinks that she will ask him to tell her about her father. She will scavenge any anecdote, any memory. She has never asked questions before because for so many years she had denied that Michael Ernst had even existed. David, gentle and strong, builder of playhouses and teller of stories, had been her father, her open-armed and large-hearted Daddy. But all that has changed. David will have his own child. It is time for her to know more about her own father.

Mancredi busies himself loading the car. He moves slowly and curses at the ash-colored cat that trails after him.

"Tell your mother this is the last year. I sold the farm. Some developer bought it. I'm moving to Florida. Enough winter for me. I'm too old for winter."

This is his valediction then, Hildy understands, and she does not protest when he gives her two extra gallon jugs of cider.

"I want to get rid of it," he says ungraciously.

"I'll tell my mother you said good-bye," Hildy says (although, of course, he has not said good-bye). She is saddened because she knows now that her questions will go unasked and she guesses that Mancredi had no answers, after all. "My mother will miss you."

That is true, she knows. Nina will miss this tie to her past. She will see Mancredi's departure as an erosion of her own history, a severing of a fragile and tenuous connection. Hildy knows how closely her mother clings to fraying friendships, to oddly fragmented relationships. Nina sends cards to colleagues who have moved across the world, to friends who have vanished to live in distant cities where they have married men Nina will never meet. In brief, scrawled messages, she recalls shared ties. "Remember our days in the Milo Company?" "Didn't we have great times that summer in Bennington?" "Whatever happened to Jolie?" With Mancredi's leaving, a grouting has been loosened, a gap exposed; she will feel the chill emptiness.

The cider is in the early stages of fermentation and has a sharp, tart taste. Seth fills paper cups and they drink it during the drive home. They stop drinking as they approach the parklands that border their own suburb. The police of their village are vigilant and have no love for the youngsters who drive around in cars that sell for half a year's salary. The cider is technically nonalcoholic, but they do not want to have explain that to an officer already angered by having to work on Thanksgiving. And only last week there was a death caused by a drunken driver who lost control of his car coming down Schoolhouse Hill. An old woman on her way to the grocery was struck, and although there are those who say she had Alzheimer's and did not look to see where she was going, the general consensus is that it was the driver's drunkenness that caused her death. They drive especially carefully down that hill, and Hildy glances at the school and wonders why it is that elementary schools are so often built on the crest of a hill.

"This road is murder when it's icy," Seth mutters. He will not travel this road in the winter because always he avoids situations he cannot control.

They carry the cider and chestnuts into the kitchen, which is steamy and fragrant. The turkey is roasting and Nina, flushed and smiling, kneels before the open oven. She pours a cup of water across the golden skin and bastes the huge bird until it shimmers. Three newly baked apple pies cool on the sideboard. David cuts up the salad; he slices tomatoes into freshly bleeding quarters that he tosses onto a green hillock of shredded lettuce. He has arranged the carrots and celery in small islands, carved peppers into narrow rings, diced scallions and radishes. His large freckled hands sail across the counter to pluck up one vegetable and then another. His salads are famous. He is attentive to color and freshness, to the shape of each ingredient. He smiles as he works. He is satisfied, pleased to be preparing food for his family and friends. He has a talent for love and affection. He hums "Puff the Magic Dragon" and pinches Nina as she kneels, holding her basting spoon aloft.

"Your mother made a wonderful stuffing," he reports exuberantly to Hildy. "Wait till you taste it."

"Stop it, David." Nina giggles and Hildy frowns.

"Good," she replies shortly. His exuberance embarrasses her. She wishes he would not wear that ridiculous red apron. "Come on," she says to her friends. "Let's go upstairs."

Seth grabs a jug of cider, a stack of paper cups.

In her room, Hildy curls up on the bed and Seth and Alison settle down on the thick red carpeting in the long-established postures of their friendship. Seth lights a joint and passes it to Alison; he also pours each of them a paper cup of cider. They are surprised at how well the grass blends with the tart drink.

"I'm not coming home for Thanksgiving next year," Alison says. She watches the blue smoke curl in a spiral tendril. The University of California at Berkeley is Alison's first choice. She has chosen it because it is across the continent. Her future is programmed and season-coded.

"I'll come home for a month in the summer and stay with my mother and her current significant other. That's what she calls them, I'm not kidding. I'll spend December break with my father and his Barbie doll," Alison tells her friends. She is a small girl; the straight hair that falls to her shoulders is the color of corn silk and her skin is blanched. She wears faded jeans that hug her narrow hips, and her pale-blue turtleneck sweater is of a double-weight cashmere that flattens her small breasts.

Alison's father and mother have each remarried twice since their divorce during her freshman year in high school. Each has had a new baby — Half Brother Number One and Half Brother Number Two, Alison calls these children. There are also stepbrothers and stepsisters who drift through Alison's life and whom she seldom introduces to her friends. Alison wept a great deal that first year after the divorce (Hildy thinks that her tears washed all color from her friend's face and left her skin pallid with grief), but she no longer weeps, although her lips are twisted into a thin, bitter line and her voice is brittle with wry cynicism.

"Who's at your house today?" Seth asks.

"All of them. Half brothers and stepsisters. My aunt's ex-husband and their kids. A friend of my mother's who just left her husband and their two kids. I can't keep up with it." She lifts her hands and begins to count on her fingers, but she runs out of fingers and takes a deep drag of the joint.

"I wish there was a rerun of *The Waltons* on," Hildy says moodily. "I want to see this family where they have this married couple who will be married forever and who have all these children, all of them their own."

"Yeah, *The Waltons*," Seth says. "A real turn-on. You know what that series was? It was science fiction."

"No," Hildy objects. "It was more like a documentary. A candid look at a vanishing phenomenon: the family, folks, a mommy and a daddy and their kids straight from the days before people slept in the streets, the time when you bought your clothes in stores, not out of cardboard boxes on the streets." (She fingers her own heavy green sweater that she purchased from a vendor who had spread his merchandise on the street outside of Ramon's; she had tried it on standing on the sidewalk and using the restaurant window as a mirror.) "There are no rules anymore. You buy a computer out of a van on Third Avenue, your hash from the cleaning lady. You want to get your dog walked, adopt a kid — tack a note on the supermarket bulletin board."

"Hey, come on, Hildy, don't go heavy on us. This is Thanksgiving," Seth says.

"Yeah. I remember. Let's go downstairs then."

Slowly, languidly, they uncurl their bodies, unwilling to abandon the slouching position they assume at every opportunity. They stand and smooth their hair, tug at their clothing. Alison pulls her sweater down so that she looks like a flaxen-haired Dutch boy, a pale, androgynous wraith. They each take a final puff of the joint and then, with practiced skill, Hildy opens the bedroom window, Alison fans the room with a magazine, and Seth lights the small scented candle that will kill the lingering smell of the pot.

The guests have converged in the large living room and David Roth happily dispenses drinks, pleased that he remembers individual preferences. Logs straddle the andirons in the flagstone fireplace, and Arnold Roth and Ted Goldfein, Seth's father, kneel on the hearth and carefully place strips of newspaper between the crevices, arrange dry kindling strategically in corners. The two doctors concentrate on this effort as they might on a patient stretched out on an examination table, but when Ted at last lights a long wooden match and passes it to Arnold, who places it against the crumpled newspaper,

the logs do not ignite. They try again and this time the kindling
sparkles — fiery stars dart forth — but still, there is no blaze. Hal
Cosgrove, who has been watching, moves forward. He kicks at a log
and lights two matches that he tosses indifferently into the fireplace.
The flame catches and spreads, the kindling crackles comfortingly,
and Arnold moves the screen in front of the brightly burning fire.
Everyone claps and Hal bows from the waist.

Edith and Nina walk through the room offering small frankfurters,
bite-sized knishes, miniature egg rolls. They are especially attentive
to blue-haired Claire Silberman, their husbands' mother, who has
flown up from Florida for the holiday. She sits on the couch beneath
a portrait painted by Amos Roth. It is a famous painting of a small
boy with coal-black eyes who wears a man's coat into which his
emaciated frame seems to disappear. His shoes are unmatched and
he clutches a brown paper bag, unwieldy but light, because it seems
to float from the child's hand. Amos Roth painted it from a photograph that appeared in *Life* just after the liberation of the concentration camps. He called it *Young Survivor*. But those who study the
painting closely see that the child's face resembles the boyhood photographs of David Roth, and if they do not notice it themselves,
Claire Silberman points it out to them. Now she explains the painting to Seth and Alison. She speaks quickly, breathlessly, as though
fearful of losing their attention.

"My Amos always thought of his sons when he painted," she says.
"You can see that he had their faces in his mind. He said that he
wanted to show that his sons, American-born, were brothers to that
poor boy in the photograph. He kept that magazine picture for years
before he painted the picture. He wasn't a religious Jew, my Amos,
but he believed in continuity, connection."

"But we all want that, don't we?" David asks quietly. "We want
to bring the past into our own futures. Generation after generation."

Almost involuntarily, his eyes flash to Stacey, and Nina, watching
him, knows that he is thinking of his child, his own real link between past and future, the daughter whose eyes will perhaps match
the hazel eyes of the young survivor — David's eyes. She recalls a
lecture they had attended at which a Jewish philosopher had ad-

vanced the opinion that with each birth of a Jewish child, a statement is made for Jewish survival. Their baby, which is carried by Stacey Cosgrove but which will be born to Nina and David Roth, will be such a statement. She looks at the painting and imagines a small girl with David's eyes, with his pale, freckle-spangled skin, and for the first time she thinks of a name for the child. Rachel perhaps. Or Leah. Or Sarah. A name that is definitively Jewish. (Hildy's name had been chosen by Michael Ernst, who was indifferent to generational continuity, to Jewish survival, and, in the end, indifferent to Nina and Hildy.) She moves toward David and takes his hand in hers and smiles to show him that she cares, she understands.

John Cowper and his family are the last to arrive. They knock sharply but thrust the door open before Nina can reach it.

"Happy holiday! Happy Thanksgiving!" John shouts exuberantly, and Mandy thrusts a large bouquet of roses at Nina.

"My wedding bouquet for your centerpiece," she says. The roses are white and their big soft petals drop to the dark-green carpet. The twins, Samantha and Eric, dash into the living room and surround the Cosgrove children, who sit quietly beside Arnold Roth's two sons.

"Remember us?" Samantha challenges them gleefully. "Pant. Grunt. Pant, pant. Grunt, grunt."

Evan and Andrea laugh, the memory of the summer day in the playhouse restored to them, but Jared begins to cry, and Stacey lifts him onto her lap. The others disappear into the study, trailing after the Roth boys, who want to play with the computer.

Mandy and John, it develops, were married the previous afternoon in the city clerk's office in lower Manhattan. They had been carrying the marriage license around for weeks, and it was Mandy who noticed that it would expire the day after Thanksgiving.

"We didn't want the hassle of getting another one, and besides, we had a free afternoon. We were the last wedding of the day. The clerk was really pissed." She makes these harsh observations in her musical, very soft voice, and then, as though the short speech has exhausted her, she sinks onto the sofa, her hands automatically clasped across the large expanse of her abdomen. She is in the last trimester of her pregnancy. Her ankles are swollen and bulging veins map blue striations across her legs. Her doctors have cautioned her about toxemia, advised her to modify her schedule, but Mandy continues to teach and give readings.

"I don't let anything interfere with my work," she told Nina. "Women shouldn't be asked to separate their lives out; we have to weave everything together. That's why I always took my kids to my readings." She spoke with the fervor of the absolute believer, with the passion of the artist who is convinced of the value of her own work. (Nina, who is always in doubt about her own compositions, her own skill, had envied her then and envies her now.)

"I hope you're staying off your feet as much as possible," Arnold says. He is not Mandy's obstetrician. She will be delivered by a nurse-midwife who works with the two women doctors who minister to all the women in Mandy's support group, but his professional concern is reflexive.

"When I can," she replies. "Actually, I have one more reading to give in Boston and then I'll just lie around all day and play Ceres."

Ceres, the earth mother, David remembers, and he remembers also the first line of Mandy's poem about Ceres. Not a very good poem but one that he will always remember because he read it in the hospital waiting room where a woman wept and the hands of grown men trembled as they turned the pages of their books.

"I wouldn't undertake a drive to Boston, if I were you," Arnold says mildly.

"Getting pregnant, becoming a mother, doesn't mean you stop living," Mandy retorts.

"But it does mean that a new dimension of responsibility comes into your life." Edith speaks in her even, professional tone. "A mother must think of her child first."

"I don't believe that. I think that when a woman thinks of her own needs, when she satisfies herself, she is, by natural extension, doing what is best for her child. Happy mother, happy baby," Mandy insists.

"Not always." Alison speaks so seldom that her gravelly voice surprises them and they turn to look at her, but she lowers her head and falls silent as though regretful that she has said anything at all. Edith notices how she clenches and unclenches her fingers; she marks the enervated pallor of her skin. Alison is quite clearly the unhappy child of a happy mother.

"But often enough." Mandy will not be easily vanquished. "Nina's done it. I'm doing it. And we haven't done too badly. What do you think, Stacey?" With effortless malice, she tosses the question to Stacey, who blushes and shrugs.

"I don't know. I'm not a poet. I'm not a dancer. I don't worry about it. I worry about other things." Her voice fades. She will not share her worries about "other things" with the strangers in this room. Her eyes burn and she is briefly fearful that she might cry. Hal moves to stand behind her, places his hand at the nape of her neck, and skillfully strokes her parched skin with his cool fingers. As always, he does not understand her grief but he knows how to assuage it.

Nina summons them into the dining room just then, and they take their seats around the laden festive table. They sit according to generations, rather than families. Hildy, her friends, and the children face the adults across the glittering array of crystal, china, and silver. David carves the turkey, and when the younger children are served, Hildy cuts their meat. She moves unobtrusively from place to place, and she adjusts Andrea's white linen napkin so that it completely covers her blue velvet skirt.

"Hildy would make such a wonderful big sister," Claire Silberman says wistfully. She is a woman who always gives voice to her thoughts. Her yearnings take precedence over the sensitivities of others, and her own losses are deeply felt. She was so young when she was widowed by Amos Roth. Nathan Silberman's death was a second abandonment. She feels her own deprivations so keenly that she is indifferent to those of others. She has only two grandchildren, and Arnold's sons are neither handsome nor affectionate. It grieves her that she will not be a grandmother (that Hildy will not be a big sister) to David's children. It is of lesser import to her that David and Nina will have no children of their own. It is of no import at all that her words may have hurt them.

Stacey watches David's mother as she arranges the food on her plate. Deftly, she shears the turkey of its glazed golden skin and surrounds it with a double helping of broccoli (which, after all, is so rich in calcium). The blue-haired woman with the petulant voice will be her baby's grandmother. She is newly bewildered by the configuration of relationships this pregnancy has engendered. The child she is carrying will embrace men and women who are strangers to Stacey; she will be at home in unfamiliar rooms and she will pray in a language Stacey does not understand. Stacey looks down at the food she has selected so carefully, and a wave of nausea washes over her. John Cowper moves to fill her wineglass but she shakes her head.

"I never drink when I'm pregnant," she says.

"You make it sound as though pregnancy is your career," Mandy says snidely (although her voice is so very soft, as always). "Like the cops on television who say, 'I never drink on the job, ma'am.' " She sips from her own wineglass.

An uneasy silence falls across the table. Jared spills a glass of grape juice and they watch the long red stain spread, and then, in relief, there is a flurry of activity. Alison and Hildy reach across the table with napkins and mop up the stain. Nina produces a place mat to cover it. Jared cries and Stacey goes across the table, rescues him, and kisses his fingers one by one.

"Why are you crying? You're such a good boy. No one cares about spilled juice. Nina doesn't care. David doesn't care. Hildy doesn't care." She soothes him with the litany of their hosts' indifference while Claire Silberman moves the place mat and says, in an aggrieved voice, "But that's a very good cloth. And grape juice stains."

"What does that stain remind you of?" Edith asks Jared in her best play-therapy tone. "I think it looks like a duck."

"No. It looks like a rabbit. See — two ears," Andrea submits.

"No. Two clouds intersecting." Evan is proud to be using this large word and he leans across the table to show what he means. "See. One cloud, two clouds."

"I think it looks like two breasts," Samantha interjects. "See. One breast, two breasts." She giggles exuberantly and Eric, her twin, smiles in complicity. He is her ally, even in fantasy, even in calculated, provocative rudeness.

Nina serves coffee and pie in the living room. They sit in a circle facing the fire to which Hal adds another log and some kindling. The firelight brushes their faces with a golden glow.

The two pregnant women, Mandy and Stacey, sit on the comfortable green easy chairs. Mandy's swollen feet are elevated on a small footstool, and a grease stain glistens on her rust maternity blouse.

David puts a record on. *A Chorus Line.* "I can do that!" a singer proclaims, and Andrea leaps to her feet. She curtsies, smiles, and then tap-dances and sings along with the record. Her heels click. She twirls and turns. It is a routine she learned in her dance and rhythm class. Her blond curls bob, and she thrusts her small body forward and taps out a rapid sequence, her black patent-leather shoes twinkling. The blue bow that matches her blue velvet skirt flies off her hair, and they all clap appreciatively.

Stacey's feet twitch as Andrea dances, and her face burns with pride. David watches Stacey and Nina watches David watching Stacey. They are wrapped in a cocoon of wistful vigilance. Abruptly, Nina moves to the stereo and turns the music up.

Hildy, her eyes closed, smiles, and Nina wonders whether she too is thinking of a distant Thanksgiving. Hildy was a small girl then, studying dance, and Nina had choreographed a small piece for the two of them, a simple sequence to the tune of "We Gather Together." They had both worn brown leotards and she had run up long skirts for each of them, of a gossamer organza in the colors of the fall harvest: deep gold blending into a pumpkin orange. Hildy's hair had been long then, and for the dance she wore it like Nina's in a single plait.

They had danced together before this hearth, the fire hot against their backs as they bent and swayed, lifting their arms to each other in thanksgiving and then gliding past each other as though chased by the autumn wind. Their family and friends had applauded and Nina had felt herself at one with Hildy, her sweet daughter, her small, lovely sister. Remembering that day, that feeling, she leans down to the rug where Hildy lies curled up. She puts her arm around her daughter and feels her relax into her embrace. Briefly, they are linked in softness and touch; but Hildy stiffens, pulls away, and Nina sits alone, her arm outstretched, the warmth of the fire grazing her open palm.

And then Hal rises and pulls Hildy to her feet. They dance exhibition style. Hildy follows Hal's lead easily, picking up his improvised, intricate steps. Like practiced partners, they anticipate each other's movements and smile theatrically as they whirl and dip. Alison and Seth rise, but they dance at each other rather than with each other. They never touch but move their bodies in rhythmic apposition, partnered yet alone.

Laughing, giddy, Mandy and Stacey dance together, slowly, ceremoniously, their protruding bellies touching. Mandy moves laboriously, clumsily, but Stacey is light on her feet, and when Mandy sinks back into her chair, Stacey dances over to Hildy and Hal. Smiling, she takes her husband's hand, and, as Hildy steps back, they dance with the accomplished precision of the long-married. When the music stops, Hal lifts her hand high in triumph and places his other hand on her abdomen. Stacey laughs but David turns away. He moves across the room and stands beside Hildy.

"Happy Thanksgiving," he says.

"Happy Thanksgiving, David," she replies softly.

"Hey," he says gently, daringly, "you used to call me Daddy. Remember?"

"I remember." She takes his hand and they stand together in a circlet of firelight, their heads bowed as though in prayer.

Nina, watching them, feels her heart turn. She freeze-frames their posture in her mind's eye. Andrea stands beside her and she leans down and scoops the small girl up into her arms, kissing the child's flushed cheek, pressing her hand against the golden tangle of her curls.

13

It snows on the first day of December. The big flakes fall slowly, almost reluctantly, and the sky is the color of anthracite. By noon a thin glistening sheet of frost covers Schoolhouse Hill, and children in rainbow-colored nylon jackets coast down the slope on large red and yellow plastic saucers, screaming in joyous hysteria as they gather speed they cannot control. Stacey's next-door neighbor hangs a wreath on her door, and the first of their Christmas cards arrives, from a woman with whom Stacey took a psychology class at the community college and who has since moved to a small city in the Midwest. At dinner, Andrea proudly announces that she must have a red dress because she has the largest part in the holiday pageant. The other girls will wear white because they are only snowflakes, but Andrea is the narrator. She loves the word and repeats it again and again in a high, happy voice. *Narrator. Narrator.*

"Of course you'll have a new dress," Stacey assures her.

The approach of Christmas (as always) fills Stacey with a mingling of anticipation and apprehension. She wants the holiday to be a happy time for the children, but already she feels a nagging uneasiness. The previous year there had been a fierce argument at her brother's home and her sister-in-law Cathy had wept bitterly, angrily. Evan had quarreled with an older cousin, and throughout the day, Rose Carmody had stood at the window, staring out at the street, now and again lifting her blue-veined hands to her eyes, although Stacey noticed (with relief) that her mother did not weep.

Stacey wants this year to be special. She thinks it important that her children harvest happy memories of this festival, which will, perhaps, be their last Christmas in the East. She wants them to recall their aunts and uncles singing and laughing, their cousins playing games, their home resonant with holiday joy. She wants them to open many gifts and litter the floor (which she will polish to a high glow) with brightly colored holiday wrapping. Stacey will cook a large and extravagant dinner (already ambitious recipes clutter her bureau and are tucked between canisters on the kitchen counter), and the children will remember the aroma of cooking and baking when they are settled in California and have threaded the huge fir tree (which will surely grow just outside their wide-windowed house) with glittering lights.

"I want a party on Christmas Day," she tells Hal. "The whole family and some friends here for Christmas dinner."

"It won't be too much for you?" he asks.

The baby is not due until March, but Stacey is almost as large now as she was when she reached term with Jared. Arnold Roth is not concerned. He has told her that a disproportionate increase in weight often occurs in a fourth pregnancy and he has cautioned her (unnecessarily) to be careful of her diet. But despite the increased weight, Stacey moves with light-footed grace. The fatigue that shadowed the earlier stages of her pregnancy is gone, and she is possessed of an electric energy, a swiftness and smoothness of movement. She sails from chore to chore, from errand to errand, as though buoyed and vaulted forward by the weight she carries. Her unveined legs retain their shapely slenderness, and she is proud of them and wears very thin high heels whenever she goes out.

"I'll be fine," she assures Hal.

"All right." He believes Stacey and relies on her as he has always believed her and relied on her. And now she speaks with a new certainty, a determined authority. When she sits, she holds her back very straight and crosses her legs as Nina Roth does. Hal smiles bitterly in recognition. Stacey has always been a good student, and Nina, after all, is an accomplished teacher.

Hal, too, is absorbed in plans for Christmas. Business has been slack at Ramon's, and Herb Green, the owner, has asked Hal to think of ideas that will attract the young, single trade. Herb, who thinks of expanding and updating the restaurant, wants the young accountants and lawyers, the teachers and advertising trainees, who share apartments on the East Side or live alone in studios so small that they scrape their shins on tables when they get out of bed, to become regular patrons. Fear and loneliness haunt these young people, Herb Green knows (because he himself is both fearful and lonely), and they would welcome a place where they feel comfortable and recognized, where they can regain the atmosphere of the sorority and fraternity houses, the eating clubs, which they think of with wistful nostalgia.

Hal has come up with the idea of Mistletoe Week. Sprigs of mistletoe will be hidden about the bar and restaurant, and free drinks or desserts will be awarded to those who find them. A spirit of gaiety and unbuttoned holiday affection will prevail. Finders will be encouraged to kiss their companions, to introduce themselves to their neighbors. Perhaps a Mistletoe Queen will be crowned.

Although when it first occurred to Hal the idea was shadowy, as he discusses it, it becomes inflated, its possibilities expand. He expounds with an enthusiasm that gathers momentum as he speaks. His excitement is contagious and self-generating. It is a gift he has had since boyhood, this ability to improvise and then communicate a buoyant and persuasive optimism. Even Stacey (who understands him and is thus wary of him) is often swept along on the current of his exuberant expectations.

Herb Green appreciates the possibilities of the holiday theme. He himself will spend Christmas week in Florida, but he relies on Hal to order specially designed napkins and place mats, to place ads in the local newspapers, to talk the idea up.

Hal will have very little time to help Stacey, but that does not worry her. In practical matters, she seldom counts on his help. She invites her parents and her brothers and their families. Hal's sister, who is newly widowed, accepts her invitation as does his niece, who is newly married. Hal himself invites his lawyer friend, Andrew Kardin, his wife, Nancy, and their two sons.

Hal decides to take Christmas Day off. Already the mistletoe theme is a success. Each night, after their shopping, the young singles wander into the bar, pile their packages on empty stools, and glance expectantly around. Christmas Eve will be busy enough. Every dinner reservation is filled, and he is sure the bar will be jumping. He may even telex Herb Green in Florida and tell him that he has decided not to open at all on Christmas Day. Such daring is Hal's own Christmas present to himself, and he smiles at the gamble.

He and Stacey argue about whether or not to invite the Roths.

"They invited us for Thanksgiving," she says.

"They don't even celebrate Christmas."

"They may decide not to come, but I think we have to invite them." Stacey is righteous and determined.

"We'd love it if all of you could join us for Christmas dinner," she tells Nina the following week as they wait for Mandy, who is to have lunch with them. Nina has a strong urge to bring the two pregnant women together, to listen intently as they discuss their thoughts and feelings. Serving them elegant cheese soufflés with salads of endive and broccoli (conscious always of the need for calcium), she is party and partner to their condition, the restlessness of their nights, the awkwardness they experience dressing and undressing, the small flurries of wonder and excitement that daze them inexplicably and unexpectedly.

"Christmas Day? Oh, I'm so sorry. We can't come." Nina coughs nervously and explains that Arnold Roth's son will celebrate his bar mitzvah that morning and afterward there will be a reception. But they will try to stop at the Cosgroves later in the afternoon. They will, of course, have presents for the children.

Stacey is at once disappointed and relieved. She is also confused.

"Aren't bar mitzvahs on a Saturday?" she asks.

"The Torah is read three times a week. On Mondays, Thursdays, and Saturdays. You can have a bar mitzvah on any one of those days. Christmas is on a Thursday this year so that really works out well. Edith and Arnold have a lot of friends who don't travel on the Sabbath — Saturday," Nina explains. She glances at her watch in annoyance. Mandy is always late except (as John Cowper drily observes) for her classes or her poetry readings.

The phone rings but Nina ignores it. Hildy will answer it and, of course, the call will be for her. Nina will not ask her daughter who

called. The parameters of privacy are strictly observed in this strange
season of their lives.

"Mom, it's for you. Tina wants a class rescheduled."

Hildy glides into the room, sinks into the chair opposite Stacey,
and pops a peanut into her mouth.

Nina takes the call in the hallway and Stacey and Hildy listen
openly, without self-consciousness. They are strangely relaxed with
each other, like friends or sisters who have peeled away the last layer
of social pretense and enjoy a natural, companionable ease. They do
not even feel the necessity for conversation. They recognize each
other as co-conspirators, symbiotic partners in a daring undertaking.
They are sharers of a secret that they do not discuss but of which
they are always aware.

"I like your top," Hildy says. Stacey has added a hand-crocheted
white collar to the soft violet maternity sweater she borrowed from
her sister-in-law Cathy, who has twice miscarried during the last
trimester of pregnancy.

"The collar does something for it," Stacey says. "A little touch
makes the difference."

"Yes, I know," Hildy agrees.

Her mother and Stacey are both believers in the little touches: the
tightly furled bud in a delicate vase, long ferns arranged in a ceramic
bowl in the guest bathroom, orange tangerines forming a pyramid in
a deep blue bowl, lace at the throat, copper at the wrist. That much
Nina Roth and Stacey Cosgrove have in common.

Hildy and Hal have discussed that during their muted exchanges
over cups of bitter coffee, their treacherous trading of family habits
and history. Stacey's husband and David's daughter have been thrust
onto each other's turf, and slyly, shyly, they explore the mysterious
terrain, serving as guide and support to each other. Hal has told
Hildy how Stacey tapes postcards from the Museum of Modern Art
to the bathroom wall, where the moisture loosens them and they
hang at odd angles until they fall. Hildy, in turn, has told him about
the photograph of her father, Michael Ernst, that Nina keeps in her
studio, hidden beneath a pile of faded leotards. Stacey's yearnings,
Nina's sorrow and loss, are mysteriously balanced.

Hildy and Stacey continue to listen to Nina's conversation without embarrassment. Mandy arrives as Nina hangs up.

She tells them, during lunch, in her quivering, whispery voice, that she and her family have no place to spend Christmas Day.

"What about your family?" Stacey asks.

"We don't get along. We're on different frequencies," Mandy replies.

Mandy has written a long poem about her struggle for freedom from her family, her determined severing of ties that clutched and obligated. She has (she wrote in a searing line that Stacey remembers, although the poem itself repelled her) cut herself loose from the "glue of her mother's sour kisses, the restraint of her sister's muted sobs." But now, as Christmas looms, she is gripped by a depression, a sense of aloneness, which she acknowledges and then unleashes on her friends.

Mandy's answer stuns Stacey, who sees family relationships as inviolate. A blood connection cannot be denied; a shared childhood cannot be ignored. Stacey tenaciously pursues her relationship with her brothers and their families (although she knows that her sisters-in-law, Cathy and Audrey, mock the courses she takes, ridicule her aspirations for her children). She is solicitous of her parents (who, abstracted in their own sadness, are indifferent to her; Rose Carmody has never commented on this new pregnancy, and her father has been sullen and disapproving).

"Come to us," Stacey says quickly, spontaneously. Her own invitation surprises her. She is intrigued by Mandy, but she does not like her.

"All right. Thanks." Mandy accepts with condescending indifference. She is bewildered by the Roths' relationship with the Cosgroves, mystified as to why Nina thrusts her and Stacey together. Still, the twins like the Cosgrove children, and it will be a way to get through the holiday.

Mandy seldom cares who it is who helps her get through any given day. Her talent (in which she has absolute, unswerving faith) absolves her from mundane responsibilities. The mechanics of practical survival are assumed by friends and acquaintances who always miraculously appear to rescue and protect her, to carry her sleeping children to waiting cars, to invite her home to carefully prepared meals.

Motherhood is incidental to Mandy's life. It most deeply involves her when, like a skilled alchemist, she translates her feelings and experiences with the twins, her reactions to her own pregnancy, into her work. She cannibalizes Eric's nighttime fears, Samantha's wild tempers, her own ambivalence about childbirth and childrearing; she chews them in a fierce gnashing of imagination and spits them out in wrenching poems, which other women read with a shock of recognition.

Andrea is pleased when Stacey tells her that the Cowpers will be joining them for Christmas. Like Stacey, she is caught up in a fever of pre-holiday preparation. She is her mother's joyful confederate, her consultant on decorations and gifts. Now, in the afternoons, they sit side by side at the kitchen table, pasting last year's Christmas cards (which Stacey scrupulously saved) on sheets of colored oaktag. They string popcorn on lengths of dental floss that Stacey dips in pots of food coloring. They giggle when the coloring betrays them and the bright red dye yields pale pink chains, which they string defiantly across the bathroom door. Flushed with their own industry and their own pleasure, they compile gift lists. They go together to the neighborhood mall, Stacey swaying majestically in her thin high heels, her black cape flaring, and Andrea pert in her plaid coat. They carry their purchases home and wrap them in the red and white striped wrapping paper that Stacey bought on sale last January. Stacey has a talent for such small economies; she imagines that they provide ballast against Hal's extravagances.

Hal watches Andrea wrap the package of Magic Markers she bought for Samantha. Primly, his daughter cuts the paper, snips the tape.

"Samantha told me on Thanksgiving that she didn't have Day-Glo colors," she tells Hal. He is moved that Andrea remembers, that she is capable of such sweet attention to detail. She is wonderful, this angel child, this princess daughter of his.

"What do you want for Christmas, doll?" he asks.

"A quilt. A pink quilt. For my new bedroom in California," she answers promptly.

Andrea sees that bedroom clearly. The wallpaper will be patterned in a pink plaid and there will be a thick white rug on the floor. Soft cushions and huge stuffed animals will be arranged on the pink spread, and her soft, sheer white curtains will be trimmed with edgings of pink satin.

Hal stares at her sharply. Why is she talking about California? He and Stacey have not mentioned the move to the children; they have not even discussed it with their families.

"When are we going to California?" he asks Andrea.

"In the happily ever after," she replies with a giggle, and he understands that this is part of the secret world of talk and laughter that Andrea and Stacey create during their long afternoons together. Dreamily, mother and daughter exchange fantasies. Stacey tells Andrea that she imagines herself visiting Italy, walking along the Arno wearing a broad-brimmed sunhat fashioned of a gauzy fabric. (She went alone to see *A Room with a View* and sat through the film twice.) Andrea wonders what it would be like to sail down a snow-covered mountain, to feel the rush of wind at her face, the frozen slopes beneath her feet. They reassure each other.

"You'll go to Italy, Mommy."

"You'll fly above the snow, Andrea."

Hal has listened to their soft-voiced trading of dreams and secrets, of mystical "Maybe we coulds . . ." and wistful "Wouldn't it be wonderful ifs . . ." His wife and daughter have a secret language, a mysterious code of time warps. Their imaginings begin "Some wonderful day soon . . ." and conclude "in the happily ever after." No, Stacey has not divulged their plan to Andrea. He relaxes, but that night he tells Stacey that soon they must decide what they will tell the children.

"About what?" She has spread the red velvet for Andrea's dress across the bed and is pinning a tissue-paper pattern to the fabric.

"About the baby." He is irritated that her attention is not focused entirely upon him, that she continues to secure the pattern with glinting steel pins, frowning because the velvet (which is a damaged remnant) tends to bunch up.

"I know. It's a problem. We could tell them the truth if they could understand, like Hildy. But they're so young." She pricks her finger and sucks the droplet of blood that so exactly matches the fabric.

"Yes."

He does not add that even now, after all these months, there are times when he himself does not understand what they have done, what they have undertaken. He awakens in the night and stares at Stacey, her pregnancy so hugely silhouetted in the darkness, and listens to the gentle whistle of her breath. He feels then that his wife is a stranger to him. She has abandoned him, in sleep, in dream, while David Roth's child grows within her, maturing in the womb that sustained his own children. He forces himself then to contain his anger, to harness his resentment. Sometimes he pretends (and almost believes) that the child is his own. But then he reminds himself that he has agreed to this incomprehensible arrangement, that soon it will be all over and they will be on their way to a new beginning, a new life. Still, he worries.

"Then what can we tell the children?" he persists.

"We could tell them that we thought it would be better if the baby stayed with Nina and David while we got settled in California. They'd understand that. And then we'd be caught up in the excitement of moving and getting settled and maybe they'd stop thinking about it. You know how children are, how quickly they forget. The baby wouldn't be part of their new life. When they're older, we could explain."

Her voice does not falter as she weaves this scenario, although she is cutting the fabric now. Courageously, she moves her scissors, carving the skirt and bodice. Her finger is still bleeding, but the blood blends into the fabric, and scraps of velvet litter the floor and bedspread. She does not hesitate (but then Stacey rarely hesitates), and her face is flushed when she finishes at last. She removes the pattern and holds her handiwork up for his inspection.

"What do you think?"

He does not know if she is referring to the dress or to the explanation they will offer the children, but now he is weary and suddenly bored.

"Fine," he says. "Fine. It looks great."

He switches on the television set and watches sullenly, weighed down by the oppressive sense of betrayal that has been familiar to him since boyhood.

The next day he sees a quilted pink comforter in a store window. He goes in and buys it, unable to resist the white organdy ruffle. "I just wanted to price it," he explains later to Stacey, who requires no explanation; it is perfect for Andrea, for the dream room that will be hers. He imagines Andrea's chin nestled against the delicate snow-white frill. After all, they can afford it. Not that he has to use the five thousand dollars that David Roth has already paid to Stacey and that she deposited in a new account in a neighborhood bank. Still, its existence gives him pleasure, allows him a careful pride. Hal enjoys the thought of money, the touch of currency. Even when their account is low, he carries a wad of bills in his wallet.

He pays for the quilt in cash and experiences an almost sensual pleasure at the feel of the bills between his fingers as he passes them to the saleswoman, who compliments him on his taste, on the swiftness of his decision. That same afternoon, he buys himself a sport jacket, rich blue corduroy with a western yoke. It is a steal because he buys it from a street merchant, but still it is expensive. He does not worry. There will be a bonus from Herb Green because the mistletoe idea is clearly a success. The jacket is a little tight, but he will lose weight in California. He models it for Hildy (who is waiting when he arrives at Ramon's) and makes her laugh when he does a cakewalk singing, "California here I come, right back where I started from."

Stacey chooses a tree that is larger than those they have had in previous years. It takes up too much room in their small, cluttered living room but they shift furniture. The couch must be moved to accommodate it and Stacey helps Hal to push it forward, despite his protests. He feels the strength and power of her body, energized and invigorated by the life within it. Her face is flushed and her lips are pursed in the ferocity of the effort, but when the couch is moved at last she laughs with exuberant pride. The children clap.

"You see," she says, "we can do anything."

"Anything. Anything." Jared laughs and jumps up and down.

"Anything. Anything." Andrea and Evan imitate him.

Stacey smiles. This is her family at holiday time, laughing and sharing. This is how she has dreamed them; always she has wished for them the childhood that she herself, daughter of a grieving, half-mad mother, never knew. And Hal, watching her, smiles too.

In bed that night he unbuttons her nightgown and studies the gentle rise of her pregnancy, the striation of blue veins that map her pale flesh. He passes his hands across the opalescent fullness of her breasts, rests them gently on the wine-colored nipples that stare blindly at him. He rests his head against her, her hand stroking his hair, her voice murmuring sleepily, and he feels the slight, almost tentative movement of the fetus brush against his cheek like an electric impulse. He lifts his face then and kisses her nipples. Milky tears leak out and he licks at them. Stacey shifts her weight, clasps her hands about his head, whispers softly into his ear.

"Hal, my Hal." She is reminded (again, yet again) that her husband was a boy who grew up in a house without a mother, a boy who could not read and dared not admit it. The chronicle of his deprivations, his deficits, saddens her, causes her heart to turn. She cradles his head until he falls asleep and then, slowly, eases herself free of his weight, covers him, and pads barefoot into the living room.

The tree's branches form velvet arches against the darkness and the pine needles fill the room with the wild, wintry scent of the greenwood. She drapes the lower branches with silver bulbs and turns the switch on. Her nightgown open, she crouches beside the tree; she sways and hums and crosses her arms about her abdomen to cradle the child unborn.

"See. See," she whispers. "How pretty. So pretty."

Then she unplugs the extension cord and lies down in bed beside Hal, who, still sleeping, rests his hand lightly on her head. Thus crowned by his tenderness, she plans the Christmas menu. She will roast a large turkey and make a stuffing of sage and chestnuts, apples and parsley. The words seem magical to her and she repeats them oh, so softly. Sage and chestnuts, apples and parsley. Above the softness of her voice, she hears Andrea call out in her sleep.

"Oh, yes," the child cries gladly. "Oh, yes. I see. I see."

What does Andrea see? Stacey wonders. Does she see herself soaring above snow-covered crests or, snuggled like a sleeping princess beneath a pink satin comforter, awaiting a magic kiss? Stacey falls asleep at last, saddened because she is exiled from her daughter's dreams, because her children (all her children) will wander down paths she cannot follow.

The Roths are also caught up in the holiday season. Chanukah falls two weeks before Christmas this year. They exchange gifts, as is their custom, only on the first night. Nina and David give Hildy a miniature smoky topaz on a delicate gold chain. She dangles the shining gemstone over the gently flickering candle and watches its color change. She is pleased, they know, and they are pleased by her gifts to them: a leather pocket calendar for David and a handwoven scarf for Nina.

Nina tosses David his gift and it falls softly into his outstretched arms. Laughing, he rips off the paper and reveals a stuffed camel, bowlegged and long-lashed.

"Doesn't he remind you of that camel we rode in Beersheba?" Nina asks.

"Oh, he does. He does," David replies, and in turn he gives her his gift. An identical camel tumbles out. They laugh at this coincidence of thought and action. Hildy laughs too. Their childishness pleases her and their gaiety is contagious.

"I'm calling mine Golda," Nina decides.

"Then mine is Meir."

David grins. He balances a camel on each shoulder and runs away. Nina chases him around the table and both camels fall. Hildy snaps them up.

"Behave yourselves," she tells them with mock gravity. She touches the topaz and smiles benignly. She is the mischievous changeling who tolerates the vagaries of her aging parents.

Nina and David lie in bed that night, each holding a camel. Stealthily, David tries to steal Golda. Nina slaps his hand. She reaches for Meir and he bites her wrist. They roll across each other, laughing and playing, baring their teeth and making small guttural sounds until at last he silences her with the tender pressure of his lips against her own. The stuffed animals fall to the floor as they make love. They fall asleep, at last, in each other's arms, and in the morning they laugh to see that Meir has fallen on top of Golda and his thin legs straddle her clumsy hump. Smiling demurely, Nina separates them and hurries to dress. She must prepare some notes before she catches her train.

Nina's dance students are rehearsing for a showcase performance and she travels into the city several days a week to work with them. She feels a new urgency about her work and often she works the dancers too hard. One afternoon, she glances out the window of her studio and sees that a light feathery snow has begun to fall and the sky is already darkening. She has extended the rehearsal time beyond the allotted hours. She apologizes.

"We have so much to work on. There's just not enough time," she tells the five young women and the three young men who make up her class.

They nod wearily, but she wonders if they understand that in that single sentence she has given them a cruel synopsis of a dancer's life. It is important that they know that there are so few years when the stage is truly theirs, when they are young enough and strong enough and beautiful enough to create the magic of movement that binds them to their audiences and stirs and excites the critics. Of all the arts, it is dance that demands vigor and energy, garnered strength and supple swiftness. Dance is a discipline of youth and of those who, through all the years of their lives, know how to preserve the secrets of their youth.

Nina's students are disciplined and determined. They are young and beautiful, and her heart aches as she watches them. She sees herself in their faces, their movements. She remembers herself as a young dancer (just beginning to claim solo roles, to gain brief mentions in reviews) walking through Mancredi's apple orchard with Michael Ernst's arm about her waist. Once they had danced amidst the trees — a lover's dance, a game of tag, leaps over low-hanging boughs, a slow waltz on dry, sweet meadow grass.

She was twenty, at the very beginning of her good years, her best years. Already, her race with time was beginning and, already, she had lost. The alarms she had set as a child (practicing her pliés in the back room of her father's pharmacy, on the living room carpet) had failed to sound. A year later she was a mother and then a widow but still a dancer, always a dancer.

But she knew what her limits were and she accepted those limits with the same discipline and control that had informed all her professional life. She juggled her life, divided herself between Hildy and the remnant of her career. Her parents, the pharmacist and schoolteacher, had always been bewildered by her talent. They had sent her to dance class only because of a vague notion that it would improve her posture; her gift had exploded upon them, invaded their lives, their aspirations for her, for themselves. Still, they did what they could to help. They supplemented her meager income with generous gifts and an allowance. They baby-sat for Hildy and cared for her when Nina was in a performance. They sighed with relief when she married David Roth, and within two months they retired and moved to a condominium in Arizona.

Nina stands before her students as a teacher, a choreographer. She chides and cajoles and urges them to repeat a movement.

"Once more," she pleads gently. "Once more from the beginning."

They are dancing to an Elizabethan *pavane*, and as the slow, stately movements proceed, Nina dances with her students. Her body, so proud and obedient, dips and sways; her arms are clasped at her breasts and wing out with fluid precision. Her head is held high, almost immobile, although the topknot into which she has twisted her black hair trembles ever so slightly. The others watch her admiringly, never breaking step, studying her movements. She is so good, so very good. She could have been great. With the arrogance of youth they do not forgive her the forfeit of her talent. Their faces are set in masks of proud determination. They will not be trapped by life. They will not make her mistakes.

When the class breaks at last, the snow is falling in thick swirls, and the sound of their steps as they race down the street is muted by the soft whiteness that blankets the pavement.

After each rehearsal, Nina dashes uptown. David gives an annual party for his employees and always Nina selects gifts to accompany the cash bonus. She consults with David and thinks carefully about each choice. She buys a gourmet cookbook for the newly married receptionist, a travel guide for the newly divorced designer. She selects a plaid wool robe for their aging, motherly bookkeeper, and in that same department, she finds a gift for Stacey. Like Stacey, she wraps each gift at home, using the wrapping paper she purchased at the Metropolitan Museum of Art.

Hildy does not help her. Hildy is too busy. She has papers due, college applications to complete, appointments in the city. Their home is a rest stop for Hildy, a place to change her clothes, to eat, to sleep. But Nina, these days, is too busy to worry about Hildy.

In addition to everything else, she has promised to help Edith with the cooking for the bar mitzvah. On principle, Edith wants the cooking for the reception to be done by family and friends (a conceit that Nina accepts because she loves her sister-in-law and understands her), and so when Nina arrives home she busies herself with mixing bowls, skillets, and saucepans. She has promised to make spiced chicken wings and sweet-and-sour meatballs. Already her freezer is filled with carefully sealed and labeled aluminum foil trays, but she is not yet through. Before shrugging out of her coat, she turns on the oven, heats the oil in the large skillet. Still in her leotard and long skirt, the smell of her own sweat (the intimate odor of her work) mingles with that of the simmering vegetables and spices as she feverishly rolls clots of chopped meat into tiny fragrant balls.

Three days before Christmas, when David is out of town on a business trip, Nina walks into the den and thrusts her hand against her forehead.

"Damn!" she says with the vehemence born of exhaustion. "I forgot to buy gifts for Stacey's kids and for Mandy's twins."

"No sweat," Hildy says laconically. "I'll take care of it. I'll ask Hal what they want."

Nina stares at her sharply. She is always wary when Hildy mentions Hal Cosgrove's name.

"All right. That would be wonderful," she says finally, wearily.

"Hildy is buying the Christmas presents for Stacey's children," she tells David when he calls that night.

"See?" he says, pleased. "I told you that she would come around."

They monitor Hildy craftily for symptoms that she has weathered the shock of their revelation; they assure each other that eventually she will be a caring sister to the child who will sleep in the large room across the hall from her own bedroom.

14

On Christmas Eve, Hildy, Seth, and Alison leave school early, ducking out of the ecumenical assembly from which any mention of either Chanukah or Christmas has been deleted and reference is made only to peace and brotherhood. They are not really cutting because the assembly is optional, but even so they are titillated by a guilt that causes them to joke and giggle as Seth drives south to the city. They are happy to be shopping for toys. Alison must buy gifts for her half brothers and grab-bag presents for the many children who will be spending Christmas Day at her home.

"We're a halfway house for the newly separated, the recently remarried, the divorced," she tells her friends. "A Salvation Army of the dispossessed. Only instead of reheated turkey and instant mashed potatoes, we serve Cornish hens with curried stuffing. My mom gave me the grab bag to organize because she wants me to be involved, to be part of the family, but I keep looking around and I don't see any family. I guess she and my therapist decided it would be constructive for me to wrap yo-yos and stuffed animals."

"I thought you didn't go to your shrink anymore," Seth says.

He is driving very slowly because traffic into Manhattan is heavy, and Hildy wonders suddenly why they are going into the city at all. They could have purchased everything they needed at the mall. Still, she had offered no protest when Seth talked about driving into midtown and she offers none now. Instead, she gazes into the window of the station wagon in the next lane, where a Puerto Rican man and woman stare straight ahead, their faces frozen into masks of anger. Their three very beautiful small daughters, who wear matching purple jackets, sit quite still in the rear seat. It saddens Hildy that the parents do not turn to talk to the little girls, that they do not admire their daughters' glossy dark hair, twisted into plump curls. She opens the window and calls out to them.

"Hey, *muchachas*, you are so pretty. *Linda. Linda.*" She waves and smiles and throws kisses, but the children look at her without responding, their dark eyes smooth and expressionless as polished stones.

"I don't go to the shrink," Alison tells Seth (although she is staring at Hildy in surprise), "but my mother confers with him. I'm sort of a patient *in absentia*. My mother figures that she is being maternal when she talks to him. She's doing her duty. She's being what a mother should be — caring and concerned — and even better, it's expensive. If you pay for it, it must be worth something. She's off the hook." There is no bitterness in her voice, only weary indifference.

"Listen, don't knock it. It's better than turning motherhood into a career," Seth retorts.

Seth worries about his mother, who is always home, waiting for him, waiting for his father. What will she do when he goes away to college? He worries that she will have no one to cook for in her newly renovated huge white designer kitchen, with its double oven and oversized microwave. His father comes home for dinner only once or twice a week. His mistress, a tall auburn-haired woman who wears horn-rimmed glasses (Seth knows this because he has, more than once, followed his father and watched him run excitedly toward the woman who waited for him at the entry of small, very expensive restaurants), will demand more time when there is no longer the excuse of a son living at home. What will his mother do on Friday nights, when she has lit the candles, set out the silver cups, the olivewood cutting board, and arranged the two braided loaves and covered them with the batik cloth, dyed in a kibbutz studio, and there is no one at the table? She will weep, he supposes, as she weeps now. He hears the susurration of her sobs as he stands outside her bedroom door, fearful of entering, enraged with his father who is such a shit, enraged with his mother who should have known better, who should have done something with her life.

"There is an in-between," Hildy says.

"What's the in-between? What's Hildy Roth's first rule of motherhood?" Seth asks, accelerating so swiftly and suddenly that pale Alison pitches backward.

"The first rule of motherhood," Hildy says importantly, "is always to talk to your kids when they sit in the backseat of the car. Always. Always."

And now the car with the Puerto Rican family is alongside them again, and the mother (as though willed to action by Hildy's words, her threatening stare) swivels her head and speaks with great animation to the little girls, who smile and nod, their fat, dark curls bobbing up and down, brushing the collars of their purple jackets.

Alison claps and Seth laughs. Hildy's bitter wit anchors their free-floating sadness. They sense her strength and trust her as neither of them trusts their own families. Restored to good humor, they sing Christmas carols and Chanukah songs as they move southward. Alison sings "O Come All Ye Faithful" in her clear and fragile voice. Hildy and Seth teach her the words to "I Have a Little Dreidel."

"Hey, we're having a holiday assembly, ecumenical, right in the car," Seth observes, and their laughter is raucous, irreverent. They are hoarse and red-faced when Seth pulls the car into a lot on the East Side.

There, they make arrangements to meet when their shopping is done, and Seth leaves them to go to a computer store. He is building an attachment to his modem. His room is an electronic arsenal. He stockpiles weapons against the onslaught of loneliness. He designs communications systems that preoccupy him, divert him from his father's absence, his mother's strangulated sorrow.

Hildy and Alison head for F.A.O. Schwarz. They hold hands and continue to sing as they dash through the streets, thronged now with last-minute shoppers who clutch bulging shopping bags and pause at street corners to read tattered lists. Passersby move with swift determination. The holiday encroaches and there is little time to spare. The tall African street vendors are authoritative rather than cajoling. They jangle their chains and bracelets, thrust their merchandise forward. "Hey, buy this! You won't get a better buy."

"Hey, you got somewhere to sleep tonight. I got nowhere to sleep tonight. Give me five bucks. What's five bucks to you?" A girl of their own age, her lank fair hair matted with dirt, a cotton skirt trailing to her ankles beneath a man's tweed coat, follows them. When they do not turn, she spits and a green globule of phlegm clings to the side of Hildy's boot. "Merry Christmas," the girl shouts after them. "Merry Christmas, you goddamn bitches."

Trembling, they sprint across Fifth Avenue and head determinedly for F.A.O. Schwarz. Their spirits lift as they enter the toy store and see the brightly lit fairyland that stretches before them, the rainbow-colored animals, the dolls that walk and talk, the red car with its own motor, a life-sized Curious George and a diminutive Paddington Bear perched on the backseat.

They are plunged backward into childhood, to the vanished years before Alison's parents took her to dinner at Luigi's and told her that they were separating, before Hildy stood outside Nina and David's bedroom door with the warm, sticky blood of menarche staining her thighs, pierced by a new loneliness as she watched their two bodies move as one.

David had often taken Hildy to this store. He had been companion and protector to her then, the tall, patient man with sandy hair whom she called Daddy with such delight. It was here that he had bought her the Pooh bear that still sits on her window seat, and together they had picked out a turquoise elephant for Nina. "Gifts for my girls," he had said, smiling.

"Look what Daddy bought us," she had shouted to Nina when they arrived home, and Nina, smiling, almost laughing, had turned to David and kissed him on the cheek.

Hildy had never called David Father. It is such a distant, forbidding word. Michael Ernst, the slender dancer whose beauty of form sour-faced Mancredi had remembered for so many years, was her father, but she has no knowledge of him. She has looked at the photographs in her mother's album (including the wedding picture with Nina so very young and so oddly frail in her embroidered Mexican dress and Michael Ernst standing so straight in a loose white shirt and white slacks) and hesitantly mouthed the word. *Father? Father?* Can this boy-man whom she never knew, with whom her only connection is biological, be called her father? If so, can a woman who merely carries a baby through pregnancy but does not raise it be called a mother? Hildy's mood darkens. She feels the slow throbbing that signals the onset of a headache, and she walks so quickly that Alison pulls at her arm.

"Hildy, wait. I want to look at these."

They stand before a cunning display of anatomically correct dolls newly imported from Scandinavia.

"This is it — the perfect present for my half brothers." Alison smiles slyly. "But here's the big question: what sex to get them, male or female? Maybe a boy for Half Brother Number One and a girl for Half Brother Number Two?"

"We'll have to call my aunt Edith and ask," Hildy giggles. "Only your family psychologist knows for sure."

They study the dolls, passing their hands across the small bodies fashioned of flesh-colored acrylic that is almost indistinguishable from human skin. The limbs move, each joint performing its function with precision. The head turns, but only as far as the head of a human baby might turn. The doll can stand on tiptoe (and its tiny toenails are delicately shaped) and it can bend and it can wave. The male doll has testicles proportionate to the size of the graceful penis, which is so meticulously crafted that it has a foreskin and a slit of an eye for secretion.

"It's the exact size of a healthy infant," the saleswoman tells them proudly.

Alison buys two male dolls for the half brothers she does not call by name. They gasp at the price, but then Alison calmly hands over her mother's charge card while Hildy lifts the female doll. She holds it in both her hands and lifts it to her cheek. Its small head is crowned with soft, curling dark hair. Real human hair, the saleswoman emphasizes, and Hildy experiences a sad uneasiness. She thinks of David as he sat across from her in Luigi's and told her of the hillock of hair he and Nina saw at that Holocaust museum in Jerusalem — the hair of Jews whose heads were shaved before they were gassed. She had wondered then what the Germans did with that hair; she wonders now if they used the hair of Jewish children to fashion lifelike dolls. The absurdity of the question depresses her. "We cried," Nina had said softly that night. And, standing in this brightly lit toy store, with Christmas carols happily blaring, Hildy feels herself close to tears. Still, the silken hair is soft against her own skin. She cradles the doll, pressing it oh, so lightly, against her breast. This, then, will be the size of the baby (David's baby) when it comes to live in the bright, sunny room that overlooks the garden.

"Do you want to get it for Andrea, or that obnoxious twin?" Alison asks. She did not like Mandy's children whom she met on Thanksgiving day. She was repelled by their crafty play, the shrillness of their voices, the ferality with which they reached for food, for toys, for dessert. She does not understand that they are children who taught themselves the skills of survival; they are unmothered scavengers of care and affection.

"No," Hildy says, although she does not relinquish the doll.

"That's right. They'll each have a real baby to play with. What with their pregnant mommies."

The saleswoman hands Alison her package and smiles encouragingly at Hildy, who shakes her head and passes the doll back. It looks so vulnerable as it is replaced on the counter, lying on its back; the soft, pink vaginal lips smile in shy embarrassment.

They continue on through the store, moving purposefully among the toys and games. Hildy buys Jared a stuffed Big Bird. She buys Evan a calculator and a chemistry set. Her choices are not casual. She consulted with Hal, who told her that Big Bird was Jared's favorite *Sesame Street* creature and that Evan had been hinting heavily for either a calculator or a chemistry set.

"Get one or the other," Hal had advised. "They're both expensive items."

Hildy buys both because it is clear to her that Hal, if he had the money, would buy both. His generosity is both unwise and instinctive, just as his decisions are so often spontaneous and ill-considered. Still, Evan is a good kid, a serious kid who takes good care of his things.

Andrea's gift presents a difficulty. Hal has said that she wants a large plastic saucer of the sort that her classmates use to sleigh down Schoolhouse Hill. But Hildy thinks them ugly and dangerous. Often she has had to slam on her brakes and screech to a halt to avoid hitting a child blithely sledding down a snowy hill with no way to control the ovoid sled. Although Hal emphasized that it was something Andrea wants, Hildy thinks that it will be both a dangerous and a stupid thing to buy. The Cosgroves will be moving to California and Andrea will not go sledding there.

She worries over this as she stands amid the play equipment for winter, the sleds and toboggans, the ice skates and miniature sleighs hung with silver bells. She confides her dilemma to Alison, who has already added a stuffed raccoon and an aqua monkey, a long-legged ostrich and a smoke-colored koala bear to her purchases. She has not had them wrapped ("Let the brats fight over them," she said indifferently), and their cunning heads peek out of her large shopping bag.

"Don't they ski in California?" Alison asks. "Get her a pair of skis."

The idea pleases Hildy.

"Great!" Andrea will be able to slide down the hill, and the poles will give her control. (Hildy values control, prizes the ability to determine where she is going and how long it will take to get there.) She buys a pair of child-sized skis and has them wrapped in the gaily patterned paper — each ski separately, each pole separately. Andrea will have more to unwrap, more to be excited over.

She buys Samantha and Eric each a small overnight case. Samantha's is a deep purple and Eric's is a sunshine yellow. This selection also pleases her. The twins are forever being dropped off at other people's houses, their possessions tossed into plastic shopping bags. The cases are a gift that Nina herself would have chosen and Hildy anticipates her mother's approval. That is when she and Nina feel closest — when they approve of each other.

Now, with their obligatory shopping done, they wander through the store, reluctant to leave the fantasy world. Alison buys Hildy a tiny furry mouse and Hildy buys Alison a hand puppet in the shape of a green frog. Hildy plucks up an assortment of ocarinas, small hand cymbals, castanets, and a plastic recorder. There will be other children at the Cosgroves' and each must have a gift.

They complete their purchases at last, and, balancing their bulging shopping bags, they hurry off to meet Seth. He is waiting outside for them, stamping his feet because the weather has turned very cold.

"I'm starving," he says. "Where should we eat?"

"We're not too far from Ramon's, are we?" Alison asks. "Why don't we go there?"

"Hildy?" As always, Seth defers to her.

"Okay. Why not?" She is uneasy, but she raises no objection and they link hands and walk the few blocks to Ramon's.

The restaurant is overheated and crowded, and there is standing room only in the small bar area. Through a veil of smoke they see that mistletoe dangles from the ceiling and boughs of pine knotted with red ribbon decorate the high stools and the long mahogany bar. The patrons shout above the din of the music (Hal has hired a synthesizer on which a lean and melancholy black man plays Christmas carols) and their voices and laughter are shrill with mandatory gaiety. The bartender in a bright red shirt, a sprig of mistletoe threaded through his bolo tie, and two waitresses who wear mistletoe in their hair move with lightning swiftness. They pour drinks and serve them, snatching away empty glasses, slapping down the red and green coasters and napkins that Hal designed and ordered specially for this holiday week.

Hal himself, wearing his new corduroy jacket, moves through the room, grinning broadly. He is the host of a successful party. He shakes hands and tells jokes, pulls a mistletoe branch from under a chair and kisses the plain, dark-haired woman who has been sitting alone. He orders a drink for her and she smiles and blushes. Hal puts his arm around the shoulder of a man who stands nearby. He draws him closer, motions to the bartender, who automatically sets a beer down. He laughs and talks, and when he walks away the man and the dark-haired woman continue the conversation, their heads bent close. Hal struts proudly. He sees Hildy and her friends at the door and hurries toward them.

"My Christmas elves," he shouts. "I knew you'd come!" He encircles all three of them in a huge embrace and begins to dance a jig. Blushing, laughing, they dance with him. Those around them laugh and two other men join the dance. The musician catches the mood and strikes up music to match. The waitresses scurry about the dancers, their trays loaded with new rounds of drinks. Hal knows that hilarity generates thirst. He estimates that the bar will take in more tonight than Ramon's usually generates in a week. The first thing he will buy for the Unicorn is a synthesizer. Hell, he will even learn to play it himself. He is high on hope. He can do anything. His luck is changing and it's about goddamn time that it did.

There are no tables available, but Hal confers with a waiter and within minutes a small table has been thrust into a corner and they are seated, studying the specially printed Mistletoe Menu.

"We've been using it all week and we've been jammed all week," Hal says proudly. He recommends the Christmas Eve Special (roast duckling in a wild-cherry sauce), but they order spaghetti.

"Anything to drink?" the waitress asks.

"A bottle of red wine," Seth replies.

"Do you have ID?"

"They're with me. It's okay." Hal frowns imperiously and waves her away. "So what have you been buying?" he asks.

"Oh, Christmas presents for the kids," Hildy replies. Her feeling of unease is gone now, replaced by a fatigue so profound that when she lifts her water glass, it is heavy in her hand. She wants desperately to go home and go to sleep. Tomorrow is Aaron's bar mitzvah, and she does not want to feel wiped out.

"And we've been shopping for babies," Alison adds. "We've been buying babies."

The good humor fades from Hal's face. Anger twists his features; his lips are knotted, his eyebrows converge. He curls his fingers into fists and stares accusingly at Hildy.

"You have a big mouth," he says. "A goddamn big mouth."

There is hatred in his voice, and Seth and Alison stare at him in surprise, but Hildy moves closer to him. She is filled with compassion. She had not realized before the shame that Hal (laughing, joking Hal, with his quick answers and sly jokes) had felt throughout these months, but she recognizes it now. It is revealed in his fury because he thinks she has told her friends about the agreement between Stacey and David.

"Do you want to see our babies?" Alison continues flirtatiously. Alison is a skilled survivor of bitter family quarrels, and she knows how to navigate herself out of dangerous waters, how to sail through dangerous emotional tides. She rummages through the shopping bags and pulls out the package that contains the doll. Carefully, she unwraps it and the anatomically correct male doll rolls onto the table and lies naked, its flexible penis leaning against its rosy thigh, amid the silverware and napery.

"Jesus," the waitress says as she arrives with the tray of spaghetti platters.

"Not quite," Seth replies. "Right night, wrong kid." They laugh until tears burn their eyes.

Alison packs the doll away. "Didn't I buy a nice baby?" she asks Hal, who nods and averts his eyes from Hildy as their wineglasses are filled. The wine is rich and fruity, and they drink quickly because the laughter has made them thirsty. They eat the spaghetti and drink from their refilled glasses. Hal leaves them and checks out the bar, shakes hands with other diners, plucks a piece of mistletoe from beneath the cloth of a table where a middle-aged couple sit in silence.

"Kiss," he commands them. "It's the rule."

Obediently, they lean toward each other. Their lips touch and they smile and glance at Hal. He waves approvingly. He is the jovial maître d', a hired, competent father who makes certain that his children are laughing and talking and eating.

Hildy, watching him, understands why Stacey loves him.

"Hey, you're really good at this," she says when he returns to the table. "You're a great host." She is apologizing to him for understanding his anger, for comprehending his shame. (*And is Nina similarly ashamed?* she wonders, and she is swept with pity for her mother.) She tilts her chair back and leans against the wall, her head touching a long strip of mistletoe.

"Kiss her," Alison commands. "It's the rule."

Hal grins and leans forward. Hildy still wears her long red scarf and he lifts its fringed ends in his hand and slowly pulls her toward him. The chair is eased onto the floor and he increases the pressure. He draws her in gently, holding each end of the scarf as a rein. Each playful tug is a testament to his power. Her head is bowed and the dark cap of her hair is smooth as satin. He pats it, as though she is an obedient animal whom he controls with this red woolen restraining leash. And then he tucks his hand beneath her chin and kisses her on the mouth. It is a light kiss, avuncular and tender. The touch of his lips erases the accusation (which her friends appear to have forgotten); their intimacy, his and Hildy's, is restored, renewed. Their shared secret is safe.

Seth drains the last drops of wine from the bottle and, over Hal's objection, insists on paying the check.

"I'll let you treat when we get out to the Coast and eat at the Unicorn," he says (because Hal has told them about the Unicorn in detail now, and they believe in the restaurant he will build on a hill that overlooks the Pacific Ocean), and they make their way out through the bar, which is still crowded. They hug their shopping bags full of toys and wince when they open the door and the cold wind slaps their wine-flushed faces. By the time they reach the lot where Seth has parked, they are frozen and they huddle together in the front seat. Seth lights a joint and they pass it to each other until they are afloat, wrapped in a cocoon of warmth and calm. Only then does Seth turn the key in the ignition and start them on the journey north.

They are all anxious to be home now, and although the highway is uncrowded, Seth weaves in and out of lanes and his daring makes them laugh and cry out. Hildy's mouth is wine-bitter and a shred of the sweet grass clings to her tongue; her limbs are heavy, her eyes burning.

"Careful, careful," Alison shouts as they careen down the right-hand lane and narrowly miss the shoulder of the road.

"I'm fine. I'm fine. I'm in control," he retorts, and, as though to prove it, he switches on WNSR. Bruce is singing "Born in the U.S.A." and they all sing along.

They are nearly home now and Seth decelerates as they drive up the gentle hills of their northern county, moving evenly down the ribbons of light cast by the streetlamps as they approach their exit. Hildy, at last, surrenders to the haunting fatigue and dozes off. She awakens, dry-mouthed and short-breathed, as the car skids, turns, and thunders downward. Alison's scream sounds distant (although Alison is seated beside her, her nails ripping at Hildy's hand), and Hildy's own terror is trapped in her throat and chokes her.

The smell of their breath and their bodies, soured by fear, fills the car, and the hill, thinly sheeted by ice and silvered by moonlight, stretches in treacherous incline ahead of them. A lacy patch of frost shimmers with a blue brilliance and Seth moves the wheel with forceful desperation. Hildy smells the burning rubber and watches the telephone poles skitter by at astonishing speed. And then, as the car nears the bottom of the hill and the approaching four-corner intersection, Seth at last regains control of the wheel. The car straightens, submits to the brake, and grinds to a halt.

"Merry Christmas," Alison says.

"Yeah."

"Right."

Their voices are very soft and fear-weakened. They do not look at each other. They are so ashamed and so relieved. Hildy's mouth is tart with the aftertaste of wine and pot, with the bilious saliva of terror.

When they reach her house, she looks up and sees that David is standing at the window. He moves away as the car stops, and she feels a surge of gratitude for his vigilance. She wonders why it is that her eyes are filled with tears and her hands are trembling. She is safe, after all. Nothing happened, nothing at all. Still, the tears fall in burning rivulets down her cheeks.

She fumbles with her keys, opens the door at last, sets the shopping bags down in the hall, and dashes up the stairs. She does not turn around when David, very softly, calls her name.

15

David Roth sits between Hildy and Nina in the small sanctuary of the synagogue on West End Avenue. Arnold and Edith sit in the pew ahead of them, their prayer books open, their hands lightly touching. Edith, quietly elegant in her pale blue suit, is smiling, but David, who knows her well, discerns the finely drawn tension lines about her eyes and the very slight tremble of her fingers when she turns a page. She is nervous because Aaron is an anxious child who struggles to excel. He has, since earliest childhood, competed with Jacob, his older brother. Competition is natural between brothers, Edith has told David (who cannot remember competing with Arnold; theirs was a brotherhood of mutual protection, of playing father and son to each other), but Aaron is too intense and has invested too much in the bar mitzvah ceremony.

He practiced the cantillations with compulsive tenacity, committed his Torah portion to memory. Once, Edith awakened in the night and heard him chanting his Torah reading. She had tiptoed down the hall and watched her younger son as he stood at the window in the darkness. His fair hair was tousled, and his long, thin arms jutted out of the frayed sleeves of his outgrown cotton pajamas. He shivered, although the night was warm, and held a book out to the spray of amber light cast by the streetlamp. In a high, fragile voice, still boyishly sweet, he intoned a difficult passage again and again but could not get the cadence he wanted. At last his voice broke and he set the book down and crawled back into bed. Edith, still in the hallway, heard the muffled sound of his sobs, the stertorous breath of the anxiety he could not contain.

"I wanted to go to him," Edith told David. "But I knew that I couldn't, that I shouldn't. It's his own battle, his own challenge."

"So what did you do?" David was concerned. He identifies strongly with his brother's younger son.

"Nothing." Edith had smiled sadly. "What could I do?" Her face was wreathed with pain. She recognized her own powerlessness to allay her child's misery, acknowledged that he must proceed alone. David had admired his sister-in-law for her forbearance, for her hard-earned maternal wisdom.

He looks at his own mother now, who sits beside Jacob, her favorite grandson. Arnold's older son paints. He works on large canvases, splashing them with the rioting celebrations of color and shape that have already won him praise in student art shows. David resents his mother's favoritism, her dogged reverence for artistic talent, her negation of other achievements. In her eyes, he knows, he and Arnold, successful as they are in their own fields, are both failures. He will not repeat Claire Silberman's mistakes. His own child (so soon to be born, so soon to be cradled in his arms) will not be hostage to his aspirations, his ambitions.

Arnold rises and motions to David. The Torah ceremony is about to begin. Obediently, David follows his brother to the ark and pulls the cord that opens the red velvet curtain embroidered in gold brocade lettering. The words translate as "Know Before Whom You Stand." David recalls a fanciful serigraph executed by an artist who experimented with Hebrew calligraphy. He had drawn each character as a winged creature soaring skyward in ecstasy. His father had shown him the print; it had surely been one of the last things Amos Roth had shown him, and that, perhaps, is why he remembers it so well.

"You see," Amos had told David as he traced the intricate design, "he truly knew before Whom he stood."

Of course, artists have that knowledge, that awareness, David thinks. They are touched by God and are thus companion to Him. They too create cohesion out of chaos, beauty out of nothingness. They do not have to believe; religion is their natural dominion. They worship with the skills of their hands, the gifts of their imagination. Often David has watched Nina as she danced, as she worked through a choreographic pattern. Her face then is transfigured and sometimes her eyes are closed. She is not unlike a woman at prayer. Has he imagined it, over the long years, or does he truly remember standing beside his father in his studio and seeing him close his eyes before stretching his brush toward the canvas? David knows that his own eyes are closed when he makes love to Nina because he is then a man stretching beyond himself, a man performing an act of devotion, arched to an exertion that encompasses all his yearning, all his tenderness. He is, in that sudden surge of power, of sexual triumph, at once suppliant and creator. Often, at such moments, his voice rings out with joyous resonance. "I love you," he shouts, and Nina smiles up at him, puts her fingers to his lips. "And I love you," she says softly.

The rabbi, a tall young man, clean-shaven and clear-eyed, his knitted skullcap askew on his dark curls, removes the Torah from the ark and passes it to David. He hugs the scroll, heavy in its velvet vestments, its silver crown and shield, and trails the rabbi as he circles the sanctuary, repeating the ancient chants. Arnold and Aaron follow him, Arnold beaming with pride, Aaron shy, pale, as they pass through the assemblage of friends and relatives who have gathered on this wintry Thursday morning to watch Aaron, the grandson of Amos, assume his responsibilities in the community of Israel.

David pauses at each pew and the worshippers extend their prayer books to the Torah's velvet covering and then kiss the book itself. When he reaches Nina and Hildy, they both smile at him and Hildy touches her fingers to her mouth and allows them to linger on the gold embroidery. Nina reaches out to straighten a fringe of his prayer shawl. He is conscious of the congregation staring at his beautiful wife, his beautiful daughter, so slender and regal in their pastel wool dresses. Nina's black hair is twisted into a chignon, while Hildy's is brushed into a glistening helmet that hugs her head. He is lucky to have so much. He trembles at his temerity in wanting more. *Know Before Whom You Stand.* Again, in his mind's eye, he sees the winged letters soar skyward.

He places the Torah on the reader's stand and returns to his seat.

Nina's hand covers his as the blessing is intoned and the reading of the Torah portion begins. Aaron's voice trembles, caught between the high pitch of boyhood and the darkening tone of maturity. Slowly, it gathers strength, resonance, and at last, in certainty and confidence, it gains and sustains the ancient melody. Edith, who has been leaning tensely forward, relaxes. She sits back and moves her finger across the text. She follows her son's reading, swaying in rhythm to the melodious chant. Arnold stands beside Aaron at the lectern, listening and reading, his lips moving. David is startled by how closely, at this moment, Arnold resembles their father. His wide-spaced gray eyes are serious and heavy-browed, his chin is square, and when he smiles (as Aaron triumphs over a difficult verse — perhaps the verse that caused him to weep that distant night), small laugh lines carve their way into the corners of his mouth. He stands as Amos Roth stood at his easel, inclined to the right with his weight concentrated on his left foot. In his brother's stance David sees their father. In his nephew's voice he hears Amos again. Jacob has inherited his grandfather's talent (perhaps, perhaps), but Aaron has his gentle voice, his ease of rhythm and his joy in song.

" 'And I will bring you to the land which I promised to Abraham, to Isaac and to Jacob and I will give it to you for a heritage . . .' " Aaron chants the final verses, his face aglow, and Arnold turns to his son (who sings in his father's voice) and embraces him. The passage celebrates generations, the transmission of heritage. Arnold, too, on this day, celebrates the triumph of generations, the sweet continuity of belief, the legacy passed on intact. He is radiant with pride, and David watches his brother and thinks that this is the reward of fatherhood, this chimerical recognition and identification, this restoration of generations.

"Aaron sounds like my father," David whispers to Nina.

His eyes are moist, and in response, her fingers clamp about his own. He too will experience that joy of continuity. He will be father to a child of his own; the emptiness, the almost visceral void that has haunted their marriage, will vanish. David puts his arm around Nina and holds her close, and she smiles with such warmth, such generosity, that it seems to him her face is bathed with light.

Hildy rises. It is her "honor" to dress the Torah once again in its velvet raiment, to arrange the silver crowns and shield. She accomplishes this with grace and kisses her cousin, her uncle. And, when she returns to her seat, she kisses Nina and David, her lips light as butterfly wings across his cheek. They are surprised, relieved, pleased. She is softening; soon (as Edith promised) the bad time will be over. Hildy sits very still. She is remembering the terrible speed of the car as it catapulted down the hill. She is thinking of the ease, the simplicity of death, of the arduousness, the complexity of birth. She is thinking of the silken hair of small children.

The rabbi's sermon is brief but incisive. David is impressed by his erudition, the depth of his thought. He is knowledgeable and confident of his authority. David seldom attends services at the large synagogue in their own suburb, although he and Nina have been members for many years. He does not like the rabbi, a tall, overly thin man with cold, pale eyes who is given to facile explanations, to superficial expositions. There are questions that David would ask him if he could trust the answers.

He listens carefully now, as this young rabbi earnestly extends a mandate to Aaron. Aaron, the rabbi says, is living proof that Hitler failed in his war against the Jews, but if he does not actively embrace the Jewish cause (and, by extension, the human cause, the rabbi adds somewhat rapidly), Hitler will have triumphed and another Jew will have been lost. Aaron listens, wearing the half-smile of nervous attention and embarrassment peculiar to bar mitzvah boys, but his gaze is serious, intent. David wonders if his nephew is thinking of Amos Roth's portraits of survivors and refugees.

A thought occurs to him. He has attended bar mitzvahs where the bar mitzvah boy was "twinned" with a Russian Jewish child who could not celebrate his own bar mitzvah. Perhaps bar mitzvah children should be "twinned" with a child lost in the Holocaust who would never chant from the Torah. No. It would evoke too much sadness on a day of joy. It would accomplish nothing. Only life can invalidate death.

Hildy too listens with great absorption. She thinks of the doll, of the human hair that covered its skin-smooth skull. She wonders if the children cried when their heads were shorn (but of course they did). The rabbi is right, she decides. There had to be a victory over those tears, those terrible deaths, that soft, soft mountain of silken hair.

The service is over and there is a chorus of mazal tovs, a warm and bewildering exchange of kisses and embraces before they rush through the cold streets to Edith and Arnold's apartment for the reception.

Every surface in the large, attractive apartment is covered with food and flowers. A woodwind quartet plays softly in a corner of the room and the guests talk and laugh against the background of the gentle music. A group of men (Arnold's fraternity brothers grown bald and portly) harmonize when "Jerusalem of Gold" is played. Friends and relatives who have not seen each other for a long time, whose only link is their acquaintance with Edith and Arnold, greet each other warmly.

Nina circulates through the room, accepting embraces, embracing in turn. Fatigued at last, she joins two women who are perched on the window seat. Ina and Irene, both cousins of David's and both named for the same grandmother, contrive always to be on opposite sides of an argument. They are both small and dark and intense, and always, it has seemed to Nina, they shoot their words like lethal bullets — they do not know how to converse.

"She has no rights," Ina says vehemently. "She gave any rights to the baby up when she signed that contract."

Nina's stomach contracts and her hands are as cold as ice. She knows that they are talking about the court case that has been much in the headlines, the case involving a woman who had agreed to become a surrogate mother and had then fought to claim the child. She herself has followed the case carefully (turning the page of the newspaper swiftly when Hildy entered the room), and each new development worried and disturbed her.

David, however, has not been troubled. He sees no parallel between their situation and that of the unfortunate couple who entered into the ill-fated agreement. They had "hired" a woman, establishing contact with her through an agency. It was an impersonal, legal arrangement. Stacey, on the other hand, is their friend (at least, she has become their friend), and they have been so very careful. Every avenue was explored, every kindness and consideration extended. Stacey is warm and stable and generous.

"She has the same right as a woman has who has agreed to allow for the adoption of a baby. There is a cooling-off period when she can change her mind. Why shouldn't the same rule apply to surrogacy?" Irene asks. "Oh, the whole thing is ridiculous. A woman renting out her womb, being used as an incubator. What do you think, Nina?"

Nina struggles to find her voice. She stares at the chirping, quarreling cousins and remembers that they each have three children. She is angered by the arrogance of their judgments, by the blindness of their perception. They are like the well-fed who cannot understand the pangs of the hungry but who argue endlessly over food-distribution programs. Is it so difficult for them to understand the yearning of a man and a woman for a child — a child who will be biologically linked to them?

"I think," she says carefully, "that each situation is different. I don't think surrogacy is something that can be argued in a single generalization. It may be wonderful for some people and horrible for others. Like adoption. Like conventional families. Anything can turn into a fairy tale and anything can turn into a nightmare." She thinks of lonely Alison and bitter Seth, of happy Andrea and of John Cowper's son, Terry, who refused to spend Christmas with his father.

She is relieved when the conversation is ended as Claire Silberman raps a glass authoritatively with her spoon and asks for silence.

"Please, everyone. I want to make a toast to my grandson."

The guests all turn to look at her. There is a rare softness in her eyes, an unnatural quiver in her voice.

"Your grandfather would have been proud of you today," she tells Aaron. And then she validates David's imaginings. "When you chanted your Torah reading I thought that it was my Amos's voice I was hearing."

She kisses Aaron, and there is a subdued smattering of applause. Some of the women wipe their eyes. David turns and sees that the young rabbi is standing beside him, smiling pleasantly, his hand outstretched.

"I'm Rabbi Cohen," he says. "And, of course, you're Dr. Roth's brother. I can see the family resemblance."

Like Stacey, at their initial meeting, the rabbi has perceived the similarities between the brothers despite the difference in their coloring, their stature. But then, the rabbi is in the business of continuity, of family connection.

"Not everyone thinks Arnold and I look alike," David says. "I was very impressed by your sermon, Rabbi."

"By its brevity, I assume."

David smiles, and as though by arrangement, the two men walk to a quiet corner of the room and sit opposite each other.

"I wonder if I could make an appointment to see you sometime," David says.

"You have questions to ask me, Mr. Roth?"

"Legal questions. That is, questions pertaining to Jewish law."

"Ah, *halachic* questions. Ask away. If I can answer them I'll save you the trouble of a journey. And if I need to research them I'll have a head start. So what are these questions?"

Has the rabbi sensed the urgency in his voice? David wonders. He plucks a chicken wing from the tray offered by a smiling waitress and recognizes Nina's special sauce, the blend of honey and soy lightly laced with orange juice.

"My wife made these," he tells the rabbi, who is also eating one.

"Yes. I noticed your wife. She is a very beautiful woman. And your daughter is also very lovely."

"Thank you."

"Now for your questions, Mr. Roth."

"They are hypothetical, of course."

"Of course."

The rabbi does not tell David that his life is punctuated by hypothetical questions, always asked in low and urgent tones, by men and women whose faces are pale with anxiety (as David's is now) and whose hands are damp with nervousness.

"How does Jewish law view the question of surrogate motherhood?"

The rabbi sighs.

"That's a difficult question. It's such a new concept that we don't

have any real Responsa on it. Of course, we'd worry about the integ-
rity of the family and whether a surrogacy arrangement endangered
it. There would be questions of jealousy, maybe even of adultery to
be considered. And I imagine we would worry about poor women
being exploited by women in a better financial situation. It's complicated. Very complicated."

"But if there were a contract into which the surrogate mother had
freely entered, which guaranteed her rights, protected her — wouldn't
that make a difference?" David persists.

"Jewish law frowns on any trade in human life. For example, there
can be no sale of organs, no prostitution. By extension, this might
affect the legitimacy of such a contract. And then, of course, the
rights of the child would have to be considered. It's not an easy
question, Mr. Roth. On the other hand, we take very seriously the
commandment to be fruitful and multiply, and there are those rabbis
who believe that any procedure which guarantees Jewish continuity
and fulfills that commandment is sanctioned. In such a context perhaps, in particular cases a surrogate arrangement might be countenanced." The rabbi averts his eyes as he speaks and David wonders
if the conversation embarrasses him. He is a very young man and
David notes that he does not wear a wedding band.

"Let's say that the surrogacy is acceptable. Would the child be
Jewish if the surrogate mother were not Jewish?" he asks.

"Ah, on such questions Jewish law is very flexible," the rabbi replies. He is on familiar territory now and speaks rapidly. "An infant
can be converted by immersion. If it were a male child there would
be circumcision. We do it all the time in adoptions. It's no big thing."
He selects another canapé from a proferred tray, licks his fingers,
adjusts his knitted skullcap. "You would be surprised at the stories I
hear," he confides.

David wonders if the rabbi has converted infants conceived through
genetic engineering, babies born in this age when so many conven-
tions are in suspension and life can be conceived in a petri dish, eggs
harvested from ovaries and sperm frozen in carefully labeled plastic
containers.

"Life is central to Jewish law," the rabbi observes. "You know
every commandment can be suspended to save a life. The only ex-

ceptions are prohibitions against murder, idolatry, and perverted sexual practices."

"I see." David wonders if the rabbi would consider the single night he and Stacey spent together, that night of such tenderness and subdued, purposeful passion, a "perversion" according to Jewish law. Surely, he would consider it adulterous. Still, that is something David will never reveal. It is enough now for him to understand how his child may become Jewish, may legally belong to the Jewish community.

He and the rabbi relax into a discussion of their work, of David's visit to Israel. The rabbi himself has recently returned from a convention there on genealogy, which, it seems, is his consuming interest.

"Did you go to the Museum of the Diaspora?" David asks.

"Oh, yes. Were you there?"

David nods. "I spent a couple of hours at the computer," he says. "It was strange to watch my family's history flash across the screen. Birth dates, death dates. Names repeated generation after generation. Amos the son of Nachman dies and Amos the son of Eli is born. David and Miriam. A nineteenth-century Kayla Yehudit and a twentieth-century Carolyn Jane."

"No one can say we're not tenacious," the young rabbi observes smilingly. "Names are important to us. They signify our survival as a family, as a people."

"Aaron was named for my father, Amos," David says musingly. "My mother did not want the exact name because my father died so young. A superstition, I suppose."

"Superstitions serve a purpose, offer us a sense of control, I suppose, over the irrational, the unpredictable. Aaron chanted so well and he was so apprehensive. But that's not unusual. Boys from accomplished families are often more nervous. They feel that more is being demanded of them, that they have a special tradition to uphold." He glances up at the painting by Amos Roth that dominates the living room. In muted grays and greens, in a red the exact shade of weathered brick, Amos had painted the small village of his birth. With deft strokes of his brush he had recreated the small stone houses at the edge of a forbidding forest and the synagogue, a square red building with a peaked roof and rounded windows. He had, in that landscape and later in the portraits of the survivors, captured a vanished world. In his work imagination triumphs over destruction. The past endures.

This is where we came from, the paintings of the village say. *And this is who we are,* the portraits aver. *In spite of everything. Because of everything. We are not rootless, without past and purpose.*

His father's paintings are a legacy, David knows, and he is suffused with an odd contentment. That legacy will live. He will pass it on to his own child.

"We're all very proud of Aaron," he tells the rabbi softly.

Edith carries in the birthday cake and they gather around her. The pianist plays "Happy Birthday" and everyone sings as Arnold kisses his wife and his sons, in turn, drawing them close in an insular circle of love. The music changes to a lively hora and friends and relatives join hands and encircle them in a joyous dance. They sing, in gentle affirmation of their linkage, of the chain unbroken, of their joy sustained. Edith dances with both her sons, and then suddenly Nina is in the center of the circle and everyone claps as she whirls about with wild grace. Her hair escapes its knot and tumbles around her shoulders. She snaps her fingers authoritatively as she dances and the others imitate her, picking up her motion, her rhythm, so contagious is her exuberance, her abandon. David sees her as gypsy, as matador.

He plucks up a napkin and dances into the center of the circle, matching her steps, taunting her, holding the napkin aloft and lowering it as he prances before her. Now she becomes the bull and he is a matador. She holds her hands to her head to form horns and charges him. He escapes and steals up behind her. They hiss and tease each other, their wild games permissible in this joyous circle. All around them others imitate their game. The adults are joyous matadors and the children laugh and dash through the room, drunk on their parents' wildness, at the spectacle of adults playful as children.

Nina's face is flushed and David's forehead is beaded with perspiration. They are breathless and laughing, and when the music stops she collapses in David's arms and allows him to lead her to the couch where Hildy sits, smiling wonderingly. They return to her like flushed and excited children who rush toward a calm and tolerant parent, and she, in turn, offers them each a tissue to wipe their faces and goes to get them cold drinks and slices of birthday cake.

16

It is late afternoon when David, Nina, and Hildy leave the bar mitz-vah party for the drive north. A pale mauve sunset etches its way across the slate-gray sky and the cars on the highway move in slow, solemn procession.

"Is it too late to go to the Cosgroves'?" David asks worriedly. He does not want to offend Stacey by arriving too late, but he does not want to offend her by not arriving at all.

"We told her we would be late," Nina points out. "What do you think, Hildy?" Nina's hair is once again pinned into a neat chignon, but the flush of excitement has not left her cheeks and she rests her hand on David's shoulder as he drives.

"I don't care." Hildy, in fact, does care. She wants to give the children their gifts, to hear their screams of delight and their giggling thank yous. And she wants to see Hal make his children laugh, to make her laugh, to break the spell of melancholy that settled on her in the synagogue that morning. "But I think they'll be disappointed if we don't show up at all."

"Oh, we should go," Nina decides, and David nods and switches into the fast lane. Still, it is almost dark when they pull up in front of the Cosgroves' small frame house. Laden down with their brightly wrapped packages, they hesitate for the briefest of moments before ringing the doorbell. It is Andrea who opens the door, and she flushes with pleasure when she sees them. She wears a crimson velvet dress, and a crown sculpted of aluminum foil is perched on her golden curls.

"Merry Christmas!" she says excitedly. "Merry Christmas!"

"Happy holiday," Nina replies, kissing her on the cheek. "I hope we're not too late."

"Oh, no. Everyone is still here," Andrea says and proudly leads them into the noisy and crowded living room. The hum of voices dies down and is replaced by an uneasy silence. Their entry has disrupted the boisterous rhythm of the afternoon, the conviviality that follows a festive meal. The Cosgroves and their guests have been talking easily, arguing with good-natured gusto, having had several hours to take each other's measure, to weigh and balance the conversational scales. The arrival of the Roths upsets the hard-earned gains of the holiday afternoon, the casual jocularity, the easy intimacy. The room is overheated and the guests are flushed. They have eaten well, and even now they nibble from the small dishes of nuts Stacey has placed around the room. Andrew Kardin and John Cowper hold small tumblers of brandy.

"Hey, glad you could make it. Terrific that you could come." Hal, the beaming host, shakes David's hand vigorously, grins at Nina and Hildy, takes their coats.

Cathy and Audrey, Stacey's sisters-in-law, covertly study Nina and Hildy. They render silent judgment of Nina's peach wool chemise, of Hildy's full-skirted, pale green cashmere dress. They mark the sheen of Nina's pearls, the delicately crafted links of Hildy's long gold chain. Their own costumes have been chosen for brightness and gaiety. They are women who revel in the rush of color, in the shimmer of satin and the iridescence of taffeta, in the bright encrustment of beads and sequins that form flowers and birds on their bodices and skirts. This is a holiday and they have dressed for it; they are proud of their extravagance, of their radiant festivity.

Even Mandy wears a royal-blue maternity dress, wildly embroidered in the Indian fashion with threads of gold and silver and twinkling slivers of mirror. Enthroned in the only armchair, next to the huge tree (Nina has never seen such a large tree; it overpowers the small living room, and its wide-flung branches hung with blue and silver ornaments reduce all the furniture to shabby miniature), Mandy resembles a fertility goddess in the act of dispensing judgment and advice.

Stacey in a black skirt and a crimson velvet blouse (fashioned from the fabric that remained when Andrea's dress was completed) hurries toward them. She kisses each of them on the cheek and sweeps them into the room, introducing them exuberantly to her family.

"My friends, the Roths. David, Nina, and their gorgeous daughter, Hildy. Dad, David is an inventor. He designs all sorts of switches and stuff. You may even sell some of them."

The owner of the hardware store nods with respect. He extends his hand and David shakes it, pleased that the older man's grasp is firm, that his gaze is steady. He holds his hand a moment too long, recognizing that this, perhaps, will be the only time he will ever look into the eyes of his child's grandfather.

Stacey does not introduce her mother, who stands at the window, her face pressed up against the glass. She is a sallow woman, and the navy-blue dress she wears hangs loosely on her body. Her hair, neatly parted down the middle in the bob of an obedient schoolgirl, has faded to the color of ashes, and her eyes, blue like Stacey's, like Andrea's, glitter with a febrile intensity. For whom is she waiting at that window? Nina wonders. The woman turns, looks at her family, and asks in a thin voice, "Are they coming? Why don't they come?" Then, without waiting for an answer, she again presses her face against the glass.

Samantha and Eric hurtle into the room, followed by Jared and Evan and a group of other children. Cosgrove cousins, Nina supposes, and the children of the lawyer Andrew Kardin and his hard-eyed, brassy-haired wife. All the children wear crowns of aluminum foil, although some have already been torn and Jared's slips to form a band about his forehead.

"Presents! More presents!" Samantha shouts greedily. "Let's open the new presents."

They encircle Hildy, who piles all the packages into a pyramid. She counts the children and decides, with relief, that she has enough gifts for all of them. There will even be an extra ocarina, which she herself will play. Smiling, she shouts their names, tosses the gifts to them, aiming wide so that they scurry like voracious small animals to pluck them up. The larger gifts, those for the Cosgrove children, she withholds for last, although Jared pulls insistently at her skirt.

"Mine, where's mine?" he asks plaintively. He has Hal's dark coloring, and when he is disappointed his face darkens and his lips knot into a tight pucker of discontent.

"Wait," Hildy replies impatiently. Of the three Cosgrove children, it is only Jared whom she dislikes. He resembles her (always Stacey has cut his dark hair into a close-fitting helmet), and it annoys her that Seth and Alison have commented on this, wondering if they were related.

"They're just friends, acquaintances. He's no relation," she had protested angrily, and then she had wondered if, in point of fact, that is true. The child Stacey will bear will be Hildy's sibling and sibling also to Stacey's children. Then perhaps there will be a connection. The thought wearied her and she gave up thinking about it. It was of no consequence.

But she does know that the baby (whose unborn presence is so palpable today as Stacey sails through the room, large-bellied and light-footed, aglow as though the child within her generates a radiance) will not look at all like her. The genes are against it. David's sandy hair and Stacey's golden curls almost guarantee a fair-haired child. Always Hildy will have to explain the relationship or ignore it and leave others to speculate. Perhaps, like Alison, she will not call the child by name; it will be an anonymous and thus unimportant presence in her life.

Andrea pulls Jared away, a rough yet protective gesture. She places her hand on his head.

"Wait your turn," she says. She is Stacey's daughter and Stacey's apprentice; she mothers her younger brother, combining affection and officiousness. She tosses her head and the tattered aluminum-foil crown (which she herself fashioned for each child) trembles.

The children are delighted with the assortment of instruments. Excitedly, they experiment with them, clashing the small cymbals, coaxing melody out of the ocarinas and the recorder, jubilantly clicking the castanets.

The twins seize their gifts with exclamations of approval. They immediately jam the overnight cases with the other presents they have received that day and then try to pull the zippers closed. Scraps of fabric and paper jam the teeth and Samantha begins to cry in frustration. It is Stacey who laboriously, clumsily kneels (although Nina too moves forward) to help them, and she arranges their things and zips the cases closed.

"There," she says and wipes Samantha's eyes. "Everything is all right."

Mandy remains seated, her eyes closed.

Now Hildy reaches for the larger packages and extends the individually wrapped skis and ski poles to Andrea, who shakes her head.

"No. Give Jared his first."

Hildy blushes. Andrea has caught her out. Defeated, she gives Jared his gift, and he squeals with excitement as he pulls the wrapping off and then clutches and hugs Big Bird, who is almost his size.

"Mine! Mine!" he screams in triumph and jumps through the room showing his new acquisition to his aunts and uncles, to Hal and Stacey and to Mandy, who leans forward and presses her face against the furry yellow surface.

Evan is pleased with both the chemistry set and the calculator.

"Two presents," he says, marveling at his good luck, at their generosity.

Cathy and Audrey exchange knowing looks and Cathy pokes her husband. Nina feels a rush of discomfort. Have they been too extravagant, too conspicuous? Is their generosity perceived as patronization? She recognizes that she is in unfamiliar territory and thus ignorant of customs and mores.

Finally, Hildy gives Andrea the skis, and the child's face blossoms with pleasure. Rose-colored petals rise at her cheeks and her blue eyes glitter like cornflowers moist with dew. Hildy shows her how the skis can be fastened, how the poles have cunning leather straps for carrying and storage. But Andrea requires no instruction. She affixes the slats of gleaming golden wood to her black Mary Jane shoes, holds the poles properly, and propels herself across the room. The wood of the skis scrapes harshly against the rough, raw wood of the floor.

"I'm skiing!" Andrea shouts. "Watch out, everyone! I'm skiing! I'm flying!"

Her crown skitters off her head as she vigorously digs her poles into the floor and thrusts herself forward.

"She is skiing! She is flying!" the Kardin youngsters shout.

Eric beats the drum loudly. Samantha clangs the cymbals. The other children play the ocarinas, click the castanets. They trail her, a primitive, atonal orchestra in a cacophonous rite of childhood, countenanced on this day of gifts and joy when adult rules are briefly suspended.

Stacey, who stands with Jared beside the tree, claps, proud of her daughter's joy, her daughter's imagination. Andrea is special. In her crimson velvet dress, her silver crown, with the gleaming skis strapped to her party shoes, she is a snow princess, a miniature majestic presence.

Andrea is almost in the center of the room where the hardwood floor glows beneath its new layer of wax. Her face aglow, she bears down upon the poles and gives herself a powerful push. Then, poles aloft, she glides with new and surprising speed across the polished, nonresistant surface. The long black extension cord for the tree's lights snakes out and her ski catches it, jerks it loose from the socket. The tree sways unsteadily; its ornaments jingle, its blue and white lights sputter, and then the room is plunged into darkness.

Stacey moves quickly, fearful that the tree may topple onto Jared. She thrusts him toward the wall, and her hands grasp through the darkness for the trunk, too loosely set in the rough clay base. She claws air and shifts her direction, kicking aside debris, but her heel (that slim high heel on the cut-out pump that she bought for this special day) catches on the treacherous wire. She trips and falls forward. Her arms flutter; her body is weighted and distended as she pitches forward, and her face is moon-pale. Like a misshapen, huge wounded bird, she falls and her body hits the floor with a dull and terrifying thud. Her scream fills the room, rising above the children's noisy music, Hal's muttered curses, the rustle of voices, and nervous laughter.

"No!" she shrieks. "No!"

Silence crashes across the room. They are still as statues, immobilized by danger. It is not for herself she is screaming, they know. She is screaming for the child she carries, for the terrible vulnerability of that unborn, that so precariously sheltered and nurtured life.

"Mama," Jared whimpers. "Mama."

David (who stands beside Stacey's mother at the window) shivers convulsively. His fingers are ice-tipped and his shirt is grafted onto his body by a sheet of cold sweat.

This cannot be happening, he thinks wildly. No. No. They have come too far for this to happen. His baby, his child, will not, cannot die unborn. No. No. *No*. The negating words freeze unspoken on his lips. His fingers are balled into fists and his eyes burn. The wraithlike woman who stands beside him in the darkness reaches out, touches his hand. Her fingers are so thin, yet so warm against his own fear-chilled flesh.

He moves away, extricates himself from her touch, distances himself from her presence. A necrotic odor emanates from her body, an encroaching stench of despair and defeat. He will not share it. He will not submit to it. He moves through the crowded room, through the darkness toward Stacey.

Nina, who stands beside Mandy's chair, stares unseeingly. Her heart pounds with arrhythmic beat and her breath comes in painful gasps. She is certain of disaster but she wills herself to calm. Automatically, she breathes through her mouth, slow, measured inhalations that battle the nausea that washes over her.

And now, as her eyes accustom themselves to the darkness, she sees the golden tangle of Stacey's curls, her widespread legs, and she sees that Stacey has fallen facedown. Her arms are pinned beneath her body, encircling her abdomen, cushioning and shielding the protuberance of her pregnancy.

Nina's horror fades and she leans against the chair, weak with relief, faint with gratitude. Their baby has not been harmed. Her certainty of disaster, within this split second, has been replaced by her certainty of survival. She is a dancer, after all, and she understands the body's defenses. She herself has fallen so many times and thus she understands the power of that protective self-embrace when the arms are lifted as a shield.

Oh, no. Stacey is fine and their baby is fine. In the darkness (with the children's aluminum-foil crowns glittering like stars) Nina smiles and understands that she loves that unborn baby, that she was terrified for its safety, just as she loves Hildy and is terrified for her safety, each morning and each evening of their lives. Like all moth-

ers, she is balanced always on a taut and teasing high wire of fear
and hope, of courage and trepidation.

Now David finds her. His arms encircle her, battle her fear, comfort her. He cannot approach Stacey, but still fearful and heavy-
hearted, he holds Nina close. She huddles against him and he soothes
her and thus calms himself.

"It's all right," he whispers. "I'm sure it's all right."

He feels the tremor of her shoulders and knows then how much
she cares about this unborn child, his child, who will redeem the
losses of the past and stand witness for the future. He passes his hand
across Nina's face and feels the heat of her tears. He has, during
these few hours, heard his wife's joyous laughter and felt her febrile
sorrow. And she, clinging to him, remembers his playfulness as they
danced together. Even now, suffused with the fear of the moment,
she feels herself protected and loved, and she marvels at the fortunate joy of their life together, of this tent of their togetherness into
which they will gather the infant, loved by them even before birth.

Hildy, crouching among the children, watched Stacey fall, mesmerized; dream and reality intermingle. Surely she has imagined this
scene before (Stacey's scream, Stacey's fall), played it out in the
nether region of her own forbidden fantasy. She has thought, in the
darkness of sleepless nights, of Stacey encountering an accident and
the baby miscarried on a wave of pain, drowned in a pool of blood.

Hildy weeps. Hot tears of shame streak her cheeks. Oh, God. She
does not want to hate. She does not want to wish for death. She
does not want Stacey (who has never been unkind to her, who has
tried so hard to reach her — *What are you reading, Hildy? How is
school going, Hildy?*) to suffer. She does not want to betray her mother.
Or David, who was and is and will always be so good to her. He is
her daddy. *Daddy.* She says the word aloud very softly, although it
cannot be heard in this room that is suddenly wild with noise as
instructions are shouted, advice offered.

The lights flash on as Hal reconnects the extension cord. The blue
and silver bulbs twinkle again amid the fragrant green needles of the
conifer boughs. Hal kneels beside Stacey. His face is grave, his voice
calm and caring. Gently, he turns her, helps her to sit up.

"Are you all right, Stacey?" he asks. "Sweetheart. Are you all right?"

She smiles. She is very pale and her lower lip is flecked with blood. He dabs at it with his handkerchief and she stares in surprise at the small stain.

"I guess I bit myself when I fell," she says. "That was stupid."

Andrea is weeping.

"It's my fault, all my fault. But I didn't mean it," she says again and again. A child's threnody — the acknowledgment of guilt, the denial of intent.

Stacey pulls her daughter to her, hugs her.

"Of course you didn't mean it. Of course not," she says.

Now she looks up and searches for David across the room. He and Nina stand together, their arms linked as though they must comfort each other. Nina's head rests on David's shoulder. It seems to Stacey that his hands are trembling. She knows that his lips are moving, although she does not hear his voice. Can it be that he is praying?

"I'm fine," she says, and her voice is loud and clear. "I'm just fine."

As though to give proof to her words, the child she carries shifts position in one of those sudden, energetic fetal movements that makes Stacey feel as though the world itself is in upheaval within her womb.

Hal helps her to her feet. She pulls her fingers through her hair, straightens her scarlet velvet blouse, adjusts the narrow strap of her high-heeled pump. Color floods back to her face.

"It was stupid to wear those heels," her sister-in-law Cathy says. Cathy, whose heavy legs are mapped by the blue varicosities of her own pregnancies, is annoyed by Stacey's vanity, by her ebullience.

"Oh, Stacey knows what she's doing. You can rely on Stacey." Her father (who has always relied on Stacey, who relies on her still) puts his arm around her, chucks her under her chin.

"That's my grandkid you've got there," he says. "So be careful." It is the first time he has referred to her pregnancy. Her mother remains at the window and Stacey wonders if Rose Carmody is even aware of her fall.

Samantha beats the drum loudly, commandingly.

"Are there any more presents?" she asks.

Everyone laughs except Nancy Kardin, who purses her lips and says, "How rude." She says it loudly because she is one of those women who is not content simply to be a good mother; she must call attention to the shortcomings of others, chronicle the deficits of other children.

But Nina walks forward with a large red box.

"I almost forgot, Stacey," she says. "This is for you. I saw it and I couldn't resist it. It was just right." She is talking too fast, saying too much because she does not know what to say.

"Hey. Saks Fifth Avenue. Sit down, Stace. Open it."

Hal moves a chair and Stacey obligingly sinks into it. They surround her as she opens the box and removes a long cashmere robe, the color of ivory, so soft and light that it seems to float on her outstretched arms.

She presses it against her cheek and then rises and slips it on. She cannot belt it (of course), but it falls in graceful folds across her shoulders and floats gently about her ankles.

"It's for the hospital," Nina murmurs, almost apologetically, because now Cathy and Audrey are staring at her curiously, accusingly. "I thought it would be warm."

"Don't let a baby get near that," Nancy Kardin warns bitterly. She herself has three small children, and sometimes she thinks that she will never be free of the stink of spit-up.

"We won't," Hal says. Deftly, he includes himself in this gift, in its luxurious folds, its generous intent. He puts his arms around his wife and dances her, in her red velvet blouse, her soft ivory robe, into the center of the room. He kisses her lips (where now the blood has dried) and sings softly.

" 'I was dancing with my darling to the Tennessee Waltz, when an old friend I happened to see.' "

"Hal, please."

She is serious and so he leads her back to the chair, but she does not remove the robe. She is very cold and welcomes its warmth. She plays with the long belt. This white wool is gossamer-soft between her fingers. She imagines herself wearing this robe, standing on a redwood terrace. The California sunshine will fall in buttery patterns across the ivory wool, and Stacey will stretch and lean forward and watch her children as they play beneath a palm tree. In her hand she will hold a letter from the Roths with a snapshot of the baby. She sees herself reading the letter, studying the snapshot, and thrusting both of them into the wide pocket of this perfect robe that Nina has selected with such generosity, such tenderness.

She will keep a scrapbook, Stacey decides now, a scrapbook to hold Nina's letters and the snapshots. She imagines Andrea helping her to organize it, Andrea who by that time will be old enough to understand the arrangement Stacey made with David Roth. It will be all right, Stacey tells herself. Nothing like that terrible case where the surrogate mother is battling so fiercely to keep the baby, or the case that was discussed on *Donahue* (or was it Oprah Winfrey?) in which a woman who had given up a child for adoption told how she had spent years searching for that child. ("I had to know where he was. How could I not know where he was?" she had asked pleadingly.) But Stacey will always know the whereabouts of her child. Always the letters will arrive, and the photographs, and always she will tuck them into the pocket of her robe.

Nina glances at her watch and rises.

"I didn't realize how late it is," she says. "David, we really should be going."

"Of course," David agrees. He is newly aware of his own fatigue, of the cumulative strain of this long day of interaction and celebration, of fear and relief commingling.

"I'm beat myself," John Cowper says.

The tall, lean novelist is also slightly drunk. He has been depressed all day because of his son Terry's refusal to spend Christmas with him. He is sad because he spent a long time staring at himself in the Cosgroves' bathroom mirror and realized that his hair is thinning and a network of creases lines his high forehead.

"We're getting old, David," he says. "Too old for kids and Christmas parties. Too old to be pushing strollers, worrying about midnight feedings. But you don't have to worry about that crap." His face collapses with self-pity.

"Shut up, John," David says shortly.

He turns away from John and goes into the bedroom and removes their coats from the mountain of wraps piled on the carelessly made king-sized bed.

There is a flurry of good-byes. Neither of Stacey's brothers have their names right. "Good-bye, Donald," they say to David. "So long, Tina." "Nice meeting you, Tildy." The Roths smile and do not correct them. The sisters-in-law are cool and meticulously polite.

"So nice of you to come," Cathy says, and her eyes ask. "*Why did you come?*"

"The kids love their gifts. And Stacey's robe is spectacular," Audrey tells Nina, and her eyes rake Nina's face, as though to unearth the reason why this dark-haired woman has bought such expensive gifts for people with whom she has no family connection.

Mandy and John wave. John has another drink in his hand. David hopes that he is not driving.

Andrea hugs them, and when Hildy kneels to embrace her, she kisses her wetly on the cheek.

"I love my skis," she says.

"Hey, what do you say we go skiing together?" Hildy suggests, surprising herself as well as Nina and David. But she does have a special fondness for Andrea, the golden, pleasant child who has inherited her father's easy laughter, her mother's amiable generosity.

"Really?" Andrea replies, her high-pitched question melding enthusiasm and agreement.

Hal and Stacey walk them to the door. In the crush of leave-taking, in the closeness of the narrow vestibule, David's outstretched hand rests, for the briefest of moments, on Stacey's abdomen. Again, the child within her stirs in a hard near-contraction, and he feels the life of his own creation taut beneath his touch. His fingers move against the nap of Stacey's crimson velvet blouse. His throat is dry, his face burning.

"Good night, Stacey," he says.

And she, knowing what he felt, moved by the gentle pressure of his palm, smiles and stands on tiptoe (in her very high heels) to kiss him lightly on the cheek.

"Thank you," she says to him, to Nina, to Hildy, to this family to whom she is now bonded. "Thank you for everything."

"And thank you, Stacey, Hal. It was a lovely party and we're so pleased that you included us." The seesaw of gratitude, the scale of all that they owe each other, is so precariously balanced that it cannot sustain one false word, one false move.

That night Nina dreams that David himself is pregnant. He stands before her, naked, and even as she watches, his gravidity progresses until his abdomen forms a vibrant, glowing mound beneath which his genitals are minuscule, obscured. They dangle so softly pink and submissive, dwarfed by the proud golden rise that shelters the life in formation, the life growing, exploding with strength and vitality. Dreaming, Nina watches herself stand. She wears only a loose skirt, and her bare breasts are huge, engorged. She dances, her arms widespread, and droplets of milk drip from her translucent nipples. She moves toward him, and now the drops, which are the color of moonlight, fall freely and form a shimmering pattern on his striated skin. He holds out his hands and she takes them into her own and moves back and forth before him, lovingly, obediently. The child, nurtured by him, nourished by her, continues to grow until, at last, it is visible, mysteriously luminescent beneath the carapace of his protecting flesh. She kneels then, and, pressing her cheek against him, she feels the unborn baby reach toward her and touch her, in acknowledgment, in recognition.

She is weeping when she awakens and she is surprised that her tears are only tears and not milky drops of moonlight.

17

The telephone's shrill ring pierces the silence of the snow-dense January night; it invades and then commingles with the sounds and voices of an elusive dream. Drifting between sleep and wakefulness, Nina defines the sound, recognizes its reality; with fumbling, somnambulistic clumsiness, she reaches for the receiver. The green lights of the digital clock glitter in the darkness. It is two-fourteen A.M. She shivers, pulls the phone from the bedside table, and cradles it against her body as she speaks.

"Hello. Hello." She keeps her voice very soft because David has not awakened and she is protective of his sleep. He is so weary now, drained by a new project at work, worried about his mother (who calls too often from Florida with varied complaints), apprehensive about Hildy (who, with the passing of the holiday, is once again darkly moody), and solicitous of Stacey (who grows easily fatigued and whose blood pressure is slightly high). It is only Nina who causes him no concern, who is able to coax him into relaxation. She bought a VCR during the post-holiday sales and she scours the video-rental shops for the old classics they both love. At night, they lie in bed and watch *How Green Was My Valley*, *Showboat*, Olivier's *Hamlet*.

Occasionally, they play Trivial Pursuit as they watch, using the Silver Screen deck. Nina sprawls across the bed cradling both camels. They argue good-naturedly over the toss of the die.

"You're supposed to advance three, not four."

"You're not counting right."

Tonight they played until one A.M. while they watched Pola Negri vamp her way across the screen. They have been asleep less than an hour, Nina realizes as she grips the receiver, an inventory of possible catastrophes catapulting through her mind.

"Nina. It's John. John Cowper."

"John. It's two o'clock in the morning. What's the matter with you?"

"David. Let me speak to David." There is urgency in his voice; sorrow and panic are blended into a bleating of helplessness.

She wakes David and hands him the receiver, and the long phone wire rests on her breasts, a curling plastic artery through which John's voice pulses.

"John, what is it?" David is calm. Through the years there have been other nocturnal calls from John Cowper, other cries for help through distance and darkness. He awakened them, weeping softly, when Leslie, his first wife, left him. He has called to spew bitterness at a critic's insensitivity (reading David the entire review) or at a colleague's obtuseness. And, he has called just to talk; ungoverned by time himself, he does not consider the lateness of the hour.

Nina (who tries to be sympathetic) knows that those who work alone through long hours, insulated by the silence so essential to their creativity, crave the sounds of friendship, the murmurs of understanding, in the still, dark hours of the night when doubt and desperation converge. She knows dancers who meet at midnight and are startled by the light of dawn. There are writers and artists who haunt dimly lit cafes, hovering over empty cups and glasses even after the proprietor rings the closing bell. They call each other, long after midnight, in distant cities, seeking affirmation, reassurance. They speak, therefore they are. Their voices give the lie to the fears of their solitude. She leans back against her pillow now, twists the phone cord through her fingers.

"When did it happen?" David asks. "Who called you? Is she all right?" His voice is steady, but Nina sees the creases of tension that form at the corners of his mouth, the worry that shadows his eyes.

She remembers now that Mandy is en route to Boston to give a reading, her last reading before the baby's birth. Nina had cautioned her to fly, but Mandy had insisted on driving. She enjoys driving alone at night, she had added. Ideas fly to her then; images scramble through her mind. She keeps a pad and pencil on the seat beside her. Something has happened to Mandy then.

Nina imagines an accident, envisions Mandy flung against the steering wheel, her pale face ribboned by the flickering red glow of hazard lights. She shivers, shamed at the ease with which she summons such images and frightened for Mandy, for John, for the baby so soon to be born.

"Listen, John, bring the children here. Then I'll drive up with you. No. Of course Nina won't mind." He covers the mouthpiece with his hand and turns to her. "There's been an accident. Somewhere near New Haven. Mandy's hurt. Can John leave the twins here and I'll drive up with him?"

"Yes. Of course." Her answer is swift, in atonement for her minatory premonition.

"Okay, John. Start out now. Drive carefully."

Nina gets up and puts on a warm plaid robe, fur-lined slippers.

David is already dressing, pulling a heavy sweater over his buffalo plaid wool shirt, searching for the thick socks he wears with his boots.

"What happened?" she asks.

"It's not quite clear," he replies. "Either Mandy fell asleep at the wheel or she skidded or she was forced to swerve. In any case, the car hit a lamppost, and she's at the Grace New Haven Hospital. The doctor who spoke to John said that her condition was stable."

"And the baby?"

"I don't know. I didn't ask."

"Did John ask?" Her question is accusatory. A woman would have asked at once. But then, the bearing and rearing of children is a female obsession. For women, nurturing and protecting begin at conception. She thinks of how pregnant women clasp their hands protectively across their abdomens, of how they walk with a rocking gait so as to soothe the tiny lives they carry.

"*I* would have asked," David says, and she feels the reproof in his swift reply. He will not be misjudged. He cares as deeply as she does. Never has he been indifferent about Hildy. Always he has been absorbed in her life, worried about her, just as always he will be absorbed in the life of the child who will soon (*in two months, just two months*) be born. Even now he calls Stacey three times a week to ask about her health (by which he means his baby's health).

"I know," she says, and in apology, she kisses him on the forehead and is surprised when he draws her close and kisses her with the force and insistence that presages their lovemaking (although, of course, they cannot, will not, make love). Still, she cups his face in her hands, presses her lips softly against his eyelids, his cheeks, the stubbly rim of his chin, and this is how Hildy finds them when she taps lightly and then opens the door — David half dressed and Nina in her plaid robe, their eyes red-rimmed, clutching each other, touching each other.

"What happened?" she asks. "I heard the phone."

Winter has blanched her skin, robbed it of its summer gold; it is chalked by fear now to the same color as the off-white granny nightgown she wears.

"Mandy's had an accident," Nina says. "A traffic accident just outside of New Haven."

"How is the baby?" Hildy asks, and Nina smiles at her daughter, perversely proud that Hildy has asked exactly the right question.

"We don't know," she replies. "John is bringing the twins here and then he and Daddy will drive up there together. I want to make some sandwiches and a thermos of coffee."

"I'll get the guest room ready," Hildy says.

She pads down the hall, and Nina hears the door of the linen closet open and knows that Hildy is rummaging through the layers of sheets for the patterned linens of her own childhood, the counterpane on which the seven dwarfs zealously protect the sleeping Snow White or those on which Wilma and Fred Flintstone cavort with an adorable Pebbles. Hildy seeks those sheets and pillowcases whenever children sleep overnight at their house. It is at once an act of kindness and a retreat (Nina thinks, Nina hopes) into Hildy's own protected childhood, when each happy day ended on a narrow bed sheeted with sweet scenes of fantasy.

Hildy likes children, is drawn to them. Nina remembers how she cut the children's meat at Thanksgiving dinner, how she shopped for the children's Christmas gifts with such care. It comforts Nina to

know that Hildy, who is so often moody and melancholy, angry and
caustic (poised as she is in this painful passage when she is neither
child nor adult), is possessed of such kindness. She relates to children with both ease and authority, blending playfulness and protec-
tiveness. It follows then, Nina thinks, as she brews coffee and makes
sandwiches, that Hildy will in the end (the closely approaching end)
act as both playmate and sister to the new baby. All she needs is a
period of reconciliation, a time to adjust. Already they detect a softening in her attitude. Only last weekend Hildy drove Andrea north
and they skied together on a gentle slope in a state park. It was an
invitation that reassured Nina and pleased David inordinately.

On that same day, Stacey and Nina wandered through the children's furnishings department at Bloomingdale's looking at cribs and
changing tables, passing their hands across the satin surfaces of blankets, the quilted cotton of gaily patterned bumpers, although Nina
will not buy anything until the baby is born.

"It's just superstition," she explained to Stacey. "I did the same
thing when I was pregnant with Hildy. It's one of the few things my
mother-in-law and I are in agreement on. She never bought a thing
during her pregnancies either." Nina did not explain that it is a fear
of tempting fates, of teasing the evil eye, that prevents her from
filling the room that will serve as a nursery with the bright new
paraphernalia of infant life. She acknowledges her dark and irrational uneasiness, her trepidation that if they move too swiftly, if
they are arrogant in their certitude, then they will be punished —
something will go wrong.

Instead she diverted the conversation to a discussion of Andrea
and Hildy, of the special relationship between mothers and
daughters.

Nina slices thick slabs of cheese and smiles as she thinks of Hildy
and herself, of Stacey and Andrea, linked in an interlocking circle
of love, with the unborn child at its center. Hildy has extended
herself to Andrea and she has grown increasingly fond of Stacey.
There is laughter between them and an unarticulated sympathy and
understanding.

The coffee perks and its strong rich aroma fills the kitchen. Nina
pours it into a thermos and makes sandwiches. Absorbed in the task,

she almost forgets why she is moving so purposefully through her
bright kitchen at this dark hour. The doorbell shrills and she is jarred
back to heart-heavy sadness.

Hildy flies down the stairs to open the door. Like abandoned ur-
chins, Samantha and Eric stand outside, their delicate skin wind-
bruised, their jeans limp and soggy. Neither child wears socks and
their pale ankles are ribboned with dirt. Samantha's jacket is held
closed with big safety pins and a crust of dried chocolate rings her
lips. Eric is crying. His tears fall slowly, steadily, although he stands
very still and his lean face is expressionless. Like Samantha, he clutches
a large brown paper bag. Hildy wonders angrily what happened to
the brightly colored overnight cases she bought them for Christmas.

John urges the children forward, placing one hand on Eric's shoulder, the other on Samantha's arm, but they stand rigid, immobile.
John's long face is twisted with anxiety and his hair is matted with
snow.

Nina and Hildy move together now. In efficient partnership, they
sweep the children into the house, speaking softly, comfortingly to
them. "Don't cry, Eric, everything will be all right." "Do you want
me to carry that bag, Samantha? Never mind, you can carry it yourself." They hurry them upstairs, help them change into dry clothing
(Hildy's tee shirts, bright red for Samantha, sunshine yellow for Eric,
become long nightshirts on their slender bodies), and tuck them into
the newly made bed. The twins fall asleep at once. They are sad and
seasoned veterans of nocturnal odysseys and midnight crises.

John and David, ready to leave, wait for them in the kitchen.
Nina gives them the bag of sandwiches and fruit, the thermos of
coffee.

"I hope everything is all right," she says. "Call when you get to
the hospital."

"Hey, David: drive carefully." Hildy leans against the refrigerator
as she speaks. Her words are careless, but he can see the tension in
her shoulders, the tight set of her mouth.

They leave, closing the door softly, too softly, behind them.

"John was so upset," Nina says.

"John is a slob," Hildy retorts. Contempt rims her words. She
judges her father's friend with harsh accuracy, and Nina, cowed by

her daughter's honesty, offers no protest. Together, tiptoeing lest they awaken the sleeping children, they make their way upstairs.

John and David speak very little at the outset of their drive to Connecticut. The snow stops when they reach Danbury, but a nacreous mist forms and obscures the sinuous turns; David switches on his brights and the harsh light beams across the highway thinly laced with frost. Only a single roadway lamp is lit and its glow is a feeble yellow; as they approach, it too is extinguished.

David is reminded of how once, he and Arnold had walked through the snow after Hebrew school, arriving at their father's studio at the exact moment the streetlights shimmered into muted brightness.

"Who turns the streetlights on?" David had asked.

It was a question that had long perplexed him. In Hebrew school he sat near the window and always watched and waited for the magic moment when the bulb of the streetlamp across the street began its vigilant nocturnal glow. He thought it mysterious and wonderful that the lamp was ignited by unseen hands, and it had occurred to him that perhaps it was God Himself who was responsible for the lambent light it cast. The question teased him but he feared to ask it lest he invoke his teacher's scorn and his classmates' ridicule.

"There's probably a central control for all the streetlights," Arnold had said.

"Papa?" David appealed to his father.

"Arnold could be right." Amos Roth dipped his brush into turpentine, removed it, and plunged it into water. "But not everything has to be explained. Sometimes it's nicer not to know. Sometimes it's nicer to think that it's magic. Or even beyond magic."

They watched as he took up a piece of charcoal and swiftly sketched the streetlamp, rendering it so tall and graceful, shrouded in the gathering shadows of darkness. And then he drew a bird, a fiery twig in its beak, flying toward it.

"I like the idea of a bird lighting the lamp better than your idea of a central control board," Amos told Arnold.

"Me too." Arnold had surrendered cheerfully, but it was David who claimed the drawing, sprayed it with fixative, and tucked it beneath his jacket. That night he put it in his drawer, beneath his polo shirts, and always he has kept it in the top drawer of his bureau — a secret, private treasure. It represents his father's legacy to him, the license to dream, to imagine, to be amused and bemused. It is an adult imprimatur for a child's imaginings.

Now David tells John about that conversation with his father and about the drawing, because John likes to hear such stories. Himself the unhappy child of unhappy parents, he sucks hungrily on the reminiscences of others.

"That's something to remember," he says appreciatively. "Something to be passed on. I try to share that kind of thinking, that kind of feeling with Terry. That's what you want to give your kids. The sense of wonder."

His lips curl bitterly. Terry evades John's confidences, rejects his secrets. John has told David that when Terry was away at summer camp, he wrote him several times a week, creating in his letters a small serial novel chronicling the adventures of a child as he wanders through an exciting and mysterious galaxy. *Star Wars*, only better, because John threaded his story with mythological references, knowing that Terry had a thing for the Greek myths. He imagined Terry waiting for each new episode, perhaps reading the sequential chapters to his admiring bunkmates. But at summer's end, when he picked Terry up at camp, he saw that the letters were in a shoe box and most of them had never been opened.

"Yes. A sense of wonder," David repeats. He feels a thrill of anticipation and imagines himself standing at a window with his daughter (Amos Roth's granddaughter) in his arms. It will be the hour of near-darkness, and as they watch, the streetlamp will suddenly assume its amber glow and she will ask him the same question he had asked his father. *Who turns the streetlamp on?* Then, her breath sweet against his neck, her heart hammering against his, he will point to his father's drawing and tell her the story of his own question, of Amos's explanation.

His heart fills, as he drives through the darkness, with all that he will share with his child. He will initiate her into Amos Roth's kingdom of wonder; he will frame his father's drawing and hang it in his child's bedroom. Ah, there are so many things he will share with his daughter. He will walk with her along the beach as summer ebbs into fall. He will hold her in his arms as they light the Chanukah candles. They will return to Israel as a family, he and Nina and Hildy and the child, whose hand he will hold as they cross the meadowlands of the Galilee and climb the gentle Judaean hills. He would have her understand that her own small life is interwoven with the life of her people; that within her being all the dreams of the past and all the hopes for the future pulsate in powerful confluence. *Oh, daughter of mine,* he thinks. *Oh, daughter of my people.* His lips move as though in prayer. His own musings so absorb him that he is startled to realize that John is sobbing softly, his head buried in his hands.

"She'll be all right, John," David says, but the words are sour in his mouth because he does not know if Mandy will be all right. He does not even know if she is alive. The thought chills him and he drives faster and then slows again.

"I shouldn't have let her go," John says. "I should have hidden the goddamn car keys. I knew it was stupid. I knew it was dangerous. I should have thought about the baby. Goddamn it, I want that baby, David. In spite of everything, I want it."

"I know." He speaks to John as he spoke to Hildy when she was a child — the calm, reassuring tone of adult omnipotence (which recognizes its own impotence), the effort at commiseration (when misery cannot be shared), the gentle proffering of solace (when there can be no consolation).

"The twins are great kids but they're Mandy's kids — Mandy's and Glen's. I love them, believe me I do, but they're not mine. I watch them running toward me sometimes and I realize that they both run with their shoulders thrust forward, like Glen does. When Eric laughs he closes his eyes. Just like Glen. I want a kid who laughs like me, who runs like me. I want to go on, David. Goddamn it, I want to be continued. Leaving a couple of books behind just isn't enough for me. Hey, do you know what I think the most awesome line in the Bible is? 'These are the generations of Noah.' I want someone to be able to say 'These are the generations of John Cowper.' " He laughs wildly as though to ward off David's own laughter, his contempt.

But David is not contemptuous. He understands that it is posterity for which John yearns. His future is invested in this unborn child, carried by Mandy almost to term — this inheritor of gene and gesture, of tale and talent, this guarantor of his own vitality. Twice during the past year, John has awakened with chest pains (he feels as though a metal fist beats relentlessly down upon his heart while spokes of pain pierce his arms) and both times he checked himself into the hospital. The doctors found nothing threatening, but he completed his new book in a burst of speed, sprinting toward the last page with the adrenaline energy of a runner who fears his breath and legs may be exhausted before he attains the finish line. Like David, John is the son of a father who died young, and, unlike David, he has allowed that early death to haunt his life.

"You have Terry," David reminds his friend.

"No, I don't. Terry hates my guts, or at least he thinks he hates my guts. He doesn't even want to come for weekends anymore. I don't have Terry." Bewilderment and despair quiver in his voice. He is a father whose son denies him, who tosses his letters unopened into a shoe box. David is silent. What, after all, can he say?

The lights of New Haven loom before them. They pass the Long Wharf exit and follow the signs to the hospital. John's breath comes in harsh rasps; the car is fetid with the sour scent of his anxiety. When David at last pulls up at the emergency room entrance, John leaps out of the car. The glowing red light turns his face into a fiery mask, and he thrusts his arms forward as though to fend off a barrage of maledictions.

But when David himself enters the emergency room after parking the car, John greets him with a smile of relief. He has already spoken with the doctor who examined Mandy and she is all right. A cut on her forehead had required half a dozen stitches and her ribs were bruised by the sudden impact of the steering wheel.

"And the baby?" David asks, remembering Nina's accusation. He will not tell Nina that John did not at once speak of the baby.

"They hooked Mandy up to a monitor," John replies, speaking very slowly as though he himself is still struggling to understand the doctor's revelations. "And the baby seemed fine, but there was a very slight indication of fetal distress. So they decided on a C-section — a cesarean. It's just a precaution."

John, always a quick study, automatically uses the professional vocabulary of the physician. The words soothe him, endow him with emotional distance. "The sonogram reading is good," he adds.

"Fetal distress?" David repeats questioningly.

He understands that the procedure requires ultrasound waves to be sent into the body and translated into a visual image. He imagines the sensitive electronic equipment registering the faint, brave heartbeat, the timid rumbling of the still maturing intestinal system, the stirring of tender limbs. It is possible that the voice of the fetus, crying out in fear, screaming its shock, its will to survive and endure, can be recorded on the screen. He wonders if babies, while still womb-sheltered, talk to themselves, sing softly, make small sounds of contentment or mewl their fatigue and discomfort.

Without warning, a darker thought occurs to him. He has read that pregnant women who were taken to concentration camps were selected for death immediately. He imagines the fetuses such women carried, contained *in utero*, living briefly on in the death-stiffened bodies of their mothers. Did they cry in hunger, in bewilderment, as sustenance ceased? Did they whimper as their small forms withered until at last they too were dead? Death contained in death, the womb become a grave. David shudders; to counter his macabre thought, he thinks of his own child, of the movements and sounds she makes even now as she grows and grows. His child's life will be at least one link restored to that cruelly broken chain.

"The doctor said the distress was minimal," John says. "Still, he doesn't want to take any chances. So I agreed, signed the consent."

David nods although he would have hesitated before signing, would have perhaps asked for a consultation, a second opinion. It occurs to him that should a similar situation arise with Stacey, it is Hal's permission that would be sought, Hal's signature that would be necessary on the hospital disclaimer. The thought makes him uneasy. His child's life is in the control of another man, a man whom he does not like and does not respect.

"Let's get some coffee, some sandwiches," John says. "The doctor said it would be an hour at least, probably longer."

David follows him into the almost deserted cafeteria. John buys them both coffee and fried-egg sandwiches. David cannot eat. He sips the coffee, which is gray in color, lukewarm, and very bitter, and too late he remembers the thermos and sandwiches still in the car.

He thinks of calling Nina but is afraid that he will wake her, wake the children. He will call when there is news, when Mandy has been safely delivered of the child. He also (crazily, he knows) thinks of calling Stacey. He wants to ask her if she is all right. He wants to be assured that his child is not in any danger, that everything is still, as Stacey assures him in the perky, upbeat tone she has mastered to perfection, "just great," "just terrific."

"If we lose this baby, David," John says, lacing his second cup of coffee with three teaspoons of sugar, as though to fortify himself against the bitterness that seeps through him, "I've lost everything. Mandy will never have another kid. And I don't know how long Mandy and I can last, the two of us and the twins — no balance, no purpose."

"They'll be fine," David says. "Mandy *and* the baby. I'm sure the doctor is perfectly competent."

It occurs to him that John has not spoken of the nature of the surgery, has not discussed the anesthesia or the length of the operation. He recalls, in contrast, listening to a conversation between Nina, Stacey, and Mandy, an earnest and intricate discussion of cesarean sections. All three women had been knowledgeable about incisions and had argued with animated intensity. They had spoken of anesthesia. They were all wary of general anesthesia; they were certain that they would want to be awake during the birth.

"If you can't deliver the baby naturally, you should at least experience something," Mandy, the energetic huntress who chases after experiences and sensations so that she might trap them in her intricately woven net of words, had maintained. She faithfully attended natural-childbirth classes in a SoHo loft — classes taught by a nurse-midwife who believes that pregnant women should partner each other. The loft is bathed in a soft rose light, Julian Bream records fill the room with the slow, elegant music of the classical guitar, and the hugely pregnant women, their faces glistening with perspiration, lie on brightly colored exercise mats and follow the instructions, moving their lips soundlessly, and then, in a burst of authority, urge each other on. *Push. Stretch. Breathe. Push. Stretch. Breathe.*

"I was awake during Hildy's delivery," Nina had said. "And I'm glad. Otherwise it would have been such a strange feeling. The birth is a climax, a finale." She summoned her professional vocabulary because in truth she sees the months of gestation as slowly paced movements, a gathering of strength, an intimate, internal dance, with mother and child moving in tandem toward the moment of crescendo, of birth and beginning.

"It's just wonderful to see the baby born, it's like being part of·a miracle." Stacey, who loves being pregnant, who loves the sheer accomplishment of giving birth to a child (she has said that preg-nancy gives her life purpose), had been more forthright in her ad-vocacy, in her claim of that moment of childbirth and mother-triumph.

Women, David acknowledges now, are invested in the experience of pregnancy, in the act of birth. Men are chiefly concerned about the child, the red-faced, screaming newborn, the inheritor and guar-antor of continuity. He understands why Nina has so deeply in-volved herself in Mandy's pregnancy (fearful as she is of jeopardizing the fragile borders that circumscribe her intimacy with Stacey), and he admires her courage, her commitment. Mandy will be mother to a newborn, to a child whose development nearly parallels that of the child Stacey will bear. Nina wants to harvest the sensations of the child's becoming, of the slow and mysterious gestation, the move-ments and the moods of the pregnancy she has been denied but that she struggles to simulate.

John looks at his watch. Almost an hour has passed. Through the large windows of the hospital cafeteria, the weak light of a wintry dawn etches spidery webs against the slate-colored sky. A new shift of workers comes on duty, and a tall, balding graduate student, a worn paperback copy of *Being and Nothingness* stuck in the pocket of his jeans, mops the floor near their table. They leave and take the elevator to the fourth floor, where John speaks to the pretty red-headed nursing student at the reception desk.

"My name if John Cowper. My wife is having a cesarean section." He enunciates very carefully as he does when he teaches his popular creative-writing class.

She consults her clipboard, lifts the phone, and speaks so softly that they cannot hear her. They glance uneasily at each other, shift their heavy winter jackets from arm to arm, conscious of their awkwardness, aware that they are suppliants.

"I see," she says at last, her voice grave. She hangs up.

"Your wife is still in surgery, Mr. Cowper," she reports. "Please take a seat in the waiting room."

Relieved, irritated, they go into the small windowless room where unread magazines litter a wood-stained Formica table and the red and blue upholstery of the chairs and couch has strangely faded, so that it is mapped with curious sprawling patterns of pallor. David and John sit on the couch. An elderly man, his silken white beard trimmed into an elegant goatee, his black shoes polished to a high gloss, sits opposite them, holding a bouquet of blood-red roses.

"My granddaughter is having a baby," he advises them. "But the baby will have no father." He smiles, as though proud of having presented them with a riddle they will be hard pressed to solve.

"It won't matter." David surprises himself with words that fly free of thought. He is, he realizes, very tired. "There will be a father one day. My wife had a daughter when I married her. I became her father."

"That was very good of you," the old man says in his courtly manner.

David closes his eyes and drifts into the disquieting sleep of the sedentary, heavy and nullifying, laden with mysterious images, abbreviated dream fragments. Like a traveler on a slowly moving train, he stares out the window, impotent witness to disturbing, swiftly vanishing scenes. A snowdrift, and on it a baby, a newborn, still glowing and wet with the fluids of birth. A roadside bench on which Nina and Stacey sit. They are both naked, but it is Nina who is pregnant and Stacey who gently brushes Nina's long, dark hair. His garden. Hildy and Andrea walking hand in hand toward the playhouse. He calls to them but they ignore him, disappear from his view, and he realizes that his shout is soundless. Still he repeats it. "Sisters! Sisters!"

He jerks into wakefulness, his limbs stiff, his mouth dry. The old man is gone and John stands in the doorway talking to a man who wears an elegantly tailored heavy tweed suit and carries a tennis racket.

John looks very serious and David feels a clutch of fear. Grim alternatives present themselves. The baby is dead. Mandy is dead. Both Mandy and the baby survive but they are impaired. The dark spectrum of possibilities overpowers him, and then, with sudden strength, he breaks free, strides across the room to stand beside John.

"Dr. Anders, this is my friend David Roth."

The doctor's handshake is firm. He is bright-eyed and clean-shaven; he exudes professional authority, professional optimism. Mandy will dislike him intensely, David knows.

"We have a daughter," John says (and David wonders if he is disappointed because a girl child will not replace Terry — Terry who will not visit his father or read his letters). "She's fine and the baby's fine."

"Wonderful!" David embraces John, shakes hands again with Dr. Anders.

"Can we see her?" John asks.

The doctor grins.

"You can even hold her," he says. "Come with me."

They follow Dr. Anders down the corridor to the nursery. Behind the glass are newborn infants, their bassinets arranged in serried configuration. They all wear white paper diapers and white shirts, and some sleep quietly, their damp lashes falling across flushed cheeks, and some squirm and cry, and some are bald, and some have bristly dark hair, and some have wisps of pale fuzz clinging to skulls that seem translucent in the rose-colored light that fills the room. A card edged in either pink or blue at the foot of each bassinet identifies them. Baby Girl Lawrence. Baby Boy Warren. Baby Boy Greenberg. Baby Girl Woo.

David reads each card carefully, just as he reads the legends beneath the plants in the Botanic Gardens. But, of course, he is in a garden of babies, peering into a windowed greenhouse where babies, white and yellow, black and brown, sleep, cry, smile, sweetened by talc and soured by spit-up, smelling pungently of the loose yellow bowel movements that soil their diapers. David's heart leaps. He would claim them all, embrace them all, gather them into a bouquet of delicate flesh and fragile limbs and plant them in all the sun-filled rooms of his house. He wonders which baby is great-granddaughter to the elegant old man — which infant at this moment of birth is already bereft, fatherless. Ah, but his child, the child that soon, soon will be born to him, will be so richly endowed — born to one mother, nurtured and raised by another, beloved by both. He has heard that in Israel, many girls are named Mazal, which means "luck," "source of good fortune," "blessing." His own daughter he will name Felicia. A name that will be, all the days of her life, a benediction.

"That's your daughter, Baby Girl Cowper in all her glory," Dr. Anders says, pointing to a smooth-skinned infant, her eyes squeezed tightly closed, pale lashes fringing her cheeks. Her tiny mouth is curled into a russet-colored bud, and as they watch, she flails her delicate legs.

"She's a good size," the doctor adds. "Over six pounds, although she is supposedly a week short of term. We sometimes have to put these emergency sections into an Isolette, but not Baby Girl Cowper." He smiles proudly, as though he himself is directly responsible for the infant's health, her resilience.

They follow him into the nursing station that adjoins the nursery.

"Baby Girl Cowper's Daddy wants to hold her," the doctor tells the nurse.

Obediently, she rises, gives David and John paper caps and gowns, masks, rubber gloves. She goes into the nursery and emerges with John and Mandy's newly born infant daughter. John holds her, studies her face intently. He lifts her tiny hand so that it rests within the cradle of his gloved palm, and then carefully, tenderly, he passes her to David.

David's heart stops. The baby is feather-light in his arms. Her ears are rosy shells and her eyelids are blue-veined. He weeps to see the infinitesimal nails, the perfectly formed opalescent arcs that shield each tiny finger, each tiny toe. Tear-blinded, he passes the baby back to the nurse, who smiles understandingly. She is used to emotional fathers (and surely the man who wept must be the father).

"You'll be a terrific Daddy," she says.

"Oh, I will be," he promises. "I will be."

Minutes later, he calls Nina.

"They did a C-section," he tells her. "Mandy is fine, still in the recovery room. And the baby is beautiful. A little girl. I held her. She's so tiny. So tiny."

His voice trembles and Nina, cradling the phone, smiles. She aches with love for David; his yearning has become her own. She imagines, with a stirring of gladness, a soaring of hope, the joy in his face, in his voice, when, at last, he holds his own child. She lifts a small white Gund bear from the headboard and rubs her cheek against its soft pink paw.

He hangs up and she glances at the clock. It is early but not too early, she decides, to call Stacey. Stacey will want to know that Mandy's baby has been born and that David has held her and marveled at her beauty. But she will not tell Stacey there were tears in his voice (can tears be heard?) when he spoke to her and said, "Tiny, so tiny."

18

"Do you sleep with Hal?" Alison asks Hildy this question on a February morning when an ice storm, blasting down from Canada, has caused schools to close and brought traffic to a halt. The two friends are perched on the cushioned window seat in Alison's bedroom, and they watch pellets of hail, their ovoid surfaces streaked with silver, shoot down with staccato rapidity; now and again a fierce wind delays their downward trek and sweeps them in a wild dance through the wintry sky. The ice-heavy branches of the huge oak tree that dominates the front lawn tremble and heave. A branch cracks; above the soughing of the wind, the tympanic chorus of the hail, they hear its violent splintering and watch it, weighted by its glittering burden, fall onto the snow-covered ground.

Hildy does not immediately answer her friend. The question startles and angers her, but she does not want to reveal either her anger or her surprise to Alison, who continues to stare out the window. Instead, she slips off the window seat and walks about Alison's large room. Two orange-scented candles burn side by side on the bureau. Hildy separates the flames, placing one at either side of the long, cluttered surface. She picks up a large stuffed bear and sets it down. Alison's diary is open on her desk and Hildy picks it up and reads the beginning of the last entry aloud. " 'I am alone — the rhythm of my thoughts frightens me. Why is that and why should it be?' " Hildy closes the book. "Heavy," she says. "Very heavy."

Alison does not turn. Instead she shifts position, pulls her knees up to her chin and hugs them. In her white slacks and loose white sweatshirt, her head bent so that her razor-cut fair hair tumbles about her pale face, she has the look of an ethereal wraith, at one with the wintry landscape that she observes with sad-eyed detachment.

A white silk blouse is tossed across a chair. Hildy removes the top of her magenta sweat suit and tries it on. Alison is slightly built and smaller than Hildy, but she favors oversized clothing, the loose shirts and baggy sweaters that deny her body's form and contour. The silk blouse is a perfect fit for Hildy, who buttons it to the collar (Alison wears it open, with a silk scarf at the neck) and rolls the sleeves up. She walks over to the long mirror and studies herself. She is pleased that her complexion has lost its winter pallor as a result of exposure to the bruising wind and the pale but penetrating sunlight of the ski slopes. Hildy skied every weekend in January, sometimes by herself and sometimes with Alison and Seth. (Alison, however, skied only for an hour on such excursions, and spent the rest of the day huddled in the lodge staring out at the slopes.)

Twice, Hildy took Andrea with her on day trips. Andrea is a natural on skis. Fearless and graceful, she easily mastered the bunny hill and skied the novice slope beside Hildy. She screamed with laughter when she fell, bounced up, brushed the snow off, and determinedly plunged her poles down. She repeated Hildy's instructions in her high, sweet voice, commanding her body to performance, to perfection. "Right foot forward. Slide. Left foot forward. Slide. Poles in. Poles out. Thrust and down." She plodded on with cheerful tenacity, and when at last she flew forward, swooping down the gentle incline, her shouts and laughter filled the air and caused other skiers to turn and clap. By day's end everyone on the lift knew Andrea's name.

Hildy unbuttons the top button of Alison's blouse and pulls the silken fabric tight about her breasts. Her skin shines rose-gold through the sheer material and her nipples rise like ripe berries.

"Do you like that blouse?" Alison asks. "If you like it, you can have it."

"Don't be stupid," Hildy says curtly. She removes the blouse and shrugs into her own top. "Why are you giving your things away?"

Only last week Alison gave Seth the autographed and framed poster of John Lennon that she had purchased at an auction, bidding on it with great intensity. Hildy turns and stares at her friend. Because she sees Alison every day she has not noticed how thin she has become. Now she sees the small bones that jut almost fleshlessly out of Alison's wrists, the sharp curve of her clavicle, the high cheekbones barely covered by her white, tightly drawn skin.

"Too many things weigh you down," Alison replies. "It's easier to split when you don't have too much to carry. So what's the answer? Do you sleep with Hal?"

"Don't be stupid, Alison. He's a friend of the family."

"So who says you can't sleep with a friend of the family?" Alison's laughter is brittle. The hail has turned to snow, and her laughter is not unlike the tiny flakes, wind-tossed into delicate frothing swirls. Hildy decides that if Alison's laughter were visible it would resemble the snow, weightless and crazed. "I slept with my father's best friend. My first time. He did it for me, he said. He wanted my first time to be good. Doug. That's his name. You've met him, Hildy. He worries a lot about firsts. He taught me to ride a bike and he stood by when I first took off on my own. He took me to my first opera. I wore a velvet dress and Mary Janes, and during intermission he bought me a Coke. The opera was *Carmen*, and Doug's wife, Lori, his first wife, was very nice when I had to go to the bathroom in the middle of the second act. She even waited outside the door. I'll bet if Lori was still married to him she would have waited outside the door while we were in bed together. And I slept with my mother's second husband, although I don't think you can count him as a friend of the family. I mean, when they marry into the family they sort of lose the 'friend' status, don't they — at least until the divorce?"

"Was he married to your mother when you slept with him?" Hildy asks. She is uneasy with this conversation, with Alison's revelations.

"They had already split, but he still kept stuff at the house and he came by once when she wasn't home. And it happened. But even if they were still together it wouldn't have been incestuous. He wasn't my father. Hey, you could even sleep with David, Hildy."

"Cut it out, Alison." Hildy's uneasiness is deepening into a dark anger, which she struggles to control.

"The laws of incest don't apply, Hildy," Alison continues. "Anyway, laws don't apply at all anymore. There are no rules. No guidelines. Don't you realize that?"

She slides down from the window seat and stretches her arms upward in a languid, feline gesture. She stalks the room, straightening the teddy bear that Hildy set down on its side, closing her diary, hanging the blouse in her closet. She restores order with feral determination, and her green eyes glitter like polished jade.

"Look at the city," she says, dangling a stray pink sock in one hand, searching the littered carpet for its mate. "It's a casbah, a bazaar. Sales without receipts. Roving peddlers. Three cartons make a counter, turn your back and there are no cartons, no counter. Buy a watch, walk two blocks. The watch stops ticking. Go back and the man who sold it to you isn't there, never existed. There are no guarantees, no warranties. The rules do not apply. Musicians don't need recital halls and you don't need tickets to listen to them. They play where they please. We listen as we like. Now drop a ten-dollar bill in a violin case, now walk away. You do as you please and so do they. No program. Don't be square. Programs belong to another age. Now everything is cool — easy, so easy. You want a meal, a home-cooked dinner? Pop a cardboard box into the microwave and three minutes later you've got it. Lasagna, burritos, veal marsala, meatloaf like Mama used to make in the days when there were mamas and they made meatloafs." Now Alison's laughter is loud and harsh.

She pulls open her jewelry box and dumps it onto the bureau. Pins and necklaces, bracelets and brooches, rain down in a confusion of metals, a twinkling of gemstones. Earrings skitter across the laminated surface like small bright jackstones. Alison scoops up a jade pendant, plows her fingers through the tiny hill of jewelry until she finds the earrings that match it.

"Here, take these, Hildy. You always liked these." Her voice is strident, imperious.

Hildy is frightened now. Her heart is pounding. She wonders if Alison is on anything, although she is certain that her friend has never done drugs, has never gone beyond the occasional joint. But her certainty fails her; she had, after all, not known that Alison had slept with either her mother's second husband or Doug, the friend of the family as Hal is the friend of Hildy's family — but no, that's not right, the comparison does not balance; Hal is Hildy's friend, Stacey's husband, but he is not and has never been a friend of the family. Distracted, she ignores Alison's outstretched hand.

"Stop that, Alison. I don't want your earrings, your pendant. They're yours. You can't give them away."

"Oh, you can give anything away, anything," Alison replies. "Old husbands. Boring marriages. Boring children. Or if you can't give them away you can send them away — to shrinks, to Europe, to schools in states so far away you have to change planes in Albuquerque to reach them. There's nothing in the rules that says you have to keep something because it's yours. And everything can be replaced. I can get a new pendant tomorrow. Today. Whatever we want is ours, Hildy. Anyone can have anything. New husbands. New wives. All of them slim and rich and fascinating. Read the personals in the back of *New York Magazine* — an emotional street bazaar on slick magazine paper. Like I said, no guarantees, no warranties. The new husband, the new wife, they look just as good on first sight, on first sell, as that crummy watch looked when you bought it. And there are always new children. Some of them are thrown in like a bonus with the new marriage. Or you can have your own. Didn't my Ma and Pa present me with Half Brother Number One and Half Brother Number Two — so adorable the way they run around the house hugging their anatomically correct dolls?

"Did I tell you that they're crazy about those disgusting dolls? There aren't even any rules for dolls, Hildy. Dolls shouldn't have goddamn penises and vaginas. Dolls are supposed to have little hearts under their clothes like my good old Raggedy Ann."

She plucks up the rag doll sprawled on her bed and tears its dress off. The red heart, fissured and faded, is exposed and she presses it to her cheek.

"And," she continues, her voice rising to a piercing shrillness Hildy has not heard before (always Alison speaks so softly, her words so weighted by the heaviness of her moods that they must strain to hear her), "if you don't want to have your own new set of kids, you can adopt, or, if you don't want to adopt, you can pay someone else to have a baby for you, like the woman who's always crying in front of the television cameras, 'I want my baby. I want my baby.' It's not her baby, for God's sake. She's just the baby machine, the incubator, the walking womb. She's all mixed up. She thinks she can bring the rules back, but she can't. She broke them herself. No one can bring the rules back. We've gone too far. Too far. And it won't stop snowing. Goddamn it! It won't stop snowing."

There is desperation in her voice, and she returns to the window and kneels again on the blue cushioned seat, her face pressed against the cold glass to which the snow mockingly adheres in lacy patterns. And Hildy, watching her, sees that she is weeping.

"Alison." Hildy moves toward her friend, her arms outstretched, but when she reaches the window seat she does not touch Alison, who remains curled in a defensive knot, her body rigid.

"It's all right. I don't give a damn whether you're sleeping with Hal or not. I don't even want to know. I'm sorry I asked you."

"No. I'm not sleeping with him. I talk to him a lot because we share a secret."

"I don't want to hear the secret, Hildy. Please don't tell me the secret. My mother tells me her secrets. My father tells me his secrets, slimy, stupid secrets. The shrink wanted to know my secrets. 'Whatever you're thinking,' he said in that stupid, pseudo-calm voice. What he meant was, 'Give me your weird fantasies, your wild moods, the wretched refuse of your teeming and diseased unconscious and I'll liberate you, you lucky kid.' I'm sorry, Hildy. I shouldn't be dumping this on you except that the snow, the goddamn snow won't stop." Her words pour out in a wild torrent, a stormy melding of anger and grief.

"It will stop, Alison. It will stop. Alison, Allie, did you take anything? I mean any pills or anything like that?" Hildy's voice wavers between fear and apology. She wonders if she should call Seth. No, Seth will be frightened. Alison's mother is in Florida. Her father is in the distant exurb where he lives with his new family in a solar-heated A-frame house. She thinks of calling her aunt Edith, but what will she say? *I'm here with my friend Alison and she's crying and talking funny.* But even as she mentally phrases the sentence, she rejects the idea. Alison is not really talking funny. Hildy understands and agrees with everything her friend has said. Alison is just a little wired, a little strung out. *That's all.* And the snow aggravates it. *That's all.*

"I don't need pills, Hildy," Alison says, and her voice is soft again; she is weakened, deflated, and Hildy is relieved. "I can get this way all on my own. No substance abuse necessary. Am I not remarkable?" She grins, the impish, wicked grin that Hildy recognizes with renewed and soaring affection.

"Me too," Hildy says. "Well, I'm not as talented as you are. I can't get quite as manic, but I don't do too badly."

They giggle, the rapport that binds them in friendship restored. They watch as a crow flies blackly through the snow to the oak tree where he perches on a bifurcated limb and stretches his huge wings. Splinters of crystalline ice fall in jagged frozen tears to the ground and the great black bird, triumphant, bellows mightily and flies away.

"But I want you to take the earrings and the pendant. The jade ones," Alison says. "Please. I want you to have something of mine when we're not together — when we go off to separate schools."

"Come on, Alison."

"And you give me something of yours. Okay?"

"Okay." She submits at last, fearful that Alison's voice will rise again to that dangerous shrillness.

Hildy sits down on the window seat and allows her friend to hang the pendant about her neck, to affix the tiny hanging earrings to her ears. She is relieved that Alison's touch is light and firm. Her fingers do not fumble with the clasp. She is in control. And when they turn again to the window, they see that the snow has stopped and the air is bright and clear.

"You see," Hildy says, vindicated. "I told you it would stop snowing."

"Everything stops," Alison replies, and her voice, once again, is melted down to the softness of resignation. "It's just a question of when."

"Now what do you want of mine?" Hildy asks. She looks at herself in the mirror and adjusts the pendant. Alison stands beside her and for the briefest of moments the two friends are framed in the glass, androgynous nymphs, the one dark-haired and olive-skinned, the other fair-haired, her complexion blanched to the color of snow. Then Alison turns and Hildy feels herself deserted, bereft.

"Do you want to go for a walk?" Hildy asks. "We could go over to Seth's."

"You go," Alison replies. Again, she is busy at her bureau, separating her jewelry into neat piles. "I have things to do."

"Hey, Allie, what do you want of mine?" Hildy asks. Already she has her jacket on and her red scarf is wound around her neck. She is eager now to leave this warm room with its scent of incense and sorrow. She is eager to feel the sharp, clean cold of the wind against her face, the biting crunch of fresh snow beneath her feet. Her eagerness troubles her; she sees it as a betrayal of her friend and tries now to make amends.

"Of yours?" Alison looks bewildered and then smiles, remembering their agreement. "Your mouse. The furry mouse I bought you for Christmas."

"Hey, anything but my mouse," Hildy replies jokingly. "It keeps my cheek warm when I sleep."

"I feel so cold when I sleep," Alison says. She shivers, although the room is overheated, thickly carpeted and cushioned; the bed is layered with two bright afghans piled atop a snow-white down comforter.

Hildy touches Alison's cheek. The pale skin is warm to her touch, even feverish.

"You okay, Allie?"

"Fine, fine." Alison's curt answer is a dismissal, and Hildy leaves the room.

She takes a long time putting on her boots, but Alison does not come downstairs. The cleaning lady is vacuuming in the rear of the house and the hum of the machine blends in with the music that floats down from Alison's room. Hildy recognizes Tracey Chapman's tender, exhausted voice. She does not know the song, although she is certain it deals with loss and loneliness.

She closes the door softly behind her and, standing on the sidewalk, looks up at Alison's bedroom, but all she can see is the glow of the candles still steadily burning on the bureau.

*   *   *

Nina, surrounded by cartons, sits on the floor of the empty room that will be the nursery and talks on the phone to Stacey. She hears Hildy open the front door and slam it shut. There is a thud, and then another, as Hildy tosses her boots into the high wooden box Nina keeps near the door.

"I know how you feel," Nina says soothingly, lifting her right leg up and down. "I'm feeling a little claustrophobic myself. But the snow has stopped and the schools should open tomorrow."

After two days at home, Stacey's children are bored. Fretful and irritable, they bicker and quarrel with each other, and Stacey, fretful and irritable herself, quarrels with them in turn.

"Thank God there are only the three of them," Stacey says, and Nina is grateful for her impatience, her honesty. With such statements Stacey issues a disclaimer, reinforces their agreement. She does not want another child. She cannot cope with another demanding voice, another mewling whine.

"The storm has messed us up too," Nina confides. "David had a business meeting in Boston and of course there are no flights. He hopes he'll be able to get an early shuttle tomorrow morning. And I was supposed to videotape the first two sequences of my new dance. I had the camera people and the dancers all set and we had to put it off twice. I just rescheduled for tomorrow. I don't know what I'll do if that doesn't work out. Two of my dancers are going off on a repertory gig."

"I wonder how Mandy is managing," Stacey says. She prolongs the conversation so that she will not have to deal with her children.

"She's probably writing a poem about it," Nina replies drily. She has visited Mandy twice since her return from the hospital, and each time the baby (whom Mandy mysteriously named Susan, as though seeking out a prosaic name that would not compete with the soaring language of her poetry) had fussed and whimpered while Mandy sat propped up in bed, writing in a spiral notebook. She has not spoken to Mandy recently. With Susan's birth, her interest in Mandy has diminished.

Stacey laughs. She, too, dutifully visited Mandy, carrying with her as a gift a carton of disposable diapers.

"Who knows if she'll remember to stock up on them," Stacey had said self-righteously to Nina. Nina and Stacey are mutually dubious about Mandy's maternal and domestic competence, scornful of her priorities. They stare disapprovingly at the twins' unmatched and unironed clothing, and they wonder if she has remembered to buy milk and eggs.

They have no such doubts about each other — which makes everything a great deal easier, they each secretly agree.

"Hildy just came in," Nina tells Stacey. She smiles at Hildy, who leans against the doorjamb and prods a carton questioningly with her foot. Her cheeks are flushed with the cold and her helmet of black hair is sleekly wet. "Well, take it easy, Stacey. The kids will probably go outside later and get rid of some of that energy. I'll speak to you at the end of the week. I'm going to be really tied up with that video — I hope. . . . Right. I'll tell Hildy. Bye."

"Tell me what?" Hildy asks.

"Andrea's nagging about going skiing again now that there's all this fresh snow."

"It's mostly fresh ice," Hildy replies. "I skidded all over the street on my way home from Alison's."

"How is Alison?" Nina asks cautiously. Betty Goldfein, Seth's mother, who seldom worries about anyone except herself and Seth, stopped Nina at the market the previous week to ask if she hadn't noticed that Alison was getting dangerously thin. Betty watches talk shows throughout the day. The four television sets in her large house are always on and she drifts from room to room. Serious, concerned hosts talk to bulimics and anorexics about binging and starving and vomiting. Betty has heard a large-eyed girl, a recovering anorexic (whose face is still skeletal) speak casually, almost coldly, of the various times she tried to kill herself. "I was sixteen then." "I tried that when I was seventeen." "Oh, you don't have to worry, I'm fine now, really fine." The girl had giggled, inviting the viewer to forgive, to be amused. Betty was neither forgiving nor amused. But she has acquired a certain icy sophistication, a layman's smug expertise.

"Could Alison be anorexic?" she had asked Nina, who shrugged.

"I hope not," Nina had replied. The question was valid, she knew, and she was ashamed because her first concern was not for Alison but for Hildy (moody, impressionable Hildy). She waits anxiously for Hildy's answer now.

"Alison's a little wired," Hildy replies. "The snow's getting to her. Claustrophobia or something. She's like on overload. What's in all these cartons?"

"Oh, some of your baby stuff that I saved. I thought that as long as I couldn't do anything else I'd sort through it today. The video's canceled again. No driving in this weather."

"I thought you don't do any of this stuff until the baby's born," Hildy reminds her.

"I'm not buying anything new. I'm just looking through things, picking out things that might come in handy." She flushes as she says this, as though she has been caught out in a foolish act, but Hildy is interested. She sits down beside Nina, who touches the delicate gold wire of one of the jade earrings.

"Pretty."

"Alison just gave them to me. Do you want to try them on?"

"Sure."

Hildy removes them from her ears and passes them to her mother. Then she reaches up for the hand mirror.

"Ugh," Nina says, grimacing at her reflection. "They're too long. I look like Elvira, Queen of the Night."

"No. It's your hair. Let me fix it."

Hildy rummages through her bag and takes out her own brush. She brushes Nina's hair back and fashions it into a ponytail.

Nina frowns.

"Now I look like a cheerleader."

Hildy giggles and brushes her mother's hair straight down.

"I'm Morticia," Nina says and presses her lips into a thin line, raises her eyebrows, and thrusts her hands like claws at a laughing, cringing Hildy.

"Oh, I'm scared. I'm so scared."

Hildy's mood lightens. She is swept back to the rainy afternoons of her childhood when she and her mother played dress-up, she clattering about the house in Nina's high heels and long dance skirts, Nina wearing David's suit jacket and his hat. She had forgotten how much fun her mother could be, how much fun she still is. Doesn't Hildy hear Nina and David laugh and call to each other, their voices rising and falling with mock lightness and depth, as they play their pretend games? Once she watched through the keyhole as David assailed Nina, holding the stuffed lion, roaring. And now she is back in the orbit of her mother's playfulness, giggling as Nina, still wearing her Morticia grimace, replaces the earrings in her ears.

Relaxed, pleased with themselves, they turn their attention to the contents of the cartons. Nina holds up a pink bunting, delicately crocheted and lined with white quilting. Michael Ernst's mother, now long dead, had made it, and Nina had dressed Hildy in it the day she brought her home from the hospital. The bunting, with its buttonholes so lovingly hand-finished into open-mouthed kisses of pink satin, still smells of the hypoallergenic detergent especially purchased because the infant Hildy had a mild form of eczema. Nina had forgotten that. Oh, she has forgotten so much, but her memories will be redeemed. Already she recalls those early days of mothering, when her life was governed by the touch and sound and scent of her newborn. And now, it will all happen again. She has been given a second chance, and it will all be so much better, so much easier. She was alone when Hildy was born, but this baby will be born into a family.

The three of them, she, David, and Hildy, will play with the newborn, care for her. She anticipates the silken touch of infant flesh, the bell-like toddler laughter, shared giggles on a snowy afternoon. Mother and daughters will be friends; sisters will laugh at their parents' foibles, mimic their laughter, sprawl across their bed and playfully toss the stuffed animals at each other. Nina fingers a pink satin buttonhole.

"Your grandmother made this," she tells Hildy. "Michael's mother."

Hildy touches it with probing fingers, as though the lovely geometric pattern will resolve a mystery. She had a grandmother who took discrete strands of pink wool and fashioned a tiny garment. For her. For her infant self.

"I thought we could use it to bring the baby home from the hospital," Nina adds. "What do you think?" It is Hildy's bunting, after all, and Hildy must give permission.

"The baby is going to come straight here, to us?" Hildy asks.

"Yes. Of course. I'm almost sure that's what will happen," Nina replies. She realizes that they have not discussed the actual logistics, but this, in any case, is the sequence of events in her own mind. With the birth of the baby the first act of this intricate life dance will be completed. Stacey's role, at least her role as prima performer, will be done and Nina, her arms extended to accept and cradle the newborn, will begin her own part, her own first movement in this long and loving dance of new motherhood.

Already she anticipates the sweetness of that time, imagines the infant in her arms, tiny hands against her neck. Sometimes, before drifting off to sleep she looks at David and thinks of the baby; her heart swells then with the miracle of it all. She will be mother to David's child who, even now, in thought and feeling, is her own.

Hildy rummages through a carton and pulls out a mobile. Carved wooden elephants and giraffes dangle from white wires. The wires are frayed, the wood has splintered, and the paint has faded.

"Junk," she says and tosses it aside.

But Nina rescues it. The mobile was a gift from their colleagues in the repertory company, the dancers who had spent that summer with her and Michael Ernst at Mancredi's farm. She will perhaps decide against hanging it over the new baby's crib, but she will surely keep it. Hildy does not yet understand the importance of these small talismans of the past, the tattered souvenirs, the colorful refuse, of faded friendships and abandoned affection.

The pile of discards grows. The plastic bibs are too stiff. The cord on the electric feeding dish is frayed. The exquisitely embroidered batiste dress, fashioned by the dance company dresser, is so brittle that the fabric cracks as Hildy passes it to Nina. She should not have starched it before putting it away, Nina thinks sadly.

In the end they dispose of almost everything in the cartons (although Hildy, mysteriously, plucks up a small golden duck and places it on the windowsill of the empty room).

"When will you get the furniture, the crib and all that?" she asks.

"When the baby is safely born," Nina replies. ("*And safely ours.*" The thought springs to mind unbidden and she frowns, angry at her-

self for this lingering uneasiness, this lingering mistrust, when everything has been worked out.) "What about the bunting? Shall we use
it for the new baby?"

"Oh, whatever you like," Hildy replies impatiently. "It doesn't
matter, it doesn't matter at all."

The dark mood, so slowly gathering since she sat beside Alison on
the window seat, briefly banished as she and Nina laughed and talked,
has quite suddenly reasserted itself. It is absurd, ludicrous, for them
to be crouching over a battered carton in this gapingly empty room,
pawing through all this junk from her unremembered infancy. She
shoves the carton and leaves the room, slamming the door. In her
own room she removes the earrings and the pendant, which seems
suddenly to weigh too heavily upon her. She lies down on her bed
and presses the furry mouse to her chest, falling asleep as the early
darkness of winter descends.

Although a harsh wind blew through the night, by dawn the storm
has completely subsided. David leaves the house at first light and
Nina imagines his Boston-bound plane winging northward through
the startlingly clear, bright air. It is almost as though the ice storm
has throttled the shadow of winter and replaced it with a cold radiance. She stands at the window and sees that the yard is littered
with fallen branches and that a large bough of the oak tree, beneath
which she and Stacey first sat so many months ago, has been almost
severed by the wind and now quivers dangerously, suspended by a
strip of bark. She will have to speak to the gardener about it. It is
beneath that tree that she will place a playpen, a baby carriage, an
infant swing. She has not forgotten how babies love to look up at
fluttering leaves. She smiles and moves from the window. All that
will come later.

Now she must work on her dance. Today the video will be shot
and she can study the movements. She is uneasy still about the way
the two women who play the mothers dance toward each other. Once
she has the videotape she can position and reposition the dancers.
She dresses quickly and decides that she will have Tina, her lead
dancer, move stage right and then glide off, rather than remain immobile as the others circle her in the very last sequence.

She brews coffee and calls her dancers, one after the other, to make sure they will all be at the studio on time.

"Ten sharp. It's great that the storm broke."

"Ten sharp." They repeat after her, their voices strained. They are tense; all their energy is reserved for the performance, which will be recorded and thus will forever bear testimony to their talent. Nina understands their terseness.

"Ten sharp," she tells the cameraman who is used to working with dancers, who understands their fears, their moods. "And don't forget to load backup lights. This is our last chance." She checks the lights off her list, relieved that she remembered to mention them. Only last week Bruce told her about a choreographer friend whose cameraman failed to bring them, and when the first set failed, they had to reschedule the taping. "All that time," Bruce had commiserated. "But they did get it done." Nina does not have the time to stage the dance again. She is done now (or will be soon, within weeks, when the baby is born) with the luxury of empty days, of long hours that belong exclusively to her, to her work.

She hears Hildy's door open and then the sound of Hildy's footsteps. The toast pops up and the coffee perks. Nina spreads the notation sheets on the table, studies the arrows that indicate the movements of her dancers. And then pleased, reassured, she pours herself a cup of coffee, butters a slice of toast. She hears Hildy on the staircase and pours her daughter a glass of orange juice (freshly squeezed by David in the dimness of dawn), places another slice of bread in the toaster.

"You're all dressed." Hildy is surprised.

"We're doing the video today."

"Right. Right. I forgot. David left for Boston?"

"Early. Very early. It's a beautiful day."

"They're predicting rain by mid-morning." Hildy listens to the radio from the moment she opens her eyes. Nina, who craves quiet, cannot understand why Hildy, like so many teenagers, must constantly be surrounded by blaring sound. Is she fearful of the silence of solitude? Does the sound (as Edith has knowingly suggested) create a barrier between herself and the thoughts and feelings that frighten and confuse her?

"I'm not worried about rain," Nina says. "Rain won't keep anyone away from the studio."

The phone rings. Of course. David will be calling from Boston to tell them of his arrival, to advise them of the time of his return flight. Nina hums happily and does a small plié on the way to the phone.

"Hello. Good morning."

Hildy collects her books, piling them into her green book bag. She places the furry mouse on top of them. She and Alison are both free during third period. She will give the mouse to Alison then. She does not wear the earrings, but the pendant rests against her loose yellow sweater. It occurred to her as she fastened it that the jade almost exactly matches Alison's eyes. Her math book drops to the floor and she stoops to pick it up. And so she does not see Nina's face but she hears the horror in her mother's voice.

"But that can't be," Nina protests. "How can that be? When did it happen? Oh, my God. Dear God."

It is David, Hildy thinks, and she dares not move. Something has happened to David. His plane has gone down. That sky. It is too bright. Its radiance blinded the pilot. She thinks that if she stands up she will faint, that the bilious vomit, surging now in her throat, will not be contained but will pour out in ugly, noxious torrents.

"I'll tell her," Nina says. "Yes, of course. . . . I'll tell her. Oh, I'm sorry. So sorry. . . . You'll keep us informed? . . . Yes. . . . Please. At any hour." Her voice is edged with misery. She hangs the phone up so softly that Hildy does not even hear the click.

Hildy rises then and stares at her mother. The color has drained from Nina's face. She presses her hands to her head and leans against the sink for support, and then, with a fierce, sudden movement, she turns the faucet on full blast and splashes her face with cold water.

"Mom, what is it? What is it?" Hildy asks in a desperate tight voice. She imagines David plummeting downward, trapped in that doomed plane, a scream frozen on his lips, the wind ruffling his sandy hair. *Oh, David. Oh, Daddy.* She has been such a bitch to him. Such a selfish little bitch.

"Hildy, I'm so sorry." Nina turns and faces her daughter. "It's Alison."

"Alison?" Relief floods over her. It is not David. He is safe. She breathes deeply. "What about Alison?"

"She took some pills. A lot of pills. Her mother found her in a coma when she got home this morning. That was Seth's mother on the phone. Dr. Goldfein is there now and they're waiting for an ambulance."

"Too many pills?" Hildy repeats the words questioningly, as though they belong to a language that is beyond her comprehension, to a vocabulary she has not mastered. "What kind of pills? Why?" But even as she speaks, in her mind's eye she sees Alison, her fair hair bobbed to frame her pale face, dressed in her loose white shirt, her baggy white pants, padding through her room. Hildy knows what kind of pills and she knows why Alison took them. Her friend had been a ghost yesterday, an ethereal spirit, laughing and mocking, ready to leap beyond a border, buoyed by her own hurt, her own bitterness, unrestrained because all rules had been abandoned. Taking too many pills only meant breaking another rule. Ah, Alison. Stupid, stupid Alison.

"Allie. Allie. *Allie.*" The grief-scream rips at Hildy's throat. She pounds the kitchen counter with her fists. She rocks back and forth, her teeth cutting into her upper lip, until she tastes blood on her tongue. And then, at last, her strength ebbs and she sinks onto a kitchen chair. Nina kneels beside her, takes her hands in her own, kisses first one then the other. Hildy's breath comes in strained gasps, and when she speaks her voice is a hoarse whisper.

"I should have done something, said something. I knew she was acting weird. Oh, God, I should have done something."

"Hildy, you couldn't have known. It wasn't your responsibility." Nina wets a washcloth and wipes her daughter's face; she passes the cold, damp cloth across Hildy's wrists, her neck. "Look, she may be all right. It's possible that they found her in time."

But Hildy will not be comforted. Tenaciously, she clings to her guilt, recites her litany of self-accusation.

"I thought of calling someone. I even thought that I would call Aunt Edith. Because Alison was talking so fast, so fast. But I didn't do anything. I came home. And this morning I put on her pendant." Perhaps Alison was counting out her pills, those bright little capsules that Hildy now remembers seeing on her bureau (and about which she had asked no questions) while Alison searched through her jewelry. This, too, she adds to her burden of complicity.

"Hildy, nothing you could have done would have helped Alison." Nina's voice is intense. She is furious suddenly, furious with Alison for placing this burden of self-recrimination on Hildy, for wounding them all with her misery, her anger.

"I don't know. I don't know." Hildy's voice is reduced to a barely audible whisper.

The phone rings. It is Tina calling from the studio, concerned about the sound system. One of the speakers seems weak.

"It's all right. . . . I checked it. But I have a backup just in case. . . . They're setting up the lights? . . . Good. I'll be a little late, Tina. I'm just leaving now."

"Leaving?" Hildy's voice is incredulous and Nina again kneels beside her, embraces her. Hildy remains rigid. Her friend may be dead and she sits in frozen imitation of that death. But she is crying; her long lashes are heavy with the moist weight of her grief and her cheeks are splotched red with misery.

"Hildy, you know that I have no choice. I must be at the studio today. I can't change the taping session. You know that." Her hands are trembling but she knows that there is nothing they can do for Alison. It is only a question of waiting, of uneasily straddling the seesaw of hope and despair, of staring out the window and silently gambling, using the vagaries of nature as stakes. *If that leaf falls she will die. If that shadow lengthens she will live.*

"I can't believe this. How can you think of work? Of your stupid dance?" Anger restores strength to Hildy's voice; accusation energizes her.

Nina turns away. She does not tell Hildy that on the afternoon she was told of Michael Ernst's death, she danced for three hours without a break, willing herself to exhaustion, affirming the discipline of life that battles the capriciousness of death.

The phone rings again and Hildy, angrily, defiantly, reaches for it.

"Oh, Seth," she says, and her sobs begin anew. "Can you believe it? Oh, Seth. How could she?"

Nina listens to her daughter's broken voice as she gathers the dance notation sheets and puts them into her portfolio, as she shrugs into her coat, as she skims her checkbook to make sure she has deposited enough to pay the cameraman, the sound technician (but of course she has; her own compulsion about detail irritates her). She is relieved that Hildy is talking to Seth, that Seth will surely come over and be with her. They are mutually diminished, the two of them; their shared anxiety will meld and thus, perhaps, be assuaged. They are brother and sister to each other as Alison (poor Alison) was sister to both of them. *Is* sister to both of them. Fiercely, Nina corrects herself. She is fumbling with her car keys when Hildy hangs up.

"You're really going?" she asks bitterly.

"I must. There is nothing we can do for Alison. Hildy, why don't you come with me?"

"No." Hildy retrieves the furry mouse from her book bag and presses it against her cheek. New anger brews and galvanizes her. "No one can do anything for Alison. Everyone is too damn busy chasing after their own lives. Her father with his Banana Republic jacket and his new wife, his new baby. And her mother always talking in that little-girl voice about getting in touch with her feelings. What kind of parents are they? And you — you're really leaving now. What kind of a mother are you? You want another baby? Try being a mother to me. Goddamn it! Goddamn you!" Hildy grabs her jacket and races past Nina, ignoring her mother's outstretched arm, not looking at Nina's pale, shocked face.

Her small red car is in the driveway, and Nina watches from the window as Hildy sprints into it, revs the engine so fiercely that it floods and dies, and then tries again, succeeds, and backs out in a swirl of flashing water and splintering ice.

"Hildy, Hildy!" Nina opens the window and calls her daughter's name, but her voice is lost in a gust of wind and Hildy neither slows down nor looks back.

Wearily, Nina closes the window, presses her brow against the glass. Tears streak her cheeks. With clenched fists she beats on the kitchen counter.

"No!" she shouts. "No!"

And then, wearing her winter coat, she rinses her coffee cup and wraps Hildy's uneaten toast in aluminum foil. She is worried, absurdly worried, that Hildy did not eat her breakfast, did not wear her boots. Before she leaves, she puts a light on in the living room. It is important, very important, that Hildy not return to a darkened house.

Hildy, driving through the white radiance of the winter day, is briefly sorry that she did not go to the hospital with Seth. But she could not face the wait there, the proximity of death, the hushed voices and the pale faces. Seth will call her as soon as he knows anything. And she will call the hospital.

Now she speeds down the highway, anxious to distance herself from the suburban streets, the landmarks of her friendship with Alison. She gives no thought to destination but continues to drive southward to the city. Slowly, her hand relaxes on the wheel and she regains her calm. A strange quietude settles upon her, weighted and swollen with grief. When it becomes too heavy to bear, she allows herself to weep, as though her tears will drain her sorrow of its terrible excess.

She thinks of going to see Edith, but her aunt will assess her misery with a professional eye, will analyze her distress even as she comforts her. Edith's consolation will be dredged with the practiced vocabulary of her profession; she is, after all, a confederate of those who abandon and betray. (Nina will call Edith today from her studio, Hildy knows, and tell her about Alison, about Hildy's reaction, and Edith will offer advice, comfort.) No, Hildy decides, driving faster now, she will not visit Edith.

A light rain begins as she crosses the bridge that will carry her into the city. It is the misty aftermath of the ice storm and, as though to atone for the fierce blasts of the previous day, it drifts down in a gentle veil, pattering lightly, companionably against the windshield. When she stops for a traffic light, Hildy opens the window and sticks her head out. The rain washes coolly across her face, dampens her hair. She opens her mouth and drinks of its sweet freshness. She drives on, knowing that she is going to Hal because Hal is her ally. He understands her and Seth and, yes, even Alison, perhaps because he is not unlike them. His enthusiasms soar and his moods, like theirs, darken swiftly, inexplicably. Hal, to whom she is linked in strange complicity (they are outsiders both, excluded from the pregnancy that so involves Nina, Stacey, and David), will know what he must say to her.

She parks the car three blocks from the restaurant and walks swiftly through the rain. And, because she has walked here with Alison, she feels her friend's absence (perhaps her enduring absence) and once again her tears fall. Passersby glance at the slender dark-haired girl who weeps as she hurries down the street.

Hal is at the register, seeding it with the small bills that will be needed for change once the lunch hour begins. He is impatient with this task and curses softly when he loses count.

"Hal." Hildy stands before him, soaked and shivering, rain and teardrops streaking her face.

"Hildy, what is it? What the hell is it?"

And, when she does not answer, he slams the register drawer shut, the bills still uncounted, and leads her into his office, locking the door behind him.

"You're soaking wet. Jesus, you're soaking wet."

He opens the closet and takes out the bath towel he keeps there for emergencies. Gently, patiently, he undresses Hildy, removing the denim jacket, sliding her jeans down.

"Arms up," he says (as he instructs Andrea when he undresses her for her bath, his voice tender, authoritative), and obediently Hildy lifts her arms and he takes off her yellow sweater.

"Sit down."

She perches on the cracked plastic couch and he unlaces her wet sneakers and removes them, peels off her yellow anklets, her flowered bikini underpants. Naked she stands and he wipes her dry, moving the towel vigorously across her body, rubbing her high breasts, her long, slender legs, the triangular black curling hair that covers her pubis, her back. He thinks of how, only last night, he had come upon Stacey naked, fresh from the shower; droplets of water glinted on the immensity of her pregnancy. Her skin was pulled tight over her huge weight, and he had felt awed and frightened because in these last stages of her pregnancy he does not recognize his wife's body; it is alien terrain and he averts his eyes, conceals his protest, his revulsion.

But Hildy, as she stands before him, submitting to his touch, his command, is so beautiful, so perfectly formed. Her skin is smooth as a child's beneath his touch.

"Sit down."

Exhausted and grateful, she obeys him.

He wipes her feet, her ankles, her shoulders, the sleek dark wet helmet of her hair.

"What happened?" he asks as he wraps the towel around her.

"Alison." Her friend's name breaks into syllables of sorrow in her mouth. It emerges as a distorted croak, a hoarse broken cry. It evokes his sympathy, smothers his desire. "She took pills. Too many pills. She's in a coma. They think she may die."

"Shit," he mutters. "Oh, shit. You poor kid, you Hildy, you."

Gently, he strokes her hair, her back, as though the rhythm itself will comfort her, soothe her.

He lowers her onto the couch, and seeing that she shivers still, he finds the old army blanket that Herb Green keeps behind the couch and covers her with it.

"Cold," she says, and he adds his own overcoat, wraps her pale feet in his scarf.

She closes her eyes. She feels herself understood, protected. *You poor kid, you Hildy, you.* Hal perceives the enormity of her grief, understands her fear. She wants to thank him but she knows there is no need. He moves quietly about the room, gathering up her wet clothing, which he drapes across the radiator. The garments emit clouds of steam. Within an hour, perhaps two hours, they will be dry.

"Poor kids. Poor kids," he mutters. He thinks of how they ordered spaghetti, the three of them, on Christmas Eve, and how they laughed and too quickly drank the red wine he ordered for them. And he remembers how fair-haired Alison, in her Dutch-boy bob, spoke so softly with such bitter precision.

"It's not fair," he says aloud (it is his frequent plaint, the protest he has made since boyhood), but Hildy does not hear him. She is in a deep sleep, motionless beneath the layer of blanket and overcoat; a foamy necklace of saliva drips down a corner of her mouth and Hal wipes it off with his handkerchief.

He leaves the office and returns to the register where, with fierce anger, he breaks open the rolls of coins and scatters them noisily into the separate metal compartments. Hours later, when the luncheon rush is long over, Hildy, wearing the dried and wrinkled clothing, her face pale but calm, emerges from the office. She approaches Hal, who sits at the bar working on the dinner menus.

"Thank you," she says gravely.

"Hey," he replies and waves his hand in dismissal of her gratitude, of his own actions. "You okay now?"

"Sort of."

"Sort of is okay. Do you want to call home?"

"I'll call Seth later."

She kisses him lightly on the cheek and leaves. The rain has stopped and the street is bathed again in that radiant white light. Slowly, like a recovering invalid whose strength must be rationed, Hildy walks to her car and slowly, slowly, drives home.

Nina sits in the darkened living room, her hands clasped in her lap. She looks up when Hildy enters. Her eyes are red-rimmed. The tears she had held back throughout the long day of harsh lights, whirling music, and her own voice shouting clipped directions to the dancers spilled out when she reached home. At each break she had called the hospital and then Seth's mother. "No news. . . . Still too early to be certain either way." No, Betty did not know where Hildy was. Nina called her own home, where the phone rang and rang. Her dancers moved to her directions and even as she corrected movements, thoughts of Hildy shadowed her mind. Always, she thought, driving home at last, mothers live suspended between two worlds — their own and the penumbral existences of their children. Always a mother steals down all the paths of her children's life, grieved because she cannot follow closer, because she cannot follow at all. She thought of the daunting vulnerability of all children, of Hildy and Alison and Seth, of golden-haired Andrea and needy, aggressive Samantha, and Jared who cries too easily. She thought of the unborn child who will be her own, whom she will nurture and shield, for whom she will stand anxiously beside silent phones and peer despairingly down empty roads. She will weep for that child one day as she weeps for Hildy now.

"Mom, you're crying." There is a new gentleness in Hildy's voice.

"Hildy, I was so worried, so frightened. But listen, the news is good. Seth just called. Alison is going to be all right."

"Oh, Mom. Oh, Mom." Relief swells Hildy's voice. She kneels beside Nina. "I didn't mean what I said. You're a good mother. Such a good mother. I'm sorry." Again her tears come and with them again a shivering and a shuddering. She gulps her sobs as she did when she was a small girl, and Nina leans forward, puts her arms around her, and rocks her gently, gently. Their faces touch and their tears mingle. They are, both of them, atremble with exhaustion.

19

Early signs of spring take Stacey by surprise. During the first week of March a vaporous warmth suffuses the afternoon air and the children arrive home from school with their jackets unzipped, their mittens trailing out of their pockets. Men and women pause as they walk down the street and lift their faces skyward, smiling as slats of sunlight shine upon their brows. Stacey, impatient with the heaviness of her body (and wearied by it after all these months, although she does not admit this), is strangely irritable. The child within her is possessed of a vigorous energy and writhes and turns during the long nights. Stacey sleeps badly and yet she delights in the fetal activity, in the force and strength exerted. She reads, in a medical magazine in Arnold's office, of a theory put forth by an neonatologist that children who were extraordinarily active *in utero* are more creative, more intelligent. And so Stacey feels an irrational pride and she places her hands on her abdomen and speaks softly. *Calm down. Quiet now. Shh.* Still, the annoyance born of fatigue persists.

But the new warmth soothes her, lightens her mood. On a morning when the children are in school, Stacey wanders outside, still wearing her faded yellow nightgown, Hal's old winter coat tossed over her shoulders. She walks across the tiny patch of grass in the rear, stooping laboriously to pick up a plastic bread bag, dirt-streaked and leaf-encrusted. In the beginning, when they first moved into this small frame house, while they were still pretending it was what the real estate agent called their "starter" house (surely they would move on to a large, wide-windowed home set between a broad lawn and a

grassy yard), they had referred to this area as their backyard. Hal had
bought an aluminum swing and slide set, which rusted and fell apart
before Jared's birth. He also began to build a patio, placing misshapen bricks (given to him by a contractor who frequented the trendy
suburban restaurant where he then worked) on the balding earth,
which he had seeded with grass without bothering to clear it of weeds.
Stacey planted bulbs along the single brick edge that Hal had managed to finish. Tulips and crocuses, daffodils and narcissi, irises and
hyacinths. She had read each box of bulbs carefully, delighting in
the names of the flowers, in the stories behind the names. In the
darkness of the night, she told Hal that the hyacinth was named for
Hyacinthus, a Greek youth beloved by Apollo; in the brightness of
the morning, she told small Andrea the story of Narcissus. It is such
knowledge that Stacey treasured and treasures still. Cathy and Audrey, her sisters-in-law, had mocked her efforts. The earth was too
dry. There was too little sun. The bulbs, which she had bought very
cheaply, were surely deficient.

They had not been wrong. Most of the bulbs had never blos-
somed, and Hal never finished building the patio. Too much effort,
he said, just to get a paved square that would barely accommodate
two chairs. And besides, the ground was too damn hard and rejected
the concrete mix. And besides, why would they want to sit in the
yard and listen to their stupid neighbors quarrel? And besides, they
weren't going to live in the house long enough even to make it
worth their while.

Stacey had not argued. She had, even then, learned that much.
When Hal's swift enthusiasms wane, she does not try to resuscitate
them.

Still, through the years, Stacey watched the bulbs that did blossom. Occasionally, she plucked the blossoms and set them on her
kitchen table in the blue ceramic vase she made in a pottery class.
Now and again, with sly malice, she has gathered the golden-hearted
white narcissi (which flowered in some abundance) into a bouquet
and presented it to either Cathy or Audrey. "You see," she told her
sisters-in-law, "they bloomed after all, even though I hardly watered
them."

Now, she stares down and sees that the unseasonable, early warmth has deceived the crocuses, and a few small green shoots courageously but prematurely thrust their way through the crumbling, winter-scarred earth. She can even see the shy, yellow beginnings of a blossom.

She steps out of her slippers but the earth is very cold beneath her bare feet, and she feels herself betrayed. She kneels and presses a finger to the tiny nascent flower. It strikes her that she will not be here next year to watch the crocus begin its journey into the light of spring. She sighs and stands, breathing heavily with the effort. She would have wanted to clear the earth around the bulbs but, of course, she cannot. Each movement is an effort. She is a powerless hostage to her pregnancy. Still, she comforts herself with silent promises. In California, she will plant a wonderful garden. Flowers and vegetables. Strawberries and blueberries and even grapes, the vines artfully draping a trellis. She and Andrea will wander together through the sun-splattered greenery, baskets in their hands, reaching up to pluck a peach, a plum, a white cherry. Already horticulture texts from the public library are strewn across Stacey's bedside table. *California Plant Life. Your Garden on the Pacific.* On nights when she cannot sleep, she props a text open on her stomach and studies the beautifully colored plates — the photographs of succulent plants and brightly colored flowers that bloom in the enchanted land that will be her home. *In the happily ever after.*

Stacey takes Andrea with her that afternoon when she visits Arnold Roth for her regular appointment. Now, at the end of this last trimester, Arnold sees her more frequently and his examinations are less cursory. On each visit, he presses his stethoscope against her abdomen, shifting the cold steel across the pale, huge swelling until at last he is satisfied.

"Ah," he says, and his lips curl into a thin, pleased smile.

He listens to the heartbeat of his brother's child, his expression absorbed, as though it is wonderful music that he hears. He passes his competent hands gently, oh, so gently, across that mountainous protuberance of her pregnancy. She has, since her eighth month, experienced the sharp contractions that he has explained to her are called Braxton-Hicks contractions. They are, he has told her, not significant of difficulty, but as they grow more frequent, he is more attentive. Such a contraction forms beneath his touch and he traces it; carefully, he palpates the area. She sighs beneath the pressure of his touch, frightened by his silence, the seriousness of his expression.

"Oh, you're fine, just fine," he says at last, sensing her anxiety. "I wish all my patients were like you, Stacey."

Like a pupil who has been praised by a revered teacher, she blushes at his words and smiles with shy pride.

"How are the children?" he askes after she has dressed and joined him in his office.

"Fine. Terrific. I have Andrea with me. It's such a beautiful day. So springy. I thought we'd do something out of doors."

"Don't let the weather fool you, Stacey. It's still winter. The first weeks of March are teasers."

"Oh, I didn't mean to go into the country or anything like that. I just thought we'd go somewhere where we can walk, maybe up to the Cloisters."

"You ought to be taking it easy."

"But I'm fine." She laughs flirtatiously. "You just said I was fine."

"You are," he assures her gravely. "But you are also in your ninth month." He glances down at her feet. Despite her great weight, she still wears her high-heeled pumps.

He walks her out to the waiting room where Andrea is perched on an overstuffed armchair. The golden-haired little girl, her plaid coat unbuttoned, is looking at *Gardens,* the magazine sent to Arnold by the New York Botanic Gardens. Her attention is focused now on a beautiful color photograph of the Madonna lily, whose white, heart-shaped petals cup together, forming a womb about the fragile golden pistils.

"Let's plant a flower like this in our garden in California, Mama," Andrea says.

"Fine," Stacey agrees good-naturedly. "Whatever you say, doll."

Arnold helps her on with her black cape.

"Take care. Don't overdo it," he cautions her.

"My mother's always careful," Andrea assures him. "And I help her. Dr. Roth, can I tear this picture out of the magazine?"

He nods assent.

"Gee, thanks." Her face blossoms into a smile. Carefully, she rips the picture out and places it in her pocket, handing the magazine to Stacey. "We'll have a nice garden in California. We're moving there."

"When?" he asks. How much do Stacey's children know? he wonders. How much will she tell them?

"In the happily ever after." She giggles. He smiles in return and shakes hands with Stacey.

A young woman, his next patient, stares at them and turns away. This is, Arnold recalls, her second visit. She was referred to Arnold by another obstetrician because she is experiencing difficulty in conceiving. Her face is pale, pinched. Stacey's pregnancy, Stacey's full laughter and unstudied poise, her small golden-haired daughter, must be taunt and temptation to her.

Stacey waves to Arnold, and as she passes the young woman, she pauses before her and says gravely, "I wish you luck."

"Thank you," the young woman says, pleased and embarrassed, caught unaware. And then, surprising herself (but not Stacey), she reaches out and touches the great rise of Stacey's pregnancy.

Stacey and Andrea do not go to the Cloisters because Stacey suddenly remembers that the exhibits there include crypts and dramatically carved sarcophagi and that doleful madonnas are positioned in shadowed archways. She does not want to spend this sunlit day walking with her small daughter through corridors where death is on display.

Instead, they take the subway to the Botanic Gardens where they walk along narrow paths lined with hedges already hung with tender fingers of green leafage. Here, too, in the South Garden, crocuses have tentatively begun to blossom; row upon row of tiny shoots, single petals hinting at the color of the full flower, press their way up through the dark earth. The sight of such burgeoning pleases Stacey, fills her with optimism. All about them life is bursting into being; the sun shines golden, her daughter walks beside her, David's child grows and moves within her. She is pleased with herself. This is a wonderful thing she has done (is doing) for herself, for David and Nina, for her family. Now, she no longer feels weighted but buoyed. She is proud of her girth, proud of this wondrous and adventurous pregnancy, of this child she will bear who will be, always and forever, of her flesh.

"Do they have this lily in the greenhouse?" Andrea asks, tugging at her mother's hand, sensing that Stacey's attention, her thoughts, have fled from her.

"We'll see," Stacey promises. "We'll see. Oh, Andrea, it's almost spring."

"But it's still winter. And I'll still get to ski some more. Up and down. Whoosh! Whoosh!"

And Andrea drops Stacey's hand and scampers up a gentle hill. When she reaches its crest, she falls to her side and rolls down, tumbling over and over amid the dank detritus of winter, her nostrils filled with the sweet scent of the warm and waiting earth.

Stacey sits on a bench and watches her daughter. Her hands instinctively rest on her abdomen and the baby moves suddenly, violently, as though in response to the lightness of her touch.

"Oh, gentle down," Stacey says, smiling.

Always, during pregnancies, she has spoken aloud to the child within her womb. Always she has imagined the babies curled and cushioned within her, as tiny companions who rely on her for life as she relies on them for purpose.

"See Andrea," she says softly now to the unborn child. "Listen to Andrea laughing."

And Andrea is still laughing when she returns to her mother. Small twigs are threaded in her hair and a clod of soil clings to the sleeve of her coat. Stacy removes the twigs and brushes the coat. Hand in hand they walk to a greenhouse where they drink watery orange juice and eat giant Pepperidge Farm chocolate chip cookies. There is no Madonna lily in this greenhouse, but they walk through tropical foliage and pause more than once to stare up through the mist-heavy air at the fronds of slender palm trees.

In the gift shop Stacey buys Andrea a crocus. It will be pink when it blossoms, the legend on the pot advises them.

"For my bedroom in California," Andrea says happily. "It will match the quilt."

The pink satin comforter that Hal bought her for Christmas is on

Andrea's bed, and each morning she carefully covers it with a sheet of thin plastic salvaged from the dry cleaning. Andrea is a careful child. She knows how to preserve the props that give substance to her dreams.

20

The warm spell vanishes as swiftly and mysteriously as it appeared. Once again the tenacious clutch of winter asserts itself and hoarfrost dangles from thin and barren branches. There is a week of nocturnal snowfalls; tiny pallid flakes fall through the night and by morning a layer of gray slush covers the ground. The cold dampness is pervasive. Wearied by winter, mocked by those few days of deceitful warmth, pedestrians walk with their heads down; they kick with booted feet at small clusters of ice afloat on sodden pathways. Motorists drive too swiftly and too close to the curb, indifferent to the splashing caused by their whirring wheels.

Children barely glance at the hills, thinly sheeted with ash-colored rime. The seasons have betrayed them. They suffer the gray cold without the compensating joy of thick white snow on which to sleigh or ski, out of which they might build squat figures or fashion forts. Andrea waxes her skis and replaces them in the front closet because Evan has reminded her that last year there had been a snowstorm as late as the first week in April.

"Do you think we'll get to ski again this year?" she asks Hildy, who stops by to bring Stacey a book from Nina.

"Maybe," Hildy says. She feels a twinge of guilt because she has been so preoccupied with Alison that she has neglected Andrea. "Listen, if there's a real snow I'll take you on another day trip."

Hildy and Seth drive north one afternoon to visit Alison in the small sanatorium to which she has been transferred. She is fine, her mother has assured them. Just fine. Her doctors think it will be good for her to see her friends.

The sanatorium is located at a distance from the main highway and is so discreetly designed that it has the appearance of a large and comfortable Tudor mansion. Here, in this northern exurb, the snow is still white and hard; a snowman stands sentinel in a large garden. They ring the doorbell and a cheerful woman in a sensible gray dress and a rose-colored cardigan welcomes them, beaming, as though she is a grandmother delighted that her granddaughter's friends have come to visit.

They enter a large living room where the decorator has clearly striven for hominess. A log fire blazes in the brick fireplace. A thick Oriental rug covers the polished floor, and the comfortable easy chairs and sofas are covered with worn but determinedly cheerful chintz. Golden drapes hang at the French windows that overlook a lawn. A snow fort is under construction. Hildy and Seth stare out at young people in brightly colored jackets, their woolen scarves sailing in the wind, who pass each other blocks of ice.

"Patients or staff?" Seth wonders aloud.

"Both, probably," Hildy replies.

Edith has told her that this sanatorium is noted for its wonderful relationships between patients and professionals, its caring, informal atmosphere.

"Just what Alison needs," Edith had added, and although Hildy disagreed, she did not argue with her aunt. Alison cannot have what she needs. She cannot have a mother and father who sit down to dinner with her and speak to her and listen to her. She cannot live again in a world where the rules are in force. These are new times. *The Waltons* and *Little House on the Prairie* have disappeared from the screen and there are no longer reruns of *The Brady Bunch* and *Eight Is Enough.* Hildy and Seth watched television hour after hour while Alison was in the hospital. They shared joints and watched divorced Kate and divorced Allie wisecrack with their children. They watched Tony Danza deliver rough but wise child care to the offspring of a working mother. They watched *My Two Dads* cope with an adolescent girl.

"The sitcom imitates life," Seth had said. "Mothers and fathers are out. Families are finished."

"Oh, they survive here and there," Hildy had protested. "What about *Cosby?*"

"And what about *Dallas?*" he had rejoined, and they had both laughed bitterly, harshly.

Waiting for Alison now, in this room that has no television set, Hildy flips through the magazines on the coffee table. She finds one of the many in-depth pieces written about the surrogate mother who reneged on her contract and sued to reclaim the child. A judge has decided in favor of the father, but interest in the case has not decreased and Hildy wonders about that. She understands her own interest, her own involvement, but why is the story still front-page news? Why is the case so obsessively discussed? This baby, conceived according to contract, whose fate has been so publicly argued and then so publicly decided, has touched a universal nerve. Opinions overflow, arguments abound. Everyone involved in the case has advocates and enemies, and everyone's heart turns when the child (who is extraordinarily beautiful and always, always smiling) is photographed as she is carried from one set of parents to the other. The article Hildy reads now explores the reactions of children to the concept of surrogate motherhood, and Hildy is so absorbed in it that she does not hear Alison enter the room, is not aware of her presence until her friend stands beside her.

"Hey, what are you reading?" Alison asks, and Hildy and Seth glance at each other. They are startled at how calm she seems (although perhaps she is sedated), how together. She embraces each of them. Alison seems to have actually gained weight and there is color in her cheeks. (Does she too scamper around and build snowmen and snow forts? Hildy wonders.) She wears a bright-blue sweater and jeans. The sweater is new. Alison's mother must have bought it — or perhaps her father's wife. It does not matter. Hildy is glad that someone who cares about her friend bought her the sweater and that Alison cares enough to wear it. She is glad, so glad, that Alison is not wearing a bathrobe tied too loosely at the waist and that her fair hair is clean and shining.

"Nothing. Some crappy article." She flips the magazine shut.

"So how you doing, Allie?" Seth asks.

"So I'm better than I was, you could say," Alison replies. "Sorry you guys had to drag up here."

"Yeah. Pretty damn inconsiderate of you, what with winter and all. The roads are a mess and there's a snow alert," Hildy says flippantly, and her laugh sounds artificial and brittle to her own ears. "Hey, I like your sweater." For a split second she is fearful that Alison will offer it to her, but Alison smiles and touches the soft wool.

"My mother brought it up. Listen, you guys. Don't be so scared. I'm okay. I'm not going to try anything like that again."

"No?" Hildy asks seriously.

"No." Alison's answer is equally grave. "I was on uppers. The first time ever. Someone at school gave them to me. The pills and the snow and the empty house got to me. And there was other stuff. I was going too fast and then everything slowed down. I was high and then I crashed. But you want to know something funny? When I woke up in that hospital I felt so calm, so peaceful. As though I was just being born and everything was all right and nothing bad had happened yet. No fighting and yelling. No slamming doors and lawyers and people whose voices I don't recognize calling the house at funny hours. My mom and dad were both there, and you know how these hospital beds have high bars, like cribs sort of? Well, I was lying there and they were standing on either side and I felt like a baby in a crib, like I was real little and they were there to take care of me and make sure that everything would be all right. And just as I was thinking that, they said together, 'Everything is going to be all right, Allie.' And I smiled. I remember how it felt to smile, to feel — well, not happy, but okay. Hopeful maybe. Hopeful that they were right. That everything will be all right."

"I think so," Hildy says. "I think everything will be all right." Her tone is urgent and Seth stares at her in surprise.

"No. It won't. It can't be. But I'll manage. I'll learn how to manage." Her voice is very sad and very quiet. Hildy is moved by the way her friend balances herself so cautiously on the thin edge of courage. "This place is good, I think. Too casual, maybe, if you know what I mean. Very big on first-name stuff. My doctor is Paul. The floor nurse wears jeans and rugby shirts and her name is Karen. But they care."

"Yeah. Well, that's terrific. We brought you some stuff." Seth holds out the shopping bag into which they have crammed the peanut brittle Alison loves (Nina drove to a neighboring town to buy it), the new *Rolling Stone*, a collection of Henry James stories (all three of them are partial to James because he is so reassuring in his emotional coolness), a small Garfield, and Hildy's furry mouse.

Alison examines everything gravely, carefully, and she takes the furry mouse and presses it to her face.

"To keep your cheek warm, like I said," Hildy reminds her.

"I remember."

They sit quietly because they are afraid to speak; they are wary of shattering the fragile peace of the moment. Hildy notices that Alison's eyes are very bright and she wonders if her friend is on tranquilizers. But of course she is; her speech and demeanor reveal it.

The front door opens and the young people who have been building the snow fort burst in. They are talking and laughing, their faces glowing, their hair wind-tossed. The room takes on the ambience of a common room in a college dormitory. A tall, smiling woman enters carrying a tray laden with mugs of hot chocolate. Hildy and Seth each take one but Alison asks for tea and Hildy sees this small request as positive, a sign that Alison is asserting herself, articulating her own preference. And then as they sit there so comfortably, holding their mugs, the fire at their backs, a pretty redheaded girl begins to cry. At first Hildy sees only her tears, but then her shoulders tremble and her mouth opens and closes in rhythmic pleas of misery.

"Oh, no," she says. "Oh, no. Oh, please no."

Hildy and Seth glance nervously at each other, and the tall woman, no longer smiling, hurries over. Gently, she puts her arm around the girl and slowly they leave the room. The woman speaks very softly to the girl but they hear her quite clearly.

"Everything will be all right," she says soothingly. "Everything will be all right."

Alison touches Hildy's hand and they both turn their gaze to the

window. Snow has begun to fall. The flakes are large and their descent is rapid. It is, they all know, a snow that will stick.

"You'd better go," Alison says. "You don't want to get snowbound
at this funny farm."

"Oh, I don't know. It's just beginning to get interesting," Seth
replies lazily, and they giggle in unison and then break into wild
laughter. They are seized by the nervous, contagious hilarity peculiar
to their friendship. Their laughter gathers momentum and they gasp
for words, for breath. The others in the room turn to look quizzically
at them and then avert their gazes as though fearful of intruding on
such insular hysteria. They are laughing still when Alison kisses them
each good-bye.

Hildy and Seth grow calm only when they leave the grounds of
the sanatorium and begin the drive southward. Thick white petals of
snow careen through the silver-streaked evening light. Seth drives
slowly, carefully, and keeps the windshield wipers moving at maxi-
mum speed.

"They didn't predict snow," he says like an aggrieved child.

"Can they predict anything?" she asks, and their laughter, newly
harsh, fills the car.

They are on familiar territory now, locked in tight alliance against
those who speak with the voice of authority and then betray that
authority by being fallible. They have been deceived. The adult world
is unreliable. Parents and teachers, adult friends, have proven themselves inconstant, unreliable, when measured against the barometer
of adolescence. Seth's mother wanders through her large and beautiful house, listening first to one weather forecaster and then to another, but their predictions vary and the snow falls without warning.

Hildy leans back. The drifting flakes, the movement of the cars,
the flashing taillights lull her into a dreamy drowsiness. She thinks
of Alison, waking in that criblike bed, turning to see her father on
one side, her mother on the other. She imagines the new baby lying
in a crib, Nina and David leaning over one side, Stacey and Hal
smiling on the other side. "Everything will be all right," they will
say in unison. The infant will be doubly protected, doubly vulnerable.

"No school tomorrow," Seth says.

"Probably not."

It is a matter of indifference to them. They are graduating seniors, poised at the edge of a new life. They do as they please. The rules, such as they are, do not apply to them.

2 I

It is dawn when the snow stops at last. Stacey wakens to the muffled metallic exertion of the municipal snowplow laboring down their street. Hal is dressing, moving with swift excitement through the half-darkness. She glances at the clock. It is not yet seven. Hal seldom leaves the house so early.

"I have a meeting," he explains before she can ask. "A friend of Andy Kardin's, he's a lawyer out on the Coast, is in town. Andy wants me to meet him. He has real know-how on financing houses, businesses out there. I'm giving them breakfast at Ramon's."

"But Herb may be there." Stacey knows that Herb Green is growing impatient with Hal's excesses, with his cavalier style of management. Like many irresponsible men, Herb is impatient with the irresponsibility of others. When Stacey stopped at Ramon's some weeks earlier, Hal was out and Herb had said, "Oh, that husband of yours — now he's here and now he isn't." Herb had laughed, but Stacey had seen the anger in his eyes.

"What do I care?" The gamble excites Hal. He does not mind seeing how far he can push Herb. Besides, this meeting marks a new stage in their plans. They are advancing steadily (he and Stacey, his wonderful Stacey) toward a real move, a new start, toward the life that should be theirs. The napkins and menus, the decorating ideas and recipes that he has been collecting for the Unicorn are toys. Today, he and Andrew and Andrew's friend, the savvy West Coast lawyer, will meet; they will spread papers across the table and study them, searching out angles, deals. Today he will enter the adult world of mortgages and contracts and deeds. He does not want Stacey to shadow the brightness of his anticipation with her doubts, her warnings.

"Go back to sleep, Stace. School's closed. I listened to the radio."

He knows that Stacey did not sleep well. The baby has shifted position and bears down close to her bladder so that she must rise several times during the night to urinate. She twists and turns, struggling to find a comfortable position. Hal is vaguely conscious of this, although he himself is a heavy sleeper.

"Okay," she says sleepily. "But you'll be careful, Hal?"

"Goddamn it. I'm always careful." He raises his voice, angry now. He hates being nagged. He slams a drawer shut and an awkwardly balanced book (Why does Stacey leave her damn books on every surface? he wonders) falls from the bureau to the floor.

"Daddy," Andrea calls to him from her bedroom. Her voice is frightened. He remembers how Andrea trembles when he and Stacey argue and he hurries into his daughter's room.

"Hey, go to sleep, Princess. It's a snow day. No school." He pulls the pink comforter up to cover her shoulders. Her curls spill out like filaments of sunlight across the white embroidered border.

"Can I go skiing later?" she asks.

"Maybe."

"Don't fight with Mommy."

"Hey, who's fighting with Mommy?"

He kisses her cheek, but Andrea is asleep again, her lips curled into a smile. He wonders if she is dreaming of California, of the redwood house in which she will have a bedroom decorated in shades of pink; or perhaps she dreams of skiing down a snow-covered slope. Andrea skis like a natural, Hildy has told him, and he smiled to think that his small daughter should be so graceful, so skilled and unafraid. In California he will take her to the Sierra Nevada mountains, and later, with her cheeks still wind-reddened, her eyes blinking against the brightness of the snow, he will drive her down to the ocean and they will swim. His heart pounds. Oh, they are moving so swiftly toward magic times.

He closes the door very softly when he leaves the house, and on the train he thinks regretfully that he should have returned to the

bedroom and kissed Stacey good-bye. Oh, well, he will make it up
to her.

Stacey stirs into wakefulness only when the children, quarreling over
the choice of channels, turn the television volume too high. No
school, she remembers gratefully. She does not have to prepare
lunches, see to the children's clothing, search for missing boots, vagrant mittens. Still in her nightgown, she pads into the kitchen,
gives them breakfast. Jared plays with his cereal and small puddles of
milk form white islands on the table.

"Jared, you're a slob," Andrea says righteously, but Stacey does
not even wipe the table. She is so tired. She will fall asleep on her
feet if she stays up any longer. Her fatigue is so profound that it
frightens her. She must have this baby soon. Its presence within her
is overwhelming; it presses against her rib cage, rolls about in her
womb, absorbs all her energy.

"Can we go out, Mom?" Evan asks.

"You'll be careful? You'll take care of Jared?" she asks wearily.

"We're always careful." Andrea is proud. She has begun to go to
the store by herself to purchase milk, bread.

"I know. I know. Be good then. Leave the door open and button
Jared's snowsuit all the way." There are other warnings she should
issue, she knows, but fatigue has obscured them. She shuffles back
to bed, finds a comfortable position lying on her side, and falls asleep
almost at once, leaving the door open. The children, still at the
kitchen table, listen to the heavy rhythmic sound of her breathing.

"Hey, Andrea, let's go over to the schoolyard. We're going to
build a giant fort. It's the last snow of the winter. That's what the
guy on television said." Evan is already searching through the closet
for his snowsuit. He finds Jared's green one-piece suit and Andrea's
bright red jacket. His own navy-blue suit is at the very bottom of
the pile.

"No. I don't want to go to the schoolyard," Andrea says. She does
not want to join in the snowball fights or the frenzied efforts to build
snowmen, snow forts. She wants to be alone in this clean white
world. She wants to ski down a snowy slope with the wind fresh and
cold against her face. "I want to practice on my skis."

"If I watch Jared this morning, will you stay home with him in the afternoon?"

"Yes." It is a better bargain than she had hoped for, and in gratitude she helps Jared into his snowsuit and zips it up so authoritatively that a seam of skin is caught in the teeth of the zipper. She loosens it quickly when he cries and kisses the tiny bruise it has left.

"Don't cry, Jared. You'll wake Mama."

"Will Mom be all right alone?" Evan asks her. "I think she'll be okay."

"Oh, she'll be fine." Gently, knowingly, they reassure each other, absolve each other of responsibility. They reproduce the ritual exchange between Stacey and her brothers.

"Will Mom be all right?"

"Oh, she'll be fine."

Of course, their grandmother Carmody has never been all right, has never been fine. Always she has been a pale wraith, peering through the window, moving like a blind woman through family gatherings, holiday celebrations. They flinch from her kiss (so dry with indifference), from the touch of her hands. But their own mother is different. She will be fine, of course she will. Still, they repeat the words to each other.

The boys leave and Andrea pulls on her heavy blue ski pants, her bright-red jacket, the white hat and scarf her aunt Cathy made her for Christmas. She finds the matching white mittens in the pocket of Stacey's black cape.

She thinks of calling Hildy but dismisses the idea. Even if Hildy wanted to take her to the state park where they have skied before, it would take too much time to get there, and besides, Andrea wants to ski alone today. She wants to tell herself stories as she mounts the hill. "Once there was a beautiful girl who lived with her mother, the queen, and her father, the king, in a beautiful palace in California. Of course, this made the girl a princess. She had beautiful golden hair just like her mother . . ." The story stops here but Andrea smiles. It will grow. She can feel it stretching in her mind, growing, the way the baby grows in Stacey's stomach. She *is* like her mother. She is pregnant with her story. The thought amuses her and she giggles.

She takes her skis from the closet. She is ready to leave. Still, she tiptoes down the hall and stands outside her parents' bedroom door. She hears her mother's heavy, sleep-thick breathing.

And then Andrea takes her skis, loops the poles over her shoulder (as Hildy has taught her), and leaves the house, closing the door behind her very softly. This is a day when the snow has cushioned all sound and Andrea is careful to preserve the white silence. Outside the house, she carefully straps on the skis and propels herself down the street, leaning heavily on her poles. Her hands grow cold and she pulls on her mittens.

There are very few cars on the street. A station wagon proceeds at a crawl and moves to the left to give Andrea more room. She lifts her poles in regal acknowledgment and continues on. The ski poles are her magic scepters, her secret source of power. She plunges them into a snowbank tossed up by a plow and is pleased to see the design they make. She is an ice princess and the poles are her powerful weapons. She slides down the small incline at the end of the street and the small burst of speed thrills her.

"I can ski anywhere!" she shouts. "I can ski everywhere. I can ski to California!"

Two women, bundled into heavy coats, their scarves drawn up to their chins, glance at her and smile.

At the foot of Schoolhouse Hill Andrea removes her skis and slowly begins to climb. She avoids the children who slide down the hill, sprawled across their red and yellow plastic saucers or perched on wooden sleds. Screams of delight edged with fear fill the air, and the soft, loose snow flies into their bright faces.

At the crest of the hill she straps her skis on again and ties the white scarf tight. The snow-covered hill, worn smooth by the sleds and saucers, glitters brilliantly. By unspoken rule, neighborhood cars avoid it on snowy days. It is the domain of the children who rule it with boisterous autonomy.

"Turns!" they scream at each other. "Take you turn. Wait your turn!"

"Stop! You went too far." The laws are established. The hill is theirs until a few feet from the bottom. Always they break their descent where a stooped elm sways.

Andrea gets on line. The voices of the other children form a dis-
sonant background to the stories she continues to tell herself. Their
words have no real meaning. She is clothing her beautiful princess
in a dress trimmed with ermine, a magical dress that will keep her
warm when she skis. Andrea moves patiently forward, and when it
is her turn she suspends the story. Now she struggles to remember
Hildy's directions as she begins her descent.

"Right foot forward. Slide. Left foot forward. Slide. Poles in. Poles
out. Sharp and down." And then her graceful glissade becomes au-
tomatic and she is flying, flying over the snow. She laughs. If she
stretches her arms out, holding her poles, she will take wing. The
children on the hillside shout, but their voices are lost in the wind.
They sail past her on their saucers, their sleds, swerving and swirling.
Deftly, she plunges her poles into the snow and slows her pace, and
then suddenly, halfway down, she thrusts with all her might and
propels herself forward.

"Poles in, poles out," she shouts and glides across a stretch of ice,
gathering speed. She is fast as the wind, faster than the stiff gust that
tears at her hat, pulls at her scarf. She is the wind. She is Queen of
the Wind. She waves her right pole imperiously, recklessly brandishing it until it slips from her grasp and rolls away. "No." She cannot
hear her own protest.

Sleds swerve to her right and to her left. Children roll off them
and plunge into drifts of snow. "Stop!" they shout to her as she
whizzes by them. "Stop!" Still she continues downhill, the cords of
fear tightening about her chest. She grips the remaining pole but
does not use it. Ejected from enchantment, she is powerless. The
spell is broken. She cannot control the relentless speed that propels
her past the stooped and sorrowing elm tree.

The cross street is in view, but she squeezes her eyes shut and so
does not see the car, the small orange Volkswagen, that moves so
slowly as it approaches a diamond-bright patch of ice. The driver,
hunched over the wheel (a salesman who has lost his way, who has
never traveled this road before), maneuvers desperately for control;
he shifts gears as his wheels hit the ice. His windshield is blurred by
frost and so he does not see the small girl in the bright red jacket
and navy-blue snow pants who comes careening down the hill. He

feels the thud of her small body as his car strikes her and then sees her at last (as perhaps he will always see her) as she is tossed, like a small ragdoll, up into the air and then down again in the fall that breaks her back and stops her heart.

The news of the accident spreads through the neighborhood within minutes. The children scurry into the schoolyard (where Evan and Jared are helping to build a snowman) and some are shouting and some are crying and some are elated with the enormity of what they have witnessed.

"Dead. She's dead," they shout, and their small voices are filled with awe. They push each other in their desperate eagerness to be the first to tell the story.

"I saw her."

"The car beeped."

"No, he didn't."

"He was going too fast."

"No, he skidded."

"I heard her scream."

"I saw the blood."

They all saw the blood, the foaming scarlet rivulet that streaked across the shining ice and faded to a soft pink even as they watched. (For days afterward, small boys would experiment, pricking their fingers and then flicking the blood onto the snow to see if it would change color or whether it was only the blood of death that faded.)

"Who?" Evan asks. "Who's dead? Who?" But their answer is briefly obscured by the screaming of the sirens on the ambulances and police cars now racing to Schoolhouse Hill.

The sirens wake Stacey and, still in her nightgown, she opens the front door. A sanitation worker hefts her garbage pail.

"What's happening? Why all the sirens?" she asks, rubbing her eyes against the day's white brightness.

"An accident at Schoolhouse Hill. A little girl on skis, they said. She got hit by a car."

"What? When?" But she turns away without waiting for his answer and looks in the front closet. Andrea's skis are gone.

"No," she says aloud, but her heart is drumming loudly, violently.

"No, it can't be. It isn't!" she shouts and her throat aches with the shrill force of her protest. "Oh, God, oh, God." She is whispering and weeping now, whispering and weeping as she plunges her bare feet into boots and drapes herself in the black cape. Her sweat-stained nightgown clings to her body and her breath is soured by sleep and fear.

The cold wind whips across her face when she steps outside. She grimaces, braces herself against it, and, like a wounded winged creature, rushes clumsily down the street.

"Andrea! Andrea!" She shouts her daughter's name; the tender syllables ricochet back to her in windy echo. *An-dre-a, An-dre-a.*

"Mrs. Cosgrove. Stacey." They come toward her, two women, neighbors whose names she cannot now recall although she has sat beside them at PTA meetings, waited on the corner with them on early-dismissal days.

She would speed by them. She has no time. There is no time. *"An-dre-a!"* But they match her pace, hurry along beside her.

"We'll come with you." She flinches against the terrible pity in their voices. Why should they come with her? Why should they pity her? No! No! She would shout the denial, the protest, but it explodes instead within her mind and she does not, she will not, break pace. Still she turns to them, spits words out through narrowed lips. "There's been an accident. Don't you know there's been an accident? I must hurry!"

"Yes. We know." Their voices brim with tenderness, glitter with tears. They flank her on either side and each takes her by an arm. She does not resist. She is powerless against their kindness, their sympathy. And she is cold, so cold. They draw near to her, as though to warm her, and so, pressed close to each other, three abreast, they run, run as fast as they can to Schoolhouse Hill.

The street is crowded but a path is cleared as they approach. Soft voices waft on the wind but she cannot hear them. Her heart is beating too loudly, too rapidly. "Too fast. So fast," someone says. "This hill. Always dangerous." "I saw her." "Oh, poor thing. Poor thing."

"Who? Who?" she shouts and looks wildly about. *"An-dre-a!"* The name is frozen on her tongue; she cannot loosen it, toss it out upon the wind. It crowds her mouth, slips back into her throat; it will choke her. She sways and her companions steady her.

"Mommy! Mommy!" Evan, clutching Jared's hand, hurtles himself at Stacey. His face is red, contorted into a knot of grief. Jared, his eyes squeezed shut, weeps; the tears force their way out, silvering his dark lashes. Stacey's arms encircle her sons, draw them into the black-winged fold of her cape. They press their heads against her; their hot tears sear through her nightgown, bruise her skin.

"Andrea's dead. Dead." Their muffled voices bleat against her body. "Dead. Dead. Andrea."

Again she sways and again her companions sustain her. She turns to them, first to one, then to the other. They nod, each in turn, their faces chalked by grief, their eyes awash with sorrow.

Her hands fly to her face; she pummels her cheeks. A scream fills the air. A terrible scream.

"Mama, don't. Don't," Evan sobs, and she understands that she herself is screaming but she cannot, she will not stop.

She moves forward, her sons beside her, clutching at her cape. A police officer walks toward them, his pad open, his hat in his hand.

"Mrs. Cosgrove?"

She does not answer. She lurches past him and runs, runs to the foot of the hill. Already Andrea's small body lies on a stretcher. Already a plastic sheet covers her.

Nausea washes over Stacey. Bitterness fills her mouth. She sinks to her knees, pulls the sheet loose, and looks down at her daughter's face. Andrea's blue eyes are open and her expression is startled. Her forehead is cut and the golden curls that cluster about it are clotted with bright red blood. A short man in a tan overcoat leans against an orange VW, his gloved hands pressed to his face.

"I didn't see her. There was no stop sign. I never saw her."

But Stacey ignores him. She passes her fingers through Andrea's hair. The blood sticks to her fingers, thick and warm. She kisses Andrea on the cheek and on the lips. She closes her eyes. And then grief claims her and she falls, weeping and weeping, across the small inert body. The child within her kicks. Her sons, frightened, pull at her.

"Mommy. Get up, Mommy. Please. Please."

Their fingers pluck at her cape. Their voices are faint pleas from afar, slivers of sound that barely pierce the density of her mourning. And then Jared pulls at her hair with such rage that she must turn her head, that she must restrain him.

"Andrea," she says to her sons. "Andrea is dead."

They throw themselves upon her, her sons, bereft of their sister, and she holds them close. They are locked together in a tangle of grief, huddled on the ground beside the small still body of the golden-haired girl in the bright red jacket.

"Dead," Jared repeats through his sobs. "Dead." His eyes are tightly closed. If he says the word often enough he will triumph over it. "Dead. Dead. Dead."

And Stacey, her body heaving, her tears flowing with scalding sorrow, rocks her sons in her arms. She makes no protest when the police officer gently helps her and the boys to their feet, although she touches Andrea's hand (how cold it is, how terribly cold) before the ambulance driver again covers the body.

Obediently, submissively, her arms around her sons' shoulders, she follows the officer who leads her to the patrol car and drives her home. Obediently, submissively, she sits on the couch while her neighbors call Hal and then her parents and then her brothers, Evan calling out each number and Jared (poor bewildered Jared) repeating them after him. Someone takes her boots off and someone else eases her out of the black cape and places a blanket around her.

"But I'm still cold," she says. "So cold."

And Evan brings her the pink quilt from Andrea's bed and places it around her shoulders.

Nina, David, and Hildy go to Andrea's funeral. Hildy, wearing a navy-blue dress to which she has affixed a white collar (because small Andrea had always noticed such details), is very pale. Guilt haunts her grief. Why did she give Andrea those skis? Why did she encourage her to go up and down the slopes? She was so little. She didn't understand. Hildy blames herself even though Hal and Stacey do not blame her; they are beyond blaming anyone.

Numbed, stunned, in those interim days between death and burial Stacey sat on a hardbacked chair in the sitting room of the funeral home where Andrea's body (dressed in her red velvet Christmas dress) was laid out. Now and again, she rose and went to the window where she stood for some moments staring down the street and then shrugged despairingly, as though she had forgotten for whom she was waiting. And Hal was consumed with anger, a stark, unfocused rage that his daughter, his darling, his princess, was dead, that he would not (ever, ever) see her again, that he would not (ever, ever) hear her laughter. At home, he turned the pages of the photograph album. In the funeral parlor, he sat in a deep easy chair or stood beside Stacey or walked the broad avenue with Evan and Jared, who grew restless in the overheated white clapboard building filled with strangers who kissed their mother and looked at Andrea (dead Andrea, cold Andrea) and wept and continued to weep.

Hal was dry-eyed, strangely controlled, during those long hours. He spoke very little. When Stacey lingered too long at the window, he went toward her, took her hands in his own, talked to her; once he even caused her to smile. It was in the night, when Stacey slept (and strangely, during that grief-drenched time, she slept heavily) and he lay awake. Only then did hot, stinging tears streak his cheeks.

The night before the funeral, he rose from his bed and walked barefoot through the darkness into the living room. He took a bottle of J&B and the photograph album into the kitchen. He sat down at the table and lifted the bottle to his lips. The drink scorched his throat, inflamed his stomach, but he drank again and then again. He set the bottle down and opened the album. Slowly, slowly, he turned the pages. Andrea, a golden-haired baby, laughed up at him. The toddler Andrea smiled shyly up at him across a birthday cake. Three candles. The cake shaped like a turtle. Andrea on roller skates whirled past him. He turned another page but he could not see because his own tears blinded him.

Grief, heavy as a stone, rolled across his heart. He slammed the album shut, buried his face in his hands, and sobbed. The sound of his sorrow was loud and guttural; to still it he bit his knuckles and tasted his own blood.

"Damn! Goddamn." The curse, loud and thick, escaped his own restraint and he looked up nervously. He did not want to waken the boys.

"Hal. Oh, Hal."

Stacey stood in the doorway, her face as white as the flannel nightgown against which her huge stomach pressed so that the fabric was drawn taut. She sailed across the room and stood before him, her hands in his hair. She pulled his head toward her, pressed it against her abdomen, against the firm expanse of her pregnancy. His sobs increased as he mourned his dead child, his lost golden princess, on this massive pillow of gestating life, which, indifferent to the wildness of his grief, the enormity of her loss, continued inexorably to grow and develop.

"Why?" The question was wrung from him; he anticipated no answer.

"Why?" Her voice was hoarse as though weakened by this question she had asked so often and will perhaps never stop asking.

Hal rose and stumbling, their arms knotted, their heads bent low, they supported each other and returned to their bed. They did not speak as they waited for the morning to come, each acknowledging that there was no comfort to be offered the other, that there was no comfort to be found, that their loss could not be redeemed. Not now. Not yet. Perhaps not ever.

Stacey wears a heavy black dress to the funeral. High-necked and long-sleeved, it was borrowed from one of the women who had walked with her to Schoolhouse Hill, whose name she now knows and will always remember. The woman is called Judith and she owns this dress because her two-year-old son died of a congenital heart defect when she was pregnant with her daughter, who is, thank God, healthy and beautiful. ("You never forget," Judith told Stacey, her fingers nervously smoothing a crease on the bodice. "Who could forget the death of a child? But when you have another child right away, it helps. They told me that and they were right. In that I was lucky. Like you.")

"Lucky?" Stacey repeated the word bitterly and Judith blushed and averted her eyes, shamed to have chosen such an inappropriate word and aware that no word would be appropriate.

"I'm sorry," she said weakly.

"Oh, you didn't know. You can't know." Stacey swayed from side to side, and, although she had eaten nothing that morning, a wave of nausea washed over her and sweat iced her body.

But now, on this chilly morning when Andrea will be buried, she is strangely calm. A black lace scarf drapes her golden hair, and once or twice she lifts her hand to a curl at her forehead and stares down at her fingers. Hal reaches for her hand. Today Andrea will be gone from them and they will be bereft even of the touch of her cold dead skin (and they have touched her often as she lay upon the bier), of the sight of her flowerlike face and her sun-colored hair. The pressure of his touch stanches her terrible and terrifying sorrow and his own.

Evan and Jared hold each other's hands. Frightened, trembling, the boys walk beside their parents and together they take their seats in the front row of the small chapel. They sit very straight, the four of them, and they look at the small coffin. Andrea (their Andrea, so brave and alone lying upon tufted white satin) demands their courage, their dignity. In the rear of the chapel, a woman cries inconsolably. Cathy. Two small girls, classmates of Andrea's (the class sits together with pale mothers and sad-eyed teachers), sob softly, bewilderedly.

The service is brief. The minister speaks of the gift of Andrea's short life, of human inability to understand divine intent. A children's choir sings "His Eye Is on the Sparrow." The chapel is very quiet. It is only when the pallbearers lift the small white coffin and Jared screams, "Where are they taking Andrea? Where are they taking her, Mommy?" that Stacey's sobs break free. The sound of her racking sorrow fills the room.

Hal's arm encircles her. All mischief is washed from his face; he is newly aged, thrust into a saddened manhood. And then he too surrenders. His features crumple and his falling tears moisten his dark beard. Those near him see that he trembles. Stacey takes Jared's hand, and Hal's hand rests on Evan's shoulder. Thus united, isolated in their grief, they walk behind Andrea's small coffin, looking neither to the right nor to the left.

Nina, David, and Hildy stand at the curb as the hearse pulls away. They see Stacey's face pressed to the window. Her lashes are heavy with tears, and as they watch they see her features contort, her mouth open wide, and they understand that she is screaming. Her silent scream haunts them as they drive north. They do not speak, and for hours after their return home, their faces remain frozen in masks of sorrowing incredulity.

One week later, Arnold calls them just as they are finishing dinner.

"I'm on my way to the hospital," he tells David who answers the phone (because he has been waiting for this call, has braced himself for it). "Stacey is in labor."

"Should we come?" David asks. This is something that has never been discussed.

"No. I don't think so. Hal is there. Just be patient. I'll call you as soon as I have any news."

They are not patient. They are gripped by anxiety. They talk to each other in unfinished sentences, pick up books and magazines and set them down, turn the television set on and then off. They are relieved that Hildy is not home and then they wish for her presence. David goes into the kitchen, presses his head against the window-pane, and prays. "Please," he says. "Oh, please. Let everything be all right."

Nina stands beside him, clutches his arm, kisses his cheek.

When the phone rings, three hours later, they both hesitate and then David lifts the receiver, but she stands beside him, her ear pressed to the phone.

"A girl. Just over seven pounds. And she's beautiful, David. Just beautiful. Mazal tov."

"And Stacey?" David asks, clutching Nina's hand, feeling her lips on his cheek, feeling his own heart throb with pride, his blood pulse with joy. Seven pounds! This new life of his own making, of his own generation, this life that will provide him with posterity, continuity, weighs over seven pounds!

"Stacey?" Arnold replies and now his voice is weary, almost faint. "Stacey can't stop crying."

22

It is dawn when Nina and David arrive at the hospital. At Arnold's suggestion (and with Arnold's intervention) they will see the baby before the start of the regular hospital day, even before the first shift of nurses arrives. They did not discuss the reasonableness of this course. They rely now on silence, on the unarticulated recognition that they are poised at a dangerous precipice; they have arrived at a difficult and painful juncture, one they could not have foreseen that distant spring day when Stacey and Nina sat together beneath the giant oak tree and ate jewel-colored fruit from milk-white dishes. Silently, they acknowledge that if they verbalize their fears, they will endow them with reality and the long shadow that has trailed them since Andrea's death will deepen into an impenetrable darkness. And, after all, Stacey has given no indication that she has changed her mind. She has, in fact, spoken very little since Andrea's death. David had called her and Nina had telephoned, had offered to visit her, to take her shopping, to do the shopping for her. She had refused politely. "No. Thanks. I'll be all right." Her voice had been flat, each mono-syllabic reply articulated slowly, with great effort. They did not press her. They respect her silence, her sorrow. They are, in fact, relieved by it. Only Hildy has uttered the question that haunts them.

They told her of the birth when she came home, perhaps an hour after Arnold's call. She had smiled, a smile of such radiance and generosity that they moved toward her, hugged her.

"That's wonderful. A baby girl." She spoke still with adolescent wonder at the reality that a baby, a real baby, had been born.

But later that night she had wandered into their bedroom where, exhausted, they watched Humphrey Bogart and Ingrid Bergman in *Casablanca*. She had perched at the edge of the bed, lifted both stuffed camels, and butted them against each other.

"Will she really give us the baby?" she asked. "It seems almost too much to ask of her."

They did not reply, although they looked sadly at her and switched off the volume on the television set. Together they watched Bogart and Bergman embrace. The print was badly worn; the blacks faded into dark grays and the whites turned to the color of gritty snow. Nina leaned forward and patted Hildy's head. David spoke at last.

"She's my baby too, Hildy. Isn't it too much to ask of me?" His question was not a question but a plea, and he uttered it in a tone so faint and sad that it seemed an audio echo of the shadowy figures that moved across the television screen.

Hildy did not answer. Before leaving the room she placed the two camels on the television set where, balanced on their slender legs, they stared at Nina and David through their long-lashed eyes.

But in the morning, Hildy trailed down the stairs after her parents.

"Here," she said and held out the pink bunting, newly washed and neatly folded into a clear plastic bag. With this gift, Nina knew, Hildy had chosen her side if sides should become necessary. (*But they won't*, she assured herself fiercely.)

"Thank you," she said gravely (not knowing how far to go in her gratitude), and she was unprepared for Hildy's swift damp kiss on her cheek and for the hug in which Hildy held David for a brief and precious moment.

Now, holding the bunting (but why has she brought it with her when she knows they will not take the baby home today, within hours of her birth?), she and David enter the hospital and inhale its ammoniacal, medicinal aroma.

Arnold waits for them at the reception desk and they stand beside him at the elevator bank. The first elevator is loaded with gurneys and cannot accommodate them. They board the second, which is filled with nurses and aides who chat animatedly with each other; they have the exuberant vitality peculiar to those who work night shifts and whose energy is sparked anew at the break of dawn. They anticipate hours of rest and leisure to be enjoyed while others work. Nina finds their good humor, their optimism unsettling because she herself is exhausted, her nerves frayed with fatigue and apprehension.

"She's a beautiful baby," Arnold tells them. "Perfectly formed, of a good weight."

"Stacey didn't have too hard a time?" David asks.

"Not too bad. She's very strong and she was well-prepared. Everything went smoothly. Hal was with her, of course, all the way through."

"Of course," David says. He remembers that it had occurred to him months ago that he might accompany Stacey to the delivery room, but he had never proposed it. It had seemed insensitive, usurpant. Yet now, he is jealous that it was Hal who first saw his newborn daughter, Hal who observed her still awash in the shimmering moisture of her long passage. Immediately, he is ashamed of his reaction. He, so newly the father of a daughter, cannot begrudge anything to Hal, who has so newly buried a daughter.

They emerge from the elevator on the maternity floor where, again, they are assaulted by a flurry of activity. Night nurses, their shift nearing completion, hurry down the corridors pushing mobile steel trays laden with medications. The floor nurse methodically updates charts and thrusts them at a weary resident. Arnold smiles at her pleasantly.

"We're just going to the nursery," he says.

"Of course, Dr. Roth." There is the barest hint of complicity in her nod of acquiescence and Nina marvels at Arnold's power.

They pass a parade of aides wheeling infants down the hall. Swaddled in pink and blue receiving blankets, bedded in gray cardboard bassinets decorated with dancing pink and blue elephants, the infants mewl piteously; their tiny faces are wrinkled with misery so that they resemble elderly gnomes.

"They're hungry," Arnold says smilingly. "They're being brought to nursing mothers."

One by one the infants are wheeled into rooms and they hear the sleepy welcomes; the maternal voices are soft and playful. ("Oh, there

you are." "Why are you so noisy, you?" "Hush. Just you hush.")
Nina and David do not look at each other.

"Stacey has a single," Arnold says, as though reading their thoughts.
"I thought it would be less disturbing for her."

"Yes, of course," they say together and giggle nervously because
they spoke in chorus.

They are, Nina thinks, all becoming experts at noncommunica-
tion, at concealing their anxieties from each other, at silently congratulating themselves on their shared sensitivity. They do not want
Stacey (so recently bereaved and soon to be bereft again) to watch
another woman nurse her infant. They are considerate of her, protective of her. Their own fears, their common worry, are denied
precedence.

Nina sees two closed doors, unapproached by nurses or aides. Which
room is Stacey's? she wonders. Is Stacey awake? Is she weeping still?
Is the white robe hanging in the metal closet of her room?

They reach the nursery and Nina's heart beats faster, although she
slows her steps so that David and Arnold precede her to the window.

"Your daughter, David," Arnold says softly and points to the infant in the third bassinet in the row closest to the window. "Isn't
she beautiful?"

With effort, as though his head has grown newly heavy, so weighted
is he by wonder and gratitude, David nods. When Nina reaches his
side, he lifts his finger, points to the baby, feels her tremble, hears
the swift intake of breath. She is startled and moved by the flesh-
and-blood reality of this infant of whom she has dreamed, for whom
she has planned, this small daughter of theirs whose life redeems the
past, ensures the future. Ah, David was right to want this child, to
have the courage to overpower the fear and emptiness that haunted
him and thus had frightened her. *Where life continues death is denied.*" Amos Roth's words. Amos Roth's legacy. Which they have
fulfilled. They have a child, a daughter.

Side by side, hand in hand, they stare at her. They are hypnotized
by the miracle of her small form, by the sudden and wondrous curl
of her tiny nostril, the twitch of her limbs within the loose swathe
of the pink flannel blanket.

Nina's throat tightens and David pulls her close, presses her against him. His body is electric with excitement, taut with joy, and that joy, that excitement, becomes her own. They stand as one, united in their absorption, their concentration. A nurse drifts through the nursery, lifts the crying infant from the next bassinet, but they scarcely mark her movements. It is their own baby to whom their attention is riveted. They would seal into their memories forever these first magical hours of her life, this spontaneous ignition of their love for her, their daughter, their own.

"Her ears," Nina says. "Look at her ears. Like tiny shells."

She had, she remembers, said exactly the same thing when she first saw the newborn Hildy. It had seemed to her then (as it seems to her now) a miracle that an organ as intricate as an ear, with its circling canals and tubes, its delicate network and complicated construction, can be reproduced in such miniature. The cartilage glistens like mother of pearl and the infinitesimal earlobes are of a deep red.

David smiles. Alone, amid the half dozen babies who remain in the nursery, his daughter sleeps quietly. The infant on her left cries, and although they cannot hear the sound of his misery, they see his flushed face, the eyes screwed shut, the pink toothless purse of his open mouth. The baby in the bassinet behind her flails restlessly; her small arms dart out of the sleeves of the white undershirt, her tiny legs twitch in an oddly rhythmic movement. In the rear of the room, a crib lies beneath an ultraviolet light and a nurse bends over it, adjusts an intravenous tube, makes a notation on a chart.

Nina pities this newborn who is not as healthy as their own baby, whose eyes open now. It seems to Nina that she is looking at them (although, of course, she cannot see yet) and that she does not cry because she can feel the protective shield of their love. The infant stretches and Nina sees the red strawberry that blossoms at her neck. She has heard Arnold say that Amos Roth had such a mark on his right shoulder, but just as Arnold cannot recall his father singing (although David remembers the songs — the melodies, even the lyrics), so David has no memory of that dermal marking. But Nina knows for certain that Hildy has such a birthmark on her back. The coincidence is chimerical and fills her with optimism and hope. She leans closer, presses her face against the cold glass.

"Ah, sweet," she says. "Ah, my sweetness." Her words are a whispered pledge of love.

"Do you want to hold her?" Arnold asks, and they nod wordlessly and follow him into the small room that adjoins the nursery.

"This gentlemen would like to hold his daughter," he says, smiling to the nurse who sits behind the desk, pointing at the baby. The heavy-set older woman, her starched cap perched on blue-gray curls, nods and hands them paper gowns and masks, nylon gloves. When they are properly robed, when David is seated on the small chair, she carries the baby out and places her in his arms.

David cradles his daughter, his face placed close to hers. Tears roll down his cheeks as he rocks her in his arms. His lips move and his voice is very soft.

"Felicia," he says. "My Felicia Miriam." He has named his daughter then for the happiness that will be hers and for his father's sister, who, in turn, has been named for other large-eyed, soft-voiced Miriams, born and buried in the tiny Polish village that survives now only on Amos Roth's canvases.

"Felicia Miriam," he repeats. The names fall together in a lyric mingling.

Nina moves to stand beside him. Soundlessly, she mouths the name. Names, she knows, are magical. To name someone is to lay invincible claim, to cross into a new dimension of caring and commitment.

David smiles. He is light-headed, full-hearted. The words of a prayer tumble through his mind. "Blessèd be God who has sustained us to this day. This happiest of days."

Nina holds her arms out and he gives her the baby. She holds her carefully, breathlessly, supporting the fragile head (so lightly indented, so dangerously soft) with the palm of her hand. The baby is feather-light in her arms and she whimpers softly. Nina's breasts ache, as though apologizing for their lack of milk. She presses the infant face, so petal smooth, to her cheek. Her eyelashes brush the fair fringe of hair that circles the baby's pale high brow. She is startled by the heat generated by the tiny body. Oh, she would hold this baby (*Felicia Miriam, Felicia Miriam* — the name is a song within her) close forever. She kisses the tiny hand on which translucent nails glow so tenderly.

"I'll take the baby now," the nurse says.

Reluctantly, impeded by new love, Nina hands the baby back to her, and she and David slowly remove their masks, their gloves, their gowns.

Again, they stand with Arnold behind the glass and proudly watch their baby. Nina clutches the bag that contains Hildy's bunting, Felicia Miriam's bunting.

They leave the hospital with Arnold, and on the steps David embraces his brother who has made it possible for them to have this child, this beautiful infant daughter, this sweet Felicia Miriam. Nina kisses him on the cheek.

"Thank you," she says. "Oh, thank you."

As they walk to the car they pass a florist's shop just opening for the day and they go inside. They send Stacey a large bouquet of yellow roses threaded through with purple irises, and on the card David writes, "Our thanks. Our love."

He buys Nina a single pink rosebud that he pins to her lapel, and she, in turn, hands him a pink Mylar balloon with the legend IT'S A GIRL scrawled across it.

Companionably, the balloon bobbing between them, they walk into the bright new sunlight and, like new lovers, marvel at the crispness of the air, the sweetness of the breeze, at their own incredible good fortune. They smile shyly at each other. They *are* newly in love, newly pledged, bonded to the infant whose sweet scent and gossamer touch clings to them.

Three blocks later they stand at a corner beside a young mother who holds her small daughter's hand. The child is crying.

"May I?" David asks gravely, and he ties the balloon to her wrist.

The little girl stops crying and looks at him in bewilderment. And then she slaps the balloon and laughs.

Her mother smiles and David and Nina grin and dash across the street. Nina sniffs her rose and they run, giggling, still holding hands, to their car.

*   *   *

A student nurse named Kathy Ames brings Stacey the flowers later that morning. Kathy Ames is a shy, pretty girl and this is her first week on the maternity floor. She is happy with this rotation and she enjoys the responsibility of bringing flowers and gifts to the new mothers. She finds Styrofoam vases for the lavish bouquets and chats with the women who sit up in bed in their embroidered bed jackets and new batiste nightgowns. They are all eager to discuss their labor and delivery, the virtues of their doctors, the names of their newborn children and how the decision about the name was arrived at. Kathy is always pleased to do them small favors because they thank her with the cheerful exuberance of those who are, at this moment, supremely happy.

She has also observed those few women to whom sadness clings like a fine film. They smile wanly at their visitors, their eyes filling with tears for no discernible reason. Some of them (those who stay only one or two nights, Kathy is relieved to note) have suffered miscarriages. Others have given birth to babies who have "problems."

The mother of the jaundiced infant whose bassinet is placed beneath the ultraviolet rays haunts the nursery. The baby is fed intravenously and it will be at least another week before she can nurse him. Still, she has refused to allow her milk to dry up but works assiduously at maintaining its flow, expressing it with care. The nurses encourage her.

"Breast-feeding is wonderful for depressed postpartums," Mrs. Hendrix, the maternity head nurse, told Kathy. "Better than tranquilizers and therapy."

Kathy Ames, new to the maternity floor, a keen and compassionate observer and a valiant warrior against sorrow, agrees with her.

Stacey Cosgrove, she decides, with the instant certitude of the naive novice, is just such a postpartum depressive. She is crying when Kathy enters, brushing her hair as she weeps. Her strokes are strong and even, as though her tears are such a natural part of her life, her grief so constant a companion, that she can accomplish all her routine chores, in tandem with her misery.

"Flowers for you, Mrs. Cosgrove," Kathy says brightly. She notes that the yellow roses almost match Stacey's hair. "Aren't they beautiful?"

Stacey nods. She reads the card that Kathy holds out to her. "Our thanks. Our love." She notes, with disinterest, that it is unsigned (an oversight that occurs to David later that morning and haunts him through the day), although she knows, of course, that such flowers, such a message, could only have been sent by Nina and David.

"Look," Kathy says, her voice brimming with false enthusiasm (she desperately wants Stacey Cosgrove to stop weeping), "the flowers match your hair."

"Much closer to my daughter's hair color," Stacey replies and then remembers (as though she could ever forget) that she no longer has a daughter. She must learn to speak of Andrea in the past tense, to say, "My daughter *had* hair that color." But not yet. She cannot take leave of Andrea so swiftly because Andrea still lives for her, still whirls through her dreams, dances into her thoughts. During the last stage of labor, when Arnold Roth gave her a painkiller and the drug caused her to drift sleepily above her pain, Andrea had come to her, soothed her.

"Push, Stacey," Arnold Roth had urged.

"It's all right, Mama," Andrea whispered.

The labor room nurse wiped Stacey's forehead with a damp cloth, but Andrea played with her hair — her magic fingers, light as air, lifting the sweat-soaked tendrils, curling and braiding them into an intricate crown. And then she had floated away, banished by Stacey's scream as another powerful contraction seized her and all her energy was concentrated on bearing down, on freeing her body of the frantic, struggling infant fighting toward birth. Stacey's final scream, when at last the painful passage was done, when the baby crowned and was pulled gently, gently, through the vaginal walls, was not for herself or for her newborn but for Andrea, vanished again and yet again.

"Good for you, Stacey. Everything will be all right, Stacey," Arnold assured her gently as he administered another injection.

"Mama. Mama." Andrea's muffled voice struggled toward her and it was then that the tears began, and she cannot stop them because she knows that nothing will ever be all right again.

Now, again, she feels the cold wind of loss wash over her and she shivers uncontrollably.

"But your daughter's hair is sort of wheat-colored," Kathy Ames persists. She took special note of the baby who was born during the night, before her shift began, and she had decided then that Stacey's daughter was the prettiest baby in the nursery, with a fringe of fair hair and her petal-smooth skin wondrously unbruised. Kathy had been intrigued by the strawberry birthmark on the infant's neck.

"Yes. You're right," Stacey agrees. Of course. Kathy Ames is not speaking of Andrea but of the baby born last night. She remembers the fair soft hair that grew like a halo about the small head. She even remembers touching a wisp of that delicate fringe when the nurse held the baby toward her as Dr. Roth hovered over her with the needle, the wonderful needle that sent her soaring above pain, above memory. "My daughter's hair is a different color." She smiles at Kathy Ames with gratitude, and with that smile her tears cease.

"I never saw hair so fair, so fine. But I'll bet it grows in thick like yours." Kathy is pleased that Stacey is no longer crying, that, in fact, she has reached for the Kleenex and is carefully wiping away all traces of tears. Kathy busies herself now arranging the flowers in the Styrofoam vase, placing ferns between the irises and roses.

"I was confused, I guess, because I only saw her for a minute last night just after the delivery," Stacey explains. It is important to her that this young nurse understand why she did not at once recognize the color of her daughter's hair. "And I guess I was asleep this morning when they brought the babies in to nurse."

"Were you?" Kathy finishes the flowers and places them on the bedside table. Then she picks up Stacey's chart. "Oh, yes. Probably you were. They gave you a shot right after the delivery. Demerol will do that, really knock you out, so you were probably totally out of it when they did the first A.M. feeding." Briefly, she wonders why Demerol was administered at all. Probably Mrs. Cosgrove suffered some real pain, perhaps even an unusual fissure. But now she seems fine and her mood is improved. Kathy credits the flowers and, of course, their brief conversation.

"When can I see my daughter?" Stacey asks. "I want to nurse her."

She is aware now of the aching fullness of her breasts; they strain against her hospital gown as though possessed of a life of their own.

The milk pulsates and pours forth. Kathy sees damp circlets form on the pale blue fabric, darkening it. She studies the chart. There is no green tab affixed to it to indicate that Stacey Cosgrove is a nursing mother, but there is also no notation that an injection has been administered to dry the flow of milk.

"You're sure you want to nurse the baby?" she asks.

"I nursed my three other children," Stacey replies. "Why wouldn't I want to nurse this baby? My daughter." Her voice trembles. She is again at the edge of sorrow, poised above a dangerous precipice, fearful that she will again be hurled into the darkness of mood that has surrounded her since Andrea's death.

Her eyes fill and her face is distorted with misery. She is newly conscious of the searing vaginal pain, the cruelly tight stitching of the episiotomy. Her breasts, so burdened, so unrelieved, throb and swell.

"I *must* nurse her," she says plaintively, "or I will be sick."

When she nursed Andrea she had, on the advice of a friend, added yeast to her diet and developed a breast infection. The milk had become impacted and her fever had risen dangerously. She had nursed Andrea (who had been a ravenous infant, the greediest of sucklings) at one breast while Hal had applied ice packs to the other. Later, they laughed about it, but she can still recall the terrible pain of that infection, the rock-hard configuration of the infected gland.

"Let me see what I can do," Kathy Ames says reassuringly. She does not want Stacey to cry again. She does not want her to grow ill. Only last night she read the chapter on breast fever in her obstetrics text. "I'll be right back."

She hurries down the hall to the nursery but it is Mrs. Dugan, an aide, who sits behind Mrs. Hendrix's desk. She is a pleasant black woman who, Kathy knows, is the mother of six children. She has worked on the maternity floor for eight years and it is whispered among the student nurses that there are times when Mrs. Hendrix defers to Mrs. Dugan's judgment.

"Where is everyone?" Kathy asks.

"Oh, they busy," Mrs. Dugan replies in her lilting Jamaican intonation.

"Mrs. Cosgrove, she's in the single, room six-ten, she hasn't seen her baby since delivery last night and she wants to see it. Also her milk is really flowing and she wants to nurse. Would it be all right to bring her the baby?" It seems natural to her to confer with Mrs. Dugan, who has the authority of age and experience, reinforced by her harsh contempt for institutional foolishness.

"Why not? The baby's due for another feeding and she's just waking up, I noticed. Sure. Take her to her mommy."

"The chart doesn't have a nursing tab," Kathy points out.

"Oh, the chart." Mrs. Dugan knows how these charts are filled out, chicken scratches racing across the sheet as phones ring and lab specimens are delivered and demanded. Mistakes are made every day. Tabs slide off, queries go unanswered.

Kathy interprets Mrs. Dugan's derision as assent. She enters the nursery, changes the infant's diaper, and carries her down the hall to Stacey's room.

"Here's Mommy," she croons to the baby. "Here's your mommy."

Stacey extends her arms and gathers in her daughter, holding her close, her open hand supporting the fragile head, her eyes drinking in the infant's perfection of form and feature. She grows light-headed, dizzied by the baby's beauty, the softness of her skin, the competent beat of that tiny heart. She unwraps the receiving blanket, removes the tiny shirt, the diaper, passes her hands across the naked infant's petal-smooth body, rests a finger on the strawberry birthmark. She counts the infant's fingers, her toes, kisses each small hand. And then she dresses the baby, who is crying now with the desperate passion of hunger.

She opens her gown and places the infant at her breast. The bud of a mouth opens and closes frantically until the lips capture the nipple and tighten about it. The small face contorts and then relaxes as, with rhythmic sucking, the milk fills the baby's mouth. The infant's pull is so energetic that the thin white liquid jets forth and trickles down the tiny cliff of her chin and drips onto the soft mound of breast flesh, coursing down in a thin sticky stream. After a few minutes (knowing exactly when to do it, although she wears no watch), Stacey shifts the infant from her right breast to her left and gently nuzzles the now sleepy mouth against the nipple until she again feels the vigorous tugging and her own relief as the milk flows easily, abundantly.

The baby is sated. Stacey feels the small body relax, hears the softest of sounds. The infant's eyes are closed; she is asleep. She does not shift position but lies motionless, comfortably pillowed on Stacey's breasts. Stacey feels her own eyes close. She is so very tired but calm, content, for the first time since . . . since. How beautiful this baby is, this second daughter born to her, this fair-haired infant. She will be like Andrea — a magical friend, a sweet sister, a daughter. She will listen to Stacey's stories and walk with her down museum corridors and through gardens slowly wakening to spring.

"Once upon a time . . . ," Stacey says sleepily and begins again. "Once upon a time." She is talking to Andrea because Andrea is within this new baby. It was Andrea, after all, who had watched the fetal growth, day by passing day, who had pressed her golden head against Stacey's abdomen, who shouted gleefully, hurling herself at Stacey, "Hello, baby! Hello, Little Sister-Brother, Little Brother-Sister." Andrea's laughter rings in Stacey's ears and she smiles. She grows drowsy and her head drops. Her hair brushes the sleeping infant's cheek. She is cushioned, insulated in the silent cocoon of her own strenuously earned fatigue.

"Stacey!" Arnold Roth's voice, sharp, unfamiliarly stern, invades her heavy torpor. "What are you doing?"

Unwillingly, she opens her eyes and smiles at him, smiles because he is her doctor, her friend. How patient he was last night, urging her on with persistent gentleness. "Come on, Stacey, once more. Ah. Now again. Almost there. Soon. Very soon." She remembers his tender coaxing and she is grateful to him, as she has always been grateful to him.

"I just nursed the baby. Isn't she beautiful?" she asks proudly.

"Yes. She is beautiful. Very beautiful." He moves forward and takes the baby from her.

Stacey smiles, closes her eyes, and falls asleep.

Kathy Ames follows Arnold from the room and gently closes the door behind her. She is unprepared for the harshness of the doctor's tone, the flashing anger in his eyes.

"Who gave you permission to bring Mrs. Cosgrove the baby?" he asks.

"She wanted to see it. She had slept through the early-morning feeding and she wanted to nurse." The girl's voice quivers.

"The chart is not tabbed for nursing," he says coldly. He is holding the baby still and she takes it from him and replaces it in the wheeled bassinet, covering it carefully, giving herself time to gather her words, to summon her excuses.

"There was no R.N. in the nursery and the mother wanted to nurse so I just assumed . . ."

"You're a student nurse. You're asked to follow orders, take instruction, not make assumptions."

"I didn't meant any harm," she says weakly. "I thought I was doing the right thing. Mrs. Cosgrove was crying. She wanted her baby."

And now Kathy Ames feels the burning of her own tears. Always, she has been exemplary in her practicals. She works harder than the other student nurses, shows more diligence, more compassion. Never before has a staff member reprimanded her. *It is not fair.* Her mental protest sustains her against this doctor's barely controlled fury, and then, quite suddenly, he softens. He leans close to read her ID badge.

"Miss Ames," he says. "I'm sure you meant no harm, Miss Ames. But you must be more careful. There are sensitive situations which are not always apparent. You are a student. You didn't realize the consequences of this particular situation. Mrs. Cosgrove was not supposed to nurse her baby for various reasons. I came just now to administer an injection to halt the milk. However, no great harm has been done, I'm sure. We will sort everything out. But you will be more careful in the future?"

"Yes, Dr. Roth." Her voice cracks with relief. Oh, he is a very nice man. That is what all the nurses have always said and that is why his anger so chilled and frightened her.

"And Miss Ames — let's keep this discussion between ourselves. No need to talk about it, to generate further difficulty."

"Of course, Doctor." Her relief turns to gratitude. No longer his victim, she is his confederate. She flashes him a smile and wheels the infant down the corridor and returns her to the nursery.

And Arnold again enters Stacey's room. He stares down at his sleeping patient and then walks over the the flowers and reads David's card.

"Oh, God," he says very softly. "Oh, God help us."

Arnold blames himself.

"It was my fault," he tells Edith, whom he calls as soon as he reaches his office, because he does not know where else to turn with his own misery. "I should have marked the chart, made sure it was tabbed correctly. I should have come in earlier to administer the injection. But I didn't want to wake her up."

"It's happened," Edith says. "Self-flagellation isn't going to do anyone any good. And is it really so terrible?" In this, as in all things, Edith strives for professional objectivity, for the psychological insight so incisively mined that it emerges sparkling with clarity. But her own question rings false. She knows the answer.

"Come on, Edith. You know better than that. Stacey nursed her baby and that means her bonding with the baby has increased, intensified."

"Stacey's never spoken of keeping the baby before," Edith points out (although, with sinking heart, she recognizes the validity of his fear). "Not for all these months."

"Andrea's death changes everything."

"We can't know that." Her protest is faint. Of course, a child's death changes everything. She places her hand on the picture of her sons that stands on her desk and, with her index finger, traces the outline of each boy's face. "You may be jumping to conclusions," she adds weakly.

"Perhaps," Arnold replies. "Perhaps."

But when he hangs up he tells his nurse, with uncharacteristic abruptness, to cancel all his appointments. He will return to the hospital and speak to Stacey. She will be awake now, rested, and they will be able to talk.

Although the hospital is only five short city blocks from his office, Arnold takes a cab and races up the hospital steps so that he is perspiring and his heart is pounding when he taps on the door of Stacey's room and enters.

Hal sits on the orange plastic bedside chair, holding Stacey's hand.

"Hey, Dr. Roth," he says convivially, "Stacey ate her lunch. All of it."

"That's fine," Arnold acknowledges. "That's wonderful."

Stacey has eaten so little since Andrea's death. Twice, Hal called him to ask if there were pills that might stimulate her appetite. She had nibbled desultorily on pieces of dry toast and sipped from tepid cups of tea that she seldom finished. She did not prepare food for Evan and Jared, nor did she serve them the casseroles and meat loafs prepared by her neighbors, her family. She could not look at meat, she said. It nauseated her. She gagged when she saw a bottle of ketchup, the tomato sauce on a neighbor's pasta offering. She remembered the crimson sheen of Andrea's blood on her fingers. She had licked at that blood, sucked at the small clot that formed on her palm (where she had touched the blood-heavy curl) and so had mingled her daughter's cold death flow with the life-warm droplets of her own saliva. How could she eat when the taste of that blood lingers in her mouth? But today she had eaten a thin hospital hamburger for lunch, emptying the plastic packet of ketchup across its surface. And then she had asked for another and Hal had dashed down to the hospital coffee shop to obtain it. Stacey has been restored to him. She is eating and asking for more.

"I have to eat if I'm going to nurse," Stacey says contentedly. "Eat and drink. Isn't that right, Dr. Roth?"

"That's right. If you *are* going to nurse," he replies, cruelly choosing his emphasis.

"Of course I'm going to nurse." She smiles engagingly at him. He approves of nursing, distributes La Leche material and an article that he himself wrote for a journal, stressing the importance of breast-feeding to the generation of antibodies. Stacy keeps a folder of this material (amid the other folders on literature and art history, on dance and music, that litter her closet floor) and over the years she has lent it to other pregnant women.

"Do you think that's wise — your nursing this baby?" Arnold asks.

"What do you mean?" But now Stacey is guarded; the ease and contentment are gone from her voice. She crosses her arms over her breasts, as though to protect them, to shield the lacteal flow that now begins again, stimulated by her own touch.

"I mean that you are not going to keep this baby. This baby will go home with Nina and David. If you nurse, you may find it very difficult to give the baby up," Arnold says evenly.

"I didn't say I was going to keep the baby," Stacey protests. "But why can't I nurse her, just for a few days?" Her voice quivers and then rises slightly. She stares at him in hurt disbelief. In another moment, Arnold knows, she will weep.

"Stacey," he says gently, "you're only going to be in the hospital for a few days. It's foolish to begin nursing the baby when you'll have to wean her so soon, so very soon. It will be upsetting to you, unsettling to the baby."

"But I want to nurse her." Her voice is plaintive, shrilly insistent, and strangely familiar in its lilting little-girl cadence. And then Arnold realizes that Stacey speaks with Andrea's voice, with Andrea's singsong charm.

"I don't see what the big deal is," Hal interposes. He smiles disarmingly. "Why can't she begin to nurse the baby here and then, if she wants, take the baby home for a couple of weeks and nurse her there? Nina and David will understand how she feels." Always Hal has depended on the forgiving understanding of others — his teachers, his bosses, Stacey herself. And now it is Nina and David on whom he counts.

Hal does not want Stacey to begin to cry again. He does not want her to go to the windows and stare down into the street with the empty-eyed gaze so reminiscent of her mother and, perhaps, of all mothers who have waited anxiously, longingly, for babies who did not arrive, for absent children who will never return home.

"We'll ask them," he continues. "Nina called. They'll be here soon."

Now he has abandoned charm and is vaguely querulous, his brow furrowed, his mouth set. Arnold is not unfamiliar with his tone, with the stiffening of his jaw. Hal is a man who has wandered into foreign territory. He does not understand the language that is being spoken and is fearful that he will betray his ignorance and thus forfeit his

role as protector. Arnold has listened to other men, bewildered and
vulnerable, pose similar questions in defiant tones, speaking loudly
as though to do battle with their wives' soft weeping. ("I don't understand, Doctor, why you would have to remove the ovary — why
can't you just remove the tumor?" "Listen, Doctor, aren't we moving
too fast? In my business we explore all the options . . .") But for
Arnold the options are always limited and the action must always be
swift.

"I don't recommend nursing this baby," he says. "But of course
you can consult with Nina and David." He sighs and then smiles.
He does not want Stacey to think that he is angry.

Stacey eases herself out of bed and Arnold marvels at her strength,
her energy. It is not a full twenty-four hours since her delivery, but
she has already eaten a full meal and now she moves slowly but
without difficulty. She selects a carefully ironed pink cotton nightgown from her overnight bag and goes into the bathroom. They hear
the sound of running water and look away from each other in embarrassment.

"She'll grow attached to the baby," Arnold warns Hal. "It will
make things more difficult for her."

"You don't know that."

Arnold does not argue. He does not want to feed Hal's obstinacy,
to allow it to harden into angry defiance. David will deal with it.

"Nursing the baby made her come alive," Hal continues. "You see
that yourself. She just needs time to get herself together — to help
her deal with what happened. It takes time. You don't know, you
don't understand." He cannot explain to Arnold (who has never lost
a child) how he copes with his misery, how he avoids drowning in
the treacherous currents of his own sorrow. He has set himself a
routine to sustain him against the bewilderment of his loss. He ra-
tions the time that he allows himself to think about Andrea. Twice
each morning he looks at his wallet snapshot — the color school
portrait taken when she was narrator of the winter pageant. "Narrator. Narrator." She had loved to say the word. She loved words, the
way Stacey does. In the photograph Andrea wears her dress of scarlet
velvet (the dress she wore on Christmas Day, the dress in which she

was buried) and her golden curls are gathered into two thick bunches, tied with narrow ribbons.

Hal kisses the snapshot each time he looks at it. Soon, he will look at it only once each morning. In the late afternoon, just before the cocktail crowd arrives at Ramon's, he has a double scotch and thinks about Andrea. Sometimes, calmed by the liquor that courses so warmly through his body, he talks to her. "Princess," he says. "How are you, my daddy's girl?" Soon he will not need the scotch.

He awakens in the night and goes into her room. It calms him to sit on her bed, to hold the pink satin comforter between his fingers, to water the crocus Stacey bought her in the Botanic Gardens gift shop. It flowered two days after her death and Hal nurses the blossom with great care, plucking away the faded petals, moving the earth in the small planter with his fingers, talking softly. "It's such a pretty flower, Princess. Really pretty."

But Stacey has not entered Andrea's room, not since she took the velvet dress from the closet and placed it, with clean underwear and lace-trimmed white socks and white dress shoes, in the shopping bag for Cathy to bring to the funeral home. Unlike Hal, she had no small routines to cope with grief. Instead, pale and trembling, she walked barefoot through the house, pausing at each window, shivering and weeping, weeping. Until today. Until she nursed the baby. It is, Hal thinks, as though the cascade of her tears has been diverted now to form the rich stream of her breast milk. The baby will suck away her sorrow and will, with lusty gulps, absorb her grief.

Stacey emerges from the lavatory wearing the pink nightgown. Her face is washed and her hair, newly brushed, frames her face in a cloud of gold. Like a small girl just after a bath, she smiles shyly at them and climbs into bed.

"How do you feel?" Arnold asks.

"Clean but exhausted."

"You're doing too much too soon," he says warningly, pleased to restore the balance of their relationship. She is his patient. He is her doctor, compassionate and authoritative.

"I wanted to look nice for Nina and David," she says.

It is then that Nina and David enter the room. Nina carries a basket of fruit that she sets down on the bedside table as she kisses Stacey on the cheek.

"How are you, Stacey? Oh, what a pretty nightgown."

David averts his eyes. He remembers the nightgown, remembers clipping the plastic tag attached to its hem.

"I'm fine," Stacey replies. "Have you seen the baby?"

"She's beautiful," they say together and smile because they have (again) spoken in chorus.

"I know. And she's so responsive. I could tell when I nursed her."

"You nursed her?" Nina's voice is very faint. She stares at Stacey as though she misheard her. David turns questioningly to Arnold.

"A student nurse brought Stacey the baby," he says, and they hear the misery in his voice.

"But, Stacey, you never planned to nurse the baby. We talked about that, don't you remember?" Nina's words are more a plea than a question. She clenches and unclenches her fists.

"I know," Stacey says, "but that was before." There is a new boundary in her life now, an invisible line. Always, events will be divided for her. *Before Andrea's death. After Andrea's death.* Her eyes fill. "I just want to nurse her for now, for this little while in the hospital."

They turn away. They cannot bear to see her tears, to perceive her terrible vulnerability, the unquenched (unquenchable) agony of her bereavement.

Nina looks at David. He shrugs, his eyes troubled, and, with almost balletic precision, they shift positions. She rises from the chair beside Stacey's bed and goes to stand beside David at the window. Hal moves past her and takes her seat. They stare at each other, David and Nina, Hal and Stacey, across the slat of sunlight that partitions the pale wood floor.

"Is it such a big thing to ask? After all Stacey's been through? Hey, is it something she even needs your permission for? I don't get it." Hal speaks in the voice of righteous bewilderment, in the whining, argumentative tone of the boy who could not express himself in writing and thus became a master of oral persuasion, of vigorous verbal denial. He is skilled at placing others on the defensive, at reversing arguments and situations.

"Hal, Stacey. It's more complicated than that. Nursing mothers grow very attached to their babies. You know that," Arnold speaks with professional calm, professional authority. Sensitive to hospital sounds, he can hear the steel wheels of the carts that carry the infants to their nursing mothers. It is time for yet another feeding.

"But just for a few days," Stacey insists plaintively. "Just while I'm in the hospital. And it will be good for her."

"Felicia Miriam," David says. "We named her Felicia Miriam." They have named his daughter, wedded her to their history, established their claim. "Felicia Miriam," he repeats.

"Such a pretty name. Felicia Miriam," Stacey says softly. Like Nina, she recognizes the lyrical quality of the two names. "David, Nina. Please let me nurse Felicia Miriam." Her voice is very weak now and her face crumples into misery as they look at her. Yet they are comforted that she accepted the name, repeated it, approved of it. They are torn with pity, for her, for themselves, for their newborn daughter.

"Hey, Stace." Hal holds her hand, raises it to his lips, smoothes her hair. But she will not be comforted. She slides down against the pillow, covers her face with her hands. He stares at Nina and David. It occurs to Nina that Hal has not repeated the baby's name, commented on it. Nor has he mentioned the baby. It is Stacey who concerns him. Only Stacey.

Arnold rises, beckons to them. They follow him out to the corridor.

"I'm sorry," he says. "You know that there is a real risk if she continues to nurse the baby."

Nina and David look at each other and fear flashes between them. They recognize the seductive power of a newborn's body pressed against adult flesh. They tingle still at the memory of Felicia Miriam's sweet breath at their necks; they smiled all day, recalling the touch of her soft, smooth skin. How much more intense, then, will Stacey's experience be. She will feel the tug of the tiny mouth (so like a tiny, succulent berry, David had said wonderingly) at her nipples. Her milk will nourish the baby and they will both be sustained by the same nourishment. They will be as one, mother and child, flesh upon flesh, still inseparable. Cushioned on Stacey's breast, Felicia Miriam

will remain attached to Stacey. Nina, who nursed Hildy, who cannot forget how infant's and mother's moistures mingled, does not
deceive herself. Arnold is right. The risk is great, overwhelming.

"What can we do?" David asks softly, fearfully.

"I don't know." Arnold's voice is low, his expression grim.

"Oh, God," Nina says. "I feel so sorry for them. For her."

Exhausted, she begins to cry. The two men stare at her.

"Oh, she's lost so much, and now to say no to this . . ." The
words are swallowed by her sorrow. They are asking too much of
Stacey, and Stacey, in turn, is asking too much of them. She is
victimized by the enormity of her loss; they are victimized by her
misery, by their own pity.

"Nina, don't." David opens his arms and she slides into them. He
presses her head against his chest and she trembles as she hears the
too-rapid beat of his heart. Holding her, calming her by moving his
large hand down her vertebrae, bone by bone, as he so often does at
night, he himself is calmed.

"I don't even know if we have any right to object to her nursing,
to prevent her. That's something else we didn't think of, we didn't
discuss." Regret and sadness are woven into the flatness of his tone.
Nina slides out of his arms, turns to Arnold.

"How long can Stacey stay in the hospital?" she asks.

"I can stretch it to five days."

"Five days." The period of danger will be defined, cordoned off.
Stacey will have time to gather her strength, to seize control. She
takes David's hand, presses it to her cheek. "Can we give her five
days, David?" They themselves will have years and years. They will
have a lifetime.

"God, I don't know. It's not that simple. Five days. And what
happens after five days?" He holds her hands so tightly that she winces
with pain, but she does not pull away.

From behind the closed door, they hear Stacey's sobs, Hal's soothing voice, and they stare at each other in misery. This they do know.
They do not want to build their joy on Stacey's sorrow. They do not
want to feel that they might have eased her pain and instead increased it.

"Please, Nina!" Stacey's voice travels out to them. It is Nina to whom she appeals because they are mothers both.

"You see?" Nina says, and David knows that she means: *We have no choice, truly we have no choice.*

"I see," he replies.

They understand the danger but are powerless to prevent it. They do not want Stacey's plea to echo in their memories. The decision they could not make has been imposed upon them.

"What else can we do, Arnold?" David asks his brother, and the words are not a question but a statement.

"All right, then." Arnold is grave in defeat. "Miss Ames," he calls to the student nurse, who immediately hurries up to him. "Mrs. Cosgrove will be nursing. I'll tab the chart accordingly."

Kathy Ames nods.

"I'll bring the baby to her now."

They return, all three of them, to Stacey's room where she and Hal sit, his hand on her shoulder. She is no longer crying, but she stares straight ahead and she is very pale.

"They'll be bringing you the baby to nurse very soon," Nina tells her.

At once the color rises to her cheeks. She turns to them and smiles. She turns to Hal and smiles.

"You see," she says. "It doesn't have to be complicated."

"Of course not." Nina is reassuring, although sadness has settled on her and doubt has etched its way into her heart. "We're going now," she adds, anxious to leave at once. She does not want to watch Stacey nurse Felicia Miriam. She does not want to be in the room when the baby is placed in Stacey's arms. "Do you need anything?"

"Oh, nothing. Thanks so much for the fruit. And the flowers." Stacey has recovered. She is effusive with her gratitude.

"I'm going too, Stace. A lot of stuff to do at Ramon's." Hal kisses her on the cheek (as does David, who hesitates only briefly).

Together, they walk toward the elevator and Hal chats easily, amiably, although he plays nervously with his heavy gold chain. He tells them that he has a meeting later in the day with a restaurant

broker from California. Things are really coming along. He has a
couple of possibilities, a couple of options. He winks and Nina nods
(he is, she knows, reassuring them that nothing has changed, that
their plans for the move to California remain in place) and smiles
encouragingly.

Kathy Ames, wheeling the baby, slows her steps when she sees
them. They pause and Nina and David, magnetically drawn to the
infant, look down at her yet again; she lies facedown but they each
touch her back, and Nina's finger brushes a tendril of that pale fringe
of hair that encircles their daughter's head.

"The elevator. Got to run. See you." Hal waves, sprints down the
hall and into the open door of the elevator.

They do not look after him, absorbed as they are in their baby.

"Felicia Miriam," David croons softly. Ah, he loves the sound of
his daughter's name. He remembers now that his aunt Miriam, Amos's
sister, had also been born at spring's beginning. The family had celebrated her birthday each year, on the evening of the first seder. The
dessert had been a birthday cake, baked with the whites of a dozen
eggs and honey from the land of Israel. It was a tradition he had
loved and that had ceased when his aunt died of leukemia during his
adolescence. He will reinstitute it in his home this year when he and
Nina host the first seder. Immediately his spirits soar. In just a few
weeks' time they will celebrate Felicia Miriam's birth with a light
sweet cake served at a festive table covered with books and aglow
with candlelight.

"Take good care of her," he tells Kathy Ames. "She's precious
cargo."

"Oh, I know," the girl assures them, and smiling, she walks on,
carefully pushing the small cart. Arms around each other, David and
Nina stand in the corridor and watch her wheel the baby into
Stacey's room.

23

"Felicia Miriam. Isn't that a pretty name?" Hildy asks.

"Oh, I love the name," Stacey agrees. "Felicia Miriam." She repeats it as though to demonstrate her approval, her acquiescence, and as she speaks she shifts the baby's position very slightly.

Stacey is wearing the white robe that Nina bought her for Christmas, although the day is unseasonably warm. The stiff hospital drapes are drawn back and she has placed her chair (because now, in her fourth day of recuperation, she prefers to nurse in a chair rather than reclining on the bed) in the center of the room so that she sits in a circlet of sunlight. The baby blinks against the brightness and a radiant aureole forms about her head. Hildy, who has not seen the baby before, is oddly shy in the infant's presence. She talks too much and too quickly and tries desperately to think of things to say to Stacey (who, in fact, is content to remain silent as she nurses).

"I'm sorry I didn't come sooner," Hildy says, "but I was finishing my senior paper." She blushes as she says this because it is not true and she is fearful that her voice betrayed the lie. She has completed her own paper (on the short stories of F. Scott Fitzgerald), although it is true that she has been helping Seth, who is writing on Brecht. Hildy has not visited the hospital sooner because she was fearful of seeing Stacey, fearful of confronting her terrible grief over Andrea's death. She is surprised now (although Nina assured her it would be so) to find Stacey so calm and so sweetly absorbed in the baby, in Felicia Miriam.

"Oh, I understand," Stacy assures her. "I know how it is when you have a paper due. That's what I dread about going back to school, although I've decided that I want to get a bachelor's degree in California. I think I can get credit for a lot of my evening extension courses. And they give credits now for life experience. But it was sweet of you to send the flowers, Hildy. I really like them."

"Oh. Great." Hildy (who has no idea which flowers are hers; Nina ordered them by phone) shifts uncomfortably in her seat. Her mother is late. Nina had promised to meet her here at four and it is now four-fifteen. "I'm surprised they let me into your room while you nurse. I thought everything had to be, like, so sterile."

"Oh, only for the first twenty-four hours, I think," Stacey replies as she lifts the baby to her shoulder and gently pats her back. "And this hospital is very relaxed. Especially with private rooms." The baby emits a tiny burp, a barely audible hiccup of repletion, and Hildy smiles.

"She's so cute," she says. "So tiny." She wonders when she will begin to think of Felicia Miriam as her sister, when she will first use the words *my sister*. How will she counter Alison's sardonic grin, Seth's bitter humor? But Alison is so changed now, and Seth (since Alison's suicide attempt, since her return from the sanatorium) is less swift to be judgmental, less harsh in his condemnations.

"She won't be tiny for long," Stacey assures her. "You'll see." She places the baby at her other breast, and Hildy watches the milk stream like a thin ribbon amid the pale blue striation of veins. Embarrassed, she averts her eyes.

"You know, my mom found the bunting she used to bring me home from the hospital. She wants to use it for Felicia Miriam." Hildy loves the combination of names.

"That's nice," Stacey says companionably. "We should be leaving soon. Tomorrow. The day after. I'm not sure." She has already stayed in the hospital longer than she had anticipated, but Arnold insisted that she needed the extra rest, the extra recuperation.

"You've been through a great deal," he had said, and she did not disagree.

"Great," Hildy says. "We can't wait to bring her home."

And it is true. Like David and Nina, she is anxious to see the baby installed in their home. They have worked swiftly, energetically, over the past few days to ready the empty room. The new crib, sparkling white and spangled with small flowers of pink and violet, made up with sheets and bumpers of matching colors, is in place beneath the large window that overlooks the garden. The changing table, its drawers filled with stretch suits and undershirts, is in place against the wall. Gleaming white plastic containers hold cotton balls and tubes of ointment. A rug of muted shades of coral and blue covers the polished wooden floor and a thick mat lies beneath it.

"We don't want her to hurt herself when she falls," David explained to Hildy. Already he envisions his daughter toddling about this bright room, sprawling across the gently colored rug. Already he hears her laughter, sees her clinging to the arms of the golden oak rocking chair on which Nina placed a coral-colored corduroy cushion.

Nina had Amos Roth's charcoal drawing of the bird carrying a fiery twig in its beak set in a frame of a coral-stained wood and David hung it on the wall opposite the crib. Next to it, in a silver frame, is an enlarged color photograph of two laughing small girls sailing down a slide shaped like a dragon.

David took that photograph in a Jerusalem park on the same afternoon he and Nina had visited Yad VaShem. Still saddened by the heartbreaking exhibits, haunted by the grim artifacts and photos of death and loss, they had decided to walk from Mount Herzl into the city. They made their way slowly, hobbled by their grief, burdened by the horror they could not assimilate. They did not speak as they walked, because there were no words they could offer each other, there was no comfort to be had. They could not speak of the mournful and mourning eyes in skeletal faces, of tattered striped uniforms, of fragments of poetry in a child's hand.

They stopped to rest on a park bench and, although the day was chilly, the playground was full of children. Cheerful and chortling, their faces wind-reddened, their sturdy bodies encased in bright quilted jackets, they clamored for swings, hoisted themselves up jungle gyms, tossed balls to each other and to their parents. They scurried up the steps of the dragon slide, laughed as they disappeared into the dragon's head, and laughed even louder as they came down the slide.

David watched the children and thought of the photograph of two small girls, dark-haired and dark-eyed, huddled in a doorway. An old man had stood beside them as he and Nina stared at the photograph and softly, so softly, he had intoned the kaddish, and David, holding Nina's hand, had also prayed. Like the old man he had prayed for the children, for laughter stilled and joy unrealized and life denied.

But here, in the Jerusalem playground, laughter trilled and there was joyful play and life surged forward. The children quarreled and made up and called to each other in the language of his prayer, and Nina and David watched them as though they were witnessing a miracle. When the two small girls, dark-haired and dark-eyed (so like the girls in the photo) mounted the dragon slide, David reached for his camera. He clicked the shutter at the magical moment when, their faces radiant with excitement, they slid down the glinting incline. The sensitive color film captured the clarity of the Jerusalem air, the fierce scarlet visage of the dragon, and the children, so vital, so joyous. It was a rare shot and Nina had enlarged it, framed it, hung it in her studio, and now she hung it in Felicia Miriam's room.

Hildy thinks of describing the photo, the nursery to Stacey but stops herself and instead walks around the room, reads the cards on the flowers and the basket of fruit, struggles to find something to say. She is relieved when Nina rushes into the room, carrying two overflowing shopping bags.

"Hi, Mom. Listen, I want to go down to the coffee shop and get a Coke or something." She is eager, suddenly, to leave the room. Stacey's calm disturbs and unnerves her. It is strangely reminiscent of Alison's behavior the day of the ice storm. The thought frightens Hildy and she averts her eyes from Stacey, who smiles her welcome at Nina without lifting her eyes from the baby.

"Sure, go ahead," Nina says and sinks into the chair opposite Stacey as Hildy hurries out.

The baby, nestled against Stacey's breast but no longer sucking, is very still, almost like an appendage affixed to the flesh or growing out of it. She neither moves nor makes a sound. Nina leans forward uneasily, chilled by a wild thought, a frightening fantasy. Is she dead? Is it possible for an infant to die at a mother's breast and then cling to it like a tenacious marmoset? Her own thought frightens her, but at that moment Stacey lifts the infant and places her on her shoulder. Her palm circles Felicia Miriam's back, gently massaging it un-til, again, the baby burps, with such softness, such delicacy, that both women smile.

"Do you want to hold her?" Stacey asks, and Nina nods and takes the baby. Stacey places a diaper on her shoulder and Nina sits down, careful to support the fragile head, so neatly fringed by hair the exact color of David's (and like David's, Nina thinks, it will grow in thick and silken). Felicia Miriam turns, offended by the sunlight, and presses her face against Nina's body. Nina feels the dampness of the infant's glutinous, cheese-smelling saliva against her russet silk tunic.

"Your blouse is stained," Stacey says.

"That's all right. I don't mind." She welcomes the smell of the baby. She wants the mother scent of sour milk, of acrid talc-dusted infant to adhere to her skin. "I wish I could nurse," she adds. Her voice is wistful. She yearns for that visceral connection with the infant. She holds Felicia Miriam close so that the warmth of the baby's body is at one with her own. She feels a sweet peace. Oh, she could sit like this forever, cradling her daughter, so sweetly sleeping, so satiated with the milk that even now dribbles from a corner of that tiny berry of a mouth.

Stacey nods. She understands what Nina means.

"Yes. Nursing is wonderful. It's made me come alive again." She is very serious as she fingers the belt of the white robe. She has brushed her hair loose and threaded a white rose through its golden thickness. With this small vanity she has laid new claim to her life. She speaks more slowly now, choosing her words carefully, and Nina, suddenly alert, looks at her as she speaks as though it is important that each syllable register, each phrase be considered.

"You know, after Andrea's funeral I felt that I was the one who had died. I walked and I talked and I tried to eat and I tried to sleep because that's what you're supposed to do when you're alive, but it made no difference. I was like a robot. The only part of me that was alive was the baby moving inside of me. Every other part of me was dead. I thought that if I cut my finger I wouldn't feel it even. I was numb. The boys were afraid of me — Evan and Jared. I know they were, although they didn't say anything. They drew away when I touched them and said my hands were like ice, and they were right.

I couldn't get warm. I sat in that overheated funeral home and I shivered. I wore your black cape indoors and I shivered. I thought, Oh, god, I'll never feel anything, ever again. Only the cold."

And Nina, holding the baby (*Felicia Miriam, Felicia Miriam,* she repeats to herself as though her daughter's name is a mantra), shivers herself and remembers the chill of the day of Andrea's burial; she imagines the winds at the cemetery, the cold earth dropping in clots on that oh, so small white coffin.

"I'm coming out of that now," Stacey continues. "I'm coming back to life, back to myself. I was so frightened. I thought that I would be like my mother. But I'll be all right. I can feel myself alive now, because my milk is flowing and because I can feel Andrea in the baby. I'm almost there. Every time I lift her to nurse her I come closer, closer. But I need time. Just a little more time."

"What are you saying, Stacey?" Nina asks. "What do you want?"

"I want to take Felicia Miriam home. To my home. I want to nurse her for just a while longer. A few weeks. Only a few weeks."

"Stacey! No. No." Nina's voice is shrill with fear. She rises and stands at a remove from Stacey.

Felicia Miriam stirs, her eyes flicker open and close again. Nina turns her back to Stacey and cradles the baby in her arms. She is dizzy with panic, with desperation. She will run from this room, clutching her daughter. She will protect Felicia Miriam from Stacey's need, from Stacey's anguish, from Stacey's terrible, insatiable grief.

Her heart beats faster and she moves toward the door and then stops herself, leans against the wall, wearied by rage. Still, her embrace of the infant is gentle but firm. Still (although she is weeping now, although she finds it difficult to breathe), she does not forget to support the infant's head. Oh, she must shield and protect this child, David's daughter and her own, their Felicia Miriam born of their will, of their vision. They cannot lose her. They will not lose her.

But Stacey approaches, her arms outstretched, her face contorted. She leans forward. She would gather Felicia Miriam into that empty circlet of her arms. Her eyes are brilliant with longing and with fear.

"Give her to me!" Her voice is high, insistent. She speaks with the authority of her grief. And then, suddenly, her strength fades and she totters and grasps the arm of the chair for support.

"Please," she whispers.

All color has faded from her face. Her skin is parchment-pale and her hair, darkened by perspiration, is the color of tarnished brass. She collapses into the chair but her eyes remain riveted to Nina, to the baby.

"I can't give her up yet," she says. "Without her, I'm not alive." She puts her hands to her face and sits on the edge of the chair, her shoulders heaving.

"You think I'm crazy, don't you?"

Nina crosses the room and puts the baby into the small cart. She wraps the blanket around her, touches the curl of the infant's clenched fist. And then she goes to Stacey, kneels before her.

"Of course you're not crazy, Stacey, but you need time. You'll be all right. You'll see."

"I am all right when I'm nursing." Stacey says. "I am. Really."

"Of course you are. You grow stronger every day. And when you're with your family you will feel even stronger."

She forces herself to say these words because she has no other words to offer. And she does not lie. Yes, Stacey's strength will be restored. Yes, the wild thoughts will be tamed and the loss, the terrible loss of Andrea, will somehow be assimilated. There will be laughter again for Stacy and quiet joy and even the comfort of memory. But not yet. Not soon. Not for a very long time.

"No. You don't understand," Stacey insists. "Nothing helps me but the baby. Without her I will die." She leans forward, grips Nina's wrists in her own. Her fingers are icy tentacles, her sorrow-soured breath is oppressive.

Nina pulls free, rises, strides the length of the room to the window. Her back to Stacey, she looks down at a newly green dogwood tree.

"I will die," Stacey repeats.

Her voice grates on Nina's ears. It violates her own certainty; it energizes a new and venomous hatred, a fierce and compelling anger. Oh, what would Stacey have them do, she and David? They are not sponges to absorb her grief. They have no anodyne for her sorrow. They cannot sacrifice their child on the altar of her grief. Stacey is not alone. Other mothers have lost children. There is a litany of tragedy. Leukemia, drowning, fires, freak accidents. Each night the television screen teems with the ravaged faces of bereft women. They tremble and weep and mourn but their lives go on. They arrive early at the school-bus stop and peer anxiously down the street. At the beach they sit too close to the water's edge. They are startled when the phone rings. But they survive. And Stacey too will survive.

"You won't die, Stacey," she says very softly.

Stacey does not reply. Instead, still wearing the white robe, she climbs into the hospital bed, pulls the covers up, and shivers. And weeps. The white rose falls from her hair and is lost amid the folds of the counterpane. Her skin is blanched. Her tears fall onto the snow-white pillowcase.

The nurse comes in and wheels the baby out. Nina gathers up her bags, gets ready to leave. She moves hurriedly, impelled by a sense of danger. It is not safe to be alone with Stacey's sadness, but even as she turns to leave, Stacey speaks.

"Nina, you must let me have her for just a while longer." Her voice is muffled. "It's not so much to ask — after everything that has happened."

"And what will you want after that?" Nina asks harshly, bitterly. Hildy, who enters the room just then, looks at her mother in surprise.

"Nothing. Nothing. I swear." Stacey's reply is hissed through clenched teeth. Stacey sits upright and clutches the sheet. Her grimace is feral, her golden hair an unkempt mane.

Nina feels a stirring of fear. She steps backward as though to shield Hildy from Stacey's sorrow, from Stacey's rage. Her own cheeks burn with fury, fury at Stacey, fury at her own impotence, her own ambivalence. But Hildy moves across the room to Stacey's bedside, eases her back down onto the pillows, wipes her face with a damp washcloth.

"Take it easy, Stacey. It will all work out. You'll see." Hildy speaks with Nina's voice, repeating the words she has heard her mother utter so many times, copying the intonation. And Stacey, in turn, relinquishes all ferocity. Wearied, diminished, her voice is reduced to a piteous plea.

"Please, Nina. Oh, please."

Nina, standing in the doorway, still holding her shopping bags, sways from side to side, fights her faintness, her nausea.

"We'll see," she says at last and leaves. Hildy hurries after her and relieves her of the bags, which she no longer has the strength to carry.

They meet that night in Edith and Arnold's apartment. They sit in the living room, Nina and David, Edith and Arnold, beneath Amos Roth's portrait of the boy survivor, skeletal and hollow-eyed, and drink coffee from the delicate Meissen cups that belonged to Edith's parents. In the den Hildy plays Trivial Pursuit with her cousins and Seth, who, in his sardonic manner, mocks the questions so cleverly that they all giggle wildly. The adults smile tolerantly at the sound of the young people's laughter, grateful for the background of normalcy it offers them. Nina, who ate little at dinner, leans forward to take a cookie. Crumbs spatter on her tan linen skirt and she brushes them absently away. She still wears the russet silk blouse, and the stain left by Felicia Miriam's spit-up forms an uneven crescent that she touches now and again, always sniffing her fingers afterward.

Arnold hands David an envelope.

"This, at least, is encouraging," he says.

David opens it and studies the baby's birth certificate. It is, he reflects, a rather small document, almost flimsy. He holds it carefully, as though it may disintegrate at his touch, and reads it through. The child's name is given as Felicia Miriam. The birth date is correct. The mother's name is Stacey Cosgrove. The father's name is David Roth. His paternity is acknowledged, even certified, he supposes, yet he feels no relief.

"Why is it encouraging?" he asks.

"Stacey gave all the information. She used the name you and Nina chose. She recognized you as the father on a legal document. That means a great deal, doesn't it, Edith?" Arnold turns to his wife for affirmation. He has, he recognizes, sailed into dangerous waters, treacherous emotional currents, and he relies on his wife to help him navigate them.

"It means she recognizes the reality of the situation," Edith says. "She hasn't created a fantasy. She does not imagine that the baby is completely her own or hers and Hal's. She knows that David is the father."

"All right," David says bitterly. "So she's rational. She gave the right answers. But does a rational woman say she'll die if she can't nurse her baby? She told Nina that she feels Andrea within Felicia. Is that rational? Come on, Edith." He is impatient with his sister-in-law, impatient with the language of her profession, which neutralizes the danger that haunts him. He looks up at his father's painting and is, as always, depressed by the threatening darkness of the sky suspended above the frightened and vulnerable boy. *He will not, he cannot lose this child.* Too many children have been lost. Too many children wept and shivered and walked with their heads shorn, their feet bare, to their deaths. Only last week he had read a review of a new Marcel Ophuls film about Klaus Barbie. The reviewer spoke of the fate of the children of Izieu whom Barbie had seized from their sanctuary and sent to the gas chambers of Auschwitz. Two of the Izieu boys had been named David. One of the small girls had been called Miriam. He was grateful then for the Jewish fidelity to names, to the new lives that offset all the terrible deaths, for all the Davids and Miriams born after the Davids and Miriams of Izieu had perished. He is father to Felicia Miriam, and he will protect her and keep her safe. She will sleep in a cushioned crib and awaken to a color photograph of laughing children in a Jerusalem park. Her own laughter will blend with theirs. Never will she stand alone and vulnerable beneath a threatening sky. He will protect her, he and Nina — they will keep her safe. She is, his newborn daughter, death denied and hope redeemed. In her tiny life, all the mysteries of his people's past, his own posterity, his father's wistful words and powerful paintings converge. *He will not, he cannot lose this child.*

"David, I'm not quarreling with you," Edith replies sadly, patiently. "None of this is rational. It hasn't been rational from the beginning."

David sighs but offers no objection. Edith is right. His yearning has propelled them into madness. All that seemed simple (because they so desperately wanted it to be simple) is now shrouded in the shadows of a complexity they cannot begin to define. Still, they cannot look back. Nor does he want to. He has a child, a daughter.

Nina sits opposite him, silent and pale. She leans forward and speaks very slowly, each word carefully, painfully chosen.

"I've been thinking about Stacey, about everything she said." She pauses. She has, in fact, thought of nothing else since leaving the hospital. Stacey's words filled her thoughts and Felicia Miriam filled her heart. Thus doubly burdened by pain and sweetness, she had rested on the daybed in Edith's study and watched the spring twilight drift across the sky, watched a mauve elephantine cloud diminish and become a deep purple sliver. An idea had taken hold, had fretted its way through thought and memory as darkness fell. Now, her voice trembling, she offers it to them.

"I can't stop thinking about Stacey, about everything that's happened to her. I feel angry and I feel betrayed and then I think, my God, Andrea hasn't even been dead a month. Not even a month. She's irrational. Of course she's irrational. What mother wouldn't be?"

"Or father," David interjects. He watches Nina through narrowed eyes, marks the sudden scarlet flush that rouges her cheeks, the brightness of her eyes.

"Or father," she agrees readily. "I don't even think it's crazy that she feels Andrea within Felicia Miriam. I know what she means." David averts his eyes. He knows that Nina is saying that she felt Michael Ernst within the infant Hildy. "Andrea was so much a part of her pregnancy." She thinks of Andrea in her Christmas dress of crimson velvet, of Stacey in the tunic cut of the same fabric, of Andrea's golden head resting on the swell of her mother's pregnancy. "She says she needs time. That's all she's asked for. Time." The word, repeated, is gentle upon her tongue. Time is magical. Within minutes muted light drifts into darkness. "She has a right to that time," she continues, although David's face is tense with anger.

"What about me?" he asks angrily. "What about my right to my child? Don't fathers have rights? I can't believe that you're agreeing with her, that you don't see the danger. Nina, if she takes the baby home we can't be sure that she will ever return her to us. You know that. We could lose her, lose Felicia Miriam!" His voice rises in fear, in anguish. He grips her wrists; furiously, his fingers bite into her flesh, punish her.

"Oh, David, we won't lose her. We can't lose her. But I don't want to feel that we gained our child by dancing on Stacey's grave." The starkness of her own image frightens her, and she falls silent and studies the rich blue and gold pattern of the Oriental carpet, listens to Aaron and Jacob argue, to Seth's quiet intervention.

"She won't die," Arnold protests. "She's being melodramatic, hysterical."

"Manipulative," Edith adds.

Their arsenal of words is powerful and, Nina knows, accurate. Stacey is, at this time, all those things: she is melodramatic, hysterical, manipulative. But none of that changes anything. None of that alters her pain, her excruciating pain, or their debt, their enormous, unrepayable debt.

"David, listen to me. I want to bring Stacey and Felicia Miriam from the hospital to our house. She would have the time she says she needs. The time she does need. She would stay with us, nurse the baby, recuperate. And Felicia Miriam would be in our home, in her own room. Her life as our daughter would begin." Exhausted, Nina leans back, touches the stain on her blouse, sniffs her fingers, inhales the faint lingering scent of the infant, sleepy and sated.

They stare at her as though she speaks in a language that is foreign to them. Their faces frozen in concentration, they consider and their eyes meet, their expressions relax. It is not unfeasible. There is (and this comforts them all) an element of fairness, of balance to it. Stacey will have the time to nurse and Nina and David will have their child.

"We can try," David agrees softly. "We can suggest it to Stacey and Hal, see if they agree." He takes Nina's hand and lifts it to his lips in gratitude, in apology.

She closes her eyes and imagines the four of them, she and Stacey, David and the baby, arriving at their home. Together, their heads bent close, she and Stacey will undress Felicia Miriam, admire her, pass her from hand to hand, each of them holding her gently, tenderly. They will carry her to the window and smile to see her blink against the harsh sunlight of the newborn spring. Stacey will nurse her, seated in the rocking chair, and Nina will change her as David looks on. It is her dance come to life: the caring, loving mothers who move with long and graceful steps, the father who drifts protectively between them, who watches over them and over his child.

"I'll call Hal now. Arrange to meet with him early tomorrow morning. I think we'll have to get his agreement first." David has not forgotten his earlier encounters with Hal; he recognizes the force of his authority, the power of his temper so deftly camouflaged by his boyish insouciance. "What do you think, Edith?" He defers to his brother's wife; she is their emotional consultant, the shrewd assessor of mood and nuance.

Edith nods but Arnold's face is wreathed in sadness. Always, he has tried to protect this younger brother, to shield him from pain. And now, his suggestion, the suggestion made with the fullness of his heart, with his keen perception of his brother's yearning, has plunged them into this emotional quagmire. And he blames himself for neglecting to tab the chart correctly, for neglecting to insure that Stacey did not nurse the baby.

"Yes, talk to Hal," Edith says.

They are conscious then that there is silence in the den. Jacob and Aaron and Seth and Hildy have stopped playing, have even stopped pretending to be involved in the game. They are listening to the conversation, judging the judgments that their parents are making. Nina wonders how much Seth understands of the situation, how much Hildy has told him. She is at once wary of his reaction and indifferent to it. All that matters, after all, is that Felicia Miriam comes home to them, becomes part of their family. The judgment of others is irrelevant. Abruptly, harshly, Hildy calls out, "It's your turn, Aaron, roll the die." David smiles bitterly, and they all shake their heads. It occurs to them that Hildy's words are prescient: they are all rolling the die, taking a gamble.

David goes to the phone. As he dials the Cosgroves' number, he stares again at his father's portrait of the young survivor and again he senses the bewilderment of the boy who has lost his parents just as he, David, may lose his daughter. Grief thickens his voice as he speaks to Hal.

"I'm sorry to call so late," he says, "but I wondered if we could meet to talk about things tomorrow morning. Early."

"Eight o'clock at Ramon's." Hal's reply is swift, as though he has been waiting for this call and has the logistics in place, his own agenda carefully prepared.

They sit across from each other at a table covered with a red cloth bisected by a gleaming oil stain. The empty room is dimly lit. Hal has not lifted the blinds and neither he nor David moves to light the small table lamp. Hal, who has not eaten breakfast (because, in Stacey's absence, the kitchen is a clutter of dirty dishes and sticky counter surfaces), munches on a piece of stale bread left overnight in a wicker basket.

"Sloppy management here," he says. "Herb doesn't know how to run a restaurant. He's too pissant cheap to hire enough busboys. We have a convention dinner booked tonight and the place is a mess. That's a mistake I'm not going to make when I have my own place. I'm not going to cut back on help."

"No, I'm sure you won't," David says. He does not want to talk to Hal about the restaurant he intends to open in California, but he is too wary to change the topic. He does not want to antagonize Stacey's husband. "How are your plans coming?" he asks cautiously.

"I've been in touch with a California lawyer about some good deals. Everything depends on how much cash I can get together. You know, after we sell the house here and figure everything out."

Hal's mention of money encourages David, fertilizes the spore of an idea that he has been nursing for days (because this is a time of desperate seeding, of a wild scattering of hope and fear), but he does not immediately respond to it.

"I can imagine," he says carefully, "that it's hard for you to focus on such things — with everything that's happened."

"It's been a bitch," Hal replies. "A bitch. I can't believe she's gone." He speaks so softly that David must lean forward to hear him.

"She wasn't an ordinary kid, you know. My Andrea. She was special. She had a shine to her. She drew, made up stories, thought things that no one else would think of. She would have been something someday. Really something."

It is, David realizes, the very first time he has heard Hal speak with sustained seriousness, the first time Stacey's husband has not relied on facile charm, on a swift barrage of coarse, enticing chatter. David had never trusted the laughing, clowning Hal (whom he had always thought capable of malicious mischief), but the sad-eyed man who sits opposite him frightens him.

"Yes," he agrees, because Hal is waiting for him to reply. "Andrea was a special little girl."

"Yeah. Yeah. Special." Hal says the word again as though it holds the answer to a question he has long been asking. "She was special. They tell us, me and Stacey, that we'll get over it. I don't think you ever get over something like that, but we're trying."

"Yes," David says. "I know."

"Both of us. Stacey's trying. She's better since the baby was born. She's talking. She has her appetite back. Last night she was burping the baby and I saw her smile. A real smile. It'll take her a while, but she'll come out of it — all the way out of it." His voice quavers. He has been fearful that Stacey would sink into a netherworld — that like her mother she would drift through life draped in the penumbra of her own sorrow. Hal has watched Rose Carmody stand at the window for too many years. But now he is reassured, optimistic. "You've seen how good the nursing is for her. Hey, do you want some coffee?"

"Yes," David answers gratefully. "Coffee would be terrific."

Hal goes into the kitchen and emerges with two steaming restaurant mugs. David takes a sip and grimaces. The coffee, obviously left over from the previous night and reheated, is bitter, almost rancid. Still, he continues to drink while Hal laces the dark, murky beverage in his own cup with sugar — one packet, then another, then a third. His greed repels David. He finds that it is helpful to him to dislike Hal Cosgrove but it is dangerous to pity him.

"It's the nursing I wanted to talk to you about," he says.

"What about it?" Hal's query is guarded, almost hostile.

"Stacey says she wants to continue to nurse the baby even after she leaves the hospital."

"That's right. She told me." Granules of sugar adhere to Hal's lips. He licks them off, takes another slice of bread. The stale crumbs rain down on his kelly-green polyester shirt and he brushes them away impatiently.

"We want to bring the baby home. To our house," David says.

"Then we've got ourselves a problem." Hal's hands (they are very large hands, David notices, and the fingers are alive with dark silken hairs) encircle the coffee mug. "But I have to do what's good for Stacey. That's all that matters to me."

"Maybe there are other things that would be good for Stacey. Like a vacation. Some time away in a different atmosphere, to rest, to be with you. Maybe you and Stacey could take a sort of pilot trip to California to check out some of the places you've been thinking of for your restaurant. It would be expensive, I know, but I'd be glad to help you. I could give you, say, another five thousand dollars." David speaks slowly, cautiously, his eyes fixed on Hal's face.

He is uncomfortable with this discussion, repelled by the recognition that he is trying to buy the baby, setting a price on his own child. But that does not matter. All that matters is Felicia Miriam and his freedom to claim her as his own, to establish himself as her father and Nina as her mother. He lay awake all night thinking about the baby, about Nina's suggestion, about his own last and wild card. As his fatigue grew, children's faces wafted toward him, floated above him like nimbus clouds colliding with each other — the laughing children in the Jerusalem park and the skeletal children of the years of terror, their eyes deeply sunk into thin and mournful faces. His brother's sons sat opposite each other over a chessboard, wearing his father's frown. Hildy dances past him and in her arms Felicia Miriam smiled as she slept.

He dozed off at last as dawn edged near and awakened to hear Nina's voice.

"We can't lose her, David. We can't."

He had rolled over and held her close. She had been crying and he licked at her tears and etched a message onto her back with his fingers.

"Don't cry," he wrote.

She read his script, smiled.

"I won't." Her voice was childish in the darkness. They have not played this game for years.

"Trust me," he scrawled.

"Write it again. More slowly."

His fingers traced the letters onto her skin and this time she discerned the words.

"I do. I do."

Thus reassured, she fell asleep.

And now, he sips the lukewarm coffee and waits for Hal's reaction. It is not long in coming.

"Five thousand dollars." Hal whistles. "That's a lot of money."

"Yes. It is a lot of money."

"But not enough." Hal's voice is hard. He rips open another packet of sugar and pours it into his mouth. Several granules snow down upon his beard and cling like shimmering diamond dust.

David was right (although he had feared to discuss this approach with Nina). He and Hal would work everything out between them. They would come to terms.

"You don't have to go much higher," Hal continues. He spits his words out in pellets of scorn. "You don't have to go anywhere at all. Listen, this is my wife we're talking about. My Stacey. This isn't a business deal here. You're not driving a bargain with me for one of your switches or gadgets or whatever the hell it is that you design. We're not in the baby-selling business. You think I let Stacey go into this just for the lousy twenty thousand dollars? It was something she wanted to do. For you and your wife. For herself. You know what she called it? A good deed, *the best deed* — that was what she said. Sure, the money was part of it. She wanted to do something for you and get something for our family at the same time, for me and the kids. And she kept her bargain. She had the baby, hers and yours. We couldn't, when all this began, figure on what would happen, what did happen." And now his voice softens; sorrow smooths its harshness, filters its anger. He cannot speak of Andrea's death. His daughter, his sweet princess, has no place in this conversation, in this dumb, half-assed exchange. His eyes are glazed and his lips twitch, but he is silent. He leans back in his chair, exhausted.

"I'm sorry," David says and recognizes the feebleness, the inadequacy of his apology. He is sorry and more than sorry. He is deeply ashamed. He has, from the beginning, misjudged Hal Cosgrove, who is, after all, a good man. "I wasn't thinking. And I want you to know that I never discussed this with Nina."

"Oh, you were thinking," Hal says. "But you were thinking wrong." His lips crease into a thin, bitter smile of forgiveness. "I know you want your daughter. But I want what's good for Stacey, what she wants, and she wants to be with the baby a little longer."

"Nina had an idea," David says. "She suggests that Stacey come from the hospital to our house. She could recuperate and nurse the baby there. We have a guest room or we could set up a daybed in the baby's room."

"I don't know." Hal's brow is furrowed and he feels a tremor of fear. He does not like the idea. He wants Stacey back in their house. He wants her beside him in their bed. He will coax forth her laughter as he mocks the talk shows that flicker across their television screen. He will cause her to moan softly as he reclaims her, restores her to their life together. She will hug their sons and shout at them and he will buy her thick paperback books that she will read with a dictionary, mouthing unfamiliar words aloud. And if she comes home with the baby (Hal does not call David Roth's daughter by name; the words *Felicia Miriam* tumble clumsily in his mind, confound his tongue), when she is done with nursing, he will lick the droplets of milk from her breast, taste their warm sweetness. "I'm your baby, your big baby," he will say (as he has said before), and she will run her fingers through his thick dark hair and speak to him softly, comfortingly. He does not want Stacey to live, even briefly, in the Roth's large, wide-windowed house where always he has felt himself an intruder, a trespasser, vulnerable to their judgment, their fragile, uneasy tolerance. His only ally in that house is Hildy, and he has not spoken to her since the baby's birth.

"We thought it might make an easier transition," David adds. "And we thought also that it would be easier for the boys, for Jared and Evan. Less confusing than Stacey bringing the baby home and then the baby disappearing from their lives." He does not add that the small boys will then have lost two sisters instead of one, that they will have to reconcile themselves to two losses. Because he remembers himself as a bereft small boy (and remembers still his father's inert form, his mother's terrified and terrifying scream), he has thought often about Evan and Jared to whom so much must be explained. "And Hal, I'm thinking about Stacey also, about what's best for her."

"No. You're thinking about your baby," Hal corrects him. "I don't blame you for it, but let's not fool ourselves. I'm thinking about Stacey and my kids."

"And about yourself," David says. Like Hal, he can invoke honesty. All their cards are on the table now.

"Yeah. About myself." Hal does not disagree. The kitchen help begins to arrive, and a delivery truck honks loudly. The day is beginning at Ramon's. Hal acknowledges greetings, waves, crumbles another piece of bread. "Look, let me talk to Stacey about it. I'll go along with what she wants."

"We haven't got a lot of time," David reminds him.

"Hey, I know that. Don't I know that?" Hal knows that Stacey cannot stay in the hospital much longer. Another day perhaps, two days at the most. Her stay has been extended this long only because of Arnold's influence.

David drinks the rest of the coffee. Lukewarm now, its bitterness is more pronounced. It leaves a metallic taste in his mouth but he drains it to the dregs, imbibing it as medicine, as punishment. They rise then and Hal walks him to the door. David extends his hand and Hal takes it. Standing in the slat of pale sunlight, the two men shake hands solemnly, as though a compact has been concluded.

"I didn't mean . . ." David begins to apologize yet again but Hal interrupts him.

"It's okay. You're playing for keeps, for your daughter. Don't kid yourself. I'd do the same thing if I could." That there is nothing he can do, that he has lost his daughter (for keeps), is acknowledged between them by their shared silence and the strong grip of their joined hands.

David takes a cab to his office and hurries past his receptionist, his secretary, into his own small bathroom where he surrenders at last to his nausea and vomits. The regurgitated coffee swirls in blackened clots in the blue water of the toilet bowl and he continues to retch, moaning softly as he gasps for breath.

"Go to their house? With the baby?" Stacey repeats Hal's suggestion, enunciating carefully, as though she has somehow misunderstood him.

"Yes." Hal is careful to keep his voice indifferent.

"What do you think?"

"I'll go along with whatever you want."

"What about the boys?"

She does not turn to face him but remains at the window looking down at the park. The dogwood, which she has been watching since her first day in this room, is budding now and the delicate star-shaped blossoms are heavy upon the fragile branches.

"They can stay on with Audrey and Mike. Audrey likes the idea. It makes her feel superior. She oozes kindness. Last night she baked a chocolate cake. It's like she's waiting for a letter congratulating her on being chosen American Aunt of the Year." Hal laughs with happy malice. He is not ungrateful for his sister-in-law's efforts but he sees them in perspective.

Stacey laughs softly but is immediately serious again.

"She won't think it's funny that I'm going to the Roths?"

"Sure, she'll think it's funny. She'll think it's weird. It'll give her and Cathy something to gossip about for at least a hundred hours."

"We'll have to tell them something soon," Stacey says, but there is no concern in her voice. Throughout the pregnancy she had worried about her family's reaction, had invented scenarios, weighed truth against falsehood, fearing their condemnation. Now their judgment is a matter of indifference to her; she thinks about it idly, distractedly. She dismisses them from her thoughts and watches two gray squirrels chase each other amid the branches of the dogwood. If the tree were in full blossom the soft white flowerlets would glide gently through the air, like snowflakes. Like snowflakes. Stacey feels tears begin to burn and she turns from the window, her breasts throbbing. She has discovered that when she weeps, her milk begins to flow as though her body's founts are warring adversaries, the sweet milk competing with the saline tears.

"Let's wait before we tell them anything," Hal says. "Let's wait and see what happens."

She does not reply, and her silence is an acknowledgment that anything might happen. They have learned, in these last weeks, not to anticipate anything with certainty. They are too vulnerable to chance; their best-laid plans may be deterred by the vagaries of weather (a falling snow, a patch of glistening ice), by a chance misstep, a careless misstatement.

"The boys can visit me there. At the Roths."

"No. We can go home. I'll get a woman to come in, to clean up. We can order in a pizza, watch TV with the boys. The baby will be taken care of. They'll have you all to themselves. We can take them out. Maybe to the Italian place with your family on Sunday. Maybe to the movies. It'll be good for them. They need it."

He does not tell Stacey that Evan is bewildered, angry. Evan's science experiment (a design rendered with magnets and the powdered iron in the chemistry set Hildy bought him for Christmas) won first prize at his school's science fair, but there was no parent present to witness his acceptance of the award. Audrey and Cathy had attended because Hal was at the hospital with Stacey. Audrey had tried to comfort Evan.

"You know, it's hard for your folks, between Andrea and the new baby," Audrey said.

"Andrea's dead." Hurt made Evan cruel. "And the baby is just a baby. She doesn't know if they're there or not. Everyone else had someone there — a mother or a father."

Audrey and Cathy do not count (although he kissed them dutifully). It is only a mother and a father who can be seduced by achievement, who recognize the beginnings of independence, who are important on such a day. Always, before, Stacey has been there beaming and proud, swift to hug him, to ask the questions and wait for his answers. ("Did you do that? Did you really do that?" "I did. I can. I will. And without you.")

And Jared (always too sensitive, always too quick to weep) wanders through Audrey's house, clutching one of Stacey's scarves. Every night he cries himself to sleep after first wrapping himself in a large blanket so that if he awakens at night and must urinate, he cannot extricate himself swiftly enough and often wets the bed.

This, too, Hal keeps from Stacey, who asks very few questions, although she speaks to both boys on the phone each day. ("Did you do your homework?" she asks Evan. "Be nice to Aunt Audrey," she tells Jared.) It will all be dealt with later. Later. When they are restored to normalcy, when they are back on track, when they are on the plane to California, ready to launch their "happily ever after."

"Maybe it's a good idea then," Stacey says at last.

She is, she acknowledges, relieved not to be returning to her own home where Andrea's plaid coat still hangs in the closet and where, beyond the closed door of her room, the pink satin comforter covers her small bed and the pink crocus (which Hal waters each morning) is in full bloom. She needs more time, just a little more time.

Later that afternoon, Kathy Ames, the pretty student nurse, wheels Stacey down to the hospital reception area where she will be discharged. Stacey holds Felicia Miriam, dressed in Hildy's pink bunting, in her arms. Felicia Miriam cries although she has just been nursed. Nina and David wait for them. Hal is caught up at Ramon's, managing the convention dinner, which is overbooked and understaffed.

Nina and Stacey sit in the rear of the car while David drives. When they leave the city limits, Stacey, overcome by weariness, hands the baby to Nina, who holds her for the rest of the journey. And so it is Nina who carries Felicia Miriam into the house and up the long staircase, past Hildy's room where Alison and Seth sit, listening to a James Taylor tape.

"We're home," Nina says brightly.

"Great," Hildy says. She stands in the doorway and blinks as though dazzled by an unfamiliar light and then goes back into her room. She closes the door gently behind her and chooses another tape.

24

They sleep fitfully that first night. Felicia Miriam's presence in the house excites and delights them and they awaken frequently and hug each other in the darkness.

"She's here. She's really here," David whispers to Nina, and she laughs, pleased by his pleasure, newly amused by the memory of his large hands fumbling with the tiny pink kimono as he dressed his daughter for the first time that evening. He struggled to make a bow but could only knot the silken ties.

"This is hard," he had complained, "Really hard."

Watching him so absorbed, his lips pursed, Nina, Stacey, and Hildy had laughed and he had shaken his finger at them.

"No fair," he had said. "Four women against one guy."

And Felicia Miriam, impatient beneath his ministrations, too long on the changing table, had emitted a piercing infant wail that increased their laughter.

Now, they hear that wail again, swiftly followed by Stacey's door opening, her feet padding down the corridor to the nursery.

"The two A.M. feeding," Nina says sleepily.

"But it's almost three."

"Stupid daughter of ours — can't tell time." Nina stretches langorously.

Hand in hand then, they lie awake and listen until they hear Stacey's footsteps as she returns to her own room and closes the door. They wait for a few minutes and then, like mischievous children, they scamper out of bed. Barefoot, holding their fingers to their lips, they hurry down the corridor and glide into the nursery. Felicia Miriam, fed and changed, lies on her stomach, her legs curled beneath the pink thermal blanket. She is asleep but her lips are puckered; she stirs and kisses the darkness. David straightens the blanket (which does not require straightening) and Nina opens the small olivewood music box that she has placed on a table near the crib. The soft tinkling sounds of a gentle waltz fill the nursery. David, in the striped pajamas that are too large for him, bows to Nina from the waist. And she, in her pale green nightgown, smiles and curtsies. She takes his arm and allows him to lead her into the circlet of moonlight that pours into the center of the room. They dance slowly, elegantly, to the music so soft and delicate, moving toward the baby's crib. They reach it as the music stops and together they look down at Felicia Miriam, whose blue-veined eyelids flutter briefly beneath their gaze.

"She's so beautiful," David says hoarsely. He wonders if he will ever become accustomed to the miracle of this baby, to the knowledge that he has a child, that a part of him lives within this sweetly sleeping infant.

Nina plays the music box again and the strains of the waltz trail after them as they tiptoe down the hall to their own room.

It seems to David that he has barely slept (although a glance at the bedroom clock tells him that it is five-thirty) when he again hears the baby's cry. This time Stacey does not awaken (although he waits for the sound of her footsteps), nor does Nina. He himself rises and goes to the nursery.

Felicia Miriam is crying lustily. Her tiny face, screwed up in misery, reminds David of a raspberry.

"Hey," he says to her as he lifts her from the crib, "don't cry. Daddy's here, my raspberry girl."

Her diaper is soiled and the odor gives him an odd satisfaction. He puts her on the changing table and, mysteriously, his movements are deft as he removes the dirty diaper, wipes her body clean, and gently spreads cream across the tiny smile of her vagina and into the narrow rectal crevice. He is moved by the miracle of this anatomy in miniature, by the privilege and responsibility that gives him such intimate dominion over his daughter's tiny form. He kisses her flailing feet and her hands are in his hair as he bends over her. Light as butterflies, he feels them on his head.

"Raspberry girl, raspberry girl," he croons softly, but she begins to cry again and draws her legs up to her stomach. She is hungry. He takes one of the bottles out of the case of prepared formula, balancing her on his shoulder, and settles himself in the rocking chair to feed her. She sucks strongly but within minutes her eyes close and she sleeps within the cradle of his arm as he rocks gently back and forth, holding the barely diminished bottle in his other hand. He hums and the melody is the half-remembered Yiddish song Amos Roth sang in his studio as he painted. David holds his daughter and looks up at the charcoal drawing of the bird. He remembers the name of the song now: "Raisins and Almonds." He sings the words softly and Felicia Miriam shifts slightly and sleeps on in his arms.

The door to the nursery opens and Stacey stands there. She stares at him, her eyes still sleep-glazed, her hair disheveled.

"I thought I heard her cry," she says.

David eases himself out of the chair and carries the baby to the crib. Stacey watches him as he sets her down without disturbing her sleep and covers her, and then she moves to stand beside him. She touches the sleeping infant's face with her finger, as though to assure herself of its warmth, its reality.

"I changed her and gave her a bottle," David says. "Was that all right?" He seeks her reassurance although they have spoken about a relief bottle for this early-morning feeding. He does not want her to feel usurped, invaded.

"Fine," she says. "Fine. I was so tired I guess it took me a while to hear her."

"I'll have to set up an intercom system," David suggests. "They have really sensitive mikes and receivers now; we'll put them all through the house." Already he plans the network of wires, the cunning gadgets that will monitor his daughter's every move and link her to them by even the faintest of sounds.

"Good," Stacey replies. "That will keep her safe."

David is unprepared for the sadness in her voice, but then he realizes that she is thinking of the child who had not been kept safe, and in sympathy, he puts his arm about her shoulders and walks her to the door. There they turn again, both reluctant to leave the sleeping baby, and see that with the sun's rising, long splinters of pale light are scattered across the crib and illumine Felicia Miriam's out-turned cheek and the soft halo of her fringe of hair.

Now they smile in shared wonder and return to their beds, each listening for the soft closing of the other's door.

David slides into bed beside Nina, who awakens and wrinkles her nose.

"Yuch," she says sleepily, "What's that smell?"

He lifts his hands and realizes that the dark gold remnants of Felicia Miriam's bowel movement rim his fingernails. Grinning, he makes a claw of his hand and thrusts the offending fingers at Nina, who slithers away, laughing and holding a pillow up in defense.

"Grr," he growls. "You can't get away. The baby monster is coming to get you."

She seizes one of the stuffed camels from the headboard and tosses it at him, but he leaps across it and rips the pillow away.

"Hello, Baby Monster." Defeated, she smiles up at him, her long dark hair caping the white sheet, her green nightgown slipping away from her breast.

They make love then, in the half light of dawn, and afterward, although Nina falls asleep almost at once, David lies awake, suffused with a new contentment. His newborn daughter sleeps peacefully in his house, his wife lies beside him. He is, at that moment, at one with himself, and he does not close his eyes but watches the morning light grow brighter and brighter.

Nina carries Stacey's breakfast tray up to her that first morning.

"Watch out. You'll spoil me," Stacey says as she sits up in bed. But the truth is that she is grateful for the tray. She is exhausted. She had forgotten the fatigue that attends the caring for a new baby — the nights of interrupted sleep, the depletion of energy, the moody nervousness.

"What's wrong with being spoiled?" Nina asks.

She sets the tray on the bedside table and perches on the edge of the bed.

"The carriage I ordered is here," she reports. "David was here

when UPS delivered it. Would you believe, he couldn't figure out
how to get the hood up?" She laughs and Stacey giggles. They are
thus locked in a feminine complicity, amused and scornful of mas-
culine clumsiness.

"Well, he managed to change her all right this morning," Stacey
reports.

"He'll get there," Nina predicts indulgently. "He just loves the
baby." Immediately, she regrets her words. Stacey turns her head,
closes her eyes. "Are you all right, Stacey?" she asks.

"Fine. Just tired." She lifts her coffee cup and sets it down after
taking only a few sips.

"You know what," Nina says. "You stay in bed this morning and
rest. I'll take Felicia Miriam for a walk in her new carriage. And I'll
bring her back for the eleven o'clock nursing. How's that?" She is at
once asking Stacey's permission and trying to establish a routine for
the time that Stacey will spend with them. It is a delicate high wire
that she treads; she would befriend Stacey and mother Felicia Miriam. She must struggle still to maintain the same uneasy balance she
has managed for all these long months.

"It's not too cool?" Stacey asks worriedly.

"No. No. It's beautiful out." She stifles the annoyance that wells
up within her. *Does Stacey think she would risk taking the baby out if
the weather was not fine?*

"All right then." Stacey sinks gratefully back against the pillows
and Nina hurries out. "Oh, Mrs. Ludovico is downstairs if you need
anything," she calls over her shoulder.

"All right." Stacey knows and likes the motherly Italian woman
who helps Nina in the house and who has now agreed to give Nina
several additional hours each week.

Nina goes into the nursery and dresses Felicia Miriam in a yellow
terry-cloth stretch suit. She herself wears yellow sweatpants and a
yellow shirt.

"We're twins," she tells the baby who looks up at her. "Mother
and daughter twins." Felicia Miriam whimpers as Nina bundles her
into a snow bunny outfit. Her head is so small that the hood slides
off, and Nina finds a tiny knitted cap and ties it beneath the chin.
Fine wisps of hair slip out beneath it onto the infant's high forehead

and Nina brushes them down with the soft silver-backed brush she used for Hildy all those years ago. "Hey, you're beautiful. Do you know you're beautiful?" she asks, but Felicia Miriam has drifted back to sleep and does not awaken when Nina carries her downstairs.

"Oh, so beautiful." Mrs. Ludovico stands at the bottom of the stairs and beams at Nina, at the baby. Her face is wreathed in a smile of admiration and Nina feels shy and proud. She smiles down at her daughter. She is so beautiful and so good.

Mrs. Ludovico holds the door open and Nina settles the baby in the high coach carriage. Although the day is warm, she puts up the hood and covers Felicia Miriam with the blue carriage blanket of Shetland wool that Edith had used for her sons, passed on to her by Claire Silberman, who had used it for both David and Arnold. Faded now, slightly frayed at the edges, it is still thick, and although it is newly laundered, Nina thinks that the soft fibres must retain the scent of the other small lives it sheltered and the loving hands that smoothed and folded it, year after passing year.

She releases the brake and wheels the carriage down the quiet road. A neighbor working in her garden glances up as Nina approaches the house.

"Lovely day," she calls.

"Marvelous," Nina agrees. "Perfect for the baby's first walk."

"Oh, let me see." Nina does not know this neighbor well, although she knows that her children are grown and that many years ago, long before Nina and David moved onto this road, an adolescent son had been killed in an auto accident. The woman hurries to the carriage and peers into it. Her face softens with the tenderness peculiar to older women who, as they look at small babies, are suffused with memory and longing.

"Isn't she lovely?" she says. "Isn't she perfect?"

"We think so," Nina says. "But I guess all parents think that about their new babies." This is, she realizes, her first public proclamation of her motherhood, and she is surprised at the lightness of her voice, of the surety of her words.

"Oh, she is," the woman assures her. "You're so lucky, Nina. So very lucky."

"I know."

Her spirits are high now, inflated by that luck, by her recognition
of their good fortune. No awkward questions have been asked because there are no awkward questions to be asked. Felicia Miriam is
hers and thus recognized as her own. Her neighbor gives her a sprig
of forsythia and she grins and tucks it behind her ear.

"Wait." The older woman snips another spray and drops it onto
the blanket. Thus garlanded, she walks on toward the small neighborhood park that overlooks an abandoned quarry.

She hears the hum of a car motor and steers the carriage to the
edge of the road, but the car slows and brakes behind her.

"Hey, Mom." Hildy pokes her head out of the window of Seth's
car and then opens the door and bounds out, Alison and Seth following her.

"No school?" Nina asks.

"Two periods off for teacher's conferences," Hildy says. "Listen, I
want you guys to meet Felicia Miriam and I want you to tell me she's
the cutest baby you've ever seen."

Obediently, Alison and Seth lean over the carriage.

"Hello, Felicia Miriam, you're the cutest baby I've ever seen,"
Alison says.

"Listen, Felicia Miriam, I'm going to be completely honest," Seth
adds. "I've seen cuter, a lot cuter. I mean, it pays to be honest at
the beginning of a relationship."

Hildy picks up a twig and tosses it at him.

"Okay," he corrects himself. "Maybe not the cutest but the
sexiest."

"Hey, don't corrupt my sister." Hildy is stern, protective, and she
herself stares at the sleeping baby. *Oh, God, she is so little, so vulnerable.* She smiles but she is afraid that she will cry. And Nina, one
hand on the carriage, touches Hildy's arm, smoothes back her hair,
grateful that Hildy does not flinch from her touch, surprised that she
knew Hildy would not flinch. They are united now in their love for
and awe of this infant who has come into their home, into their
lives.

"We have to get going if we're going to make it to the village and
back in time," Seth says impatiently, and as swiftly as they

descended upon her they scramble back into the car and, waving, drive off.

Nina smiles and wonders what, if anything, Hildy has told her friends about this baby.

She walks on and by the time she reaches the quarry park she is tired.

Nina brakes the carriage beneath a maple tree on whose slender branches the delicate young leaves of early spring are loosely furled. She sits down on the stone bench and stares into the still waters across which flocks of birds soar in the linear pattern of their spring migration. A community of terns nests amid the willows on the opposite shore, and Nina and David, who often walk along this path, have occasionally caught a glimpse of the majestic white sea birds. Her hand on the carriage, she gently rocks it and then looks up to see two terns flying in tandem, interrupting the flight lines of a flock of long-tailed swallows, who obediently part to allow them through.

Nina gasps at their grace and beauty and Felicia Miriam stirs. Her eyes open and before she can cry, Nina lifts her from the carriage and wraps the blue Shetland blanket about her.

"Look," she says and holds the infant up, her face turned to the beautiful white birds who sail across the sky into their cove beyond the willows. And the infant is quiet, her small face radiant in the rush of sunlight; her eyes are open and, it seems to Nina, they follow the path of the birds (although she knows, of course she knows, that their range and focus are not yet strong enough). Still, she holds Felicia Miriam aloft, light-headed now with the thrill of beauty shared. Oh, she has so much to give this baby, to share with her. Smiling, she sits down on the bench and cradles the blanketed baby in her arms. She leans forward and takes up the spray of forsythia. Cosseted by the sun's warmth, she brushes the infant's face with the soft and fragrant flowers and places a tiny blossom at the trim of her bonnet.

When Nina returns to the house, she carries Felicia Miriam up to Stacey, who changes her while Nina leans on the opposite end of the changing table.

"Oh, such a tired baby," Stacey says, because the baby's eyes are closed and her limbs are heavy with drowsiness, "Did you have a nice walk, tired baby?"

"We saw two beautiful terns, didn't we, little thing?" Nina speaks in the lilting, childish tone peculiar to mothers who chat with warm affection to their infant children. Her voice is not unlike Stacey's own, with its playful, singsong intonations. Felicia Miriam, indifferent to them both, sleeps on, nor does she awaken when Stacey places her at her breast; she nurses with her eyes closed, emitting a tiny whimper when she is shifted from one breast to the other.

Nina leaves the nursery and goes to her studio. The time she spent with Felicia Miriam has energized her, stirred up ideas that she is eager to work through. She had feared that the obligations of this new motherhood would deplete her, but instead she is invigorated, fired with a sense of purpose and eager to work because she is newly aware of constraints on her time. She studies the video yet again and makes notes for revisions. She dances through a new solo in which Tina sweeps across the stage, cradling an infant. She remembers herself in the park, lifting the blanketed baby, and, smiling, she works that gesture, that urgent maternal invitation to beauty and wonder, into the dance. She does not break her session when she hears a car drive up the circular driveway, although she does look out the window and sees Hal comb his hair before walking to the door.

Hal and Stacey sit in the den. Felicia Miriam is asleep in her crib and Hal has not asked to see her. He has brought with him a report on the space shuttle that Evan wrote for school and that the teacher gave a gold star and two happy-face seals. Stacey reads it slowly. In all things now, she measures her pace. She is at once recovering from her grief and gathering her strength. Her hands are steady as she unfolds Jared's nursery-school painting. With broad and wild strokes he has painted a black background interlaced with writhing swirls of crimson. She thinks of the black tar of Schoolhouse Hill beneath the thin sheeting of ice and of Andrea's blood staining it with a crimson thickness; she fights a surge of nausea and forces herself to listen to Hal.

"It's a fire engine, he said. When I told him I couldn't make it out too well, he told me that was because it was moving too quickly down the street. He told me that slowly, like I was an idiot or something." Hal laughs at Jared's precocity and Stacey smiles weakly. She places both Evan's report and the drawing on the coffee table.

Hal has also brought color snapshots of restaurant sites in California and these Stacey studies with interest. She is especially interested in the landscaping of the exteriors.

"Oh, currant bushes," she notes. "And those are leopard lilies. And mariposa tulips."

She knows the names of the flowers because she so carefully studied the flora of California in the oversized picture books she checked out of the library, which she and Andrea had flipped through during those long and lazy afternoons of her pregnancy when they lay sprawled across her unmade bed.

"You can go on *Jeopardy!*" Hal says. "The category is California flowers, and remember, contestants, phrase your answers as questions." He strokes his imagined mustache and smiles engagingly in his Alex Trebek imitation. Andrea had always giggled ecstatically when he imitated the quiz master, when he mocked the categories and the questions, and, remembering that now, they are silent and fearful of looking at each other.

"You all right?" Hal takes her hand and links his fingers through her own.

Stacey nods. She does not tell Hal that sorrow attacks her like a small scurrying animal, darting across her heart suddenly, unexpectedly. To thwart such surprise invasions, she lies in wait, sets traps, schools herself to evoke Andrea's name in moments of calm.

"Hey, I've got to go. Got to be there in time to set up for happy hour."

He kisses her on the cheek and leaves. Stacey waits for a moment but she knows that she cannot counter the depression by herself. She goes to the nursery and lifts Felicia Miriam from her crib. She holds the compliant baby close. The baby is her shield, her protection against the sharp-toothed rodent of sorrow that would gnash away at the thin carapace of calm that shields her from despair. She is still holding the baby when there is a knock at the door. Judith, her new friend (bonded to Stacey because she too buried a child, wearing the same black maternity dress she had lent Stacey for Andrea's funeral), enters. She is a plump, smiling woman and she nods approvingly at Stacey.

"Oh, the baby is so beautiful," she says. "You'll be fine. You'll see.

Having a new baby helps so much. And you're lucky to be staying with such good friends."

"Yes," Stacey says. She is pleased to see Judith. Judith is proof that a loss as enormous as her own can be sustained, that recovery, even triumph, over the madness of her grief (and she recognizes that madness even as she battles it), is possible. And Judith is right. The new baby is her relief, her panacea, and yes, she is fortunate in her friendship with Nina and David. She and Felicia Miriam are jointly in their care, jointly sheltered beneath the mantle of their tenderness.

That evening David sets up the intercom system. With great precision he installs the network of wires and speakers. Hildy helps him. She holds the ladder and hands up his tools and dashes up the stairs as each receiver is installed to make sure the sounds from the nursery are transmitted. She speaks in a very soft voice from a position near the crib.

"Do you read me?" she says. "Over and out."

Felicia Miriam awakens at the sound of her voice and Hildy lifts the baby. Her diaper is wet and Hildy changes it.

"Operation dry Pamper in progress," she says. "This is cool. Smelly but cool."

Nina, David, and Stacey hear her through the intercom and laugh. Hildy's humor, her acceptance, normalizes their situation and they are grateful to her. They experience a new ease, a hesitant optimism.

That night Nina and David again awaken when Felicia Miriam wails with hunger. The intercom picks up the sound of the baby's cry and Stacey's swift steps. They hear her comforting whisper as she picks the baby up, changes her. Even the creak of the rocker as she nurses is transmitted. And then, after she has returned to her room, David rises and goes to the nursery. He picks Felicia Miriam up and carries her back to their bedroom where Nina waits for him expectantly.

She has arranged their menagerie of stuffed animals in a large circle on the sheets and David sets Felicia Miriam down in the center.

"Here's our baby, here's our sweet."

Nina inclines her head to the baby. Her long black hair blankets the small body. She kisses each tiny toe, kisses the tiny strawberry

marking tucked into the cleft of the neck. And David, leaning across
the stuffed animals, kisses her, and his large fingers curl about the
wisps of pale hair that fringe his daughter's brow. One by one he lifts
the animals and dangles them above the baby, and Nina laughs as
he repeats their names.

"Meet Tigger," he says solemnly, holding up a long and fluffy tiger.
"And Golda and Meir." He balances the Chanukah camels on each
arm and then he bends his head low and nuzzles Felicia Miriam,
kisses the firmness of her small stomach, the tender cushions of her
knees.

Nina lies across the bed, watching them, her head resting against
a turquoise elephant. She smiles at the game and David lifts Felicia
Miriam and places her on Nina. The baby falls asleep against the
softness of her breast and Nina listens to the rhythmic sound of her
breathing, feels the light and steady beat of the infant heart. Her
arm encircles the baby. She would lie like this forever, at one with
their daughter, her husband's loving and laughing face close by her
own. She is half asleep when David gently takes Felicia Miriam and
carries her back to the nursery. Her breast, where the child rested,
is very warm, and she touches her own hand to it and sinks into the
deepest and sweetest of sleeps.

They settle then into a daily routine, the baby's care and feeding
evenly distributed, their own small idiosyncrasies marked and monitored. Stacey, ever the avid student, observes the small habits of the
household. She listens for the small sounds that mark the domestic
rhythm: the clatter of Hildy's car keys as she tosses them into the
bronze bowl on the hallway table when she arrives home, the cham-
ber music Nina plays as she drinks her morning coffee, the opening
of the windows when David rises each morning and their closing
when he goes to sleep each night. She recognizes different steps upon
the staircase: Hildy's light-footed gambol, Nina's slow and even gait,
David's heavy tread. Felicia Miriam's anguished wails of hunger and
discomfort, the faint chirps of her infant contentment, are added to
the domestic polyphony.

And Stacey grows stronger. She walks more swiftly and no longer
feels the need to sleep in the afternoon. She delights in dressing

Felicia Miriam, in speaking to the baby as she carries her through the garden, wheels her down the road in her high and elegant coach carriage.

"I am getting better," she tells herself. "I will be all right."

She laughs more frequently during Hal's visits and asks more questions. She claps when he does his imitation of Johnny Carson for Mrs. Ludovico, and she giggles wildly when, minutes later, after the housekeeper leaves, he does an imitation of Mrs. Ludovico. And although the rodent of sorrow still trails her, the incursions are less frequent. And there are moments when she can think of Andrea, and although the sadness is there, it does not frighten her.

Herb Green gives Hal tickets for the preview of an off-Broadway musical that a patron of Ramon's is producing.

"Do you want to go?" he asks Stacey.

She hesitates, but she sees the eagerness in his eyes and at once she agrees.

"Sure," she says. "Why not?" And with her acquiescence, she feels a glow of anticipation. They will go out. To a restaurant. To a show. She will wear makeup and perfume and her flowered blue dress and her white high heels. Normalcy, gaiety, beckon them. Nina and David can give the baby relief bottles.

"Of course," Nina says when Stacey tells her about the show. "Have a terrific time."

Stacey looks pretty in the flowered blue dress.

"It's not too tight?" she asks worriedly. As always after her pregnancies, she has retained some weight.

"No. Not at all," Nina assures her. "But let me fix the hem."

She kneels before Stacey and places a few stitches where Stacey's heel has caught at the fabric.

She hums as she works. "Memories" from *Cats*.

Nina picks up the lyric and she and Stacey sing together, their voices blending and rising and then, as she finishes the hem and snaps the thread, edging so terribly off-key that they break into embarrassed laughter. They are still laughing when David, carrying Felicia Miriam, enters the room.

"Look at those silly giggling mothers," he gravely tells the baby. "Just look at them."

"Your daddy has no sense of humor," Nina retorts. She feels mischievous and lighthearted. She dashes into her own room and returns with earrings, dangling flowers carved of turquoise that look wonderful with Stacey's dress.

When Hal beeps his horn and Stacey leaves ("Have fun," they call after her), Nina waves from the window although David remains in the doorway, holding Felicia Miriam, who has fallen asleep on his shoulder.

Hildy is also out that evening and Nina realizes that this is the first time they have been alone in the house with the baby.

David carries her into their bedroom and sets her down, still sleeping, on their bed. Again they form a cordon about her with their stuffed animals and they lie on opposite sides of the bed, their arms extended, their fingers linked, fencing in their sleeping child and the colorful menagerie that stands guard over her.

"Oh, God," David murmurs, "I don't think I've ever been so happy."

They are reluctant to disturb the sleeping baby, and so Nina goes downstairs, makes coffee and sandwiches, and carries them up to the bedroom. They eat at the small table near the window that overlooks the garden. It is not yet dark and Nina can see the playhouse. The pine trees that grow too close to it must be pruned. She remembers Hildy running toward it, a tinseled cardboard birthday hat perched on her dark hair. She imagines Felicia Miriam peering into it, the sunlight turning her fair hair to gold.

"I hope her hair stays light," she tells David.

He grins.

"I just hope some more grows in."

"Stupid. Of course it will."

She rises and places a light blanket about the sleeping baby. Felicia Miriam's face is flushed and it seems to Nina that her skin, which she touches oh, so lightly with her fingertips, is unnaturally warm.

"It's just a warm evening," David says when she mentions it.

They drink their coffee and the phone rings. It is Hildy telling them she will stay over at Alison's.

"Fine," David says. "Fine." And as he hangs up the baby awakens, her strident wail piercing the silence. Nina hurries to her, lifts her in her arms, but Felicia Miriam does not stop crying. She writhes against Nina's embrace, and her tiny face, screwed up in anguish, is flushed and mottled, her skin burning against the touch of Nina's hand.

"She has a fever," Nina says and her voice quakes with fear. "David, she has a fever."

"You can't know. Maybe she's hungry. She's thirsty." He rushes frantically from the room and returns with a bottle.

They force it into the baby's mouth but she does not suck. Nina forces her lips open, spurts one drop then another of the formula against her tongue, and Felicia Miriam's lips close about the nipple. Relieved, they keep their eyes fixed on her and on the measurement delineation on the bottle. One ounce. Two ounces. And then she stops, thrusts her tongue against the bottle, and begins to cry again, kicking her feet, her body rigid and burning in Nina's arms.

They carry her into the nursery and change her. They take her temperature, Nina's hands on her body, David holding the thermometer in place. He reads it.

"A hundred and three," he says in a croaking, frightened voice. "Goddamn it. A hundred and three."

"Infants run high temperatures," she says reassuringly, but her own heart is racing and her mouth is dry.

David calls the pediatrician. His service answers. He is not on this evening and his partner is out on a call, but he will call them as soon as possible. The operator's voice is calm, untroubled. She is used to speaking to frightened, hysterical parents. The terror in their voices does not disturb her.

"The baby is barely three weeks old," David tells her, his voice quivering.

"I'll have the doctor call," she repeats. "I have your number." She would soothe him with her efficiency, but he is not soothed. His desperation intensifies and he hurries to Nina, who walks back and forth across the room trying to calm the crying baby, and then back to the phone.

He calls Arnold, who listens carefully.

"Listen," Arnold say, "fever is a frightening thing in an infant, but it's not always dangerous. The important thing is to bring it down as soon as possible."

He instructs David to bathe the baby with a solution of alcohol and water. He prescribes a quarter of a tablet of infant aspirin, dissolved in glucose water.

"Do you want me to come up there?" he asks.

"I don't know," David says, but the truth is that he does want his brother to come. He hears Edith's voice in the background.

"Let me call you back in an hour. Edith just remembered that Jacob ran the same kind of fever when he was only ten days old. It lasted for an hour and vanished as quickly as it came. That happens sometimes with infants. I'll call you back."

David fills a small basin with the alcohol-and-water mixture. Nina holds Felicia Miriam firmly on the changing table while he bathes her with the soaking washcloths and swiftly wraps her in a large hooded towel. Her screams and cries seem to grow louder. His daughter's misery is more than he can bear, and he looks at Nina. Her hands are steady, but her eyes are bright with tears and she bites down on her upper lip.

Nina holds Felicia Miriam on her lap while he dissolves the aspirin in the glucose water in a tiny spoon. And then she holds the baby's lips apart while he forces the spoon into her mouth, above her tongue. She screams in protest, screams and gags and fights for breath. And then she vomits, the thin milky streak spewing from her mouth in a projectile stream, spattering Nina's shirt, his fingers.

"Damn!"

Again, he grinds up the aspirin and again they feed it to the baby. This time, weakened and wearied, she swallows it. Now they repeat the sponge bath, and her sobs and wails become weaker and then drift into quiet. They marvel to see that she is asleep. Nina slides her into a fleecy pink sleeping bag and places her carefully in the crib.

"She's still warm," she says worriedly.

"Yes." His voice is toneless.

He sits in the rocking chair and she settles herself at his feet. Their eyes are riveted on the sleeping baby. The nursery is dark, illuminated only by the small nightlight, but they can see the faces of the children in the Jerusalem playground. Their mouths are open in laughter; their teeth are very white and their eyes glitter.

"Please. Please," he says aloud. *Please let my daughter grow into just such a laughing child. Please give her health and joy. Please let her be all right.* The unspoken words, the silent prayer, fill his mind, take possession of his body. His knuckles are white as they grip the arms of the chair, and cold sweat glazes his skin. Shivering, he averts his eyes from the laughing children because he has remembered that each of them is haunted by a small ghost and he cannot (not now, as he sits in this darkened room) bear to think of pyramids of children's shoes, of soft hillocks of children's hair.

"I can't ever imagine being without her," he says.

The words, heavy as stones, fall upon Nina's heart.

"Shh. David. She'll be all right. She'll be fine."

"I didn't know it would be like this." His voice breaks with misery. He is an initiate into the mystery and terror of parenthood. Never has such a tiny life been dependent on him, a life so bonded with his own, so invested with love and dream and hope.

Leaning against his knees, she reaches for his hand, presses it to her cheek. He feels her tears, hot against his palm.

And then the phone rings and Felicia Miriam whimpers. Nina hurries to the bedroom to take the call and David lifts his daughter, presses his lips to her forehead. Again, he takes her temperature, holding her firmly, holding the thermometer in place. He can hear Nina talking to Arnold.

"She slept quietly for over an hour," she says. "That's good, isn't it?"

And then she is in the room and standing beside him as he removes the thermometer. She changes Felicia Miriam (who, miraculously, has stopped crying) as David stands beneath the lamplight and squints at the mercury line.

"Ninety-nine point six," he says, and wonder and relief mingle in his voice. "Almost normal."

Nina is weak with relief. The baby's body is cool but she is pale, listless. The brief fever has exhausted her. Still, she sucks hungrily at the bottle Nina feeds her and falls asleep again as soon as David (who must hold her after the feeding, who must feel her moist breath against his neck, her small heart beating against the pressure of his finger) sets her down in the crib and covers her.

They leave the door to the nursery ajar and return to their own room. On their bed, within the protective circle of stuffed animals formed for their daughter, on the counterpane that carries her scent, they cling very close to each other, nor does David release Nina when again the phone rings. The pediatrician is at last returning their call, and David recounts the baby's fever, its stabilization.

"Yeah. I guess it was a freak thing," he agrees. "Of course we'll keep a close watch on her."

He hangs up and looks at Nina, who is smiling.

"A freak thing," she repeats. "See, I told you our baby would be all right. I told you she'd be fine. Our little girl. Our darling."

And then her eyes close. She is asleep. He covers her and calls Arnold, and then he goes again into the nursery and sees that his daughter sleeps quietly, threaded to her flowered sheet by a shaft of moonlight.

They do not tell Stacey about Felicia Miriam's sudden fever. There is no need to worry her. She enjoyed her evening at the theater and over breakfast she tells Nina about the plot of the musical, which appears to be excessively convoluted.

"I may have missed parts of it," Stacey acknowledges. "I lost my concentration here and there."

She had felt, last night, in her flowered dress and high heels, Nina's earrings dangling, like a traveler newly returned to familiar shores, pleased to be back yet still disoriented, still hesitant. The normal world, the world of men and women sitting expectantly in a darkened theater, smiling and applauding, was still strange to her. She had looked down at her flat stomach and wondered what had happened to her pregnancy. She had watched a boy and a girl sing a duet on stage and thought: Oh, Andrea would love this, and then she had remembered that Andrea was dead. Still, she had held Hal's hand and laughed and clapped and felt herself slowly, slowly, become part of that audience, so intent on pleasure, so absorbed in life. She had taken her first uneasy steps forward, and when she returned to the Roths' home she tiptoed upstairs and stood barefoot in the nursery beside the crib.

Ah, sweet, she had thought as she removed Nina's earrings and held them in her hands just above the baby's head, like amulets of benediction.

Hal has brought Stacey the notebooks that contain her poems and her scattered journal entries. She reads them this morning with absorption, as though they are the work of a stranger and she is encountering them for the first time. Some are more familiar to her than others. She reads the entry she made after returning from New York, after spending the night with David Roth (after conceiving Felicia Miriam, she reminds herself punishingly). "I have done it — I have really done it. This is the beginning, then, of a new life for our family and for the Roths. Oh, how excited I am. Oh, how proud I am!" She marvels at her naïveté, her exuberance. Oh, how young she was, just over nine months ago. How very young. She had not yet wiped blood from her dead child's face, she had not yet heard the sound of earth upon the small white coffin. Now, the rodent of sorrow attacks her, sinks its cruel teeth into the soft and yielding heart of her grief. In defense, she gathers Felicia Miriam into her arms and carries her onto the porch, striated now by the pale light of the spring sun.

Still, that afternoon, Stacey turns back to the poems. She is reading her notebook when Nina returns from a rehearsal in the city, flushed with excitement. The rehearsal went well and she found an adorable hat and sweater fashioned of pale green angora for Felicia Miriam. Stacey holds the baby while Nina dresses her.

"Adorable," Stacey says, and Nina picks Felicia Miriam up and dances the length of the porch with her.

" 'Greensleeves was my delight,' " she croons, but Felicia Miriam squirms in her arms, and Nina sets her down in the carriage and sits beside Stacey on the porch glider.

"What are those?" she asks Stacey, pointing to the notebooks.

"Oh, stuff I've written. My poems," Stacey replies. "My journals."

"For courses?"

"Mostly for myself. But I read that sometimes people submit this sort of thing for credit. I think there's a program at San Francisco State College that gives, like, advance placement for what they call 'life experience.' " She laughs harshly. "I think I deserve a couple of credits for life experience."

Nina ignores the bitterness in her tone.

"Mandy would know about that. I think she did a semester out there, teaching or advising or something. And she'd be able to evaluate your work."

"Yes. I guess so." Stacey snaps her notebook shut. There are some poems she fears to read — poems she remembers writing at her kitchen table while Andrea drew lacy hearts and smiling stars; poems about mothers and daughters and fairy tales, all of which end in the happily ever after.

That evening Nina calls Mandy and invites her to visit. It will have to be in the late morning, Mandy says, because she is so busy; Nina hears the excitement in her voice, the breathless impatience. Wonderful things have been happening, Mandy whispers huskily, mysteriously. She must tell them all about it. They choose a day when Nina will not be going into the city for either classes or rehearsals, and Stacey begins to copy the best of her poems into a new notebook.

25

Stacey waits for Mandy in the garden, seated on a chaise that is shaded by the tender new leafage of the oak tree. Once again, the small redwood table is spread with the strawberry-shaped milk-glass plates and the blue ceramic bowl is filled with fruit. Stacey notices that there is a small chip on the bowl, exposing a centimeter of whiteness, not unlike a baby's first tooth, and she slides her finger across the imperfection. Nina has sanded it down so that it is smooth to her touch, and she is moved that Nina (busy Nina, who schedules rehearsals and classes and prepares careful meals and quietly sees to the running of her home) should have taken the time for such a small task. But then Nina is careful and meticulous in all things, Stacey thinks with admiration tinged by a resentment, which shames her because Nina is kind and she is possessed of warmth and generosity, although it is sometimes obscured by that same meticulousness, that deceptive aura of control.

Even now, she can hear Nina's voice through the open window as she places an order with the butcher, reading from a list. Stacey, who is familiar now with the household routine, knows that she reads from a list taped to the refrigerator and that as she speaks, she moves about the kitchen, wiping counter tops, removing the dishes from the dishwasher, watering her plants. Stacey, who abandons one task in favor of another, who dumps the laundry on her bed and lies across it to read a chapter in a book or write a page in her journal or even to watch a television show, marvels at Nina's control, her organization. Somewhere in the house a vacuum cleaner hums as Mrs. Ludovico moves from room to room.

"A large roast beef," Nina says. "Oh, enough for fourteen people. And a small turkey. And two soup chickens. Three pounds of chicken livers. Two shank bones."

Nina, Stacey knows, is ordering the food for the seder. She has explained the holiday to Stacey (who was, in fact, familiar with it, having taken a course in comparative religion, but she listened carefully, politely) and even discussed the menu with her, displaying uncharacteristic nervousness. Nina is uneasy because her parents will be coming east from Arizona and David's mother will be coming from her home in Florida to celebrate the holiday with them. Her own parents, always passive and accepting, do not cause Nina anticipatory unease but always she has found her mother-in-law judgmental and disapproving.

She told Stacey about her uneasiness late one afternoon as they sat together in the nursery. It has become Nina's habit to sit with Stacey then. She brings her a mug of beer (because it so enriches the milk) and she herself has the cup of tea that refreshes her after her drive home from the city. They speak softly as Stacey nurses the baby, both of them smiling at the barely audible infant sounds, the languid movements of Felicia Miriam's small limbs. Always, Nina keeps a diaper on her shoulder and Stacey passes the baby to her as she herself buttons her blouse. Nina burps the baby and holds her close before placing her, sated and often asleep, into the crib. Thus, they are partners, sharing mothers in the ritual of sustenance.

"Why should you care what your mother-in-law says?" Stacey asked Nina. "I worried about my family at the beginning, but now I know that the important thing is the baby. She's the only one who counts. Your mother-in-law will go back to Florida and she'll tell her friends that you and David have a daughter, and maybe people will think she's adopted or maybe they'll think something else, but it won't really matter to them. And pretty soon, it won't matter to her either. The only people who matter are you and David and Felicia Miriam. Just like I'm not going to waste time worrying about my parents, my brothers, my sisters-in-law. The only people who matter are me and

Hal and Evan and Jared and Andrea." And then, without missing a
beat, swiftly she corrected herself. "Evan and Jared and Felicia Miriam. That's what I meant."

Now, as Nina's voice continues to waft out to the garden, Stacey
turns her head and lifts herself slightly in the chair. She sees that
the baby is still asleep in the blue coach carriage that David placed
beneath the oak tree that morning. The spring sunlight, filtering its
way between the newly formed leaves, dapples the hood of the carriage with lacy star-shaped patterns.

Golden stars of sunlight, Stacey thinks and writes the words down
on the pad she holds on her lap. It occurs to her that if she lowers
the hood those golden stars of sunlight will spangle her daughter's
brow and turn her fringe of fair hair a richer, deeper hue, closer to
Stacey's own color, closer to Andrea's color. She turns her gaze from
the carriage and looks across the garden to the playhouse, where a
gardener is pruning the hedges. Briefly, she watches him and then
her lids grow heavy. Nina's voice trails off and, swathed in the new
silence, warmed by the sun, Stacey falls into the luxurious, heavy
sleep of the recovering invalid.

She is awakened by the light clatter of the fruit knife against the
white glass dish. Mandy, wearing a loose dress of gauzy Indian cotton, draped with a batik scarf, her hair pulled back and held in place
by high silver combs, sits opposite her. She slices a large peach into
rosy crescents and smiles benignly at Stacey. She wipes her fingers
on Nina's pretty flowered linen napkin and reaches into her faded
Greek shoulder bag.

"A present for you," she says, smiling. "It's a poem I wrote as soon
as I heard the baby's name." She hands Stacey a large white envelope. "One of my students, she does terrific calligraphy, copied it out
for you." Always Mandy has a student available with a cunning,
obscure talent offered to her as an acolyte's tribute. Mandy wears
their batik scarves, munches their homemade granola, uses and loses
their hand-tooled leather bookmarks, their beaded purses.

Pleased, Stacey opens the envelope, notes the poem's title, "For
Felicia Miriam," and the graceful India ink letters that dance across
the cream-colored linen paper. It is a simple yet elegant poem, and

the last line (which the calligrapher designed as a wreath of swirling letters) reads "Felicia, my daughter. Miriam, my friend. Felicia Miriam, dear sister, sweet sister."

"It's beautiful," Stacey says.

"I thought you could frame it, maybe in walnut, and hang it in her room." Mandy often gives her own poems to her friends as gifts, always suggesting, with the arrogance that is now natural to her, the frame she herself would prefer.

"Yes. I think Nina would want to hang it in the nursery," Stacey says and carefully places the poem in the envelope.

"Nina? What does Nina have to do with it?" Mandy asks impatiently.

Stacey looks at her in surprise. She has assumed, for weeks now, that Mandy and John understood her arrangement with the Roths. She based that assumption on their close friendship and the ease with which John and David discuss the most intimate matters. But she sees now that Mandy is openly bewildered, and hastily, she steers the conversation away from her own baby.

"How is Susan?" she asks. "Does she sleep through the night yet?"

"No. She gets up two or three times. But John goes to her most of the time. He's very good with her. He and Elizabeth both."

"Elizabeth?"

"Oh, I didn't tell you about Elizabeth. She's one of John's doctoral students. She's living with us now as a sort of lodger-cum-babysitter. She pays for her board by doing some childcare. The twins are wild about her. She's very artistic — see, she made my scarf. And she's made all sorts of great stuff for Samantha. A god's eye for her wall, throw pillows. And she's terrific with Susan too. Gives her bottles, changes her. All that sort of thing." Mandy furrows her brow, as though trying to think of other talents Elizabeth has demonstrated in the care of her children, and then shrugs in defeat. "Eric likes her too," she adds, "which will make it easier."

"She gives bottles? Aren't you nursing Susan?" Stacey asks. She remembers the long poem Mandy wrote on the joys of nursing a newborn; she even recalls a visual image from that poem, of the infant as a novice voyager sailing on the huge pale ship of a maternal breast. She had thought the simile wonderful and summoned it (as she often summons fragments of poems she has memorized) when she nursed Felicia Miriam. Once, moving the infant from the right breast to the left she had murmured, "Now to another ship, sweet sailor."

"I gave it up," Mandy replies. "I only nursed for a couple of days. It was too much strain after the cesarean. Also I rethought the whole philosophy of nursing and I decided that it reinforces a negative image of women. The breast is perceived as a spigot and the mother becomes a nourishing automaton — her body is simply an anchor for this faucet that delivers milk on demand. My thinking has changed a lot since I nursed Eric and Samantha. And of course, philosophy aside, it's just as well that Susan's on bottles now, considering I'm going to be away for so long."

Mandy studies the slices of peach that she has arranged in a circular pattern on the white dish. Finally, she selects one and sucks at it, allowing the golden juice to color her lips and glide in slender rivulets down the corners of her mouth.

"Away?" It is Stacey's turn to be surprised. "Where are you going?"

"I've been invited to a writers' colony in Arizona. A marvelous place. All desert and mountains with small cabins for the writers in residence. Absolute peace and solitude. And of course, they arrange for readings at colleges throughout the Southwest. It was so strange — I'd been dreaming desert poems and then I received the invitation . . ." Mandy's wispy voice is full of wonder. Her very dreams presage reality. She is a prophetess who, through her visions, ordains her own future. "I'll be away for about three months, maybe four if I can arrange for an extension."

"Yes. John told David about your plans." Nina has walked so quietly across the grass that neither Stacey nor Mandy heard her approach. She carries a tray laden with a crystal pitcher of iced tea, on which sprigs of jade-colored mint (almost the exact color of her loose linen dress) float, and tall glasses patterned with butterflies. She sets the tray down on the redwood table and pours the tea without asking if they are thirsty. "Isn't that a rather long time to be away from the children?" she asks, passing Mandy a glass.

Mandy shrugs.

"Elizabeth will be there. They love Elizabeth."

"I see."

Nina does see. In her mind's eye she visualizes Elizabeth, the eager young graduate student (about whom John has spoken with dangerous enthusiasm) acquiescently typing John's new novel, dressing and feeding John's infant daughter, playing merrily with John's stepson and -daughter (the difficult children who are easy with her), and at last, ministering to John's loneliness. "Poor John. Poor dear John," she will say as she comforts him, kissing his fingers, stroking his hair. "Wonderful John. Oh, I never knew it could be so wonderful," as her teacher, her mentor, guides her hands, trains her body. Nina dislikes herself for her own cynicism, but she knows her judgment, her prediction, to be correct. Swiftly, she changes the subject.

"Isn't Felicia Miriam beautiful?" she asks Mandy, and Stacey realizes that Mandy has not even glanced at the baby about whom she wrote the elegant poem.

"She's lovely," Mandy agrees. "I wrote a poem for her. I thought Stacey would want to frame it and hang it in her room, but Stacey said she'd ask you how you felt about it." Caught up in an enthusiastic explanation of her own plans, Mandy has confused Stacey's response.

"What I said was that Nina would have to decide what goes into Felicia Miriam's room." Stacey corrects her stiffly. She does not want Nina to think that she has been dissembling, that she has deliberately created a false impression about her future with the baby, that she has translated into words her fantasy that Felicia Miriam is hers alone, a fantasy to which she surrenders to forestall encroaching attacks of misery.

"Yes. You did say that," Mandy agrees. "You know, Stacey, you shouldn't rely so much on other people's judgment. You should express yourself. You did some nice things in your house." She speaks in the gentle, condescending tone she reserves for her students. "And I remember those clever aluminum-foil crowns you made for all the children on Christmas Day."

"The crowns," Stacey says. *Her hand upon Andrea's guiding the scissors, showing Andrea how to press the glittering foil onto the cardboard.* The small mouse of pain begins again to nibble at her heart. She braces herself against her own sorrow, against the feral rodent that lies deceptively dormant and then attacks her with sharp teeth that tear at the tender sutures of her forbearance. She remembers (and now that nibbling is a ferocious angry gnawing) Andrea in her silver crown and scarlet dress, the gay Christmas princess skiing across the waxed hardwood floor, practicing for her flight through snow, her strenuous climbs, her swift and magical descents. Sweet, graceful Andrea, speeding and sliding, downward, downward.

With trembling hand, she sets her glass down, plucks out a sprig of mint that she sucks as though it had medicinal powers, and listens to Nina who is so calmly explaining everything to Mandy.

"It isn't that Stacey relies on my decorating advice," Nina says. "It's that Felicia Miriam's room is here; her home will be this house. She will be our child, mine and David's."

This is the first time since they sat opposite Hildy at Luigi's all those months ago that she has spoken to anyone of their arrangement. She listens to her own voice now, as though to discern any chaotic irrationality in her words, any startling incoherence in her revelation. But what she has said seems clear and logical, and although her throat is dry and her hands tremble, she is comforted. They do not have to explain what they have done. They do not have to apologize for what they have done.

"You mean Stacey and Hal conceived this baby for you and David?" Mandy asks, and there is muted disbelief, the slightest intonation of accusation, in her whispery voice.

Stacey is very pale, but Nina's cheeks are flushed with anger. Who is Mandy to demand explanation, to level accusation? Still, with effort, she keeps her voice level as she replies.

"No. David and Stacey conceived this baby. Felicia Miriam is David's child. And my own," she adds. "As though she were born to me." She remembers the night of Felicia Miriam's swift and sudden fever and how she had felt the merging of fear and love, the tender tyranny of her new motherhood, her frenzy and her passion. Felicia Miriam is her own — perhaps even more than her own (and this thought, so new to her, is startling) than if she had given birth to her. They are bonded to their daughter, she and David, by their yearning and by their love.

"I see. Stacey carried this baby for you," Mandy says. She lifts another slice of peach and eats it. Her lips curl and her brow is furrowed. She prepares to do battle. She marshals her resources, assembles her arguments.

"I wanted to do it," Stacey says softly. She looks at Mandy appealingly and blanches beneath the scorn in her friend's gaze.

"You wanted to become a surrogate mother?" Mandy asks. She spits the words out as though they are tainted.

"That's not how we think of Stacey," Nina protests, and now her voice is raised. "We think of her as a wonderful friend who has given us a wonderful gift." She reaches out and touches Stacey's hand, but Stacey pulls away, rises. She walks over to the carriage and rocks it gently, gently, biting her lip, smoothing back her hair.

"Is that how you think of it, Stacey?" Mandy asks.

"I don't know," Stacey says faintly. She returns to the chaise and leans back, shielding her eyes with her hand. *A gift.* The words echo in her mind. That was how she had thought of her Andrea, her golden daughter. And that was how the minister himself had spoken of Andrea at the funeral. "We thank God for the gift of this child's brief life," he had said, and Stacey in her black dress (with Felicia Miriam within her, moving and shifting, impatient for life) had listened to his words and had tried so desperately to believe him. *Thank you, God, for the gift of my daughter's brief life.* The words had frozen in her mind. She could not believe them. She could not say them.

"You don't know." Mandy's tone is harsh, derisory. This is how she answers her challengers on panels, her shy questioners at college readings. She is a partisan for all women. Her rhetoric is honed, her passion cultivated. She writes odes to Ceres, tributes to Hecate. "But you must know that a baby can't be given by a woman as a gift. Babies belong to their mothers, with their mothers. They are bonded to them." She is warming to her argument now. "Women aren't biological machines, their wombs aren't incubators that can be rented out at will. How could you have agreed to this, Stacey? How can you go on with it? You have rights."

"Shut up, Mandy!" Nina's voice rings with anger, trembles with fury. Rage like a ramrod rigidifies her spine and the pallor of fury chalks her face. "What do you know about this? You want to teach others? You want to give lessons to me, to Stacey? Take a few yourself. Get your own goddamn priorities in order. Like maybe a woman who's nine months pregnant shouldn't risk her life and her baby's by driving on an interstate highway in the dead of winter to give a stupid reading."

"Who are you to tell me what to do?" Mandy retorts shrilly. "Who are you to judge me?"

"You judge everyone else. Stacey. Me. David. You sit in my garden and eat my fruit and tell me you're going off to Arizona and leaving your kids — your twins and, God help us, a newborn baby — and then you deliver a canned feminist lecture on motherhood. You know all about it, don't you? If you bear a child you're a mother. Poof — magic. Run off and write a poem about it. Even better, leave your children and write a lot of poems about it. What kind of a mother are you, Mandy?"

"I'm a mother who carried my children for nine months. I felt them move. I felt them grow," Mandy replies. She shoves away the plate and stares at Nina with hatred.

"Terrific. Terrific reasoning." Nina is relentless now. She fires her words like deadly arrows aimed at Mandy's impassioned protest. "That's enlightened. The biological relationship is more important than anything else. So what about adoptive mothers who raise and nurture and love children born to other women? Are they lesser mothers because they didn't give birth to their children? How can they compare to a woman who gives birth and then leaves her children, goes off to Arizona?" She is almost shouting now and her face is inflamed with her fury. She lifts a knife to cut a cluster of grapes, but her hand is unsteady and the blade cuts into her thumb. She welcomes the pain, the thin ribbon of blood. She looks defiantly at Mandy.

"You know, Nina, that there's a special relationship between a pregnant woman and her baby," Mandy says, speaking again in that soft wisp of a voice that gives her a muted authority. She has regained control. She will not defend herself against Nina's accusations. Why should she? They are irrelevant to her. It is the abstract that interests and engages her. "A woman talks to that baby, tells stories. I wrote poems to Susan. I felt her. She was part of me. No matter where I am, she will never stop being part of me. Don't you feel that, Stacey?"

"Yes," Stacey replies. "Yes."

She is weak now, depleted by pain, exhausted because her grief is exposed, the open wound of her loss drains her strength, the gnashing of sorrow is inexorable, unremitting. She looks across the garden to the playhouse and she remembers how Andrea trotted across the lawn, carrying a bouquet of daisies. Andrea, who had rolled down a hill in the Botanic Gardens, her face bright with the promise of that false spring. "*See Andrea*," Stacey had whispered to the baby she carried, and she remembers how Felicia Miriam had stirred within her then. Had Felicia Miriam pressed her face against the uterine wall, as though it were a window, as though her purblind eyes could see that sister, that forever vanished golden-haired sister, roll down the hill, shouting and laughing until she lay quiet at last in a pool of sunlight?

"You see?" Mandy is triumphant, vindicated. She pops a cherry into her mouth, takes a sip of her iced tea.

"What is there to see? What have you shown me that I didn't know before?" Nina retorts contemptuously. "I know the special feelings a woman has during pregnancy. I don't deny them. Oh, God, I remember them. But I know that there is more to being a mother than that. There are all the years and the caring and the worrying and the joy and the understanding and the trying to understand. And I will have all that with Felicia Miriam just as I had it with Hildy, and I will never feel less for her than I feel for Hildy. I know that. Stacey knows that. Don't you, Stacey?"

But Stacey, lying so pale and inert on the chaise, makes no answer, and wounded, threatened, Nina plunges on. She would strike at Mandy, wound her as Mandy has struck and wounded.

"It's true that you gave birth to Susan, Mandy. And to Eric and Samantha. But how can you be a mother to them when you are at a writers' colony in Arizona and Elizabeth cares for them, changes them, feeds them, wipes their noses, and tells them stories and plays with them? Perhaps you are turning Elizabeth into a surrogate mother of a kind. Who knows? She may even become a surrogate wife?" Her attack is cruel, she knows, but Mandy has provoked it with her own swift judgments, her own cruel indifference to their pain, their dilemma, their yearning — David's yearning become her own. Can

Mandy understand the sorrow she shared with David as they stood in the corridor of the memorial museum on Mount Herzl and stared at the photos of vanished children? Can she comprehend their feelings when they heard the laughter of the children in the Jerusalem playground? Can she imagine the depth of their love for their daughter, their beautiful baby? Nina is close to tears now, but she must not weep. Oh, no. She must not weep. She must not betray her vulnerability to Mandy, who sits upright in her chair, who tosses her head so that her wispy hair whips her cheeks, whose face is ablaze with the fire of anger.

"I don't live by your standards," Mandy shoots back. "I live by my own credo. John and I talk about things, decide them. I don't have to justify the way I live for you, to you. I'm not like you. I wouldn't want to be like you. I don't have to live in a suburban fortress. I don't have to have a big house and fill it with expensive furniture. My values are different. Matching glassware doesn't matter to me. Mothers and babies matter to me." She drains her tea and twirls the glass in her hand.

Nina clenches her fists. Rage engulfs her. Protests, objections, careen through her mind. She is battered by the injustice of Mandy's words. To be a mother, to have a baby, was all that mattered to her all these months and all that matters to her now, at this moment of searing truth, of devastating exposure. Her stomach hurts and she crosses her hands across it in the ancient gesture of the pregnant woman. She feels the bitterness of deprivation, the ache of emptiness. Her body had been invaded by disease; steel instruments scooped out the uterus that would have cradled the babies who will never be born to her. She cannot conceive or carry another child, but she can be a mother. She is a mother. The pain abates and the words break loose.

"Do you think babies don't matter to me, Mandy? Do you think I don't love Felicia Miriam? My God, she was conceived out of my love, out of my need, mine and David's. She is part of me. Stacey knows that. Do you think Stacey would have even considered having the baby if she didn't know that?" She is screaming now, her throat raw with passion, even with hatred. Who is Mandy to judge her, Mandy who left her children at home on a wintry night to drive down a dangerous highway, Mandy who will leave her husband and children to fly to Arizona where, in luxurious desert solitude, far from Susan's urgent crying, Samantha and Eric's quarrels, she will write elegaic descriptions of motherhood? Nina cannot imagine leaving Felicia Miriam, just as she could not imagine leaving Hildy during her childhood years. How could she leave Felicia Miriam, whose feverish body had seared her own flesh, branding her with love, welding her to the recognition that she would do anything for this newborn daughter of hers? *Anything. Anything. Anything.* Now the tears come and she weeps without shame, without caring.

"Nina." How soft Stacey's voice is, how pitying.

"Don't you think I wanted to have my own baby? Do you know what it is to want a child as badly as David and I wanted a baby? For David never to have a child of his own?" Her voice breaks as she thinks of David's longing, of his hunger, of how she held him close, so close that she was infused with that longing, that hunger. "We had to have a child," she finishes in a whisper. The large eyes of the thin-faced children in the photographs at Yad VaShem, the sad gaze of the child survivors in Amos Roth's paintings, had implored them to have a child; the clamorous laughter of the children in the Jerusalem playground had impelled them to have a child. "*Listen*," David had said as they sat in the pale wintry sunlight and listened to the children. "*The chain is not broken*." *Look*, she thinks now, her eyes fixed on the carriage. *The chain is not broken.*

"Yes," Mandy says bitterly, unmoved by Nina's tears, Nina's screaming. "You had to have a child. You couldn't just adopt. You had to hire someone to have your baby for you."

"Hire?" Stacey repeats the word faintly, piteously. She stares at them miserably. She is a bewildered and reluctant audience at a performance that pains and embarrasses her.

They do not answer her. The air is electric with their antipathy. It is clear to Nina (and the clarity at once relieves and exonerates her) that just as she has disliked and disapproved of Mandy, so Mandy has disliked and disapproved of her. Like marionettes, controlled by the strings of their husbands' friendship, they had bobbed politely about each other, suspended above the reality of their veiled enmity. But they can no longer pretend. The battle lines are clear.

"You don't have to hire anyone, Mandy," Nina says. "No. You're lucky. Besides, that wouldn't be your style. You don't operate that way. What you do is insinuate yourself into other people's lives. Your problems become their problems. Mandy must have time to write. Mandy must do a reading. Nothing is more important than Mandy's poetry unless it is Mandy herself." Flushed, her face still wet with tears, her shirt soaked with perspiration, Nina taunts. Her attack is her defense.

"Shut up! Shut up, you bitch!" Mandy's empty glass is clenched in her hand and she hurls it at the tree. It shatters on impact and the bright slivers of crystal rain soundlessly down on the soft grass, bounce radiantly off the thick tangles of roots that snake their way across the lawn.

Stacey and Nina jump to their feet and hurry to the carriage, although the glass shattered several feet from where the sunlight dances with liquid swiftness across the upturned dark hood. Felicia Miriam, wrapped in a pink thermal blanket, sleeps on.

"All right. All right," Stacey says in that same faint and broken voice. She goes back to her chaise and curls up on it, her face turned away from them.

Nina and Mandy kneel, and together, not looking at each other, they pick up the shards of glass.

"Listen, this was stupid. I'm sorry. Really sorry," Mandy offers.

"What I meant was . . . ," Nina interposes, and their voices meld.

Their backs are to Stacey. They do not see her curl up as though in pain. They do not see her cover her ears with her clenched fists, but they hear her strangulated cry.

"Stop! Stop this!" Stacey pleads and her words gurgle forth like muffled bubbles. "I don't want to hear what you're saying. I don't want to hear it. Please. Please."

Nina wheels around. Stacey's body, folded into itself, does not move. Her golden hair is a tangle of knots, her face concealed from them.

"Stacey, I'm sorry." Nina kneels beside the chair, but Stacey does not move, does not answer.

Mandy too moves forward, hesitantly, fearfully.

"Stacey, we just exploded. We didn't mean anything." Once again she speaks in husky tones, at once apologetic and appealing, but still, Stacey does not respond.

Wild thoughts career through Nina's mind. She remembers a dancer in a repertory company who suffered a breakdown on tour. She sank down onto the stage and could not, would not, rise. Catatonia, it had been whispered, and the word, so ominous and foreboding, had caused the dancers to look nervously at each other and huddle in small groups. Someone had looked it up in a dictionary of psychiatric terms. Catatonia, they learned, was a near vegetative stage of immobility, of nonresponse. The word leaps out at Nina now as she encircles Stacey's shoulders, hugs her, whispers to her. And still Stacey utters no sound, makes no movement. On either side of the chair, across Stacey's inert body, Mandy and Nina stare at each other. Now fear replaces their anger; mutual concern dulls the edge of their revealed hostility, their open enmity.

"What should we do?" Mandy asks.

And then, before Nina can answer, Felicia Miriam begins to cry. Faintly at first, the baby's waking moan invades the quiet garden, and then, rhythmically, sobs bellow forth, gathering strength and vibrancy. And Stacey, as though energized by the sound of her child, lifts her head, and a smile comes to her lips. She rises and moves from the chaise to the carriage. Still smiling (although her face is tear-streaked), she lifts Felicia Miriam and holds her in her arms. The baby, flushed with sleep, angered by her hunger, kicks at the pink blanket. Beads of sweat pearl her forehead and the fair fringe of her hair is damp. Stacey takes up a dry diaper, wipes her face, loosens the blanket.

"But you're overheated, you silly thing," she says in the confidential tone peculiar to those mothers who speak softly, cajolingly, to their infants. "And you're hungry too. Aren't you? Aren't you?"

She sits down, the baby's head frantically darting back and forth, in search of the nipple, even as Stacey unbuttons her blouse. Already her milk is spurting forth, and when she leans back and places the baby at her breast there is quiet, broken only by the sound of urgent sucking and the cawing of a crow, standing sentinel on a distant tree.

Mandy and Nina look at each other. For the moment they are no longer at odds. Their eyes are soft with pity as they watch Stacey lift her hand so that the baby's eyes are shielded from the sun.

Stacey, who as she nurses rests her fingers lightly on the strawberry rise at her baby's neck, is indifferent to their presence. Their argument, their wounding anger is forgotten. It is Felicia Miriam who absorbs her, Felicia Miriam who banishes the invasive rodent of sorrow and again (yet again) closes the open wound of loss.

She burps the baby and the three women smile at the surprising loudness of Felicia Miriam's hiccup. Nina carries her indoors to change her.

"You'll want to speak to Mandy about your poems, your journals," she reminds Stacey on her way into the house. They are intent now on restoring an aura of normalcy to this meeting. They will not, they cannot, forget what has been said, but something must be rescued, something must be redeemed. And so Nina goes upstairs to the nursery, and Stacey opens her notebooks and passes them one by one to Mandy.

In the nursery Nina undresses Felicia Miriam. It is not enough for her simply to change the infant. She must care for her, revel in the petal softness of her skin, the perfect formation of each limb, the miracle of each shell-like ear. Tenderly, deftly, she rubs the baby's body with a fragrant pink cream. Baby Magic, it is called. "Magic Baby," she whispers into Felicia Miriam's ear. Using a soft cloth, she washes the baby's face, although Felicia Miriam slithers and protests. She notices for the first time how long and straight Felicia Miriam's lashes are — like David's own, like Arnold's and those of his sons. She presses her own face close to the baby's. She would have those long lashes brush her cheek — just so do David's lashes flutter against her in love — but Felicia Miriam closes her eyes. She sleeps, as Nina finishes dressing her in a pale green stretch suit, as she brushes her fringe of hair with the silver-backed brush with Hildy's initials on it.

She sings to the sleeping baby. "Hush, little baby, don't you cry." And Felicia Miriam does not cry. She sleeps. Nina hums. The melody that David loves, the old Yiddish song Amos Roth sang as he painted. "Raisins and Almonds."

Still humming, holding her daughter close, she dances, moving barefoot across the nursery floor, cradling the sleeping infant, inhaling the sweetness of her skin, listening to the rhythmic lightness of her breath.

Mandy turns the pages of Stacey's journals. She reads carefully and Stacey watches nervously.

"I thought of maybe submitting these to a program at a college that gives credits for life experience," she explains. "What do you think?"

And Mandy, the teacher who has studied many such journals, read many such poems ("Chronicles of Wounded Women," she called them in an essay she wrote for an academic journal of feminist studies), reads carefully, noting strengths, weaknesses.

"You have a gift for words, Stacey," she says approvingly.

"I love words," Stacey says. "Weaving them together. I used to try my poems out on Andrea. She didn't understand them but she liked to listen." Soothed and relaxed, she can speak of Andrea calmly now. The baby's lips, so urgently sucking, kissed away her despair. "So you think it's okay to submit these for credit?"

"I think so. You'd have to type everything up and get it into some order, but I think they merit consideration. Of course, it depends on the school. Some of the state university departments are more lenient than others. You know John sits on an evaluation committee." She wonders if it would be a conflict of interest for John to evaluate Stacey's work. Perhaps he could give it to Elizabeth, who does not know Stacey. Effortlessly Mandy assigns Elizabeth roles she once claimed for herself.

"I'll be going out to California. I thought I'd try one of the state schools there," Stacey tells her, gathering her work together.

"You mean you'll leave the baby here with David and Nina and go out West?" Mandy asks.

"Yes."

Stacey looks up. She can see the nursery window from her chaise. Mandy follows her gaze and together they watch Nina as she dances with Felicia Miriam. She has loosened her hair so that it capes her shoulders and the baby's fair head is pillowed on its silken dark thickness as she bends and sways in the mother dance of her own composition.

Mandy leaves before Nina returns to the garden. She kisses Stacey and promises to write her from Arizona (a promise that seems important, although they both disbelieve it) and takes a peach.

"For the road," she says jauntily.

Stacey rises and walks over to the carriage. The sun has moved and the tall coach carriage is in the velvet shade of the tree. Stacey smooths the flowered sheet, folds the blanket. She wheels the empty carriage into the sunlight and rocks it with gentle rhythmic gesture, humming and swaying. She is rocking it still when Hildy returns from school with Alison and Seth.

The three teenagers stand at the garden gate and watch her, before walking stealthily to the front of the house. Alison and Seth ask Hildy no questions. They accept the presence of Stacey and the baby in the Roth home as they accept all the strange confluences introduced into their lives by parents who weep softly in the night, who hold whispered phone conversations at strange hours, who wander from room to room, staring vaguely at television screens, unaware that the volume has been switched off or that the language being spoken is incomprehensible to them.

26

The nursery has become the heart of the household. The intercom system that David installed carries the slightest sound to the receivers that are in place in every room. Seated at dinner, they smile to hear the sweet, soft voice that Felicia Miriam has only now, in the third week of her life, discovered. They spring to their feet when her frantic cry tells them that she is hungry or uncomfortable, and then they smile ruefully at each other, acknowledging the absurdity of their anxiety. Sometimes only one of them goes to the baby, but occasionally two of them tend her together. Nina and Stacey or Nina and David; by tacit agreement Stacey and David do not go into the nursery together. More and more often, Hildy trails after them, and her presence pleases them. They clap when Hildy dances about the nursery with Felicia Miriam in her arms.

"Don't worry," she sings in reggae rhythm. "Be happy."

And they all sing it together, their bodies swaying, laughter wreathing their faces.

David still rises each and every night, after Stacey has nursed Felicia Miriam and he has heard the door to her room close. Sometimes, if Nina is also awake, he carries the baby back to their bedroom and settles her in the center of their bed. Lying beside her, they speak very softly, as though they are telling each other secrets. They smile and place their fingers in her tiny palm and feel her reflexive grasp. They kiss her. They cannot wait for her to return their kisses, to look up at them with love. They surround her with the bright stuffed animals. They spread the animals out and place her atop the uneven mattress of plump bodies, faces crafted of strips of felt and plastic. David nuzzles her.

"Who will she look like?" he asks. "Bacall? Candice Bergen? She has that sophisticated look."

"No, no. Princess Di. Fergie. Stephanie of Monaco. She's royalty. Yes, your highness. No, your highness. Duchess Felicia. Lady Miriam." Nina giggles and sinks to her knees on the bed and bows in mock obeisance to the bemused baby.

One night there is a tentative knock at the door and when David opens it Stacey stands there. She looks at them shyly.

"I'm sorry," she says. "I went to the nursery and Felicia Miriam wasn't there. She's all right?"

"Oh, she's fine. She's fine," David says, standing awkwardly in the doorway in his pajamas. "See."

Nina holds up the baby and Stacey nods.

"That's all right then," she says, and she goes back to her room. It bothers David that her voice was muffled, that an expression of wounded sadness flickered across her face.

He returns to the bed but the gaiety of the game is gone. Within minutes he carries Felicia Miriam back to her crib and then lies beside Nina in the dark, imagining Stacey, sleepless and alone in the guest-room bed. Oh, he is sorry for her, so sorry for her, but he wants her gone — gone from his house and from his daughter's life. Still, it is only a matter of time, just a little more time.

On nights when Nina does not awaken, David steals down the hall and enters the nursery. They do not draw the curtains in that room and the silver moonlight streaks the infant's delicate features, slides in radiant shafts across the curl of her body. David leans against the crib and stares down at his daughter.

"My Felicia." He forms the words soundlessly, gratefully. His fatherhood is still a miracle to him.

Occasionally, Nina follows him into the nursery and places her hand over his on the bar of the crib. They stand together then, attentive sentinels, cloaked in silver moonlight, and watch their child sleep.

*   *   *

Stacey spends a Sunday afternoon with Hal and her sons. They have dinner with the rest of the family at an Italian restaurant. They struggle now to reestablish old routines, and Stacey returns to the Roth home exhausted by the effort. She feels the fatigue of an actress who has performed a difficult and demanding role. Her efforts at small talk have drained her and she feels oppressed by the unasked questions that hovered over the dinner table.

She sinks down on the couch beside Hildy, who is sorting index cards for a term paper.

"Hey, you look wiped out," Hildy says with the disarming honesty of the adolescent. And then swiftly, as though reading the question in Stacey's eyes, she adds, "Felicia Miriam is fine. Mom gave her a relief bottle about an hour ago."

Hildy herself changed the baby twice. She loves taking care of Felicia Miriam; she is fascinated by her sweetness and vulnerability. Sometimes Hildy helps Nina and Stacey (who accomplish this task together) bathe the baby. She holds the fleecy hooded white towel and watches Nina powder Felicia Miriam and then spread a pink cream across the tiny limbs, within the smiling flesh behind her knees, even into the tiny crevices between each toe. Hildy imagines herself as an infant, imagines her mother's long, graceful fingers moving across her own tiny body with such caring diligence, such gentleness.

Only yesterday, Hildy had come home at twilight and found Nina and David on the terrace, their chairs flanking Felicia Miriam's carriage. The baby cried just then and David lifted her from the carriage and held her against his shoulder. He pressed her to his own body, at this hour of waning warmth and light. His large hands enveloped his daughter and he rocked back and forth on his heels. It seemed to Hildy, as she stood in the gold-dusted shadow, that she could remember David lifting her in his arms all those years ago. Yes. She even recalled the roughness of his chin against her cheek, the smell of the sea-scented skin freshener that he has not used since her childhood.

She and Nina had moved simultaneously to the carriage; their hands had met as they reached together for the pink thermal blanket. The singleness of their thought and gesture caused them to laugh, and together, each holding one end, they carried the blanket to David, who wrapped the baby within its folds. Together then, the four of them had stood in a circlet of fading sunlight. They formed a rondelle of love, an enchanted family in which ties of devotion prevail over ties of blood. Hildy had understood then that she was not David's child just as Felicia Miriam was not Nina's child but that they are daughters both to the tall man and woman who have chosen them both as they have chosen each other. She had, standing beside them, beginning to shiver, felt the melting of a long and inexplicable bitterness. She understood then Alison's feeling when she awakened in her criblike hospital bed and saw her mother and father bending over her. Like Alison, Hildy has been restored to the certainty of her childhood.

Now, relaxed, pleased to be taking a break from work, she smiles at Stacey.

"Hey," she asks. "How did Evan and Jared like our baby?" (She too has laid claim to Felicia Miriam. "Hello, sister, little sister," Hildy said when she changed her. "My sister," she said proudly when she introduced Felicia Miriam to her friends.) But although Stacey's sons' relationship to the infant is even closer than Hildy's, the boys saw her for the first time that day.

"Oh, they thought she was adorable," Stacey replies.

She does not tell Stacey that Evan and Jared were almost uninterested in the baby. They looked at her as she lay in the crib and touched her very tentatively when Stacey held her. Evan placed a finger on the strawberry mark and asked if it could be removed.

"When will she walk? When will she talk?" Jared had asked. "Stupid baby. Can't walk. Can't talk."

Both boys had been more curious about the intercom system than about the baby. Felicia Miriam has not come into their home nor have any preparations been made for her arrival. She is not part of their lives. In this Edith has been proven right. To Evan and Jared, the word *sister* means Andrea, and that in turn means a sadness and loss that weights their hearts and engorges their throats. Jared no longer looks for Andrea, but Evan sometimes speaks to her in the darkness of the night. "Where are you?" he asks. "I want to touch you. I want to play with you." He cries very quietly then and asks his father with angry insistence the next day when Stacey will return home, when they will all be back in their house. "I want her! I want her!" he shouts and stops only when Jared too begins to cry and imitate his chant.

But that afternoon it had been the intercom that absorbed him.

"How does it work?" he had asked.

"It's a wire in the wall. Something like that," Hal had explained, waiting impatiently for Stacey to bring the baby back to the nursery. (He himself never holds Felicia Miriam, although he visits almost daily.)

"No. Actually, it's the sensors," David interjected and Hal frowned. His irritation at the correction (he hates to be contradicted in front of his sons) is compounded by his annoyance at David's constant presence whenever he is near the baby.

"What's he afraid of, that I'll run off with his kid?" Hal asked Stacey roughly, and she (newly mired in sadness by his question) did not reply.

"Stacey, is your family — I mean, like your parents and your brothers — are they going to see the baby?" Hildy asks curiously. She knows that Nina is uneasy about discussing Felicia Miriam with either David's mother or her own parents, who will be arriving for the seder.

"I'm not sure," Stacey replies.

Her brothers and sisters-in-law have pressed her but accepted her excuses. While in the hospital she maintained that she was too tired, too depressed to accept visitors. Now she says that she does not want to impose upon the Roths by having company of her own. She knows that they think her convalescence at the Roth home strange, even bizarre, but neither they nor her parents have asked for explanations, nor have they discussed the baby. It is, Stacey thinks, as though they know, without being told, that this baby is peripheral to their lives; transient and unseen, she will vanish.

They were quiet at dinner when Hal told them about the move to California. He thinks Andrew Kardin has found a buyer for their house. He can hardly wait to see Herb Green's face when he gives notice at Ramon's. He has lots of options on the Coast (how he loves that phrase). They can take off anytime Stacey is ready. It's up to her. Next month, the month after.

"The kids should finish the semester," Audrey had said righteously.

"What the hell? Jared's in nursery and Evan is such a super student it doesn't matter if he misses a couple of weeks," Hal had retorted.

Stacey had been silent, but they have, since Andrea's death, grown accustomed to her silence. Her grief insulates her against their concern, their curiosity. They see her as half-mad, but it is a madness that they understand and condone. *To lose a child.* The words strike at their hearts and Cathy and Audrey speak them in whispers. They are married to the sons of Rose Carmody. They understand the consequences of such a loss.

Now, Stacey, unwilling to think about her family, turns the conversation back to Hildy.

"What did you do today?" she asks.

"Not much. Studied for an exam. Helped a little with the baby. And, oh yeah, I helped my mom get the Passover things out. She always gets uptight before the seder." Hildy's tone is condescending, but this is the first time in years that she has actively participated in the rituals of preparation. She found herself taking pleasure in the small routines, listening with interest to the stories David told about the seder plate brought over from Poland, the silver kiddush cups that have been worn by polishing and use to a shimmering fragility.

There is a small crack in the gold-rimmed white china plate where a severed fragment was scrupulously glued. It had been chipped by Amos Roth's mother when she was a small girl, and she told Amos how she had wept as she mended it, sitting at the scrubbed pine table in that kitchen where copper-bottomed pots hung above a huge black iron stove. That house, that kitchen, are vanished now. The village itself, that small hamlet of Jews, is no longer; it exists only on old maps, as an entry in the computer at the Museum of the Diaspora in Tel Aviv. But David held the white china seder plate in his hands and told Hildy about his grandmother, and then he told her how, after their arrival in America, they had pawned the silver kiddush cups — pawned them and redeemed them and pawned them again. And Hildy had laughed. As Felicia Miriam will laugh, in turn, at the idea of pawned silver cups, at the idea of a great-grandmother who wept because a china plate was chipped. But with that laughter the stories become their own, to be told and retold on spring afternoons when cartons are opened and memories begin.

"When is the seder?" Stacey asks.

"Next week. Sunday night. I'll give you a book about it."

"All right. Sunday night." Stacey repeats. She sees it as a boundary, a clear delineation. A week. Tomorrow she will begin to wean Felicia Miriam, who is already accustomed to relief bottles. The flow of her own milk will gradually lessen over the seven days of withdrawal. And on the day after the seder she will return to her own home, her own life. She sees her own departure with dispassionate clarity. She will not turn around when she reaches the flagstone walk.

"I'm going back to my own house on Monday, after the seder," she says solemnly to Hildy.

"We'll miss you, Stacey." Hildy is not dissembling. She likes Stacey and she will miss her.

"I must," Stacey says. "It's time." Felicia Miriam will be a month old. Already she emerges from the sentient, self-contained cocoon of infancy and assumes a personality. She coos and soon she will laugh, and that laughter will bind Stacey to her with joy and recognition. She must leave while she can, before she is unable to break the tentacles of love, before the infant has a voice that will echo in Stacey's ear, resonate against her heart. All this is clear to her. She will have had Felicia Miriam for four weeks, which means (she calculates unwillingly) that *Andrea will have been dead for five weeks.*

The teeth of sorrow tear at her, but she knows how to dull the edge of the assault. She will go upstairs and look at Felicia Miriam, touch her soft skin, the pale wispy tendrils of her aureole of hair. She has lost a daughter but she has borne a daughter. Judith (who has herself lost a son and borne a daughter) was right. Life balances life. She will not be reconciled; what could ever reconcile her to Andrea's loss? And surely she knows (as Judith knows) that one child can never replace another. But she will be comforted. Her life will not be an imitation of her mother's.

Stacey and Hildy walk upstairs together, companionably, their arms about each other's waists. They are sisterly friends. They are bonded together by Felicia Miriam, and they go together to her room. They stand together in the doorway and watch her sleep in a cornucopia of moonlight. Then, gently, Stacey closes the door and she and Hildy separate and go to their rooms. "I am all right," Stacey says aloud in the darkness. "I will be all right," she amends in a whisper.

Stacey's sleep that night is dream-haunted. She is walking, holding Evan and Jared by the hand, through swirling mists to a pool of soft light where Andrea, wearing her crimson velvet dress, waits. But as she walks she hears an infant cry. *Felicia Miriam.* She drops the boys' hands and whirls about, but she cannot see the baby. She rushes toward Andrea, but before she can reach her the mist thickens and the child vanishes. The boys too are gone. Stacey has lost them. She has lost all her children.

"Come back," she calls piteously. "Oh, come back."

She awakens then; she is sitting up in bed, her arms outstretched. She stares into the darkness, and she is frightened because she feels herself lost and alone, because she is in this strange house that is not her home and her sons and her husband are at a distance. And because Andrea will never, never call to her. Not ever again.

Fighting for breath, she gets out of bed and, barefoot, wearing only her pink nightgown, she hurries to the nursery.

David, in pajamas and a robe, stands at the changing table. He has changed Felicia Miriam and now he lowers his head to her and nuzzles her bare stomach.

"Here comes Daddy," he warns and dives again, pursing his lips against her skin, sucking noisily, lovingly, at her tender flesh, at the healed navel, that inturned umbilicus, the dimpled and enduring scar of her physical attachment to Stacey. And then he turns and sees Stacey.

"Stacey. Are you all right?" Her face is waxen-white in the darkness and her hair is unkempt.

"I had a dream," she said, and the flatness of her voice frightens him. "About Andrea. About the boys. And the baby was crying. Crying and crying."

"She was crying," David replies reassuringly. "You must have heard her on the intercom."

"Yes. I suppose."

She watches him while he dresses the baby in a fresh undershirt, his large hands fumbling with the snaps.

"In the dream they were lost. I couldn't find them." Again, she feels a wave of terror and moves to stand beside David, who is fitting the baby into a yellow stretch suit. He steps aside and she completes the small task. She wipes the baby's face with a damp cloth, brushes the pale fringe of hair, using the silver-backed brush; its bristles are as wispy as the tendrils that lie flat now against Felicia Miriam's curiously high forehead.

"Flower face. I found you, flower face," she whispers, and the baby (whose eyes remain a cobalt blue) stares seriously up at her. David feels a stirring of fear. He moves closer, as though to protect his daughter from Stacey's febrile touch, from her urgent, wild whisper. But, almost magically, her face is eased of tension and she smiles.

"Oh, she's so beautiful," she says and lifts the baby.

David's heart stops. He is fearful that she will leave the room with his daughter, that he will have to chase after her and pry the baby out of her arms, but she only carries Felicia Miriam to the rocking chair and sits down, holding her close. And then, as David watches, she places her against her breast. Sleepily, weakly, the baby nurses. David sees how his daughter's face presses so naturally into the mother-of-pearl softness of Stacey's breast, so intricately laced with veins of the palest blue.

Stacey rocks back and forth. It is herself she is soothing, her own distress she is calming. *Only a dream. Only a dream.* Felicia Miriam is asleep and she carries her back to the crib. Again, she and David stand side by side and look down at her.

"You will always know where she is," David says, and although he speaks softly, she hears the urgency in his tone. "Always."

She does not reply, although she is grateful to him. He understands and he would offer her solace.

Stacey does not dream again that night and she awakens in the morning feeling so refreshed that she arranges to meet Hal for lunch at Ramon's.

"I'm going to come home next week," she tells him, and he beams at her across the table.

"Great. Terrific." His face is alive with pleasure, relief, excitement. They will move forward from this dark time; they will live where sunlight glistens on mountains and ocean, far from ice-coated hills and flatlands studded with small gray gravestones. He spreads the color snapshots of locations for the Unicorn sent by Andrew Kardin's colleague in California. Stacey studies a photograph of a cafe near Saratoga in which small tables are set in a garden, bright with freesia and fuchsia.

"We could be happy there," she says huskily.

"Sure."

"Oh, Hal, am I doing the right thing?" she asks, and he looks at her steadily, in sorrow, in sympathy.

"Come on, Stacey," he says at last. "We have to make our own rules. Whatever you decide to do is the right thing."

They sit a few minutes longer, although their meal is finished and the coffee in their cups has grown cold. The snapshots are fanned out across the red cloth, each obscuring the other, like carelessly scattered playing cards in a child's game.

27

As the seder approaches, the household is gripped in a fever of activity. Nina sets up a bassinet in the kitchen and carries Felicia Miriam downstairs each morning. She talks to the baby as she cooks.

"A little more salt in the soup. What do you think, Felicia Miriam mine? Oh, pepper. I forgot the pepper. Thanks for reminding me, you clever kid. World's youngest gourmet cook." She scoops the baby up in her arms and holds her in skillful embrace while she adds the seasonings. The steam rising from the pot assaults them both, and Felicia Miriam grimaces, averts her head. Mrs. Ludovico laughs.

"Good baby," she says approvingly. "Smart too."

"Good baby?" Nina is indignant. "Marvelous baby. Wonderful baby. Smart baby? No. Brilliant baby. Genius." She dances through the kitchen with the baby at her hip and then places Felicia Miriam in her pink and white infant seat atop the wooden counter.

She polishes the silver kiddush cups and the flatware used only on Passover that belonged to her own grandparents and that her mother had given her when her parents moved to Arizona.

"It's only plate," her mother had said. "Not sterling. But your father and I gave it to my parents for their thirtieth anniversary. We saved for two years to buy it and they loved it. They had never had matching silver for Passover before. It was important to them." Nina knew that her mother was telling her that she wanted this set of silver-plated flatware to be important to her. It was a gift of love.

It is a gift of love. She holds up a large serving spoon and polishes it to a high luster. And then she holds the spoon in front of Felicia Miriam so that the baby's face is mirrored in the gleaming metal.

"They saved for two years to buy it. Isn't that marvelous?"

The baby screws her eyes shut against the brightness and stirs restlessly.

"She's hungry," Mrs. Ludovico says without turning round. "Listen. Soon she's going to tell you she's hungry."

And yes, Felicia Miriam's face grows very red and she bellows out her hunger in such urgent wails that Mrs. Ludovico, laughing, holds her as Nina hastily washes her hands and readies the bottle.

Stacey, who wanders into the kitchen just then, takes up the chamois cloth Nina discarded and continues the silver polishing. She watches Nina feed Felicia Miriam the bottle as she works. She congratulates herself because she feels no surge of pain and because her breasts do not throb at the sound of the baby's cry, at the sight of her feeding. Her milk has significantly diminished and Felicia Miriam is almost weaned. Stacey nurses only once a day now, and she no longer rises at night. It is Nina or David who awakens now and feeds Felicia Miriam the bottle and then carries her, more often than not, down the hall and back to their bedroom where (Stacey surmises) she sleeps between them until dawn. Stacey approves of this. She and Hal always slept with their infant children. And even now she carries Felicia Miriam, when she is alone, upstairs with her, into her own bed in the guest room and lies beside her.

Yes, she thinks, spreading the polish on the dessert spoons, it is growing easier. It is sufficient now for Stacey to hold her daughter close when the dusky-skinned shadow of sorrow creeps toward her. She marks her daily progress carefully, with great absorption, like an invalid who, throughout a successful convalescence, continues to measure temperature and pulse at regular intervals.

The phone rings. The call is for Nina. A rehearsal must be rescheduled. Nina talks on the phone while the baby sleeps on her shoulder. Nina's cheek rests on her fringe of fair hair and she speaks very softly because she does not want to wake her daughter. Stacey, watching them, watching Nina hang up and brush her lips across the sleeping infant's forehead, struggles against an onrushing wave of sadness.

It's all right. It's all right. Still, the melancholy clings to her until Nina, smiling and rueful, hands her the baby.

Hal will not come to the seder. Audrey and Mike have tickets to a musical and he has volunteered to stay with their children and Evan and Jared.

"It's only fair. They've had our kids all these weeks," he tells Stacey, who raises no objection although she knows that Audrey often uses teenagers to baby-sit.

It is clear to her that Hal does not want to share in this family celebration. He has, from the beginning, resisted intimacy. Although he has visited almost daily during the weeks Stacey has spent with the Roths, he has, with almost prescient skill, timed his arrivals so that Nina and David are not at home. Often, though, Hildy has been there and Stacey, Hal, and Hildy have shared snacks, watched television together. Hal has initiated Hildy into the game in which he turns the volume off and creates his own dialogue for the characters who drift across the screen. Stacey and Hildy giggled as Hal spoke in a falsetto and then in deep bass tones. But when Nina and David arrived home they turned the volume back up.

"What's the joke?" David asked.

"Oh, just something on the tube," Hal replied. As always, he left very shortly after they arrived. He is not comfortable with David. How could he be comfortable with him? There are too many unarticulated secrets and sorrows between them.

Stacey understands Hal's uneasiness, his reluctance, and does not press him. But she herself will go to the seder. She sees it as a valediction of a kind. On that night, Felicia Miriam will be surrounded by her extended family, by the grandparents and relatives who will love her through all the years of her life. Stacey wants to see her daughter insulated by their affection, cosseted by their caring warmth. It will make it easier, she thinks, and she smiles bitterly at the thought that follows. *Can the impossible be made easier?* But, of course, her leaving is not impossible. Rending and wrenching, but not impossible. She has weathered worse. The worst. Yes. The very worst. And now she allows herself to weep for Andrea without holding Felicia Miriam as a shield against her grief.

On the day of the seder the activity in the house is frenetic. The doorbell rings and rings again. Flowers and extra chairs are delivered. Edith arrives early to help, and the house is filled with the voices of women. Mrs. Ludovico argues with the greengrocer who has neglected to include the asparagus in his delivery.

"It is what they are like," she tells Stacey, who has volunteered to help set the table. "These men. They don't understand."

The house has become a battle station, and the women coordinate their efforts against attack and calamity. A tablecloth is misplaced and then found. The wine delivery is delayed but arrives at last. And through it all, through all the commotion and talk and work, Felicia Miriam sleeps in her bassinet in the kitchen, waking only to be fed and changed.

"She's so good," Edith marvels. "Oh, my boys were never so good. I should have had a daughter. Why didn't I have a daughter?" And her words trail into an uneasy silence because Stacey has come into the kitchen for more glassware — Stacey who bore two daughters. Yet Stacey, looking so well in her navy-blue sweat suit, her golden hair tied back, does not react to her words. In the end, Edith decides that she did not hear them.

Felicia Miriam is more restless in the afternoon. Nina places her in the infant seat on the counter and the baby's eyes follow her as she beats the egg whites with the mixer. They form stiff white hills in the glass bowl.

"See that," Nina tells the infant. "Like snow. And they're for your cake. You're going to have your very own cake." She adds the sugar. A single granule clings to her finger and she puts it in Felicia Miriam's mouth. The baby grimaces at the unfamiliar taste. "Silly baby. Foolish Felicia. Foolicia. Not to like sugar." Nina sings. "Foolicia. Foolish Foolicia." The melody is of her own invention and she sings it as she blends the sugar and the egg whites. A careful folding is crucial to the success of the sponge cake she will serve as dessert — the cake that within the tradition of the family marked the springtime birthday of Amos Roth's sister Miriam and will now, and through all the years to come, celebrate the birth of Felicia Miriam. Nina's voice grows louder, merrier. She is intent on her task; she is, at once, recreating family history and establishing a new tradition.

The phone rings yet again. David calls to say that he has been delayed at a meeting and cannot pick Nina's parents up at the airport.

"Damn," Nina says, and Felicia Miriam cries. She lifts her from the infant seat and holds her while she talks to David.

"Here, I'll take her." Stacey relieves Nina of the baby and carries her up to the nursery crib, placing her beneath the blanket as the problem is resolved. Hildy will drive to the airport. The door slams as she leaves.

Stacey is very tired, but instead of lying down she sits in the nursery rocking chair, the notebook that contains her poems on her lap. But she cannot concentrate. Felicia Miriam is restless. The house is permeated by the aromas of cooking and baking — the roasting meat and turkey, the soup that Mrs. Ludovico is reheating, the blend of fish, carrots, and onions. The invasive odors nauseate Stacey, and then Felicia Miriam, who has slept only briefly and lightly, awakens and begins to cry.

"All right. All right."

Stacey speaks softly to her daughter and deftly changes her. And then she dresses her in a delicate white dress of embroidered batiste, knitted pink tights, and a matching hat and sweater. The baby is pliant, as though soothed by Stacey's touch, pleased by the soft fabrics that cover her. Her eyes are open and her features have lost the somnolent look of infancy and are more clearly defined, her expression newly aware.

"Sweet. So sweet," Stacey murmurs, and she carries her downstairs. The kitchen is frenetic with activity. Pots and pans clatter and Nina, Edith, and Mrs. Ludovico speak in the pleasant yet vaguely distracted tones of women who are busily involved in a common task. Stacey thinks of going in to show them the baby in all her finery, to tell them that she is taking her for a walk, but the phone rings, a glass dish is dropped, Nina curses softly, and Edith laughs. Stacey leaves the house by the front door, closing it softly behind her.

She settles Felicia Miriam into the large coach carriage and maneuvers it out onto the street. Passersby smile at her and she smiles
back. She enjoys her power as she pushes the large coach, so unlike
the small utilitarian carriage she used for Evan, Andrea, and Jared.
This regal coach is high above the ground, and Felicia Miriam lies
within it like a small royal presence, on flowered sheets, beneath a
coverlet woven of feather-light pink and silver wool.

When she reaches the park that overlooks the quarry, she settles
the carriage beneath a tree and sits beside it on a redwood bench.
The clear water is shadowed by the branches of overhanging willow
trees, and nesting birds trill in extravagant chorus. Stacey takes a
thick paperback book (Hal's gift to her, brought as penance, the
night he told her he would not attend the seder) from her large
white pocketbook. *One Hundred Years of Solitude.* She likes the title,
and the author's name, Gabriel García Márquez, rolls about like a
melodic poem in her mind. She will study Spanish in California.
She has always been good at languages. She will study Spanish and
French and she will write delicate quatrains in both languages. She
sees herself sitting at a desk, surrounded by dictionaries, in a pleasant
room that overlooks a large garden, a garden wondrously overgrown
with brightly colored flowers.

She opens her book, but before she can read a single page, a young
woman pushing a smaller carriage approaches the bench, hesitates
shyly for a moment, and then sits beside Stacey. She is very pale
and her long brown hair is tied back into a lank ponytail. Her dark
slacks are too tight and her blue blouse hangs too loosely. Stacey
recognizes her instinctively as a new mother who is still adjusting to
the logistics of caring for a baby, whose body has not yet recovered
from the imbalances of her pregnancy. She is new to the loneliness
of a long day spent with only an infant, unbroken by the sound of
an adult voice, and she rocks the carriage with a nervous desperation. She turns to Stacey, shrugs, and smiles.

"Your first baby?" Stacey asks kindly.

The woman nods, grateful for the question, the expression of interest, hungry for conversation.

"Yes. My first. A little girl. Robin, we called her. Oh, my name
is Lisa." Her voice cracks as though from disuse and Stacey remem-

bers how she walked through the house, talking to herself, reciting poetry aloud after Evan's birth. New mothers are unprepared for the solitude, the vast abyss of stillness across which they wander in bewilderment during the first weeks and months of their first child's life. There is no such silence with a second child and a third. There has been no silence at all with Felicia Miriam, which is why Stacey is so grateful for the quiet of this day, this very last day.

"And what about you — is this your first baby?" Lisa asks.

"Oh, no," Stacey replies in surprise. "She's my fourth."

"Oh, I thought because the carriage was brand new."

"Oh, yes, the carriage is new. We had to get everything new for this baby. After three children things get so worn, so frayed. Besides, it's fun to shop for new things," Stacey says (and feels a vague bitterness because she did not shop for any of Felicia Miriam's furnishings — an exclusion that she both understands and resents).

"Yes. That's exciting. I love that coverlet."

"My mother made it," Stacey lies. Rose Carmody has never made anything for any of her grandchildren. She has never held any of them in her arms, although she studied each infant gravely as though to seek out a sign that did not reveal itself.

"It's beautiful. Are your other children boys or girls?" Lisa asks. Her baby has stopped crying and she sits back on the bench in relief.

"My oldest is a boy. Evan. He's nearly eight. And then there's Andrea. She's almost six. And Jared. He's four. Felicia Miriam evens everything out — two boys, two girls." She smiles complacently and feels a surge of happiness, of satisfaction. She is not lying. She is creating her own brief and happy truth. And she is protected because she recognizes that that truth is ephemeral, that it exists only as long as she can make this young, sad-eyed woman, whom she will never see again, believe her. "All the children are very excited about the baby," she adds.

"They're not jealous? I read that older children get jealous of a newborn."

"Oh, no. They all want to take care of her. Especially Andrea. She dresses and undresses her. See." Stacey pulls the coverlet back slightly so that Felicia Miriam's sweater and the embroidered skirt of her batiste dress, floating above the knit tights, are revealed. "Andrea chose this outfit."

"That's beautiful. Although the stretch suits are more comfortable, aren't they?"

"I suppose so. But these little dresses are better for the warm weather we have in northern California."

"Oh, do you come from California?"

"Actually, we just moved there. We came home for the holidays to see family and do some shopping." The life she has invented for herself takes on new dimensions, assumes a new reality. She talks on with great fluency, with attention to detail. She describes her redwood house that overlooks a canyon, family trips to San Francisco, dinners at Fisherman's Wharf.

"Oh, we'd love to go to California," Lisa says. "We had planned to travel, to go to Europe and Mexico, to the West, before we had kids, but then I got pregnant and that was it." Her voice is wistful, laced with longing for places she will not soon visit, languages she will not soon hear spoken. "Of course," she adds hastily, "we're very happy with Robin. We think we're very lucky. And we are thinking of going west for a vacation."

"Oh, you're young. You'll manage," Stacey assures her. "And if you're ever in the Saratoga area, come by my husband's restaurant and have lunch. It's called the Unicorn. Everyone in town knows about it even though we just opened. My husband had such creative ideas for the menus, the decorations. We serve the most wonderful meals in the garden — the tables are shaded by orange trees. I let the baby sleep there sometimes when I help with the books or the ordering."

"You leave her out there alone?"

"Oh, no. Andrea loves to watch her and she's very responsible. She sits at a table with her construction paper and her Magic Markers — she's very creative — and if she has to, she rocks the carriage and Felicia Miriam goes right back to sleep." Stacey's voice is stronger. Her story is gathering momentum, accruing reality. She closes her eyes and sees Andrea's face so clearly, the intent set of her lips, the thoughtful cast of her eyes as she selects a color, decides on a design.

She sees Andrea standing on tiptoe to rock the carriage. If she listens hard enough she will hear her voice calling, "Mom, come quickly, the baby is crying."

And now Felicia Miriam is crying, stirring and writhing beneath the pink and silver coverlet. Her sobs come in syncopated gasps, jolting Stacey from reverie into action. She rises, shifts the baby's position, loosens the ribbons on her hat, and rocks the carriage. The baby's crying does not abate.

"Perhaps she's hungry," Lisa suggests. There is a note of superiority in her tone. Her own baby, despite her inexperience, sleeps peacefully.

"No, I nursed her only an hour ago." (In fact, she has not nursed the baby at all today, relying entirely on bottles, and this lie, unlike the others, shames her, causes her to blush.)

"Oh, you're nursing also," Lisa says approvingly.

"Oh, yes. I nursed my other three children. I nursed Andrea until she was almost two." That at least is true. She had nursed Andrea longer than Evan and Jared because she had been reluctant to give up the long sweet moments of their togetherness, of her daughter's gentle, playful nuzzling, the touch of the chubby arms about her shoulders, her face buried in Andrea's golden curls. "But I've already begun to wean Felicia Miriam. I'm going to school and there just doesn't seem to be enough time, between classes and helping my husband with the business and driving the boys to their games, Andrea to her dance and art lessons . . ." Her voice trails off as Felicia Miriam whimpers again.

Stacey touches the baby's forehead. It is disturbingly warm. The tiny legs flail, and her face, screwed into a knot of misery, is mottled.

"I must take her home," Stacey says. "She feels a little warm. I'm sure it's nothing, but you can never be too careful with an infant."

"Of course," Lisa agrees, but there is disappointment in her voice. She does not want Stacey to leave. She does not want to be abandoned again to the silences and loneliness of her new motherhood. "I hope I see you again. I come here almost every afternoon."

"Oh, I hope so," Stacey says. "But I'm not sure. We're going back to California soon and I have so much to do. But yes, maybe I'll be here again. Maybe." She thrusts her book into the large white purse, releases the brake on the carriage. "But remember, if you're ever in Saratoga, California, ask for the Unicorn. I'll guarantee you a table in our grape arbor."

And then she is off, walking rapidly, not hearing Lisa, who calls after her, wanting to know her name.

Don't be sick, she commands Felicia Miriam, who is quiet now, so quiet that half a block from the Roths' house, Stacey pauses and checks her again. She listens (her own heart beating with arrhythmic rapidity, her hand ice-cold) for the baby's shallow breath; she looks (her own eyes burning with fear) into the baby's calm, cobalt-blue gaze.

It is only after Nina has put the sponge cake into the oven that she and Edith set the table. They have done this together every year since Nina's marriage to David, and they relish the small rituals. Nina places the Elijah cup in the center of the table and Edith fills it. Nina sets out the silver and Edith carries in the china. They take a sensual pleasure in the smoothness of the fine linen napkins, the intricate design of the huge lace cloth, the sparkling fragility of the crystal. They laugh and talk as they work, now retelling one family story, now doubting the authenticity of another.

"These kiddush cups look pretty good for having knocked around pawnshops year after year," Edith says.

"They are beautiful though." Nina holds one up to the light, runs her finger across the slender stem.

"Yes. I'm glad we have them. And it works out exactly right. Four cups. Two for my boys, two for your girls. Claire will approve."

Claire Silberman had been scrupulously fair. Before her move to Florida, she had summoned her sons and their wives and given each family two silver cups. The seder plate she gave to Nina and David, the embroidered matzoh cloth to Edith and Arnold.

"To be passed on," she said sternly, "to your children."

She was not giving them possessions. She was vesting them with history, making them custodians of continuity. The silver cups, the chipped china plate, the faded embroidered cloth, wrapped in layers of newspaper and tied with the tattered string she saved from bakery boxes, were not objects — they were evidence of survival, of vitality.

"Claire never approves," Nina replies. "I can't imagine Hildy ever polishing silver, and it's a little too early to tell about Felicia Miriam. Gee, she's been quiet for a while. You carry on. I'll run upstairs and check her."

"Isn't Stacey with her?"

"Yes. But I'll just look in on them."

She does not tell Edith that she is suddenly overcome with a hunger for the baby, an urge to see her and touch her and hold her close. She had been gripped by similar feelings during Hildy's infancy, but she had forgotten them — forgotten how she had recognized from the very first moment she held Hildy that her daughter was welded to her, connected to her more fiercely than she ever had been during the long months of gestation. And now it is Felicia Miriam who absorbs her, for whom she feels this tenacious longing, this passionate vigilance.

She dashes upstairs. The doors to both Stacey's room and the nursery are closed. Cautiously, because she does not want to wake the sleeping baby, she opens the nursery door and tiptoes across the room. The crib is empty.

She stares into it. Her toes and fingers are points of ice. She touches the fresh quilted pad that lies across the flowered sheet as though her eyes have deceived her and she will feel Felicia Miriam's back, run her fingers down the tiny vertebrae. (*"Like pebbles,"* David had said, *"like tiny, tiny, sea-smoothed pebbles."*)

She hurries across the hall. Of course. Stacey has probably taken the baby into her own room, is even now lying in bed with her. Nina knows that Stacey often does this, and it would be only natural that she would do it on this, her last afternoon with Felicia Miriam. She knocks but there is no answer. She opens the door. The guest room is dimly lit and only Stacey's open suitcase is on the bed. Nina looks around. She opens and closes bureau drawers, peeks into the closet. She does not find what she is looking for. Stacey's big white purse is gone.

"Edith!" The shrillness of fear is in her voice. She leans against the doorjamb and does not move as Edith comes running up the steps. "Nina. What is it? What's wrong?"

"The baby's gone. The baby and Stacey."

"Oh." Edith's face is wreathed with relief. "She probably took the baby for a walk in the carriage. It's such a gorgeous day."

"Without telling me?"

"All right, she should have told you, but it's no big deal. Maybe she didn't want to bother us."

"Edith, listen to me. It's not as simple as that. Stacey's been so moody, so depressed. David found her in the nursery the other night. That is, she came in all distraught in the middle of the night. She's been having nightmares."

"Nina. Listen to me. I'd worry if she wasn't moody and depressed. If she weren't having nightmares. She has lost one daughter. She is giving up another. It's devastating. She will be all right. Eventually, she will be all right. She's strong. She's resilient. She'll build a new life. But this must be a terrible time for her." Edith speaks breath-lessly, insistently, as though the force and speed of her words can will Nina to calm.

"And in this terrible time, she can do anything, anything," Nina says. It is not of Stacey she is thinking now, she knows, but of her-self. Oh, she would have done anything, anything, for the infant Hildy, to keep her safe, to protect her. And she would do anything, anything, for Felicia Miriam, to keep her safe, to keep her theirs.

"Come, Nina."

Edith takes her sister-in-law's hand and together they go down-stairs. Edith leads her out to the porch and they lean against the rail and stare beyond the slate path, to the wide sunstreaked road. And together they see a shadow darken it and then the high coach car-riage that Stacey is pushing swiftly, her white bag swinging against her hip, her body bent so that she can peer into the carriage even as she wheels it. Nina and Edith wave to her and she waves back. Edith goes into the house and Nina hears her call something to Mrs. Lu-dovico. She herself remains on the porch, a smile fixed on her face, and Stacey, walking up the path, at once discerns the relief in Nina's eyes, hears the rasp in her voice.

"We were just wondering where the two of you were," Nina says, but the lightness of her tone is edged with the vestige of anger, the remnant of terror.

"I took Felicia Miriam for a walk to the park near the quarry," Stacey explains. "I would have stayed longer but she's fussy — at least she was — and she felt warm, but maybe I was imagining it." Her voice is grave with worry, weighted with guilt. She is being punished for her lies, for the bargain she had no right to make.

She lifts the baby from the carriage, and Nina takes her and balances her small, unsteady head against her palm while her lips brush the high white forehead. Felicia Miriam is cool and she falls asleep as Nina holds her, her breath soft and moist within the safe cove of Nina's inclined neck.

"I think she's all right," Nina assures Stacey. "Maybe she was overdressed." She does not mean this as criticism but as reassurance. Stacey blushes and Nina swiftly adds, "It's so hard to know how to dress a baby in this weather. But she looks so beautiful in that little dress."

"I wanted to see her in it," Stacey says and turns away. But Nina hears, in the words that she does not say, her mute mourning. Stacey will not see Felicia Miriam in sunsuits and dungarees and starched party dresses and brightly colored overalls. She will have no memory of Felicia Miriam in a crimson velvet dress.

"Of course you did," Nina replies, and she holds the baby closer. She wants to comfort Stacey, to tell her they will send her photographs of the infant grown to toddler, but she restrains herself. This is a dangerous day. They tread a delicate high wire, and an extra word, an uneasy glance, may jeopardize the balance they have strained so hard to maintain.

They enter the house together then and go upstairs to the nursery.

"Should we take her temperature?" Stacey asks, and although Nina does not want to wake the baby, she agrees. Oh, she will agree to anything Stacey asks today because Felicia Miriam is safe within her arms, and soon, soon, they will have her to themselves.

Nina hands Stacey the thermometer and she and Stacey each read it in turn. It is normal and they smile at each other in embarrassment and relief. Mothers of infants are always so worried, so overly concerned. They forgive themselves, they forgive each other, and they feel the exhausted calm of swimmers who have been caught in dangerous waters but have come to rest at last on a safe shore.

Nina undresses and changes the baby, talking softly to her, apologizing.

"Oh, did we wake you up? Oh, how bad we are to wake you up."

She gives the baby to Stacey, who carries her to the rocking chair where, seated, she places her at her breast.

The front door opens and closes and they hear the excited murmur of voices, the clatter of Hildy's car keys as she tosses them into the bronze bowl.

Nina kneels and kisses the nursing baby's head. New hair is growing in, crowning the scalp with tufts of golden cloud. Briefly her eyes meet Stacey's, and then she hurries downstairs to greet her parents.

28

Stacey prepares carefully for the seder. She washes her hair and brushes it vigorously as she dries it so that it falls naturally into curling golden folds. Although the door to her room is closed (Felicia Miriam is asleep and will sleep for several hours), she can hear the holiday activity of the household, the rushing footsteps and slamming doors, the ringing phones contrasted by the carefully muted voices. Nina's mother speaks in a chirping birdlike tone (which surprises Stacey because Nina's own voice is so rich and firm), while her father's statements resonate with irritable authority. Hildy is shy and flirtatious with these grandparents whom she so rarely sees. Stacey listens as they walk down the long hallway past her room.

"Do you want to see my room?" Stacey hears Hildy ask them, and she is disappointed for Hildy, who is trying so hard, when they decline.

"We're too tired, dear," the grandmother chirps.

"I just want to lie down," the grandfather says. "After all, a six-hour flight is a six-hour flight."

The door to their room (a larger guest room at the end of the hall) closes and Hildy's step is slow upon the stairs.

Will they be similarly insensitive to Felicia Miriam? Stacey wonders, although she realizes that, of course, it will not matter. Nina's parents live in a distant state and they will see this new granddaughter only infrequently. Still, she feels the beginning of a sadness. She would have wanted the baby to grow up in the heart of a large, warm family, adored by grandparents, coddled by aunts and uncles. Andrea had loved her role as the petted darling of Stacey's own family; how she had flitted, certain of their affection, their admiration, from aunt to uncle, scrambling upon laps, perching on shoulders, demanding and dispensing kisses, playfully shaking her golden curls.

Stacey shakes her own head vigorously as though to banish the memory and glances at the clock. It is only a quarter to six and Nina told her that the seder would begin at seven. The extra time unsettles her and she paces her room, looks out at the garden. The bushes near the playhouse have been pruned and a small path is being cleared. She is looking down at the landscape of her daughter's childhood. She turns away, toys with the idea of going into the kitchen, offering Nina and Mrs. Ludovico her assistance, but she hears David's mother (who had arrived earlier) talking too loudly to Edith and she decides against it.

She does not want to confront Claire Silberman nor does she want to meet Nina's parents. She wonders how much Nina has told them about the baby, if, in fact, she has told them anything at all. Stacey is sorry now that she stayed for the seder. She is an awkward, alien presence in their midst, inhibiting their celebration, shadowing the Roths' joy in their daughter; bitterly, she recognizes that she impedes them from sharing that joy.

She tries to think of small tasks that she might accomplish, but she has already packed her clothing and only her white robe and the navy-blue dress she will wear to the seder hang in her closet. She has gathered up her books and magazines from the bedside table, her cosmetics and toilet articles from the bureau, leaving out only a small picture book about Passover that Hildy had lent her. Already her presence in this house, in this room, is vanishing. Tomorrow, Nina will thrust the windows open and Mrs. Ludovico will change the linens, and she will be gone, nullified.

She wishes now that she had left some tangible evidence of her existence, of her love, in the nursery — a wall hanging, perhaps, or a plant, even a cushion, some small talisman that would bear proof of her fleeting presence, of her care. The thought is foolish, she knows. After tonight, she will cease to exist for the baby she bore and suckled. She will be (as she must be, as she agreed to be) a transient presence, arriving at infrequent intervals, uncomfortably

identified as a close friend who must be dutifully kissed, carelessly
hugged. She is bound to Felicia Miriam, but Felicia Miriam will not,
and should not, be bound to her. She understands this, yet she repeats it to herself again and again as though it is a lesson that must
be learned anew, a catechism that must be memorized.

She readies herself for the onslaught of misery and lies down upon
the bed. Staring up at the ceiling, hearing Felicia Miriam's light and
even breathing on the intercom, she anticipates tears, but her eyes
remain dry. She congratulates herself. She grows expert at vanquish-
ing grief, at overcoming separation and deprivation. She reaches for
the book on Passover and opens it purposefully. It is, of course, meant
for children, and the simple clarity of its language, the large print
on the glossy white paper, the colorful illustrations, soothe her. She
reads it with the absorption of a child, playfully sounding out the
words, studying the illustrations.

It recounts the story of Moses, and Stacey looks at the picture of
the baby in the neatly caulked basket hidden amidst the bulrushes
and reads that his mother, Jocheved, wept to part with him but she
knew that she was doing what was best for the baby. Stacey is comforted. She too is doing what is best for her baby (and what is best
too for Evan and Jared and Hal). She turns the page and studies the
picture of the Pharaoh's daughter who rescues the infant. In this
illustration the Egyptian princess is depicted as a tall and lean young
woman whose dark hair is intricately plaited, and Stacey decides that
she resembles Nina. The thought amuses her and she reflects that
the princess, like Nina herself, mothered the child born to another
woman. And, of course, Moses grew to young manhood in the palace, but he was not seduced by power or riches or by the culture that
was not his own. In the end he returned to his people. He sought
out and claimed his natural birthright. ·Perhaps, Stacey thinks, Felicia Miriam will one day seek her out, return to her. And now, at
last, her tears do fall because she is shamed by the childish foolishness of her fantasy, the desperate irrationality of her hope. *Crazy
person. Stop thinking like a crazy person,* she tells herself.

"Stacey." Hildy is knocking at her door, calling to her. "Are you
ready?" Hildy, who has herself so often felt excluded or intrusive,
worries about Stacey, understands her uneasiness.

"In a minute. Wait, I'll open the door."

She slips her robe on and lets Hildy in. It does not matter to her that Hildy sees that her eyes are reddened and knows that she has been weeping. She has a right to her grief, her misery. Perversely, she hopes that tomorrow or the next day Hildy will tell Nina and David about her tears. She wants them to know how deeply she cared; she wants to punish them (and this she acknowledges without qualm) with her love.

Hildy sits on the bed while Stacey dresses. Hildy turns the pages of the picture book and Stacey wonders if she too identifies with the Moses story — if she perhaps sees herself as the vigilant older sister, the sweet singer, Miriam, who in the illustration wears a white dress not unlike the loose gauzy white cotton skirt and blouse Hildy herself wears. But Stacey does not mention this. Instead, as she slips on the navy-blue dress, she asks Hildy about her grandparents, about the trip home from the airport.

"Oh, they're fine," Hildy replies. "There wasn't that much traffic, but they get tired so easily."

"Did your mother tell them about Felicia Miriam?" Stacey asks. That is the question that absorbs her, and she buttons her dress and studies herself in the mirror as Hildy struggles to answer.

"No. Not yet. I mean, they know that the baby's here and that you're here. Like, I guess they think you're a friend who's staying here because you have some kind of problem. They haven't gone into the nursery yet or anything. I think my mom wants to wait until after the seder, like maybe tomorrow when they're not so tired, to explain everything to them. You know, they're older. They might not understand all this so easily."

"I know," Stacey says, and she wonders if she herself understands it at all.

"It's better to tell them when they're rested."

"And when I'm not here," Stacey says. "It's all right, Hildy," she adds swiftly because Hildy is blushing painfully and Stacey understands that all this has been discussed and weighed very carefully, that Edith has been consulted. "I understand that it's awkward and difficult for them. And for you."

"They want to make it easier for you too," Hildy says miserably, and she turns the pages of the book and closes it at last, tossing it across the bed.

"Oh, well," Stacey replies. "Oh, well." It cannot be made easier for her, but she will bear it. She has borne worse. She is newly confident of her strength. She is, after all, leaving a daughter who is alive and who will live an enchanted life; she is not burying a daughter, a golden-haired child who has so arbitrarily, so inexplicably, died. "How do I look?"

"Terrific," Hildy says. She thinks that she would like to comb Stacey's hair, which, during these last weeks, has grown too long. She would pull it back from her face as Andrea used to, but because she remembers Andrea so diligently brushing and combing, she says nothing. Then Stacey, as though reading her thoughts, brushes her hair back and holds it in place with the tortoiseshell headband that gives her the look of a schoolgirl.

"How's that?" she asks. She is nervous. Her body is aquiver with tremulous energy and her voice is uncertain; she feels herself suspended between laughter and tears. Quite suddenly, she picks up her wallet and fumbles in it for the snapshots of Evan and Jared. She studies her sons' smiling faces. They give her ballast, reassurance. Tomorrow she will be with them. *They* are not lost to her.

"You look terrific," Hildy says. "Just fine."

She watches as Stacey kisses each snapshot and replaces them in her wallet. Does it also contain a picture of Andrea? she wonders. Does one carry around a snapshot of a dead child?

"Oh, Stacey," she says, and her words are an apology for her cruel curiosity, an acknowledgment of Stacey's pain, of Stacey's losses.

"I'll be all right," Stacey says. "Don't you worry."

Together then, their arms about each other's waists, they descend the thickly carpeted staircase and greet Alison as she arrives.

The table is beautifully set for the festive meal. The snow-white lace cloth, so faintly mapped with fading stains of other seders in other years, covers its vast expanse. The polished flatware gleams and the silver cups, filled to the brim with red wine, stand at each place setting. They are all different and each, Stacey knows, has a history. She has listened to Nina tell of the cups that were pawned and the cup that she and David discovered in a small shop in Flor-

ence. It is important that she remember these stories. They will become Felicia Miriam's heritage, her family history. Each year at this
season, Stacey's daughter will touch the silver cups, the linen napkins and matzoh cloth, the chipped seder plate, and she will feel
herself part of a tradition. And each year Stacey, caught up in Easter
feasts and finery, will imagine Felicia in this room, among these things.

Stacey looks at the gold-rimmed china seder plate and (testing
herself now so that she will not have time to think of years gone by
and years to come) struggles to recall the significance of the hard-
boiled egg, the bright-green sprigs of parsley, the roasted shank bone,
the clumsy bitter horseradish root, the chopped apples and nuts. She
summons to memory the explanations on the pages of the children's
book on her bed, but there is no time. Already the room is filling
with guests, and she must smile, acknowledge introductions, greet
those who are familiar to her. The new faces dizzy her and she de-
spairs of matching names with faces. Her mouth aches with the effort
of the forced smile, and she leans heavily on the back of a chair.
Oh, Hal was right not to come. She should not have stayed. It is
too much, too much.

"Such beautiful flowers," Betty Goldfein says, admiring the sprays
of forsythia that Nina arranged in smoked glass vases and surrounded
with white carnations from Israel.

"Stacey helped me," Nina says (and this, at least, is true; Stacey
did cut the forsythia and help to arrange them). "You met Stacey at
our Thanksgiving dinner," she reminds Betty. She wants to establish
the normalcy and the continuity of this abnormal and soon-to-be
discontinued intimacy. She takes Stacey's hand in her own and leads
her across the room to where Claire Silberman stands with the elderly couple who, of course, must be Nina's parents, Stacey realizes.

"Claire, you remember our good friend Stacey Cosgrove," Nina
says. "And Stacey, I'd like you to meet my mother and father, Mr.
and Mrs. Milstein." She makes the introduction carefully. She does
not want Stacey to feel slighted, and she wants her to know the
family that will be Felicia Miriam's, the grandparents who will celebrate her birthdays, year by passing year, who will rejoice in her
growth, who will carry her picture in their wallets (as perhaps Stacey
herself will).

"Ah, you must be the mother of that little baby we've yet to meet," Nina's mother says pleasantly. "It's wonderful that you've been able to stay with Nina and David." If she is bewildered by the arrangement (and surely, Stacey thinks, she must be) she restrains her puzzlement, her curiosity. Just so, bemused but smiling, she has accepted Nina's career, her early marriage and motherhood. She is, as Nina had described her, pliable and acquiescent.

Claire Silberman, elegant in black silk, takes Stacey's hand, looks hard at her.

"I remember you from Thanksgiving," she says. "And now you have yet another little girl. How nice. I hope she's as pretty as your older daughter. She spilled a glass of grape juice then, I remember. Did that stain ever come out, Nina?"

"Yes." Nina squeezes Stacey's hand in regret, apology, but Stacey simply smiles back at David's mother.

"You have such a good memory," she says quite clearly. "Yes, now I have two little girls. Two daughters. And they are both beautiful, I think." She does not look at Nina, although she hears the swift intake of her breath, feels the pressure of her hand. They are all playacting tonight. She too has the right to a scenario of her own choosing.

Stacey takes her seat between Hildy and Seth. Edith and Arnold, who sit across the table, smile encouragingly, comfortingly, at her. She takes her cues from them, rising as they do when Nina lights the candles and blesses them, when David intones the prayer over the wine. She does not attempt to follow the prayer in English, in the book at her place, but instead studies their faces. She is memorizing their gestures — the way Nina encircles the tall silver candlesticks so that the flimsy gray sleeves of her dress fly dangerously above the flickering flames, the way she presses her fingers to her eyes as she murmurs the prayers. She marks the way David lifts his silver wine cup (that much-traveled, much-lost, and much-redeemed legacy) and passes it to Hildy, who drinks from it and passes her fingers across its engraved surface. Felicia Miriam will, one day, repeat each motion and Stacey wants her imaginings to be accurate. She must observe carefully tonight so that each springtime she will draw her memories from a wellspring of authenticity.

"Let's begin then," David says affably. He is proud of this beautifully set table, of these symbols of continuity. If he approaches the
intercom receiver subtly placed on the wall near him, he will hear
his infant daughter's sleep-bound breathing. He explains that it is
their custom to have each guest read a portion of the story. Of course,
they will sing portions of the Haggadah. Arnold begins the reading
in Hebrew, and then Aaron, who is the youngest, is called to ask
the traditional four questions.

"Aaron's eternal role," Claire Silberman says slyly. "Always the
youngest, the baby of the family."

"Well, that's hardly a permanent situation," Edith retorts. "It is
subject to change." Edith is equable with most people, but her mother-
in-law irritates her, tempts her into argument.

"Oh, I suppose so. Eventually you'll have grandchildren," Claire
says. "I'm not anticipating any more grandchildren of my own. Or
perhaps you're going to surprise me, Edith?" Malice coats her words
but her smile does not falter, and neither her sons nor their wives
answer her, although they exchange looks.

Stacey listens to Aaron chant the questions and realizes that, of
course, this role, in only a few years' time, will fall to Felicia Miriam.
"Wherefore is this night different from all other nights?" And will
her daughter ever ask, "Wherefore am I different from all other children?" And how will they answer her — oh, how? Aaron's voice,
high and sweet, deepens occasionally, without warning. He blushes
and glances at Edith, who nods her encouragement, her approval.

The reading resumes, and slowly the story of the exodus unfolds.
They go around the table, breaking now and again into song. Stacey
(who loves stories, who loves words) is caught up in the text and she
follows the movements of the others. She too lifts a finger to point
to the shank bone, the matzoh, the bitter herb, as each is explained.
Her face is flushed and she feels lightheaded. She too has drunk two
cups of wine. Hildy nudges her. It is her turn to read. She smiles
shyly as Hildy helps her to find the place.

"Who is like unto the Lord our God, who dwells so high, who
looks down so low, upon the heavens and the earth. He lifts the
lowly and supports the needy and sets them among the princes of
His people," she reads without hesitation. She pauses for breath and

continues. "He makes the barren woman dwell in her house as the joyful mother of children." This last sentence she reads very slowly, as though uncertain of its meaning, and then, her voice thickening, she repeats it. "He makes the barren woman dwell in her house as the joyful mother of children?"

She has turned the words into a question, and she looks at Nina and David as though seeking an answer, but their eyes are lowered. Across the table from her, Edith and Arnold toy with their wine-glasses and restlessly turn the pages of their Haggadahs. Then Seth's father picks up the reading, realizes that it is a song, and leads them in a rollicking melody that breaks the strange tension that fell upon them as Stacey read.

Swiftly then, the first part of the service is concluded and they recite in feverish unison the blessings over the matzoh and the bitter herb and the strange combination of apples and nuts. Hildy plucks up a cutting of the raw horseradish root and dips it into the brick-colored mixture (and now Stacey, the good student, recalls that indeed it is symbolic of the bricks the Israelites were forced to make by their harsh Egyptian taskmasters) and passes it to Stacey.

"Try this," she says. "But be prepared. It's very strong."

Stacey does try it but she is not prepared. The bitter taste causes tears to come to her eyes.

"It stings, doesn't it?" Alison asks.

She and Seth and Hildy too dab at their eyes with their napkins, but Stacey cannot stanch her tears and she must, at last, leave the table and hurry into the kitchen, where kindly Mrs. Ludovico wets a cloth with cold water and presses it against her eyes. Still the taste does not leave her tongue, and its bitterness invades her heart, even as she tastes the fish and the soup, as she rises to help Nina and Mrs. Ludovico, Hildy and Edith, set out the turkey and the roast, the salads and vegetables.

"Oh, no, Stacey," Nina protests when she comes into the kitchen. "We want you to relax, enjoy yourself."

There is laughter in the kitchen. Edith and Hildy recall an incident from a bygone year. Nina and Mrs. Ludovico work at a counter with companionable intensity, arranging the serving dishes, garnishes dancing from their fingers onto the large platters. Stacey stands alone in the doorway and then, unnoticed, she goes upstairs to the nursery.

Felicia Miriam is asleep but she is perspiring. Stacey removes one of her blankets and opens the window slightly. Then she thinks again (these spring evenings grow chilly quite suddenly) and closes it. The baby stretches, moans softly, and then curls again into the fetal position. Her fair straight eyelashes are stuck together by tears that have long since dried. Her hand, curled into a fist, beats lightly, only once, upon the flowered sheet. Stacey leans forward, her arms outstretched (although of course she will not touch the sleeping child), and she smiles because always she has been charmed by these small tentative movements of her infant children — she their joyful mother.

"Is everything all right, Stacey?" Soundlessly, David has entered the room. He stands behind her in the darkness and his voice is heavy with concern. But it is not the baby he stares at. His eyes are riveted to Stacey, and in them she sees his sorrow and his fear, and she is sorry to have caused them both.

"Yes. Everything is fine. I thought I heard her cry."

"No. The intercom would pick it up. I have it turned on high. You know, because of all the noise at the table."

"It's a lovely seder, David," she says.

"Yes. Nina worked hard. But then, Nina always works hard — at whatever she does."

He speaks very softly, fearful of waking the sleeping baby, and Stacey understands that his words are meant to reassure her. Nina will work hard at being a good mother to Felicia Miriam. She, the barren woman, will dwell in this house as the joyful mother of children. Stacey need not worry.

"I know."

They go downstairs together then, but they keep their distance from each other on the wide staircase. Already they have begun to separate from each other, to pace out a distance.

Laughter and talk fill the dining room. Dishes of food travel from one end of the table to the other. Alison, Seth, and Hildy argue politics vigorously with Arnold and Dr. Goldfein. Nina's mother shows Claire Silberman a photograph of her condominium.

"Very nice," Claire says. "If you don't mind living so close to other people. But we always valued our privacy."

"I wish Hildy would visit," Nina's father complains. "I have one grandchild and she doesn't want to visit."

"Maybe we'll all go west this year," David says. "Maybe for Thanksgiving."

"That would be wonderful," Nina's mother trills. "And you too, Claire. You too."

"Only if Arnold and the boys and Edith come."

"Yes. Why not? Why shouldn't they come?"

Their words form magical threads. Their plans are tightly woven to form a safety net of their own assured continuity. Year after year, at wonderfully set tables, at times of joy and festival, they will gather together and talk and sing and laugh and quarrel over incidents that happened long years ago. Always they will plan for years to come. And Felicia Miriam will be at the heart of their contentment, swallowed by their love, insulated by their security, their traditions. Stacey understands this and she understands, too, that this is all to the good. Felicia Miriam will have a good and happy life. She chews determinedly on her turkey, drinks yet another cup of wine, tastes the sugar-sweetened dish of carrots, and wonders why it is that the bitter taste adheres to her tongue and settles, like a leaden fire, upon her heart.

The table is cleared. Hildy and Alison carry tray after tray of dishes into the kitchen. Mrs. Ludovico brings out huge bowls of fruit and nuts, cups and saucers, cake plates. Coffee and tea are served and there is a search for sugar tongs and nutcrackers, which Nina (of course) finds in the silver chest.

And then, as the coffee is being poured, they hear the sound of Felicia Miriam crying. Fragile and reedy, her wail pours out of the receiver, and because David has increased the volume, they hear its resonance, its unrelenting sweet vigor.

"Such timing," Claire Silberman says slyly.

Stacey is on her feet, and Nina too is halfway out of her chair. A glance of complicity, of shared concern, flashes between them.

"I'm sorry. I'll see to her," Stacey says quickly.

"Why don't you bring her downstairs?" Betty Goldfein suggests. "I'd love to see her."

"Yes, why don't you?" Nina's mother chirps.

Stacey glances at Nina, who nods.

"All right, then."

She hurries upstairs and changes Felicia Miriam and feeds her a small bottle of Similac. Greedily, lustily, the infant sucks at the rubber nipple: the transition from breast to bottle has been so easily (too easily, Stacey thinks) accomplished.

"You don't need me anymore, do you?" she murmurs playfully as she places the baby on her shoulder and feels the new solidity of her body, the roundness of the clinging arms. "Oh, yes, you do," she says as a burp is emitted, a puncture of relief, contentment.

Stacey dresses Felicia Miriam in the pretty white batiste dress and brushes her fringe of fair hair. She carries her downstairs, cradled in her arms, one finger concealing the small birthmark.

"Oh, the baby." Their smiling faces turn toward her expectantly, admiringly, gratefully. Hildy and Alison rise and encircle her.

"Mom," Hildy calls. Her voice ripples with joyous conspiracy.

Nina emerges from the kitchen, carrying the high golden sponge cake, spangled now with strawberries and flaming birthday candles.

"Happy birthday," they sing gaily. "Happy birthday, dear Felicia Miriam. Happy birthday to you!"

There is a sudden flash of light as Seth takes a picture of Stacey and the baby. Felicia Miriam fixes her serious cobalt-blue gaze on the bright candles, and Nina and Stacey incline their heads and together, laughing, blow the candles out.

Everyone claps, but Claire Silberman looks at them in bewilderment. She alone has not risen from her seat.

"What is this?" she says. "I don't understand." Her voice is petulant. The cake, the singing, have startled her, violated her sense of propriety.

"Don't you remember, Mom? We used to have a cake every year for Aunt Miriam's birthday. A sponge cake. And then we'd sing."

"I never liked your aunt Miriam — you know that." She is aggrieved that her sons have forgotten her ancient enmities.

"We just thought it would be nice to have a birthday cake for the new baby," Edith says quietly.

"But who is this new baby to us?" Stridently, she asks the question they have all studiously avoided.

Her sons do not answer her and Nina busies herself with slicing the cake. Only Hildy and her friends look at each other, untroubled, unembarrassed.

Stacey stands in the doorway, her lips frozen in a smile she can no longer control. She holds Felicia Miriam close as though to protect her from the onslaught of questions (which are not asked), the curious and puzzled glances. Light-headed, her tongue thick with the bitterness that haunted her throughout the meal, she fights back a wave of nausea.

"If you'll excuse me," she says, "I'm not feeling very well."

She turns and hurries upstairs where she places Felicia Miriam, still in her white embroidered dress, in the crib. She goes to her own room and stretches out on her bed in the darkness. Minutes later, there is a light knock at the door.

"Stacey?" Nina's voice is soft, diffident.

"It's all right, Nina. I'm just not feeling too terrific. I just want to sleep."

"All right."

A few minutes later there is another knock, but this time Stacey does not answer. She does not know whose footsteps retreat or who it is who opens the door of the nursery and closes it very softly. She lies quietly and, still wearing her navy-blue dress and her very high blue heels, falls into a sleep so light that she drifts in and out of wakefulness. The door is not fully closed and she hears the clatter of dishes as the coffee and dessert dishes are cleared. The singing and reading resumes. David laughs gently.

"Ah, Hildy," he says in a tone Stacey has not heard him use before — he is proud, amused. Hildy has said something clever or perhaps something outrageous. Sleepbound, Stacey smiles.

There is a brief quarrel between Arnold's sons.

"You did."

"I didn't."

"They are tired," Edith says.

She awakens again because the front door opens and closes as the guests leave, trilling their farewells, their thanks.

"A wonderful seder."

"We had a super time."

"You must come again next year."

"Oh, we will. We will."

Next year. The words skitter like small jagged stones across Stacey's heart. She will not be here next year. She will be across a continent. She will not see the infant grown to toddler; she will not hear the voices raised in song, celebrating her child's birth. Already, she feels her own loneliness; already she is pierced by the pain of this new loss, this new separation. Exhausted, debilitated, she sleeps again, fully clothed like a traveler who, at the end of a journey, cannot summon the energy to undress.

The house is quiet when she awakens again. She rises and goes into the hallway. Every door is closed and the darkness is impenetrable, thick, layered with the dreams of many sleepers. It seems to her that from behind the closed doors, she can hear their rhythmic breathing, even discern the word spoken aloud, the muted moan and the abrupt laugh breaking free of dream. Their feast has exhausted them. Their sleep is embroidered with the songs they have sung, the stories they have told; it is deepened by the wine they have drunk.

Stacey steals downstairs, tiptoeing in her high heels. The table has been cleared, but the flowers, the sun-colored forsythia and the tall white carnations, glow softly in the darkness. Wine has been spilled and the fresh stains are crimson-bright against the white cloth. The fragrance of the flowers mingles with the scent of the melted tallow. Stacey grips the back of a chair. She feels faint; vomit wells up in her throat and she forces it back. A silent scream grows within her. She is back on that ice-bright hillside, Andrea's blood staining the embankment, Andrea's blood crimson-bright against her porcelain skin. She is back in the funeral parlor and flowers and candles are arranged about the small white coffin. She wears Judith's tentlike black dress and the baby within her is stirring and kicking, comforting her with life.

"No," she says. "No." It is not a scream she utters but a whimper.

Again the wave of nausea sweeps over her and she hurries into the kitchen to the sink. Onto that stainless-steel surface, she regurgitates everything she ate that night. Her eyes tear with the exertion as she retches again and again, bringing up the wine, the chicken, the fish; she is divesting herself of their nurturing and nourishment; she is purging herself of promises she cannot keep, of assurances she cannot grant. Exhausted, her throat aching, she opens the cold-water faucet and splashes her face, her neck. And then she takes a sponge and scouring powder and cleans the sink of her sour vomit, scrubbing furiously as though she would erase every trace of her presence, of her bilious, unremitting sorrow.

She leans against the wooden counter on which the pink and white striped infant seat still rests. She carries it upstairs. Only when she is back in her room, still clutching the pink and white seat so that its plastic frame cuts into her flesh, does she speak aloud the words that resonated in her mind as she crouched over the sink.

"I can't," she informs the darkness, and she does not recognize the sound of her own voice. It is so sad, so coated with a strange commingling of relief and resignation.

The words are an acknowledgment and a confession. Her strength has waned. She has fought her grief but in the end she has been subdued, her small arsenal depleted. She has made up so many stories, dreamed so many dreams, crafted rationalizations out of spiderwebs of hope, but she knows now that they are of no use to her. She dreams of loss and walks through swirling mist, but the soft light is teasing, evasive. She will awaken to emptiness. And she knows, because she is Rose Carmody's daughter, that to chase after shadows with outstretched arms is to embrace madness.

She sways back and forth now, like a keening woman. Too much has been asked of her. She did not know. She could not have known. But now it is all clear to her. They will have to understand that she is not who they thought she was, that she cannot do what she thought she could do. She cannot help herself. She cannot give up the child she carried, the child she gave birth to in a swirl of pain and grief and triumph, whose soft mouth sucked at her breast. It is too much to ask of her. Mandy was right. She cannot (and if she could, she would not have the right to) offer this child as a gift, an exchange. It was crazy, mad, to think that she could. She is not God, *to make a joyful mother of a barren woman.* She made a bargain, yes, but it was a wild bargain and she had no real recognition of its terms. She is, she must be, free of it.

Oh, please. She has lost one daughter. Over that loss she had no control. She cannot lose another. (And over this loss she has control.) Despite her promise, despite her commitment and their goodness — and they are so good. They will understand this when it is explained to them. They do not know about the rodent of sorrow. They do not know about the shadow of madness, about a mother's face pressed against a cold windowpane. They will understand. They will forgive. She relies now on their love as they have relied on hers, and from that reliance she takes new strength, new resolution.

Thus energized, she moves resolutely through the room. She slings her white purse across her shoulder and puts on her terry-cloth slippers. She takes up her valise but sets it down again. It can be collected later. And now she walks down the hall, her steps cushioned. As always, the nursery door is partially open and she slips soundlessly in. She reaches up and turns off the intercom.

A door opens at the far end of the hallway. She remains very still. Someone goes to the hall lavatory. She waits. The silence is broken by the sound of a toilet flushing, a faucet running, and then the same footsteps make their way back down the hall and the house is again shrouded in stillness.

She does not hesitate. Desperation has made her daring; she is feverish with energy, determination. Now, at last, she knows exactly what she must do. She lifts the baby from the crib. The infant's eyes flutter open and then she puts her head down on Stacey's shoulder (light as a flower, it rests there) and slips trustingly back to sleep. Hurriedly, Stacey jams diapers, stretch suits, and undershirts into her purse. She plucks the pink thermal blanket from the crib and drapes it over the baby.

Soundlessly, carrying the infant seat, she descends the staircase and glides through the darkened house. She goes to the kitchen and takes three bottles of Similac from the carton. She finds the black cape (the mantle of her pregnancy) in the hallway closet and shrugs into it awkwardly. Her fingers close around Hildy's car keys that are, as always, in the bronze bowl on the hallway table. She opens the front door, closes it very quietly, and steps out into the night. The cold night air startles her and she holds the baby close as she hurries to the car.

She places the infant seat in the car, straps Felicia Miriam (who miraculously, quiescently, does not awaken) into it, and tightens the seat belt around it. And then she settles herself in the driver's seat, studies the unfamiliar dashboard, and at last, without turning the car lights on, pulls out of the driveway. Her heart is pounding, and despite the chill air, she is soaked with sweat. She looks back when she reaches the corner, fearful that the windows will be ablaze with light, that Nina and David will be shouting after her, calling the police, calling Hal. But the house is dark and a new calm settles over her. She turns the corner and switches the lights on. She has a full tank of gas. She can go anywhere, she can do anything. She turns the heat on.

"We're all right," she tells the sleeping baby. "Oh, we're fine." And then, inexplicably, she begins to cry. The tears flow and she presses harder on the accelerator, speeds down streets that are unfamiliar. A red light looms ahead but she cannot brake in time and shoots past it, barely missing a car about to turn.

"Oh, God," she says aloud. "Oh, help me."

The tears have frayed her new confidence, have washed away that surge of certainty. She is on a highway now, moving north. The exits are unfamiliar to her but their names calm her and she reads them aloud as they approach.

"Campfire Road. Twin Pines Drive. Overlook Circle." The pastoral names are soothing, and when she sees the lights of a small motel, she has stopped crying. She pulls into the parking lot. Her mind pulsates with the explanations she will offer the motel clerk (who will surely wonder at a woman with a baby arriving in the middle of the night — no, not the middle of the night, the early hours of the morning). She is rushing to her husband who became ill on a business trip and she finds that she is too tired to drive. She is taking her baby to visit her grandparents and she lost her way and has been driving aimlessly. There is a grain of truth to both stories. She is too tired to drive and she has been driving aimlessly. She does not want to go home to Hal and the boys. Not yet. She wants some time alone with her daughter, some hours alone with her baby. She has never been alone with Felicia Miriam, free of nurses, of Nina and David. Perhaps she will say just that to the motel clerk. "Can you give me a room? I want to be alone with my baby." Oh, no — he will think her mad. And she has been mad. It was madness to enter into this agreement with Nina and David, madness to think that she could ever give up her baby. She understands that now. Calmed, she combs her hair, puts lipstick on, and, with Felicia Miriam in her arms, enters the reception area.

There was no need to worry. The clerk is a sleepy, bored college student who looks disinterestedly up from a heavy textbook when she enters. He asks her no questions but takes her credit card, verifies it (she holds her breath because Hal is often overextended, but it is all right), and, perhaps perceiving her fatigue, drives her down the court to her room.

"See, it's got everything," he says and puts on the light, opens the bathroom door so she can see how clean it is. She is not the first woman who has come to his cubicle in the middle of the night, swollen-eyed and carrying a baby. Stacey fumbles in her purse, but he waves her away and leaves. She sees that he walks with the slightest of limps.

She locks the door after him and puts Felicia Miriam in the middle of the double bed. She switches off the overhead light and studies the room in the glow of the small bedside lamp. The floor is covered with worn blue-gray carpeting and the matching polyester drapes have been cruelly faded to the color of ashes. The Formica dresser and tables are scarred by signs of transient carelessness, by the indifferences of the harried and dispirited traveler. They are etched with cigarette burns, the pale rings left by bottles and glasses. Stacey opens the drawers of the dresser one by one, and in the bottom drawer she finds a child's yellow sock, frayed at heel and toe.

She goes into the small bathroom where she slips off her shoes and her dress and washes her face with soap and very hot water. She wants to take a shower but she is afraid to disturb Felicia Miriam. Instead, she sponges herself with the wash cloth, but as she wipes herself dry with the thin towel, Felicia Miriam awakens.

Stacey hurries to her and swiftly changes her, talking softly.

"Do you know where you are? Ah, you don't know where you are. It doesn't matter. You're with me. With Mommy. With your mommy."

And then she slides between the sheets, lifts the baby, and places her at her breast. She turns off the bedside light, and Felicia Miriam roots desperately until she discovers the nipple and claims it with her soft lips. Stacey bends her head low and the infant's fingers grip a tendril of her hair. Here, in this quiet enclosed darkness, alone, unseen, they are as one. Their breath and touch mingle. They are mother and daughter, cleft together, as they were, as they will be.

Stacey smiles and touches that fringe of fair hair and shifts Felicia Miriam to her other breast, and when the baby, sated, sleeps again, she does too. Felicia Miriam's head rests on her shoulder, and her milk-scented breath is a warm vapor at Stacey's neck.

It is dawn when David awakens. Nina stirs beside him but she does not wake up. She is exhausted, he knows, by the preparations for the seder, by the serving and long cleanup. Still, it had been a wonderful evening. Even that small scene with his mother and the birthday cake had not really marred it. It had been wonderful to gather family and friends together, to feel past and present meld, to hear familiar laughter, familiar song. It had been wonderful to see Felicia Miriam stare so seriously at the candles and to know that year after passing year, as they celebrate this festival of spring and freedom, she will look at the candles lit in celebration of her birth.

"Who is this baby to us?" his mother had asked. Today he will give her the answer. He will tell her, "This baby is my daughter, your granddaughter, our Felicia Miriam, named for the happiness she brings us and for all the Miriams of our family — all the soft-spoken, gentle-eyed women who covered their eyes as they blessed the Sabbath flames and sang sweetly of raisins and almonds; the Miriams who have died and those who were never born. She is Amos Roth's granddaughter who will, one day, look at the survivor children in his paintings and understand her past and know that she links generations, that her small life defies so many deaths. She is my baby, mine and Nina's. Ours. Our darling."

He smiles, touches Nina's shoulder. Of course, he will not say all this to Claire Silberman, although he wishes that he could. Lying there, in the half-light, he is aware of a strange silence, an almost palpable absence of sound. Of course. He misses the barely perceptible hum that emanates from the intercom. Damn. The battery must have worn down. He swings out of bed and hurries barefoot down the hall.

The door to the nursery is ajar and this relieves him. Stacey must have awakened during the night and realized that the intercom was not functioning. He goes into the room, which is alight now with the silvery gloss of dawn. He approaches the crib where he can see the small rise, the nest of bunting and blanket in which his daughter sleeps. Ah, he will not disturb her but he must look at her. He loves to watch her as she sleeps; never is he free of this need to look at her, to reassure himself that she truly exists — his daughter, *flesh of his flesh, blood of his blood*. For him, still, even after all these weeks, the thought is awesome.

He smiles. How still she is. How quietly she sleeps. And then he bends low and the smile freezes into a grimace because the crib is empty and his daughter does not sleep beneath that soft mound of blankets. He hurries then across the hall, knocks lightly on Stacey's door, and then, scarcely waiting for an answer, thrusts it open. He sees at once the valise that she discarded in the center of the room. And he sees her empty disheveled bed and he smells the acrid odor of sweat. It seems to him as he stands there trembling, fully aware now of what has happened, that the air itself is thick with fear and betrayal and disappointment. His knees shake. Again he is abandoned. He was a boy whose father slept and vanished into death. He is a man whose daughter slept and vanished. A small moan escapes his lips, a childlike sound because, like a child, he confronts a loss so profound that it is beyond comprehension.

And then Nina is beside him, her arms around him, her eyes taking in the disordered room, the abandoned valise, the open door of the nursery, and the crib that stands empty in the silver light of a dawn they will never forget.

"Oh, no," she says and her voice is so stricken that his own heart stirs. "It can't be. It isn't."

Weeping, her knuckles pressed to her lips, she walks back to their room, and he supports her, his hand about her shoulders, although he cannot understand how he himself has the strength to walk.

He calls Hal. The phone rings once, twice, three times. On the fourth ring Hal picks up, his voice thick with sleep, irritable.

"Hal, it's David Roth. Is Stacey there?"

"Stacey? No. No. Isn't she with you?"

"No. She's gone. And so is the baby."

"Shit," Hal says, and David hears the anger and fear in his voice. "When? How? She had no car. No money. She's not here. Where would she go?"

"She didn't say anything about this to you?"

"Are you crazy?" Hal's voice is harsh, explosive.

"We have to find her," David says. "Maybe the police."

"Wait," Hal says. "A couple of hours. We'll try her brothers. Judith. Maybe her parents. Let me make some calls."

"What did he say?" Nina asks. She is hugging herself, rocking from side to side.

"He said. He said. What does it matter what he said? They're not there. We have to find them." He is dressing, swiftly pulling on his slacks, a shirt, shoes without socks, and she too dresses, her frenzied speed matching his own. David is right; they must search for their daughter, their sweet, sweet baby.

They see at once that Hildy's car is gone, and they look at each other with new fear. Stacey is driving, alone with the baby, along unfamiliar roads in a car that she has never driven before. David remembers that the signals on that car are quirky: they must be turned on with a particular pressure. He imagines Stacey trying, failing, swerving wildly to avoid an oncoming car, a truck. And Felicia Miriam beside her, sliding, falling. No. No. He must grab control. He must stop thinking like this and do something.

He and Nina get into their own car and drive slowly, glancing from side to side. The streets are empty. They pass the *Times* delivery truck and watch the papers, wrapped in blue plastic, sail through the air. David is glad that they cannot read the headlines. He anticipates horror, disaster. Often there are front-page stories about vanished children, stolen infants. Some of the children are never found.

They have been kidnapped by strangers, by distraught fathers, anguished mothers. Oh, God. Let Felicia Miriam be found. Let her be safe.

Aimlessly, they drive up and down the streets of their town. David pulls up next to a phone booth and calls the police station.

"Have there been any accidents involving a small red Pontiac?" he asks. He explains that he is anxious because his daughter has not come home.

"No. No accidents. Want to give me your name?" The desk officer is not unused to such calls. Nor is he surprised when David hangs up.

They drive on. They go to the train station, but Hildy's car is not in the parking lot. The early commuters stand on the platform at a distance from each other, and the roar of the oncoming train stifles the scream that David can no longer control.

"I don't know what to do," he shouts. "I don't know where to go. I don't know where to look."

And Nina, crying now, encircles him with her arms; his dropped head butts against her breast again and yet again.

At last he turns and drives in the direction of their home.

"Turn here," Nina says suddenly at the narrow lane that leads to the quarry park.

He obeys her and drives to the wooded enclosure. He parks when he can drive no farther and together they walk along the edge of the quarry. The heron, which he has never seen before, sweeps across the still water, flying low so that its reflection is mirrored, its motion recorded. They mount the gentle incline where benches are placed and where there are ruts in the soft earth, formed by the wheels of baby carriages. They lean against the railing and look down at the stagnant waters. The quarry has been fenced off because it is a sheer drop to the pit below, and the neighbors were fearful and worried about the safety of the children.

"You don't think . . ." David cannot formulate the sentence.

"No. Of course not. Never." Nina's voice rings with certainty. Of this she is positive. Stacey would never willfully harm Felicia Miriam. She loves the baby, as they do. She could never, never hurt their child, her child.

"Don't even think it," she says fiercely. She grips his hand, brings it to her lips, and bites into it, drawing blood, tasting it.

"No, no. You're right." He holds her close and they cling to each other as the rising sun beats down and turns the dark waters the color of molten gold.

The phone is ringing when they enter the house. It is Hal, his voice hoarse with relief.

"It's okay," he says. "Stacey is here. With the baby."

"They're all right?" David asks. "The baby is all right?" At this moment that is all that matters, all that he needs to know.

"She's fine. She's sleeping."

"And Stacey?" He asks this even as he steadies himself against his own weakness, his sudden fear that he will fall if he is not sustained.

"Tired. You know. But fine."

"Can I talk to her?"

"Just a second."

The receiver has been covered and he hears muffled whispers. Nina moves close to him, and Hildy, in a flowered nightgown, stands at the top of the stairs and looks down at him.

"David, listen. She can't talk. She's — like, she's very upset. She wants me to tell you that she's really sorry but she changed her mind. She just can't go through with it. She wants to keep the baby."

And David, gripping the receiver, feels a scream begin at the back of his throat. But his vocal cords are paralyzed; his breath comes in stertorous gasps.

"David. David, are you there? Goddamn it, David, she's sorry. We're sorry. But what can we do? Who knew? Who could have known?"

But David does not answer because he cannot. Sorrow coats his tongue and the unspent scream weakens him so that he cannot hold the receiver. Nina rushes to him and Hildy dashes downstairs and takes the phone.

"Later. We'll talk later," she tells Hal. She does not know what has happened, but once again, she and Hal are allies. They are buffers against the terrible emotional storm that rages around them.

Nina leads David to the sofa and sits beside him. They lean back, their hands linked, their faces frozen into masks of grief. They are enervated, like the newly bereaved who cannot yet comprehend the enormity of their loss.

29

Exhausted, and because it is still so very early, and because they do not know what else to do, they go back to bed and, miraculously, fall asleep. He awakens because he thinks he hears his child crying, and the sound of her misery energizes him, fires him with compassion and urgency. Her sobs are rhythmic, punctuated by rasping gasps, and he realizes that it is Nina curled up beside him who weeps and trembles. He gathers her into his arms, and like small children, they huddle together beneath the heavy quilt. He presses his cheek against hers and their tears mingle.

"Oh, God," he says. "How could she let us come so far and then do this?"

His voice is plaintive, like that of a bemused child. All his kindness, all his care has been nullified.

Now it is Nina's turn to comfort him. She runs her fingers across his face, kisses his eyes.

"It will be all right," she says. "We have to wait. We need time. She needs time." She tries desperately to believe her own words.

"Goddamn it, we had an agreement. We signed a contract." His voice is suddenly harsh, almost brutal. He has soared to a peak of anger, but within minutes, she knows, he will plunge again into the flatland of despair. "I won't lose my baby," he says fiercely. "I'll never give her up."

"It won't come to that, David," she assures him and holds him close.

She glances at the bedside clock. It is only hours since Stacey stole out of their home, since they last saw Felicia Miriam. Why, then, does she feel this aching emptiness, this sinking conviction that they are losers at a game that perhaps they had no right to play?

Nina and Hildy drive to the Cosgrove house that afternoon. They bring Stacey's suitcase and clothing and diapers for Felicia Miriam.

Evan answers the door.

"My mother isn't home," he says. "She took the baby to the doctor."

"Is she all right?" Nina asks. "Is the baby all right?" A new apprehension clutches at her, constricts her throat, causes her hands to tremble.

"Yeah. Sure," Evan replies. "How you doing, Hildy?" He does not forget that it was Hildy who bought him his chemistry set, his calculator.

"Okay. You guys having fun with the baby?"

"She's okay." The sullenness of his answer is rooted in bewilderment. His mother was not supposed to bring the baby home. The baby was supposed to stay with Hildy's family while they got settled in California. And now all of a sudden the baby is in his house and she is crying and fussing. She sleeps in a bureau drawer lined with Andrea's pink quilt. There is no carriage, no infant seat. They don't even have a crib. This baby does not belong in their house.

"Thanks, Evan." Hildy pats his head and he grimaces, but he does not pull away. Hildy is beautiful. And she smells wonderful. The baby is ugly and she stinks.

"But the baby is all right?" Nina asks yet again.

Again she is gripped by the terror she felt as she and David drove through the deserted suburban streets. Felicia Miriam was gone and they did not know where she was. *Let her be safe,* Nina had prayed silently. She could not articulate her fear, her despair. If she gave voice to her anguished premonitions, she would frighten David and endow them with reality. She waits, dry-throated, for Evan's reply.

"I told you already. My mom said it was just for a checkup." He is aggrieved that she does not believe him, that she repeats the question in that tight, nervous voice. And he is tired of talking about that baby who has kept his mother from him and Jared all these weeks. His mother had asked him if he wanted to hold her, but he had shrugged and walked away. His father didn't hold her either and somehow that had pleased Evan, had justified and reinforced his sullen anger.

"Don't you want to hold your sister?" his mother had asked.

His sister. Andrea had been his sister and he was mad that that baby was wrapped in Andrea's pink comforter. He had begun to cry then and Jared, copycat Jared, had cried too. But he does not want to think about that now.

"Listen," he says. "Here are your car keys. My dad said to give them to you when you came. The car's parked on the corner."

"I know," Hildy says. "I saw. Thank you." She pats Evan's head, in sympathy, in consolation.

Nina is glad that Hildy must drive her own car home. She chooses a less direct route and, on a quiet, unfamiliar street, parks and sits with her hands covering her face, swaying from side to side.

"Oh, my baby," she whispers. "Oh, my Felicia."

Hildy is already home when Nina arrives, and she pulls her mother into the kitchen.

"Stacey called," she says. "Evan told her you were worried and she wanted you to know that the baby is fine. She sounded, like, weird, sort of confused. She said you could call her if you wanted."

"What would I say to her?" Nina asks, and Hildy stares at her. She has never before heard her mother's voice so dulled by misery, so muted by hopelessness.

That evening they go to the second seder at Edith and Arnold's home. By tacit agreement, neither David's mother nor Stacey's parents ask any questions about Stacey and the baby. Nina understands that they are protecting themselves from the burden of knowledge. Their ignorance exonerates them. Her parents' pattern is long established. Always they have avoided asking her questions so they would be spared their own disapproval at her answers.

"It's nice to have just the family, the second night," Claire Silberman says. "Your father always preferred that."

Her sons do not reply. She has created her own mythology around

Amos Roth's preferences, his likes and dislikes, and they do not argue with her.

"Although he liked a large family," she adds. "He loved children. Who knows — maybe if he had lived . . ." Her voice trails off as she imagines the children who were not born to her, the grandchildren who are denied her.

"Please, Ma," Arnold says impatiently.

"I am not saying anything wrong. Children are everything. Nothing else is important. Nothing." She drinks another cup of wine, florid with the virtue of her conviction.

Irritated, David looks up at his father's painting of the child survivor. He notices for the first time that the skeleton-faced child has eyes of cobalt blue. He has read somewhere of a mystical poet in Israel who believes that every Jewish child born since the Holocaust contains the spiritual spark of a child lost during that terrible time. It is a theory not unlike that of the philosopher whose lecture he and Nina attended who argued that the birth of every Jewish child represents a posthumous victory over Hitler. If Felicia Miriam, his daughter, his darling (his heart swells with love, throbs with grief), is lost to him, that spark too will be extinguished, that victory abrogated. His child will be a stranger to his people and they will, both of them, live their lives searching and bereft.

Again, he studies the boy in the painting and a wild thought comes to him: his father anticipated Felicia Miriam's eyes, the solemnity of her infant gaze, the straight fair lashes, dew-bright with her tears.

He leaves the table and goes to Arnold's study. With trembling fingers, he dials the Cosgroves' number.

"Hello," Stacey says, and he hears Felicia Miriam cry. That thin, reedy wail triggers a longing and misery he cannot contain.

"Stacey, is Felicia Miriam all right?" (*Let her be all right, let her be safe,* he had prayed during the dawn hours of his worst fears, but now he wants more than that, oh, much more.)

"Yes. She's fine. Really, David."

"Stacey, listen. We miss her. We want her. She's part of us. We love her. She's ours. Our baby. Please. Please." His voice breaks. He is pleading now, powerless to conceal his pain.

"David, I'm sorry. I'm so sorry. I never meant for it to be this way. But in the end I couldn't do it. I must have been crazy to have thought I could. We both must have been crazy." She is crying now. She is crying and Felicia Miriam is wailing. Their misery surges through the earpiece. He clutches it and bites his lip. He does not know what to say. She is right. They must have been crazy, both of them. But still the child has been born. His child. His. And Nina's. In Stacey's sobs, he hears Nina's misery. They are, both of them, mothers, like Rachel at Ramah, weeping for their child.

And then Hal is on the phone.

"David, I'm sorry. Stacey is too upset to talk."

"You think I'm not upset? But we have to talk. We have to settle this." They will not soften him; he cannot be dissuaded, deterred from his love for his child. Already pity has weakened him. He has been victimized by his compassion for her. Stacey is young. She will have other children. But he will never father another child. Nor can he imagine any other child claiming his heart, his love, as Felicia Miriam has. He has been pledged to her from the moment of conception, but Stacey carried her with the clear intent of giving her up. Surely, he and Nina are more deeply bonded to this child born of their yearning. And yet. And yet. He cannot, he will not articulate the emotional arguments that Stacey can offer. Not yet.

"Let's meet tomorrow and talk about it," Hal suggests. "At Ramon's. Five o'clock. Five-thirty."

"Hal, take care of my baby."

But Hal has hung up and David returns to the seder table and sits beside Nina. She knows at once, from the pallor of his face and the tremor of his fingers, that he has spoken to Stacey.

"I'm sorry," Hal says. "Let me say that straight off. I didn't mean for this to happen. Not any of it. I didn't want this whole deal from the beginning. I agreed to it because Stacey wanted it. And it made sense in a crazy way. Then . . ." He pauses. He too sees his life split in two. *Then.* The glory days of hope before Andrea's death. *Now.* The grim struggle to survive their grief, their loss. "But a lot happened. Now Stacey wants to keep the baby. More than that. She says she has to keep the baby. That's what she wants, so that's what I want."

"As simple as that," David retorts bitterly. "Nothing is that simple, Hal. You know that. We made an agreement. We have a contract. Your house is up for sale. You're talking deals in California."

"Sold," Hal corrects him. "The house is sold. Stacey doesn't even know that yet, but it wouldn't matter to her if she did. And I'm still talking deals in California. Just talking. Nothing is signed. So what I say is, let's forget the contract. I'll return the payment you already made and we'll keep the baby."

"Are you crazy? That's not what I want," David replies. He struggles to contain his fury. Does Hal really think that his daughter's life can be settled with these few words? The stupid simplistic bastard. He stares across the table at him with hate. He hates Hal's slicked-back hair, his twisted gold chain, his goddamn open smile. He hates those large hands that drum now on the table, each finger furred with silken black hair. He does not want those hands to touch his child, his fragile, blue-eyed daughter. "You can't return the money and walk away as though everything is all right. I want Felicia Miriam. She's my daughter. Mine. She has nothing to do with you." He slams his hand down on the table and the water glasses shiver at the fierceness of the impact.

"She's Stacey's daughter too. And Stacey needs her. God, you know how she needs her." Hal is pleading now, and David leans closer, savoring his discomfort, seeking out the flaw his misery may betray. "She cried all night. She says that she didn't know how it would be. She thought she would be strong enough but she's not. That's what she says and I know it's true. She's a fighter. She was fighting her own feelings in the hospital and all that time at your house, and if she says she gives up, I have to believe her. And I have to help her. She can't give the baby up. I told that to Hildy this afternoon and I'm telling it to you now. We'll do whatever we can to make it easier for you. You can see the baby, visit her, whatever. But she stays with us. That's it. *Finito.*"

"We'll see," David says. "We'll see." His words are monitory, threatening. He is newly calm. "When was Hildy here?"

"Just an hour or so ago. She's all broken up."

"I know."

He does know. That, he reflects, is one of the odd side effects of this experience, that Hildy has been restored to them, that she is once again child to them both, sharing their love, their pain, interceding for them with Hal who, mysteriously, has become her friend, her ally. But that is not enough. It will never be enough. Not now. Not since the very first moment he held Felicia Miriam in his arms, touched the rise of the strawberry mark at her neck, and realized that in this tiny being, his daughter, his own history, his own immortality were concentrated. His love for Hildy is not diminished, but Felicia Miriam has filled a vacuum in his life. If he loses her, that void will fill with his bilious anguish.

"Look, David, I don't like this whole mess. But I have to do what Stacey wants, what she needs." Hal's tone is conciliatory, sincere. He is telling the truth, the simple truth.

"What about you?" David asks. "How do you feel about the baby?"

"I don't feel about the baby. I feel about Stacey," Hal answers flatly, and they stare at each other, as though a new and painful truth has been thrust upon them.

"Hey, Hal, can we go over this stuff?" Herb Green stands in the office doorway holding a sheaf of receipts. He frowns, taps his foot impatiently. He is renovating a house in the Hamptons and resents having to come into the city to check the books at Ramon's, but he knows that Hal is careless, indifferent to detail.

"In a couple of minutes," Hal says without turning around. He has already decided that no matter what happens, whether they go to California (and they still may do just that — he has other ideas of how to get the money: Andrew Kardin knows people, Stacey's brothers may want to invest) or not, he is not going to hang around Ramon's much longer. He holds out his hand but David does not take it, and Hal is angered that Herb Green sees this rejection. "Listen," he says to David, "I'm not looking for any trouble."

"Trouble?" David repeats, and he laughs harshly, bitterly. The word is so weak, so inadequate. It bears no relationship to his fury, his grief, and (yes) his terror.

He leaves then, and Hal slowly and deliberately drains his water glass before going back to his office where Herb Green, red-faced and irritable, waits for him.

David calls Charles Norris. His lawyer, his friend, listens without interrupting, although once he sighs deeply. David imagines him looking at the silver-framed photographs of his own children on his desk, twirling his pen, drawing question marks on his yellow legal pad. There is a great deal that he must explain to Charles Norris. He describes Felicia Miriam. It is important to him that Charles Norris understand how beautiful his daughter is, how her hair matches his own, that her high forehead is so like his father's.

"But the really important thing, Charles, is that I love her. I would do anything for her. Anything." His words do not sound overly dramatic to him. It is true. He would do anything for his child. He would fight for her and go hungry for her. No effort would be too great. She comes first now in his life; her well-being takes precedence over everything else. He bites his lip and thinks of how tiny she is, how helpless, how vulnerable.

"What do you want me to do, David?" Charles Norris asks gently.

"I want my daughter. I want you to help me get her back."

"Yes. I know that." Charles Norris sighs heavily again. His profession has geared him to pessimism and his own life has sustained his sadness. He fears that his retarded daughter will outlive him. He has worked out elaborate fantasies in which he poisons his daughter and then kills himself. He knows what it means to say, "I would do anything for her. Anything."

"Can I get her back?" David needs words, not sighs.

"I'm not sure."

"But we have an agreement. A contract."

"I warned you about it then. And that contract is even more vulnerable now. That last case unhinged everything." He does not have to mention the case by name. It has haunted their dreams, dominated dinner party conversations, flashed across magazine covers. The nation is obsessed with it. Letters-to-the-editor columns pulsate with opinions, ideas, precedents. Charles Norris has followed it carefully.

"I know," David acknowledges miserably. "But surely we can do something?" His question is a plea. "We must do something." Now he gathers control, issues a statement, a directive.

"Oh, yes," Charles Norris agrees. "We'll do something. First let me review the agreement. And I'll want to talk to their attorney. There's always the chance that they're just holding out for more money."

"No," David replies. "There's no chance of that."

"We'll see. Give me some time. A few days. In the meantime, don't do anything. Don't meet with them. Don't call their home."

"All right."

David is relieved to take direction. He is grateful for the authority in Charles Norris's voice, for the cynicism that is a weapon of his profession. He hangs up and asks his secretary to arrange for theater tickets for that evening. He and Nina will take her parents out. He also invites Edith and Arnold and his mother. It reassures him that he can make such a plan, that he can organize such an evening. Everything will be all right. His desperation was premature, unfounded. There is hope. Even Charles Norris did not deny that.

30

Hildy does not join the family at the theater. Because Seth's computer is being repaired he must use hers for his senior project (which is already a week overdue), and that night she and Alison and Seth order in a pizza, which they eat straight out of the box as they crouch on the floor of her room. They each drink a beer and then, as the printer clatters and the long sheets cascade onto the floor in an ongoing fall, they share a joint, passing it from hand to hand. Hildy opens the window and closes the door.

"Hey, the baby," Seth reminds her. "How are you going to hear the baby if the door is closed?"

"No baby. She's not here," Hildy answers.

She studies herself in the mirror. She is allowing her hair to grow longer and looks at her own reflection as though it is that of a stranger. She acknowledges that the dark curls that frame her face give her a softer look. It was Hal's suggestion (offered weeks ago as they sat over coffee at Ramon's), but he has not mentioned it since. Their days of such intimacies are over. When she last spoke with him she avoided his gaze, and she did not say good-bye when she left. No longer accomplices, they have become adversaries. They grant each other no middle ground.

"What about Stacey?" Alison asks.

"Gone. She stole away in the night. She and the baby. We didn't even hear them leave."

Hildy lies down on the floor. She keeps her body rigid and lifts one leg and then the other, following Nina's warm-up exercise routine. Then, to reward herself she takes a drag of the joint. The smoke wafts upward as she exhales in a soft blue-gray streak.

"Felicia Miriam's eyes are that color," she says, but before her friends can follow her gaze, the thin column of smoke has disappeared. They do, however, see her tears and they draw closer to her. Seth holds her hand and Alison runs her fingers through her hair. They are accomplished at these gestures of comfort. They have, since childhood, protected each other, forming an alliance against the adults whose support they accept, whose love they acknowledge, but whom they cannot (dare not) trust.

"What's the story with the baby, Hildy?" Seth asks. "Your folks were supposed to adopt it, right?"

"That's part of it," Hildy says.

"What's the rest of it?" Allison takes a drag and switches the printer off. Her voice is controlled. She is inured to surprises, immune to the vagaries of the adult world. She is cultivating (with the help of her soft-voiced therapist, her glittering collection of capsules) an acceptance of this suspension of rules, the domestic anarchy within her own home and the homes of her friends.

"David is the baby's father. Her real father."

"They were having an affair?" Seth asks with disbelief. Nina and David Roth always seemed so happy, so together. Wistfully, he has often contrasted them with his own parents — his father who haunts Manhattan apartments that Seth has never seen, his mother who stares at television screens, indifferent to the programs, indifferent (it seems to him) to the passing days of her own life.

"No. Nothing like that. Stacey was having the baby for David and my mother. It was all arranged — worked out with her husband. They had an agreement, a legal contract."

"Oh, like she was a surrogate mother," Seth says.

"Sort of. I guess that's right. I mean for a while it was as though we were all one family — holidays together and all that. But now everything changed. Because Andrea died. Stacey changed her mind. She wants to keep the baby. But David is the father and my mom feels as though she's the mother too. She was with Stacey all through the pregnancy, and then Felicia Miriam was here — she was in our house and she became part of our lives. We all took care of her.

Stacey gave birth to her but she's our baby also." Hildy speaks ever more quickly; her words fall over each other as though speed will give them coherence. She juggles the equations of parentage. David and Stacey. Nina and Stacey. Stacey and Hal. Nina and David. She is relieved to be talking about the situation (Nina and David do not include her in their conversations; they are intent on shielding her from their misery, their uncertainty), and she is comforted that her friends listen so carefully. They comprehend her pain, the source of her bewilderment.

"So what's going to happen?" Seth asks. "I mean, are your folks going to sue?"

They are of a generation that is not unfamiliar with lawsuits. Their friends have been at the center of custody battles. Seth's mother speaks with tight-lipped bitterness of the legal options women must explore for their own protection. Often she watches television shows that feature courtroom scenes, and she goes to meetings of a group called Legal Awareness for Women. Alison has her own attorney, a kindly man retained by both her parents to advise her of her rights.

"I don't know. They don't want to. They keep hoping they'll be able to work it out another way," Hildy replies.

Still, she knows that David has called Charles Norris. She listened on the extension as he told Nina about their conversation.

"But I guess if they have to, they'll go to court. David is the father, and my mother's been involved with this every step of the way. You just can't give up a baby when you have that kind of a connection."

"But that's probably how Stacey feels," Alison says softly. "Oh, Jesus, what a mess. What an eighties mess. A biotech nightmare. Two mothers, one baby. A field day for the TV crews."

"Who says it's an eighties phenomenon?" Seth asks. He is skilled at recalling historical and literary precedents. "There was Solomon's case — two mothers, one baby. And then Brecht in *The Caucasian Chalk Circle*. I've got it right here." He lifts the long sheaf of paper spewed from the printer and tears one section loose.

"Don't read it to us. Please don't read it to us," Alison says. "Just tell it, like, in as few words as possible. And without your interpretation."

"Jesus, you guys are Philistines — Cliff Note addicts. All right. The gist of it is that Brecht took an old Chinese play — something from, like, the fourteenth century. The author's name got lost or maybe no one could pronounce it." Seth scans his own material now, jabbing at it with a ballpoint pen to make corrections. "Okay. Two mothers go before a judge, claiming the same kid. Each says that she's the real mother. The judge draws a chalk circle and puts the kid in the middle of it. The women wait at opposite ends of it and the test was for the real mother to take hold of him and get him out of the circle, but the 'false' mother can't lead him out. So one of the women does just that. She takes the kid out of the circle and the judge says that it's clear that she must be the real mother because the other woman didn't even put up a fight. But the other woman says that she wouldn't risk a fight because she would risk harming the boy. The judge rules that she's the real mother because a real mother would never harm her own child. It's not too different from the Solomon story, and Brecht switched the whole situation to the Caucasus after World War II. Two mothers, one kid. Same dilemma."

"So that's how you'd have them come to a decision about Felicia Miriam — draw a chalk circle with Nina on one side and Stacey on the other?" Alison asks. Her voice is very serious. She has learned to invest every hypothesis with reality, to translate every fantasy into possibility.

"It's as good a technique as any," Seth replies. "And a hell of a lot better than a legal circus with these shrinks discussing which mother seems to hug better."

"But it wouldn't work," Hildy says gravely. "Your chalk circle wouldn't work. Neither of them could hurt the baby. Not my mother and not Stacey. They both love her too much for that. They'd be frozen forever on opposite sides of the circle, and Felicia Miriam would be in the middle, crying and crying."

She takes a final puff of the joint and they sit quietly and watch as she crushes out the glowing end and then lights a scented candle.

Alison and Seth nod. Hildy's certainty becomes their own. Seth switches the printer back on. Its intrusive, staccato clatter reassures them. Hildy shuts off the overhead light and they lie in the darkness and watch the wisp of gray candle smoke drift fragrantly through the darkness.

Nina's parents decide to curtail their visit. They have, after all, accomplished its purpose. They have shared the seders with the family. They have gone to the theater. They have watched (with some puzzlement) a rehearsal of Nina's dance composition. Her mother thought it beautiful but she found the title bewildering.

" 'The Dance of the Mothers,' " she repeated in her birdlike voice. "I don't understand what you're trying to do, dear."

"I'm using movement to show the joy of mothering — how women nurture their babies; how that nurturing and joy can be shared with men, with each other," Nina explains patiently. She wonders if she should try to interpret each segue, if indeed she can explain the movements to her mother. She is relieved when her mother nods.

"I see. I understand," she says.

Her parents have not once during the course of their visit asked about the nursery, although Nina notices that they speak softly as they pass the closed door. Only Mrs. Ludovico enters the room to dust and vacuum, a task she accomplishes when Nina is in the city or in another part of the house. Nina is reminded that Stacey told her that she could not bring herself to enter Andrea's room after the funeral. It was Hal who stripped the narrow bed of its linens, who smoothed out the pink satin comforter and watered the crocus.

Will she and David treat the nursery with similar circumspection, isolating themselves from its memories, from the lingering scents and images that hover within its bright walls? On the last night of her parents' visit Nina goes into the nursery. She looks down at the crib and takes up the small white Gund bear (a gift from Seth and Alison) that nestles in a corner, and holding it, she settles herself in the rocking chair. Gently, gently, she pitches back and forth and watches a silver wand of moonlight dart across the flowered sheet, as though searching for the vanished baby.

She closes her eyes. Images of Felicia Miriam dance through her mind. Felicia Miriam with her flailing arms, her delicate skin. Felicia Miriam in her green stretch suit, a tiny ribbon tied to her pale fringe of hair. Felicia Miriam in Nina's arms, sucking thirstily at a bottle, burping, sliding her head into that safe maternal cave, the slight declivity between neck and shoulder. She is not gone from this room. When Nina opens her eyes she will be there, asleep in her crib. The magic thinking of Nina's childhood asserts itself. Count to ten and Daddy will be home. One, two three . . . She opens her eyes but the crib is empty.

"No!" she screams. "No!" She throws the soft white bear across the room and lifts her hands. She pulls at her own long black hair.

"Nina." David stands in the doorway. He walks toward her, his arms outstretched. Gently, he pries her fists open. Long strands of her own hair lie curled in her palm, and he takes a tissue from the changing table and wipes her hands. "Come to bed," he says, and his voice is soft with pity.

Like invalids leaning on each other for support, they walk down the hallway to their room. In bed, they lie side by side, encased in their shared misery, their silence insulated by all the words they will not say, all the fears they dare not articulate. Each knows the emptiness the other feels. They are mutually bereft. And then Nina speaks.

"David. Are you sorry now that we did it? Sorry that we got involved with Stacey?"

"Sorry?" He hesitates. There is a picture of Felicia Miriam on his bedside table, a Polaroid taken by Arnold at the hospital that Nina has placed in a Lucite frame. He touches it now. "How can I be sorry? She's a wonderful baby. She'll be a wonderful little girl. No matter what. We've done that much."

"Yes." She is comforted, reassured. Because of them, because of his yearning, a baby has been born. They have, in concert, all of them, created a life. About this they can have no regrets, not any of them.

The nocturnal silence is deep and she pierces it with yet another question, softly asked.

"Would you do it again?"

Now he replies at once, his answer in place.

"Never. Never."

She turns to look at him. He is very pale and his face is contorted with misery. His eyes are shut and his long fair lashes are stuck to-gether by his tears.

Nina takes her parents to the airport. Their farewells are as con-trolled and restrained as their greetings. She notices that as they proceed down the runway to their waiting plane they walk very slowly. Her father's shoulders are curved as though he carries a great weight. Her mother turns and waves, and her gaze is sharp with worry. She understands that something of extreme gravity has occurred during their visit but she asks no questions, and Nina is grateful to her. Could she be similarly restrained with Hildy? Would she want to be? The decisions of motherhood must be so carefully weighed, each ges-ture measured, monitored. There is a movement in her dance when the mothers draw close and then slowly withdraw. Her choreography (much revised) now calls for them to walk backward, their faces turned toward the child who remains alone on the stage.

She drives home very slowly, reluctant to confront the silence and emptiness of the house. But the phone is ringing as she walks up the flagstone path and she hurries to answer it.

"Hi, Nina." Stacey's voice is oddly light, reminiscent of Hildy's when she has done something she knows will incur their disapproval.

"Hello, Stacey." Nina wills herself to calm.

"I wanted to thank you for bringing my suitcase. And the baby's things."

"That's all right," Nina says. "I'm sorry I missed you." She keeps her tone casual as though the slightest indication of intensity might shatter the fragile connection.

"I took the baby to the pediatrician."

"Is she all right?" Again, she struggles to communicate concern without conveying anxiety. Dizzied, she sits down and grips the phone tightly.

"Oh, she's fine, wonderful."

"May I see her?"

"Oh, yes. Yes, of course." Stacey's voice brims with relief. "Whenever you like."

"Tomorrow morning then?" Nina suggests. "Is ten-thirty good?"

She picks the hour carefully. Hal will be at Ramon's, Evan at school, and Jared at his day-care center.

"Fine," Stacey says. "Terrific."

She hangs up and Nina stares at the phone and wonders why Stacey, throughout their conversation, did not mention Felicia Miriam by name.

3 1

They sit together the next morning in the Cosgrove living room and drink coffee from unmatched mugs because Stacey has already packed her china. It is raining and Nina's feet are wet. She takes her shoes off and tucks her legs beneath her long paisley skirt. Stacey, who wears blue jeans and a pale blue sweatshirt, does the same. Facing each other, in this companionable dormitory posture, they talk while Felicia Miriam naps in the room that had been Andrea's. Nina has brought a parcel of baby clothing, and as they speak Stacey reaches down and lifts out one small garment or another. She waves the undershirts and the pastel stretch suits, the delicate dresses and sweaters, as though they are small flags. She smiles. She is a benificent victor. She is grateful that Nina is not angry with her, that she will remain her friend.

Stacey does not notice that Nina's hands tremble nor does she remark on Nina's pallor, the dark circles that shadow her eyes. Still, she keeps her face averted as they talk, and Nina, for her part, keeps her eyes fixed on the closed door beyond which her daughter sleeps. It occurs to her that she can rush into that room, pluck the baby up, and flee the house, as Stacey fled that night. The thought itself frightens her, and she can no longer hold her coffee cup but must set it down. She is distressed when the brown liquid sloshes across the table. She does not want Stacey to discern the anxiety that grips her. It is important that she remain calm; she must not rescind her control. She clasps her hands on her lap and looks around the room.

The rain streaks the windows and the sills (where Hal has neglected to caulk) are wet, but the room, despite its disarray (or because of it), is bright and cheerful. There are cartons everywhere. Some are neatly packed and others have become catchalls for ordinary clutter. Jared's Big Bird peers at them over the top of an otherwise empty crate and a green nylon tablecloth is tossed across a cardboard packing case.

"I'll be glad when this move is over," Stacey says. "When we know where we're going and what we're doing." She laughs nervously, apologetically.

"Don't you know that yet?" Nina asks.

"All I know is that Hal sold the house. He got such a good offer that he felt he couldn't turn it down. And the new owner wants to move in, in just a couple of weeks' time. Of course, we still have to have the closing and everything, but Hal started the packing even before I got home."

"He didn't tell you he had sold?" Nina asks in surprise.

"No. But it was what we planned to do all along. Even before."

There is no recrimination in her voice. She does not blame Hal as he did not blame her. He followed a plan they had set in motion together, and when she altered the plan he supported her. The house is sold and they must move on.

"Do you know where you'll be moving to?" Nina asks. She is lightheaded, dizzied by the thought that Stacey has the power to put a vast distance between David and herself and Felicia Miriam. They will not see their daughter's face slowly blossom from tiny-featured infancy into the radiant, generous visage of childhood. Can it be that they will not see her crawl and then tentatively but trustingly rise and come toward them in those first rubbery steps of toddlerhood? She darkens her mind against the other images that crowd it. No. It will not come to that. They will not allow their daughter to be spirited away from them, to be transported to the other side of the continent. They will do battle for her.

"Hal's still talking about California," Stacey replies. "He's trying to get the money together." She looks away. Through all the months of her pregnancy, they never discussed money. Once the arrangement had been agreed upon, their lawyers became their conduits. Charles Norris transmitted checks to Andrew Kardin while Stacey gave Nina a fragile swan designed to hold toothpicks and Nina gave Stacey a feather-light cashmere robe. But now the charade is over. The veneer has been savagely scraped away and their relationship stands revealed in all its crudity.

"That's a lot of money you're talking about," Nina says. The words are sour in her mouth. She hates herself for what she is doing, but there is no weapon she would not use in this battle for her daughter.

"Yeah. We know. But Hal thinks he can get people to invest in the restaurant. Maybe my family. Maybe his boss at Ramon's. Something will work out. And if it doesn't we can always stay with my folks for a while."

Her embarrassment is gone and she speaks with a new assurance. She is truly unconcerned about the location of their home, the focus of their new life. She relies on Hal. They will manage, she and her husband and her sons and Felicia Miriam, the daughter restored to her.

"Nina, listen. I know how hard this is for you and David, and really I feel awful. Worse than awful. But there was nothing else I could do. It was too much for me, in the end. I just couldn't give my baby up. You understand that, don't you?" She leans toward Nina and speaks earnestly. Her cheeks are flushed and her eyes glitter like polished glass.

"I know that things must have gotten to be too much for you that night. The seder. All the people. Too much excitement, too much tension. I understand that. So does David. We don't blame you." Nina chooses her words carefully. She has rehearsed them and revised them. Indeed, since Stacey's call, she has thought of nothing else except what she had to say to Stacey, the verbal volleys she would have to fire so that she might reclaim her baby, so that she might carry Felicia Miriam home to the crib, newly made up that morning with sheets on which bright-hearted daisies blossom. "But now that you've had time to think about it, Stacey, you must see it all differently. We made an agreement. You know that. You're a good person. A fair person. We care about you and your family. We've been your friends. We tried so hard, David and myself, to do what was right, to understand you." She fingers the cuffs of her wine-colored blouse, tucks in the tendrils of hair that have escaped her loose dancer's bun. Her throat feels hoarse, as though she has been speaking for hours, pleading her cause, pleading for reason. How is it that these few sentences have so strained her, have so depleted her?

"I know," Stacey says miserably. "I know how hard you tried, and I'm grateful. But I couldn't help it. When we first met, when we first decided what we would do and made our agreement, we couldn't have known what would happen, how everything would change."

"You mean because of Andrea?" Nina asks. Her heart is heavy. The dead child's name is awkward upon her tongue, like a word at once forbidden and foreboding. Still, she does not avert her eyes from Stacey's face, which crumples now in sorrow renewed, in mourning resumed. Today all their silences must be broken. Nina cannot, she will not, allow her pity, her compassion for Stacey, to override her pity, her compassion for David, for herself, for their love for Felicia Miriam. *Their daughter. Theirs.*

"Yes. Because of Andrea. My Andrea." Stacey gulps for air. She is drowning in her own fear, her own misery. How can she explain to Nina her fear of the rodent of sorrow? How can she tell her how she left the motel after that long night and drove through the bright morning light to the city, not knowing where she would go, where she would take her baby? Aimlessly, she had driven south, speaking all the while to Felicia Miriam who slept in the infant seat. She called her by her own name and she called her by Andrea's name and she told her stories, wonderful stories. She was with Andrea again and they whirled each other toward the world of the happily ever after. She looked up at an exit sign and saw that she was at the Botanic Gardens, and so she drove off the highway and through the open but unattended gate of the park.

She parked and carried the baby, still sleeping, to the South Garden. The first flowers of spring were in full blossom and Stacey remembered how she had walked with Andrea among the tender buds on that sunlit day when she had been buoyant with joy, rushing eagerly toward spring. She sat on the same bench she had occupied as Andrea rolled and tumbled down the gentle hill. Felicia Miriam's head had rested on her shoulder, and Stacey, weary, her mouth dry, her eyes red-rimmed because she had not slept but instead had watched

Felicia Miriam sleep, had stared at the hill. She had found herself listening carefully and recognized that she was waiting for the sound of Andrea's laughter — as though it lingered still in the fragrant air. But there was only silence, and the incline that had been covered with the detritus of winter, damp dark leaves and snapping twigs, was green now, covered with sweet and tender grass. Winter was done with and spring had begun. Andrea was dead and she held Felicia Miriam in her arms. She had to go home. It was time to go home.

Stacey can say none of this to Nina. Nina cannot understand the gnawing pain that bites at her still at strange hours of the day and night, attacking her as she wraps newspapers around cups and saucers, helps Evan with his homework, kneels beside the tub to bathe Jared. She is free of its threat only when she cares for Felicia Miriam.

But Nina does not wait for her to speak. Instead, she grips Stacey's hands, her nails carving their way into Stacey's wrists.

"Stacey, listen to me. You're beginning a new life. You're young, you and Hal. You can have other children. But Felicia Miriam is our last chance to have a child. David's last chance for a child of his own. You'll have another baby." She is pleading now, pulling Stacey toward her as though she would force her to comply; she would overwhelm her with the sheer physical strength of her need, the vitriol of her anguish.

Stacey pulls away, frightened, sullen.

"What are you talking about? Another baby won't be Felicia Miriam. You can't replace one child with another."

"And Felicia Miriam won't replace Andrea," Nina shouts. "Andrea is dead. Dead!"

She is on her feet now, standing over Stacey. All her restraint is gone — the hard-earned control of her art, of her fierce discipline, that control which dominates and orders her life. She is electric with anger; her skin tingles and yet her clothing clings to her, clammy and cold. She is chilled by her own sweat and her mouth is sour with thick and evil-tasting saliva. Her strength rises and fades. Barefoot, she strides across the room and looks out at the ragged, rain-tossed garden. The thin leaves of the ailanthus tree are rain-blackened and the skeletal branches shiver helplessly in the wind.

She does not face Stacey when she speaks, but her voice rings loud and clear, resonant in its insistence.

"You must give us our baby. We must have our baby."

She is newly energized, empowered by the adrenaline of her own passionate yearnings, of her love for the infant her husband has fathered, the infant she imagined and nurtured. She is moved now to throw open the door and pluck Felicia Miriam from her bed and run with her through the rain. Triumphantly she will carry her to David and they will hold her fast, grip her in the tentacles of their love.

"I can't." Stacey's voice is piteous in denial.

"Why not? Why can't you?"

Nina whirls around and stands over Stacey, her arms uplifted, her fingers curled into fists. She hammers at the air, her muscles tensed with fury, and then she brings her hands together in a wild clap of anguish. Her mouth opens as she struggles for words but she emits only a rattling, strangulated cry.

"Oh, Nina, I'm sorry. I'm so sorry." Stacey is crying now, crying and sobbing, her shoulders heaving. Curled up on the couch, she cowers into a corner. "I can't be without her. I can't. But I don't want to keep you from her. You can visit whenever you want. You and David and Hildy. Or we can work out a schedule. I want to do the right thing. I've always wanted to do the right thing." Her voice breaks. She pities herself for her own goodness. She has been, in turn, since earliest childhood, the good daughter (mothering her own half-mad mother, consoling her father), the good wife, the good mother, the good student, juggling laundry and class schedules, keeping textbooks on her kitchen counter. She has tried to please everyone always. But now too much has been asked of her. Too much.

She clutches a pillow to her stomach and rocks back and forth, her head down, fearful of Nina's anger and her own encroaching despair.

And that is how Evan finds them when he bursts into the house, having run all the way home from school to collect his forgotten lunch. Shivering in his oversized yellow slicker, his hair matted by the rain, his face flushed and wet, he thrusts himself between the two women. His outstretched arms warn Nina away, shield Stacey.

"Leave my mother alone," he shouts at Nina. "Leave her alone!"

Then, from behind the closed door, they hear Felicia Miriam cry. Her high-pitched wail is plaintive, vibrant with infant fear, infant desperation.

Stacy struggles to her feet.

"It's all right," she says reassuringly to Evan. "Nina and I were just talking."

And Nina, shamed, sits down on the couch as Stacey hurries to the baby. Evan, his body still rigid, his eyes narrow and wary, stares at her. She knows that he must think her mad as she sits there barefoot, her clothing in disarray, her hair tumbling wildly about her shoulders, all color drained from her face. He is not far wrong. She is mad, obsessed with her love for this baby and her love for her husband who has invested so much in his child, so much love, so much longing. Perhaps it was madness that spurred them from the very beginning, that caused them to enter into this relationship that defies reason, that challenges convention, madness inspired by sorrow and — yes — motivated by courage. They had stood together and stared at the photographs of skeletal children, at the clumsy hillocks of small shoes and soft hair. They had stared at death and made a commitment, a wild commitment to new life, to a guarantor of continuity. They had thought then, in their yearning and in their innocence, that it was possible. And it might have been. And it might still be. She does not know. She knows only, as she and Evan look at each other, that she is consumed with pity for herself and David and Hildly, for Stacey, but most of all for Felicia Miriam.

Stacey emerges from the bedroom, carrying the baby. The infant's tear-streaked face is grave with new awareness. Safe in the cove of Stacey's arms, she looks at Nina, whose heart turns. She is certain that she perceives a flicker of recognition in the cobalt-blue eyes that fix her in that solemn infant gaze. She moves toward her, but Stacey holds the baby close and shifts her position so that Nina slips from the infant's field of vision.

"Can I hold her?" Nina asks softly, and then adds more loudly, "I must hold her."

Her arms are outstretched. The baby draws her like a magnet and she inches toward Stacey, who retreats.

"No," she says fearfully. She has read Nina's darkest thoughts, discerned her wildest fantasies. She knows now that reason cannot prevail, that there is no "right thing," only visceral choices. "No!"

Still, Nina advances, but Evan hurls himself between the two women, pushes at Nina with his hard small fists, driving her away from his mother.

"She said no," he shrieks. "And no is no. Go away! Go home!" He is crying now, tears of rage and bewilderment. He does not understand what is happening here in his home any more than he can understand that Andrea is gone from his life or that his father's laughter is stilled and his mother's face is wreathed in sadness. But all his unarticulated terror, all his painful confusion, is focused now on Nina. They were all right before she came into their lives. Andrea was alive. His mother was happy. Oh, she is a witch. A witch. He strikes out at her, his clenched fist hitting her in the abdomen, propelled by all the force of his anger and his fear. She doubles over in pain, sinks to her knees on the floor.

"Evan." Stacey is shocked, reproving, but still she keeps her distance from Nina, who rises slowly, still feeling the cramp of pain, still startled because never before has a hand been raised against her.

Defeated, enervated, she slips on her wet shoes. She tucks her blouse into her skirt and, with trembling fingers, pins back her hair. Thus repaired, she turns to Stacey, who stands watching her, Evan at her side. And now, without hesitation, she bends her head forward and kisses Felicia Miriam, kisses her cheek and then kisses the strawberry mark at her neck.

She leaves the house and sprints through the rain to her car. Stacey stands in the doorway, holding the baby, with Evan standing guard. Nina looks back at them as she drives away. Stacey is calling to her, mouthing the words with urgent expressiveness. Seen in the rearview mirror, through the filter of the falling rain, frozen in the frame of the doorway, she is like a character in a silent film. Nina rolls down the car window, but all she can hear is the sound of Felicia Miriam's crying and the rhythm of the rain as it falls gently onto the soft and yielding earth.

32

They are gathered again around the long rosewood table in Charles Norris's conference room, Nina and David on one side, Hal and Stacey on the other. Today, however, Arnold is not with them. It is Andrew Kardin who sits opposite Charles Norris, a copy of the contract and a yellow legal pad spread before him. It is, David realizes as he glances at the date on the contract, a year almost to the day since they signed their names to this document. He looks up and sees that Stacey too is looking at the date. He notes with sadness that she does not look well. Her face is drawn beneath the makeup she has applied so carefully. Shadows form velvet grooves beneath her eyes. She wears a gray dress. (Later, Nina tells him that she has never before seen Stacey wear anything devoid of color or brightness.) Stacey will not again be mistaken for a schoolgirl. The year has claimed her youth. She looks up and meets his eyes. Immediately, she blushes and looks away.

Hot rage courses through him. She cannot avoid him. She must acknowledge him and in doing so acknowledge all that she has done. And then, at once, his fury subsides and he is mired again (yet again) in stagnant sadness.

"How are you, Stacey?" he asks.

And now she does look at him and smiles thinly, nervously.

"I'm okay, I guess," she says. The breathlessness is gone from her voice. Her tone is flat, ironed down by experience. She has submitted, at last, to the realities of adulthood.

"And Felicia Miriam?" he persists.

"She's good. Really good." Again, she looks away. She is courageous but not foolhardy. She knows that she cannot bear the pain
that immobilizes his face as though he has suddenly suffered an odd
paralysis. Nina reaches out and takes his hand, covers it with her
own. She does not speak but nods to Stacey, to Hal, who flashes
them a benificent smile.

"Yeah. She's great," Hal interjects. "She changes every day. You
know how it is with babies. We want you to see her. You know, if
we can work everything out." He strokes his beard, clipped short
now, and fingers the gold chain at his neck. He wears a white suit
and a navy-blue shirt, and, David notes with wry malice, both his
dark hair and his beard are threaded with silver.

"We'll see," David says.

He is conscious of Charles Norris's warning glance, of the comforting pressure of Nina's hand upon his own. He looks at his wife
and is newly moved by her beauty. It seems to him that her face has
changed during this long and difficult year. There is a warmth in her
eyes, and the intensity of expression that sometimes frightened him
has been replaced with an accepting calm, often veiled with melancholy. She looks especially well today because this evening her class
will do a showcase performance of her dance and she has dressed
carefully for it, in a jade-green suit and a white blouse. He moves
his chair closer to her so that his shoulder brushes her own.

Charles Norris coughs nervously. The afternoon is warm but he
wears a dark three-piece suit, and, unlike Andrew Kardin, he does
not remove his jacket. He wipes his face with his white linen handkerchief.

"Well," he says, "we all know why we are here. I trust everyone
has had time to reread the agreement, to refresh your memories on
all details."

They nod in unison, like a class of bright and obedient children.

"All right then," he continues. "An agreement was made, a contract executed. The terms, stated as briefly as possible, were that
Stacey Cosgrove would undertake to conceive a child. The sperm for
that conception would be that of David Roth, and after the child's
birth, he and his wife, Nina Roth, would assume all responsibility
for that child. Nina Roth would become the adoptive mother. Sta-

cey Cosgrove would make no claims on the infant. My client, David Roth, lived up to all the terms of this agreement. The set fees were remitted to the Cosgroves as they came due under the schedule agreed upon and all miscellaneous expenses were paid. But now, it appears that Stacey Cosgrove wants to retain custody of the infant female, in violation of the terms of this agreement."

"Felicia Miriam," Stacey says. "Her name is Felicia Miriam."

"Yes. Of course." Charles Norris is courteous, but he does not look up from his notes. "We are meeting here today to decide on the most peaceful course of action to resolve this painful difference between my client and the Cosgroves. I have spoken to Andrew Kardin, who represents them, and he tells me that Stacey Cosgrove's position is not amenable to compromise, that she is determined to keep the infant female and to raise her as her daughter."

"She is her daughter," Hal says. "And that's what she wants. So that's what I want too. It's not only Stacey. It's me too." Harshly, he claims his role, thrusts himself into the action. Goddamn it, he's not going to be treated like a shadow in this room.

"Hal." Andrew Kardin speaks softly but the monitory tone of his voice is clear. His expression does not change. His long fingers, expertly manicured and coated with clear polish, flutter through the papers spread before him as though he is dealing a deck of cards, shuffling them with expert swiftness.

"We understand that," Charles Norris replies drily. "However, your position presents serious problems. My clients endured a great deal of mental stress, a great deal of painful disappointment. Sizable amounts of money were expended."

"My clients are prepared to return the payment made to them," Andrew Kardin counters in his flat gambler's voice.

Hal breathes deeply. He is glad that he hardly touched that initial payment and that whatever dent he did make in it he has been able to replenish with the money he received as a down payment on the house.

"And, of course," Andrew continues, "they will forfeit all claim to any other payment."

"All that is well and good," Charles Norris says, "but there was an outlay of funds for other expenses. Maternity clothing for Mrs.

Cosgrove. The obstetrician's fees during the nine months of pregnancy. The hospital bill. All of this was paid by Mr. Roth."

"Oh, come on, give us a break," Hal says irritably. "The obstetrician is your brother, David. Did he really send you a hefty bill?"

"There is a bill," Charles Norris repeats quietly.

"What's the exact amount of all these so-called expenses?" Andrew Kardin asks.

"It is somewhere in the neighborhood of six thousand dollars. I will, of course, give you an exact accounting. We would require you to make restitution in that amount."

"Six thousand dollars?" Stacey leans forward and her color is high. "David, you can't mean that." She stares hard at him as though searching his face for clues of character she had somehow missed before.

"That figure is negotiable, I'm sure," Andrew Kardin says smoothly. "The Cosgroves are prepared to grant visitation rights. Their reasonableness and generosity depend on the reasonableness and generosity of the Roths."

"No." Charles Norris's tone is level. "It is not negotiable. It is a firm figure, fairly arrived at."

"Fair?" Hal shouts. "There's nothing fair about it. You're bluffing. You're trying to scare us. Well, fuck you!"

The epithet causes them to drop their eyes, to busy themselves with the papers — and yet they are not shocked; they have anticipated it. Nina twists her gold bracelet. Stacey snaps her purse open and shut. It is new, a small white pouch of real leather, not unlike the one Nina herself carries. She has abandoned the oversized plastic shoulder bag. She no longer has need of its voluminous space for her notebooks, her paperbacks. Her life is newly organized, newly orderly.

"There is no need for obscenities, Mr. Cosgrove," Charles Norris reminds him curtly. "We give you a fair figure. If you cannot meet it we may indeed sue for its recovery if necessary. However, we are prepared to offer an alternative. My client originally offered you a payment of twenty thousand dollars. I indicated to Mr. Kardin that he is prepared to raise this amount in view of your reluctance and the difficulties you have encountered. I spoke of an additional five thousand dollars, which Mr. Kardin indicated was unacceptable. Mr.

Roth now authorizes me to offer you an additional ten thousand dollars and a forgiveness, naturally, of all expenses."

"No," Hal says and his voice is hard. "Like I told my attorney, like I told David Roth, we're not in the baby-selling business here. Not me. Not Stacey. We got ourselves into this and we shouldn't have, but we did it for the best reasons, with the best intentions. Now things changed and everyone here knows how they changed and why they changed and what my Stacey went through. Okay, we can't keep the agreement and we'll try to get ourselves out of it, but this isn't a goddamn marketplace, a baby bazaar. We don't need your money and we don't want it. You talk about me using an obscenity, Mr. Norris. Well, this whole goddamn discussion is an obscenity. Your lousy offer is an obscenity. You talk about what's not negotiable. Well, I'll tell you what's not negotiable. Stacey's feelings aren't negotiable. What she wants isn't negotiable. And she wants the baby to stay with us, so that's what's going to happen and you can bring all the goddamn suits you want to." He is on his feet now, his chair pushed back. "Come on, Stacey. Let's get the hell out of here."

Bewildered, she too rises. Her glance travels beseechingly from Nina to David, but she rests her hand on Hal's wrist. Clearly, she will follow wherever he leads.

"Stop," David says quietly. "Sit down, Hal, Stacey." He turns to Charles Norris. "I told you none of this would work, Charles."

Charles Norris closes his file folder, sits back.

"We had to try," he replies. He speaks to David, his client and his friend, as though they are alone in the room, yet it is important that everyone at the table hear their interchange, that everyone understand that it was he, acting as David's attorney, who initiated the offers set forth at this table. David and Nina are absolved.

Stacey glances at Hal. He nods and they both sit down.

"So you tried," David says. "And now we go forward. Listen, Hal, Stacey, Nina and I have talked about all this. I don't have to tell you what this baby, my daughter, means to me, to us. You know. You've seen. I've told you. Nina's told you. And we know that you entered into this agreement in good faith. None of us could have foreseen what would happen and we couldn't foresee how Stacey would feel about the baby afterwards. After . . ." Here his voice

breaks and they do not look at each other. They understand that
there are words that must not be said lest the veil of a terrible sadness descend upon them and smother them in its soft and rotting
folds. David waits, gathers strength, continues. "We know she tried
and we tried to help her. Maybe we did the wrong thing. I think
now that we were wrong from the beginning. We thought we were
right and it sounded reasonable. My brother wanted to help us and
he wanted to help you. But it was crazy and we were crazy — crazy
to think that we could make our own rules, that we could draw up a
contract with rules for love. And we'd be crazy now to think that
we could divide up that love, that there could be a sharing. Oh, yes.
We love Felicia Miriam and we'll always love her. She was born
because we wanted her. Both of us. But now we have to do what's
best for her. And what's best for her is for her to have one family,
not two families who fight over her. And even if we didn't do that,
even if everything was friendly and easy, she'd still be confused, and
we don't want that. And most of all we don't want a court case. We
don't want lawyers and television interviews and letters to the editor.
We just want her to have a normal life.

"So Nina and I will give up all rights to her. She'll be Felicia
Miriam Cosgrove, Stacey and Hal's daughter. But I still want to be
sure that she has a good life, that her family doesn't have to struggle.
So I'll honor all the terms of the original agreement plus the amount
we talked about here today. And, of course, all the expenses. We
wanted to try. You understand that. How could we give her up without trying everything, everything? But it's clear how it is with you —
how you feel, and we accept that. We have to. We love Felicia
Miriam, so we have to do what's right for her no matter how much
it hurts. And it hurts. It hurts." He is very pale and there is a rasp
in his voice, as though he must strain to speak these words. But he
continues. "I don't want to ever interfere, but I don't want her ever
to be in want. I hope you understand, Hal, Stacey. And I want you
to understand that we never thought of this as baby selling. Never."
Again his voice cracks and he turns away. He knows that within
minutes his face will shatter, that the grief he cannot contain will
spill over. Still, he has done what he had to do, said what he had
to say. They have struggled, he and Nina, and they have lost. They

are not warriors; they will not become tenacious litigants. They are bereaved and loving parents.

He holds Nina's hand very tightly. Her fingers are cold but she sits erect, her shoulders thrust bravely back, her eyes brilliant with unshed tears.

"That's very generous of you, Mr. Roth," Andrew Kardin says pleasantly. "But it's only the correct position. As you say, my clients entered into this arrangement in good faith."

"That's it, Mr. Kardin. That's the end of the discussion. I've said everything there is to say. Mr. Norris will act for me as far as further exchange of funds, the signing of any release. My wife and I must leave now. We have an appointment." David does not look at Andrew Kardin as he speaks: his words are as carefully rehearsed as Nina's dance and he keeps his voice to a monotone, as though he fears that a variation of expression, a minor deviation, will alter his resolve.

"David." Stacey looks at him pleadingly. "You could visit anytime. We could send you pictures. Like you would have if it had all worked out the way we thought it would, at first. We said we would be like one family. We said that from the beginning."

"But we were wrong." It is Nina who answers her, Nina who stands beside David. She is crying now, and she makes no attempt to restrain or wipe her tears. Her voice is muffled, cottoned by her grief, and her cheeks are aflame as though scalded by the burning drops that will not stop falling. She shivers even as she speaks, and David holds her close. "It wouldn't work. It couldn't work. We didn't know it then but we all see it now. David told you. We're doing what we think will be best for Felicia Miriam. But we're not saints, Stacey. We couldn't do what you ask us to do. We know that. We love her too much for that. When we leave this room it's over between you and us. We won't see you or our daughter again."

Our daughter. The words come so naturally to her that she is frightened, yet always she will think of the infant she cuddled and cared for as their daughter. She leans on David, faint suddenly with the enormity of their decision. And yet she knows and David knows and Hildy too (Hildy, who wept when they told her what they planned to say in this room) knows that they could not do otherwise.

And so they leave, hand in hand, and they do not look back. It is only when they are waiting for the elevator that David realizes that they have left their own copies of the contract on the rosewood conference table. But that is of no consequence. Nothing, in this moment of their loss, of their final and inevitable despair, is of any consequence at all.

33

They resume their daily routines, pacing themselves like convalescents. Like victims of a chronic ailment, they learn to take prophylactic measures, to avoid contact with places and situations that will deepen the festering infection of their grief. They do not walk in the quarry park where, on weekends, parents push carriages and strollers, and small children gambol. One afternoon, Nina sweeps all the cunning stuffed animals that have decorated their headboard into a large carton that she carries up to the attic. Only the two camels remain, and when she comes downstairs, she climbs, fully clothed, beneath the comforter, and hugs the camels to her breast. Her body is racked with a piercing pain that causes her chest to ache, although she does not weep. She is still there when David comes home that evening and he climbs into bed beside her, still in his business suit, and holds her close, kissing her hair, her face, gently removing the animals from her grasp so that he can press his own head against the soft rise of her breasts. And he does weep. She feels the heat of his tears beneath the layer of her own blouse. Thus they comfort each other, although they do not speak because there is nothing left to say.

Tentatively, they plan a vacation, a graduation party for Hildy; they ask an architect to submit plans for a skylight for Nina's studio. They intensify their work schedules. David flies to California on business and calls Nina twice each day.

"Are you all right?" he asks each time. "Really. Are you all right?"

His question, she knows, is a plea for reassurance, for an acknowledgment that they will recover, that they are recovering.

"Fine. I'm fine," she says, and she speaks too rapidly, telling him about her work, about the plans Hildy, Seth, and Alison are making for their graduation party, about a troubling call from his mother who complains of chest pains. They struggle toward a resumption of normalcy. They will be all right.

Nina plans a new taping for her dance. The showcase performance was successful, and her friend Bruce Connors has invited her students to perform at a festival in Connecticut. She has twice revised the final movement, which originally was a duet; now only Tina sweeps across the stage, holding the infant, while the dancer who plays the other mother stands poised motionless in the shadowed apron of the proscenium.

Spring in all its brilliance surrounds them. They take long drives into the country and hike along woodland trails. They find, in this long season of their recovery, that the darkness of the forest is soothing, that they prefer it to the sunlit expanse of their own garden. When she does sit outside, Nina turns her chair so that it does not face the playhouse.

One Sunday afternoon they drive to Mancredi's farm. The developer has started work. Cinder-block foundations, ranged like gravestones, stud the fields where Nina walked, so many years ago, with Michael Ernst. The slender maple beneath which she danced during the early days of her pregnancy with Hildy has been uprooted. She takes a perverse pleasure in noting that the landscapes of the past are not immutable, that the scenes of sorrow are altered and that sorrow itself fades and diminishes.

The door to the nursery remains closed. They have not yet dismantled the room, although they speak of it now and again. One night, when a spring storm rages, Nina awakens and sees that David is gone from their bed. She finds him (as, instinctively, she knew she would) at the nursery window, and she stands beside him. His arm reaches out and he draws her into the shelter of his embrace. They do not speak as they watch the wind whip across the rosebushes that form a bower near the playhouse. They move as one across the soft carpet, and Nina closes her eyes so that she will not have to see the empty crib, although David slows his step as they walk past it. They do stop at Hildy's room. Always, when she was a child, nocturnal storms had frightened Hildy, and Nina opens the door carefully. Her daughter is fast asleep, a slight smile playing on her lips. She does not stir even when a brilliant crack of lightning scissors its way across the sky. Nina turns to David. She is oddly proud that their daughter can sleep so peacefully, happily, through the raging storm.

They make love that night with febrile intensity, as the thunder rolls and the lightning flashes. It is his grief, as well as his love, that explodes within her, and her moans of pleasure are fused with the long, deep ululation of her mourning. They sleep at last, in each other's arms, and they do not awaken until bright sunlight floods the room.

News of the Cosgroves comes to them. John Cowper tells them that he has sent an evaluation of Stacey's poems to the admissions office of a state college in northern California. Mandy (who returned briefly from Arizona and is now traveling through the Canadian Rockies) arranged for this. John himself thinks of going west, but he does not want to leave his son Terry, and Elizabeth (who is so wonderful with the children) wants to complete her doctorate.

Charles Norris meets with Andrew Kardin and tells them that all monies have been transferred. Hal has taken an option on a restaurant in Cupertino and he is negotiating for the rental of a small house nearby.

"When will they leave?" David asks. Already sorrow saps the strength he has so carefully cultivated during this respite.

"A week. Two weeks," Charles Norris replies. "That's my guess. He didn't give me a date, of course."

"Of course," David says.

That night he drives past the Cosgrove house. The drapes have been removed and he watches shadows glide across the drawn window shades. Two small figures. Evan and Jared. He turns the corner and drives by again, very slowly. Stacey's silhouette appears on the white shade. Through the open window, he hears Felicia Miriam cry.

Pain rips through him, sears his chest. He clutches the steering wheel for support. He is having a heart attack. He shivers because his body is coated with cold sweat. And then Felicia Miriam cries again and he is calmed. The pain subsides. *All right. You will be all right,* he tells himself sternly, reprovingly. He presses his foot down on the accelerator and speeds away. But his mouth is open and his throat grows hoarse as he screams out the anguish that he had thought vanquished or, at least, subdued.

Nina calls Stacey some days later.

"David and I have talked," she says (although the plan she proposes is entirely her own), "and we have all this baby equipment. The crib, the bassinet, the carriage. Have you bought anything yet?"

"We were waiting till we got to California," Stacey says. She recovers quickly from her fright at the sound of Nina's voice. "You know the stuff we had from Jared was so beat-up we threw it out."

"I think it would be best if we shipped everything to you. It's silly for you to have the trouble, the expense," Nina says. "If you'll give me the address I'll have it taken care of."

"Thank you. That's wonderful of you," Stacey says breathlessly. "Let me speak to Hal." Hal is so edgy, so unpredictable. "Felicia Miriam is fine," she adds, although Nina has not asked about the baby.

"Good. Let me know what you decide," Nina says, and she hangs up without saying good-bye.

She goes up the bedroom and lies across the bed. The framed picture of Felicia Miriam is no longer on David's bedside table, but when she opens the drawer it stares up at her and she removes it and presses it to her face.

Stacey tells Hal about Nina's call that night as they lie in bed. They are both naked because the night is unseasonably warm. The room is stripped of all decoration and every surface is clear. The movers will come in the morning and in the late afternoon Audrey will drive them to the airport. This is their last night in this house, and already Stacey feels herself at a remove from it. Divested of the clutter of their lives, it is no longer familiar to her. She is repelled by the cracks in the plaster, the scarred floors, the hairline crack in their bedroom window. She feels no connection to these small boxlike rooms. She wonders what the house in Cupertino will look like. Hal says that an orange tree grows in the garden. At least he *thinks* it is an orange tree. He saw it only briefly on a lightning trip he made to settle the lease. She smiles into the darkness. It will not be an orange tree. Of that she is certain.

"Nina wants to give us everything?" Hal asks lazily.

"That's what she said. The crib. The carriage. The changing table. And I suppose the infant seat. And there's a swing. You know, the kind you wind up and strap the baby into. It plays music."

"Does the kid need all that?"

"Felicia Miriam." She corrects him gently. She wants him to use the baby's name. "Yes. Of course she needs all that. Or at least it would all be useful. It's really generous of them."

"What else would they do with all that stuff? And besides, it's for his baby, remember that."

"Our baby."

She sits up in bed and looks down at him. His hand reaches up and touches her stretch marks, lightly traces the fading ripples of flesh.

"Our baby," she repeats, more harshly now.

He does not answer, although his lips part slowly, teasingly.

"Our baby!"

She falls across him, pummels his chest, butts her head against his shoulders, and now he rises halfway; swiftly he pinions her arms, forces her down on her back. He releases her when there is no need to restrain her, when her body rises to meet him in the darkness, and her arms reach out to hold him close, moving with practiced touch, across the muscles of his back, the curling tendrils of hair that grow too long at the nape of his neck. And then he is within her, moving within her, and their lips crush all questions, all words, all accusations. She is ready, poised for his love surge, for the wild laugh, the triumphant smile he flashes at her as he buries his face in her neck, sated and exhausted.

But she is not defeated. Nor has she forgotten.

"Our baby," she says again, and he hears the plea in her voice.

Restored to power, he answers her.

"Your baby," he says, although his voice is not unkind. "Not mine. Not ours. She'll be with us. We'll raise her. But there's only so much you can ask of me, Stacey."

In the darkness, in this stripped and barren room, his honesty rings clear. And she acknowledges what she has known all along. He does not call Felicia Miriam by name. He does not cuddle her or ever hold her in his arms or smile into the small bright flower of her face. He is a man who loves his own. Andrea was his princess because he was her father, her king. (She holds the thought of Andrea a moment longer. She embellishes it. She summons Andrea in her silver-foil crown. She flashes back to Andrea, the toddler. And she feels sadness and loss, but not the terrible gnashing assault of sorrow.) Felicia Miriam will always be an indifferent presence in his home, a child to whom he will show kindness (because he is a kind man) but whom he will never be able to love. Nor can she demand that love. She cannot expect more of him.

"I don't play games with you, Stace," he says softly. "I tell it to you like it is, like it will be."

"I know."

He sleeps. She hears the steady, deep rhythm of his breathing. She gets up, slips on her white robe, and walks through these unfamiliar rooms where she has lived for so many years. Her sons sleep side by side in sleeping bags on their bedroom floor. They have, on this last night in the only home they have ever known, disdained their bed and elected for adventure. Their faces are flushed. Evan's skin is bronzed by the spring sun and Jared sleeps with his head pressed against his brother's golden skin. Stacey remembers a distant dream in which her breast had resembled a large-petaled pink and white flower at which a black-haired, golden-skinned child sucked hungrily, with the absorption of a bee consuming the sustenance of nectar. Hal's child, gifted with his coloring and his vigor, blessed with his love. As a child must be blessed. Yes. The child's natural birthright — a loving mother, a loving father.

"*We must do what is best for Felicia Miriam,*" David had said. She agreed with him then. She agrees with him now. She sees everything with startling clarity, as though she has been fitted with new and powerful glasses. She too must do what is best for Felicia Miriam.

In Andrea's room (no longer Andrea's room really but an ugly cubicle of plasterboard, a sheet of plywood covering a window they have, in the end, decided not to repair) Felicia Miriam sleeps in the drawer lined with the pink satin comforter. She grows too big for this makeshift bed and already her small hand reaches up and clutches its edge. Stacey kneels and kisses each finger. The baby does not stir, does not awaken. Stacey leans closer and lightly presses her lips against the soft cheek. Nor does she wake up when Stacey lifts her in her arms and walks through the house with her, gathering up her purse, slipping into her sandals. She sleeps even as Stacey carries her out to the car and settles her in the car bed.

Once again, Stacey is in a car with Felicia Miriam. Once again, she moves through dark and empty streets, speaking softly to her baby as she drives. She tells her a story that begins and ends in the secret land of the happily ever after. At the Roths' corner, she sings a song the words to which she thought she had long forgotten. It is a lullaby and its nonsense limerick causes her to smile.

She draws up in front of the large wide-windowed house. A small light glows in the nursery window. She goes up the door, the pink-blanketed baby in her arms, her breath moist and warm against her neck. She lifts the knocker and allows it to fall. Once. Twice. Then the hall light flashes on. She hears the murmur of voices, imagines them hurrying down the staircase.

"Who's there?" David's voice, deep and firm.

"It's Stacey." And then, more loudly, she adds the name of their baby. "And Felicia Miriam. I've brought her to you. I've brought her home."

The door opens. David and Nina look at her wonderingly. Hildy leans briefly against the newel post and then she moves forward. She glides between Nina and David and takes the baby from Stacey. Still, they remain in the doorway, Stacey and Nina and David, and together they watch Hildy carry their daughter, their sweetly sleeping daughter, up the staircase and into the nursery.